First I thought I was a writer. Then I realized I was a Jew. Then I no longer distinguished the writer in me from the Jew because one and the other are only torments of an ancient word.

—Edmond Jabès

SUNY Series on Modern Jewish Literature
and Culture

Sarah Blacher Cohen, Editor

The Slayers of Moses

THE EMERGENCE OF RABBINIC INTERPRETATION IN MODERN LITERARY THEORY

Susan A. Handelman
UNIVERSITY OF MARYLAND

State University of New York Press
ALBANY

Published by
State University of New York Press, Albany

For information, address State University of New York
Press, State University Plaza, Albany, N.Y., 12246

Library of Congress Cataloging in Publication Data

Handelman, Susan A.
  The slayers of Moses.

  (SUNY series on modern Jewish literature and culture)
  Bibliography: p. 251.
  1. Rabbinical literature—History and criticism.
2. Talmud—Influence—Civilization, Occidental.
3. Criticism. I. Title. II. Series.
BM496.5.H34   121'.68   81-16522
ISBN 0-87395-576-5   AACR2
ISBN 0-87395-577-3 (pbk.)

For my mother, Marian Handelman
In memory of my father, Milton Handelman

Contents

Figures

Acknowledgements

This book is an *intertext* in many ways. It relies on the thoughts of the many critics, philosophers, psychoanalysts, theologians, and exegetes who are cited in the footnotes and bibliography. But it depends even more on the insights and guidance of my many teachers and friends, who do not appear in the footnotes but who have made my intellectual life not only worth living but joyous. Among the many I am especially grateful to are: Murray Schwartz, who always encouraged and supported my ideas, and especially enlivened my mind with his profound knowledge of psychoanalysis; Norman Holland, who also nurtured my love for Freud; Ken Dauber and Irving Massey, who read and guided the manuscript; and Diane Christian, whose thoughts about the Bible and literature have always challenged and exhilarated me. They, along with the rest of the English Department at the State University of New York at Buffalo, provided me with an extraordinarily invigorating, creative, and expansive education. My thanks to them for my vision of literature.

The University of Maryland at College Park has been another supportive home where I have been able to widen my ideas and pursue my interests with the strong encouragement of my fine colleagues in the English Department and the faculty of Jewish Studies.

I should also like to acknowledge here the support of the University of Maryland Graduate Research Board, the Memorial Foundation for Jewish Culture, and the Graduate School of the State University of New York at Buffalo, who generously awarded me research grants and fellowships to pursue this study.

It would not, moreover, be now in the reader's hands without the efforts of Robert Mandel and Sarah Cohen, the editors of this series on Modern Jewish Literature and Culture. A very special expression of gratitude is due to Jenna Schulman for her superb copy editing of the manuscript.

And finally, to Ellen Golub at the University of Pennsylvania and Theresa Coletti at the University of Maryland, thanks for listening.

Portions of this book have previously appeared in different form and are reprinted with the permission of the following: part of Chapter 5 as "Interpretation as Devotion: Freud's Relation to Rabbinic Hermeneutics," reprinted from *The Psychoanalytic Review,* Vol. 68, No. 2. Summer 1981, through the courtesy of the Editors and the Publisher, National Psychological Association for Psychoanalysis, New York, N.Y.; part of Chapter 6 as "Freud's Midrash: The Exile of Interpretation," from *New York Literary Forum* 2 (1978): 99–112; and Chapter 1, "Greek Philosophy and the Overcoming of the Word," from *Works and Days* 1 (1980): 45–69.

The diagram of Bloom's Map of Misreading is from *A Map of Misreading* by Harold Bloom. Copyright © 1975 by Oxford University Press, Inc. Reprinted by permission.

The illustration of a page from the Talmud was obtained from the *Encyclopaedia Britannica,* 15th edition (1974).

S.A.H.

College Park, Maryland
October, 1981

Methodological Preface

The slightest alteration in the relation between man and the signifier, in this case in the procedures of exegesis, changes the whole course of history by modifying the lines which anchor his being.

— Jacques Lacan[1]

To write is not only to know that the Book does not exist and that forever there are books, against which the meaning of a world not conceived by an absolute subject is shattered, before it has even become a unique meaning. . . . It is not only to have lost the theological certainty of seeing every page bind itself into the unique text of truth . . . . the Book of Reason this time, the infinite manuscript read by a God who, in a more or less defined way, is said to have given us the use of his pen. This lost certainty, this absolute of divine writing, i.e., first of all, the absence of the Jewish God does not solely . . . define something like "modernity." As the absence and haunting of the divine sign, it regulates all modern criticism and aesthetics.

— Jacques Derrida[2]

Modern criticism is haunted indeed. If the Book of Books has lost its status as divine, the notion of the "Text"—in particular, the critical Text—has taken its place. Literary criticism has become a kind of substitute theology. Critics today, in the wake of the overthrow of all absolutes, are revelling in their freedom, and creating a variety of ideologies, sects, and systems whose true believers battle out their quasi-religious wars.

Criticism, however, has always in a sense been waging some religious war or other. Yet we little realize how deep are the theological roots of the modern science of interpretation. Modern hermeneutics has its prehistory and foundation in Biblical hermeneutics; the other major source of our concept of interpretation is Greek philosophy, especially Aristotle. One of the most important contributions of the Jews to Western culture was the concept of the divine text, a book whose contents and their interpretation were the key to knowing ultimate reality. In the West, those thinkers who have meditated on the problems of the text have always done so within the context of the Biblical tradition, or in reaction to it.

The history of interpretation, however, has been equally determined by the schism between Jews and Christians precisely over the issue of proper interpretation of the text. Christianity claimed that it had the final and validating interpretation of the now "Old" Testament text. The word literally became incarnate. The Rabbinic tradition, by contrast, based itself on the principles of multiple meaning and endless interpretability, maintaining that interpretation and text were not only inseparable, but that interpretation—as opposed to incarnation—was the central divine act.

As Christianity severed its ties with Judaism and spread into the Roman Empire, later to conquer Europe, it became allied with Greek philosophy (and a variety of intellectual and religious currents prevailing in the Hellenistic era), and a link was formed which provided the matrix for Western culture. Many of the most influential treatises on language and interpretation in the West have been—until recently—overtly theological and polemical, from Augustine to Dante, Luther, Spinoza, and so forth. Even the modern philosophers of hermeneutics, such as Dilthey, Schleiermacher, Heidegger, Bultmann, and Gadamer, are situated within the tradition of German Protestant theology. In literary criticism, major modern theorists, from Coleridge and Wordsworth to Arnold, Eliot, and the New Critics, or more recent figures such as Northrop Frye, are heavily indebted to their respective Catholic or Protestant concepts of *word, logos, text,* and *meaning.*

Recently a group of challengers to the Greco-Christian tradition of interpretation has arisen. Compared with Frye's stately static schemata of archetypal criticism, for example, Harold Bloom's tortuous "anxieties of influence" and dialectical poetic wars come from an openly avowed Hebraic bias. In contrast to Frye's use of the Christian apocalyptic mode, taken especially from his study of Blake, Bloom turns to Jewish esotericism, Kabbalah, and Gnosticism. And Freud, Lacan, and Derrida have taken over much of the contemporary critical scene, overturning classical concepts of meaning, interpretation, and exegesis. Derrida is most openly polemical in his constant diatribes against the "onto-theological" tradition of Western philosophy, seeking to undo completely the Greco-Christian tradition of thought and replace it with his notion of *Écriture—Writing.*

Little attention, however, has been focused on the Rabbinic interpretive tradition, and its possible relation to movements in criticism. Despite the Church's general rejection of the validity of Jewish interpretation, the Rabbinic hermeneutic tradition continued in force in its own right, and also exerted a subterranean influence not only on Christianity but on the subsequent history of Western thought. This lack of attention to the Rabbinic tradition might be due to a number of factors, among which are: (1) the Church's stigmatizing of Rabbinic interpretation; (2) the inaccessibility of Jewish sources to those unfamiliar with Hebrew; and (3) the exclusion of the Jews from the intellectual life of Europe until the Enlightenment. The collapse of the prestige of Christianity, especially in the last century, coincides with the entry of the Jews into the full intellectual life of Europe, and the influence of Jewish thinkers has become increasingly dominant since World War II.

To try to prove that a Jewish background has some influence on even the most avowedly secular Jews is a difficult and complicated task. Even if one leaves this question entirely aside, the fact remains, however, that there are striking and profound *structural* affinities between the work of some of our most recent and influential (Jewish) thinkers like Freud, Derrida, and Bloom, and Rabbinic models of interpretation. In fact, the genesis of this book was my chancing upon a remark of Lacan's that psychoanalysis belonged to the exegetical tradition of midrash—that genre of Rabbinic interpretation which is a searching out of the meaning of Biblical texts through methods close to free association.[3] Freud himself recognized that what distinguished his method of dream interpretation from all others was that he treated the dream as "holy writ," and assumed meaning to lie hidden in the most trivial and inconsequential details. Freud in this manner linked the Rabbinic hermeneutic mode with literary criticism, for he showed us that in a sense, every text is holy writ—has multiple meanings, none of which are arbitrary, and which must be derived through seemingly outlandish techniques of interpretation.

Perhaps, then, it is an appropriate moment to try to illuminate some of these theological specters haunting contemporary criticism. In this work, I have examined the conflict of interpretations in light of its theological background. I have sought not so much to trace the *historical* influence of Christianity or Judaism on the history of criticism as to examine by a comparative method the general *structural* models of interpretation, which may roughly be labelled *Rabbinic* and *Patristic,* and their relation to theories of meaning in certain modern thinkers.

I should like here to clarify and emphasize this description of my method. It is not, by any means, an orthodox "structuralist" approach—moreover, we are now in a post-structuralist era; nor am I a Lacanian, Derridean, or member of any of the contemporary "hermeneutical mafias." In the broadest sense, this book is itself a kind of midrash, a search for hidden elements and correspondences, a tropism or "wandering of meaning," which proceeds as much by analogy and association as by linear logic. Perhaps it should be called a "structuralist midrash." This method, though, has its own philosophic rigor, as I will show when I discuss the use to which it is put in Freud, Derrida, and Bloom.

Both Rabbinic and Patristic thought are endlessly complicated and multifaceted topics. I have sought primarily to define them in terms of their original conflict in the first few centuries of the Common Era, which laid, I believe, the basis for all future discussion. I have not ventured into the vast territory of their complex relations in medieval thought, and have only made a few comments about the Reformation as preparation for the discussion of modern criticism. Though these gaps are undeniably large, the basic structure traced here does, I think, sufficiently cover the fundamental issues which are played upon as a theme and variation throughout the history of Jewish–Christian relations.

Within the general categories I have outlined, there are endless subcategories, and always exceptions to the rule. When I speak of *Greek, Rabbinic,* or *Patristic* thought, I am, to be sure, using the terms in a broader sense than usual. I am, however, trying to define certain structures of thought and patterns of organizing reality rather than set bodies of historical literature. Thus I link together disparate figures in hitherto unperceived correspondences. For example, I have extended the term *Rabbinic* into realms where it is usually not applied. But this is part of my central thesis: that these thought patterns and structures have been displaced and re-emerge in secular thought. This commingling of "holy" and "profane" becomes part of the "heretic hermeneutic" which I attempt to define at the end of the book.

As the foregoing comments imply, this study is by no means comprehensive. To write an all-inclusive survey of the relation of Biblical exegesis to literary criticism would require more than one lifetime. Scholars in the varying fields which I touch upon—Biblical studies, Rabbinics, Patristics, philosophy, linguistics, psychoanalysis—will not, I hope, feel too roughly intruded upon. I should make clear that I approach these fields from the point of view of a *literary* theoretician; I approach the material having in mind the literary concerns that have become pressing in the last decade: What is a text? How is meaning conceived? What is the nature of signification? How is interpretation to be understood? How do we understand understanding?

Literary theory has been radically transformed in the past decade; the distinctions between genres, between artist and critic, critic and philosopher, reading and writing, text and commentary, have all been blurred. Criticism is now in what Geoffrey Hartman has called the phase of "revisionist reversal."[4] Revisionism is, of course, a reseeing, rereading, reinterpreting of canonical texts. I, too, have reread and perhaps upset the various sacred canons of Biblical and theological studies, psychoanalysis, and philosophy. I am convinced, however, that those who work in these fields can much profit from exposure to those of us whose concern is the theory of literature. Certainly the primary texts I discuss—Bible, Aristotle, Plato, Midrash, Church Fathers, Freud, etc.—are not only historical documents but daring, speculative, willful, controversial, poetic, and rhetorical visions. They make exceedingly strong claims upon their readers, and perhaps, sometimes, in order to better comprehend them, we also need to *read* strongly. As Harold Bloom puts it: "We need to read more strenuously and more audaciously, the more we realize that we cannot escape the predicament of misreading."[5]

This book, then, is an attempt to break, more than cover, ground. It is also primarily a work of theory, not an exercise in practical exegesis. Future efforts, I hope, will be concerned with praxis, but here I am focusing on the concepts of meaning that underlie exegetic techniques—that is, the hermeneutic, the philosophy of interpretation by which the exegete understands himself and his text. There is, of course, some comparison of exegetic techniques in this book, but that is not its center. When I discuss the thirteen exegetical principles of R. Ishmael as a guide to Rabbinic hermeneutics, I by no means intend to imply that therein the whole Talmud may be understood—or that Freud, Lacan, and Derrida are Rabbinic simply because some of the same principles resurface in their work. The main issues constantly are: What do these principles reflect about the authors' understanding of texts, meaning, language, and interpretation?

In Part II, I have concentrated on Freud, Lacan, Derrida, and Bloom because they are seminal thinkers and major influences on literary study today. (In addition, all but Lacan are Jewish.)

"Had I but time," cries Hamlet at the end of the play, "O, I could tell you." Had I but time, I too could tell a story which would include many others—Kafka, Wittgenstein, Marx, Walter Benjamin, Durkheim, Lévi-Straus, Levinas, Barthes, and Borges, to name a few. I leave them to future studies. As the Jewish mystics are fond of writing in passages where they can go no further: "Those who know will understand."

As to Jewish mysticism, I have not discussed it at length until the final chapter. I have not done so because I agree with Gershom Scholem that Kabbalah, for all its innovation, was not in essence different from classical Rabbinic thought. All too often, in comparative studies, those with little knowledge of Rabbinic thought proclaim all unusual and extravagant techniques of interpreting Scripture as "Kabbalistic."

In Part I, I attempt to give the historical and philosophical background to the conflict of interpretations. Chapter 1 examines some of the Greek roots of Western thought about interpretation, focusing particularly on Plato's and Aristotle's attitudes towards language, meaning, and texts in the context of our contemporary debate about metaphor. Chapters 2 and 3 discuss some major aspects of the Rabbinic interpretive system, and its emphasis on the divinity and endless interpretability of the Text. In Chapter 4, the divorce of Christianity from Judaism is examined from Paul through Origen, Philo, and Augustine.

In Part II, the displacements of these ancient theological conflicts are traced in modern literary theory. Chapters 5, 6, and 7, respectively, analyze Freud, Lacan, and Derrida in light of the tradition of Rabbinic hermeneutics. Finally, in Chapter 8, I turn to Harold Bloom, the "Kabbalist of criticism," and his use of Jewish mysticism, to formulate a "heretic hermeneutic."

The return of theology into secular systems of thought is most intentional and obvious in Bloom, but, as Geoffrey Hartman notes, "Pure secularism is simply another religion, its ghosts or god will appear at some point."[6] Hartman draws our attention to Walter Benjamin's image of a little hunchback within, directing the movements of a puppet who plays and wins chess games against all opponents; Benjamin identifies the puppet in this little parable with historical materialism, and the hidden hunchback with theology.[7] The critic, Hartman continues,

> is inexorably a figure of pathos and aesthetic play. He is a latter-day clown, close cousin to the little hunchback. The Romantic or religious passion, in all its calculating if displaced strength, may be the hump he cannot shake off. Wizened, shrunken, crippled though it may be, we know there is a power there, if only because we show it instinctive fear and keep it out of sight.[8]

It is time to bring these repressed theological specters to light. The recognition of origins—that obsession of Oedipal Greeks and Oedipal Freudians—might even prove to be cathartic. Needless to say, however, the subject requires far more—even endless—interpretation.

Note to the Reader

In addition to Notes collected at the end of each chapter, and the Selected Bibliography, this book contains three kinds of references—Biblical, classical, and Judaic. Biblical quotations generally follow the translation of the Revised Standard Version. Classical sources, primarily from Aristotle, are abbreviated in the standard manner; the abbreviations are listed later in this Note. Primary Judaic sources include the Talmud—the great collection of Rabbinic law, discussion and wisdom—and the Midrash, Rabbinic commentary and exegesis of Scripture.

Translations generally follow the English edition of the Talmud by I. Epstein (London: Soncino, 1935-48); this text is based on the Romm edition published in Vilna, 1906. Quotations from the Midrash Rabbah generally follow the translation of H. Freedman and M. Simon (London: Soncino, 1939), based on the Romm edition of 1853-58. The abbreviations used are listed at the end of this Note. All Talmudic citations refer to the Babylonian Talmud, except where noted by *Yer.*, indicating *Yerushalmi* or Jerusalem Talmud. Translations of R. Shlomo Yitzhaki's commentary on the Bible are taken from the English edition of the *Pentateuch and Rashi's Commentary* by B. Sharfman and Abraham Ben-Isaiah (Brooklyn, N.Y.: S.S. & R. Pub. Co., 1949).

The transliterations of individual Hebrew words are my own attempts at rendering English phonetic equivalents for readers unfamiliar with the language and the various scholarly translation codes.

I have also capitalized the words Rabbinic and Patristic throughout, in contrast to standard usage. I have done so because I am using these terms as designations for specific thought-systems.

List of Abbreviations

Classical References

Aristotle

An. Pr.	Analytica Priora
Gen. Corr.	De Generatione et Corruptione
Int.	De Interpretatione
Metaph.	Metaphysica
Rh.	Rhetorica
Poet.	Poetica

Plato

Cra.	Cratylus

Judaic Sources

Talmud (Babylonian)

Av. Zar.	Avodah Zarah
B. Kamma	Bava Kamma
B. Metzia	Bava Metzia
Ber.	Berachot
Chul.	Chullin
Eruv.	Eruvin
Git.	Gittin
Hag.	Hagigah
Kid.	Kiddushin
Ket.	Ketuvot
Meg.	Megillah
Men.	Menachot
Naz.	Nazir
Nid.	Niddah
Pes.	Pesachim
Sanh.	Sanhedrin
Shab.	Shabbat
Sot.	Sotah
Suk.	Sukkah
Tos.	Tosefot
Yev.	Yevamot
Zev.	Zevachim

Talmud (Jerusalem)

Yer. Hag.	Hagigah
Yer. Peah	Peah
Yer. Shek.	Shekalim

Midrash

Ber. Rab.	Bereishit Rabbah (on Genesis)
Eicah Rab.	Eicha Rabbah (on Lamentations)
Lev. Rab.	Leviticus Rabbah (on Leviticus)
	Mekilta (legalistic Midrash on Exodus)
	Sifre (Midrash on Deuteronomy and Numbers)

Other Rabbinic Commentary

Av. R. Nat.	Avot de. R. Natan
Ot. R. Akiba	Otiyot de. R. Akiba
	Sefer Yetzirah
T. El. Zut.	Tanna d'bei Eliyahu Zuta
Rashi	Acronym for Rabbi Shlomo Yitzhaki

I

HISTORICAL BACKGROUND

THE INTERPRETIVE AGON OF GREEK, JEW, AND CHRISTIAN

1

Greek Philosophy and the Overcoming of the Word

"What has Athens to do with Jerusalem?" Tertullian, the Latin Church Father, angrily demanded in his scornful repudiation of philosophy—that seductive and lovely pagan which tempted many in the early Church. But Athens and Jerusalem, the seductive pagan and the stalwart believer, came to have much to do with each other. Sometimes mutually antagonistic, sometimes holding secret trysts, sometimes publicly embracing, the history of their relationship has been stormy.

Matthew Arnold, in the nineteenth century, defined this tension between "Hebrew and Hellene" as the essential creative dialectic of Western culture. The struggle between Athens and Jerusalem indeed has taken many forms: it is the conflict between philosophy and the church, Greek wisdom and Jewish Torah, reason and faith, the secular and the sacred—or, in another transformation, Christian and Jew. It has involved the best minds of the West and spilled over into every major field of inquiry. This volatile relationship renews itself in every epoch, taking another guise, using another language, but continuing the old quarrels and flirtations.

This book concentrates more on the eras of antagonism than the moments of accommodation. Literary criticism, as a theory of the book, has always been tied to these exegetical wars over The Book—echoed them, reenacted them, and contributed to them. And neither literary criticism, Biblical exegesis, nor the history of interpretation in general can be understood without comprehending the extent to which they are rooted in Athens. We must begin then, as usual, with the Greeks. And "Greek philosophy more or less begins," writes Hans-Georg Gadamer, "with the insight that a word is only a name, i.e., that it does not represent true being."[1] Indeed, the Greek term for word, *onoma,* is synonymous with *name.* By contrast, its Hebrew counterpart—*davar*—means not only *word*

3

but also *thing*. It was precisely this original unity of word and thing, speech and thought, discourse and truth that the Greek Enlightenment disrupted. And this cleavage determined the subsequent history of Western thought about language.

One of the most important consequences of this disruption was to make the word suspect and to steer the seeker of truth away from language towards a silent ontology, or towards a purely rational system of signs, an artificially constructed ideal language such as mathematics. In the latter respect, in the quest for a purely rational sign system, contemporary semioticians follow the classical view of language. And the Christian tradition—whose philosophical roots, despite Tertullian's best efforts, became deeply embedded in Greek thought—also ultimately calls for transcendence of the word and language altogether. The central doctrine of the Church—Incarnation—celebrates not the exaltation of the word, but its transformation from the linguistic order into the material realm, its conversion into the flesh. For the Rabbis, however, the primary reality was linguistic; true being was a God who *speaks* and creates *texts,* and *imitatio deus* was not silent suffering, but speaking and interpreting. Let us, then, first examine the two Greeks whose work became the foundation of all subsequent thought on the problems of language and interpretation: Plato and Aristotle.

Plato and Language: The Cratylus

Plato's *Cratylus* has been one of the crucial texts in the history of linguistics. The ostensible debate in this dialogue between Cratylus and Socrates concerns the familiar question of whether words are "natural" or "conventional," that is, whether they contain an innate truth or whether their meanings are assigned by men through common agreement. The ultimate solution to this question in the dialogue is that words, by which is generally meant *names*, are instrumental signs—not for things, but for the forms of things. The question then becomes one of the correctness of names, not of any innate truth value. Is the instrument used to represent the object properly? This instrumental concept of the word, as Gadamer explains, banished knowledge "to the intelligible sphere, so that ever since in all discussion on language, the concept of the image (*eikon*) has been replaced by that of sign (*semeia*) which is not just a terminological change, but expresses an epoch-making decision about thought concerning language."[2] *Sign* here means the abstract relation of pointing, not an entity with any content of its own. Hence, according to Plato, language is not truth, but only "imitative sound." "A name is . . . a vocal imitation of any object and a man is said to name an object when he imitates it with the voice" (*Cra.* 423b). That is, he imitates the essence or nature of the thing; he signifies its form. There remains, however, an irremediable gap between the imitation and the thing itself. And so, says Socrates in the dialogue, "He who follows names in the search after things, and analyzes their meaning, is in great danger of being deceived" (436a). " . . . How real existence is to be discovered is, I suspect, beyond you and me—we must rest content with the admission that the knowledge of things is not to be derived from names" (439).

Underlying this attitude toward language, of course, is Platonic ontology. In this concept of true being, language belongs to the realm of the imperfect and contingent, while true knowledge is possible only in the realm of the immutable forms. Thus the progression required of us by Plato is a movement from word to thing to form. "The *Cratylus* urges us to study not linguistics but ontology."[3] Being must be known not from language, but "from itself," and the object of thought is not words, but "Ideas." Language, like the inferior sensible appearance of things, must be transcended. As we shall see, Plato's conquest of language will have its counterpart in the Church's attempt to surpass the letter of the Biblical text for the spirit. Our examination of Augustine in particular will show the effects of this rhetoric of silence in more detail. This theology of silence has, of course, its adherents in literature as well: the pure thought of ideas is silent, a dialogue of the soul with itself independent of language, and writers from Augustine to Mallarmé to Beckett have tried to achieve that goal.

But as certain contemporary linguistic theorists have pointed out, language and thought are intricately interrelated, and words have an independent cognitive function, which Plato entirely ignores. Precisely because he relegates language to inferior realms, Plato has no real problem of interpretation. As William and Martha Kneale write, for Plato "correct thinking is following out connections between forms. . . . A sentence is true if the arrangement of its parts reflects or corresponds to connections between forms."[4] The model for this sort of thinking is at bottom mathematical. So, too, the ideal is a mathematical language abstracted from objects, above contingency; number, not words, provides access to true knowledge of reality. (We clearly see the resurgence of this mathematical approach in the nineteenth and twentieth century's concept of an ideal language constructed of artificial, unambiguous symbols, and especially in contemporary semiotics, which has retained the concept of the sign and left the ontology behind.)

Aristotle and the Problems of Predication

Aristotle follows Plato both in his use of mathematical models as a foundation for his logic and in his injunction to look to the thing rather than to the word. That logical reflection among the Greeks arose in the context of the problems of geometry cannot be stressed too much. This fact is of supreme importance in the determination of the concepts of truth, meaning, and interpretation in Western thought. And herein is one of the major differences between Greek and Rabbinic thought. Rabbinic thinking arises, in the first instance, from reflection on a *text,* on *words* rather than numbers. We will, however, leave for the next chapter a more detailed explanation of this crucial difference, and concentrate here on Aristotle's ideas about language and truth as a preliminary background.

The Kneales point out that there are many important consequences of Aristotle's reliance on a primarily mathematical model for his logic.[5] First, there is an attention to general propositions, which are concerned with kinds or *classes* of things and not individuals. Furthermore, there is an emphasis on universal propositions, which are *necessarily* true. These "demonstrative" (or "scientific") premises, as Aristotle calls them (*An. Pr.* 1. 24a22–24b12), are didactic, assumed, not questioned. In a geometrical model of proof, all other propositions of the science must be deduced solely from these demonstrative premises. In the Aristotelian model of proof, the necessary premise leads to a necessary conclusion, meaning that the relation between subject and predicate is a *per se* relation; the predicate is entailed by the subject as its definition, genus, differentia, property, and so forth.

Aristotle's great contribution to logic was, accordingly, the syllogism—which is not a method of investigation but of deductive proof. One important feature of the syllogism is its dependence on a *subject–predicate* relation between two terms, as mentioned above, wherein one tries to show that the predicate is included in the subject. The subject–predicate relation becomes, then, the common form of *all* judgment and reasoning, and one of Aristotle's major mistakes is his neglect of other forms of relational inference not based on this model. Indeed, Aristotle argues that all valid arguments involve syllogistic reasoning, and the syllogism is for him the ideal model of logic and thought. For Aristotle, a proposition always indicates either the definition, property, genus, or accident of the subject, and is always concerned with a general statement such as "man is a two-footed animal," that is, with the relation of a predicate to a subject. "It is necessary that every demonstration and every syllogism should prove either that something belongs or that it does not, and this either universally or in part" (*An. Pr.* 1. 23–40b23). We shall see that one of the major accomplishments of the Rabbis was the creation of another system of relational inference independent of the syllogistic model, and hence branded as illogical by those schooled only in Greek thought.[6]

The Kneales describe the consequences of Aristotle's delimitation of logic to subject–predicate propositions in the following way:

> Aristotle's emphasis on primary substance as the ultimate subject of predication led to an overemphasis on the subject–predicate form of proposition which still restricted logical development in the time of Leibniz. If primary

substance is the ultimate subject of predication, all basic truths are of the form "This (primary substance) is (or is not) such and such," and all other truths are derivative from or dependent on these. . . . Most obviously dependent are those with some form, i.e., the universal propositions of Aristotelian logic. . . . It seemed then that the important differences between propositions were marked by the occurrence or non-occurrence of the negative particle, and by the qualifier, "all" and "some."

The Kneales further comment that Aristotle's view of the basic proposition was "over-simplified" and "a hindrance to the development of the logic of relations."[7]

Gadamer explains[8] that Hegel also criticized the classical subject–predicate proposition, claiming that, in truth, it constitutes a "blockage of thought": the subject, in effect, does not truly pass over to *another concept,* placed in relation to it; the subject's truth is merely stated in the form of the predicate. The proposition thus never really defines a new concept beyond the subject. One finds instead that the predicate is the substance into which the subject has passed over, and thus vanished. The predicate thus blocks the movement of thought and the form of the proposition cancels itself; it does not truly state something of something. And this blockage of thought, says Hegel, constitutes the speculative nature of all philosophy to the extent that in the entire history of philosophy, all speculation becomes a form of predication. Derrida, we will find, attacks the entire history of philosophy based on the Greek fathers, and especially its ontology and notion of predication.

Aristotle, as is well known, had differed with Plato concerning the latter's theory of forms. Aristotle maintained that Plato had erred in hypostatizing the forms, that is, in confusing them with substances capable of independent existence. For Aristotle, only primary substance is capable of independent existence, and those things falling under other categories are dependent. Hence Aristotle formulated his famous Categories to replace Plato's forms. In the Categories, Aristotle classified the types of being in terms of ten predicates (or "secondary substances"): substance, quantity, quality, relation, place, time, situation, state, motion, and passivity. In effect, as Gadamer notes, Aristotle totally reoriented the forms of being to the forms of assertion—the relation of assertion between subject and predicate, that something "is" or "is not" something else. But in concentrating on this form of differences between predicates, he created, as has already been noted, a very restricted logic. As Tzvetan Todorov puts it, "Aristotle's logic is a logic of classes, not of propositions; its argumentation describes the relation of predicates that make up the propositions and not the relations between propositions."[9]

All of this is to say that despite his differences with Plato, Aristotle agrees that the realm of words is not the realm of meaning and truth. Discourse and being are not coterminous. Like Plato, for Aristotle the central act of knowing is a movement *beyond* discourse, beyond talking.

Although *ousia,* primary being, the essential *what* of a thing, is the subject of discourse, the formulations of discourse are not themselves *what is (ousiai).** (It should be noted that Aristotle makes a key distinction between "first being," the *what* which denotes *ousia,* and all other things, which are secondary being, and are said to be because they are either qualities or quantities, etc., of first being. *Ousia* is the primary subject and hence also the subject of discourse. On the other hand, the formulations of discourse are not ever the *essence* of that which discourse is about.) Universals, genera, and so forth are not things but predicates common to many things, according to the view of Aristotle; the same is true of all of Plato's forms. They are not *ousiai.* Through discourse, however, one can formulate the intelligible structure or makeup of a thing (its *logos*), but this formulation is not identical with the thing itself. *Ousia* is what we always talk about, but what is never a predicate. Primary substance, according to Aristotle, is defined as that which is neither asserted for a subject nor present in a subject, and hence has an aspect that entirely eludes articulation in words.

Logos, that which we can articulate in words, becomes a central expression in Christian thought as the Greek translation for the Hebrew *davar,* and ultimately *logos* becomes transposed into the personhood of Jesus in the Gospel of John. In the beginning was the *logos.* In Aristotle, though, *logos* does not really mean *word,* but rather *reason, definition, formula,* or *discourse.* Science, accordingly, is concerned with the definition of what a thing is in terms of demonstrating the connection of its properties with the essence of the subject. Such demonstration leads to finding a thing's *logos.* However, though science operates through *logos,* definition of properties and so forth, true knowledge is not obtained through *logos.* Discourse, as we have noted, can state the "what is" that is essential to being any specific kind of thing, but it cannot state the concrete thing itself.

Nous, however, (*mind or intellectual vision,* as opposed to *speech*) is the activity, power, or "place of forms" and the real human intellectual power capable of knowing truth, and of transcending the limits of particulars to attain direct intellectual vision of things as they are. "Actual sensing is always of particulars, while knowledge is of universals; and these universals are, in a manner, in the rational psyche—or *nous* itself" (*De An.* 2. 5. 4176–22–6). *Nous,* it is important to note, is described in visual not linguistic terms, and we shall later discuss the central difference between the importance of *seeing* in Greek thought and *hearing* in Rabbinic thought, the visual versus the verbal. For the Greeks, following Aristotle, things are not exhausted by discourse; for the Rabbis, discourse is not exhausted by things.

---

*John H. Randall's discussion of the relation of *ousia* to discourse has been very helpful here. See "Ousia as a Subject of Discourse" in his *Aristotle* (New York: Columbia Univ. Press), pp. 116–123.

In practical terms, Aristotle is making a crucial distinction between treating a subject in terms of *logos* (discourse) and treating it in terms of *physikos* (natural processes). Aristotle writes:

> . . . Those who have lived in intimate association with natural things are better able to lay down such *archai* [necessary axioms] as can be connected together to cover a wide field. Those, on the other hand, who from many words are unable to see things that really are, are more detected as men of narrow vision. One can see, too, from this the great difference that exists between those who conduct their investigating as natural philosophers *(physikos)* and as dialecticians *(logikos)*. *[Gen. Corr.* 1. 2. 316. a 5–14.]

Aristotle's aim, of course, was to be a *physikos*. His logic is not a study of words, but the thought of which words are merely signs, and thought is the apprehension of the nature of things.

Aristotle: Words and Things, Rhetoric vs. Philosophy

It remains, however, to examine more closely Aristotle's conception of the precise relation between word and thing. It has been said that a few sentences at the beginning of *De Interpretatione* (16a3–8) constitute the most influential text in the history of semantics.[10] Writing against the background of the *Cratylus*, Aristotle here claims:

> Now spoken sounds are symbols of affections in the soul, and written marks symbols of spoken sounds. And just as written marks are not the same for all men, neither are spoken sounds. But what they are in the first place signs of—affections of the soul—are the same for all; and what these affections are likenesses of—actual things—are also the same. [1. 16a.3–8.]

It is immediately apparent that Aristotle's description of the relation between names (as in the *Cratylus, onoma* is the Greek word used here) and things is most imprecise. His main concern is to assert that language is conventional, as he states a few lines later in the famous definition, "A name is spoken sound significant by convention" (16a19). Also noteworthy here is the subordination of written to spoken language (to keep in mind for our later discussion of the Rabbinic concept of the holiness of a *written* text, indeed of the letters themselves, and Derrida's attack against the subordination of writing to speech). Aristotle, however, does not really specify in what manner written marks are symbols of spoken sounds, or how, in turn, these spoken sounds are symbols of the "affections in the soul." These "affections in the soul," which presumably are images of a sort, are called "likenesses of actual things," and they are not conventional but the same for all men. By *affections,* Aristotle most likely means *thoughts*.

Richard McKeon points out that Aristotle did not articulate a philosophy of language, or a science of symbols or signs. When words and language are scientifically used, i.e., when arguments are properly constructed, they are symbolic of ideas in the mind. In essence, thoughts and words are two different kinds of discourse for Aristotle. Scientific demonstrative proof has to do not with verbal discourse, but with the affections in the soul, which image things. According to McKeon, this notion leads Aristotle to construct an "outer" discourse and an "inner" discourse. The inner discourse is one which consists of mental experiences, the passions of the soul; the outer discourse is expressed in sound and symbolizes these passions, and written discourse is even further removed. The verbal, outer discourse is significant by convention, whereas the inner silent discourse is "naturally" significant, the same for all men—and, moreover, the source of meaning for verbal sound.[11]

At the heart of Aristotle's discussion is what we may call the antiverbal—or, better, anti-Scriptural—tendency of Greek thought. The Christian interpretation of the Bible, we have asserted, has primarily followed the Greeks in disparaging verbal, outer discourse. Our discussion of the conflict between letter and spirit in Biblical interpretation must wait, but the seeds of the controversy can easily be seen here. Outer discourse—especially the written—is related to inner in a more or less extraneous, albeit symbolic, way. One seeks to discard the outer letter and move towards direct perception of things in the silent images of the soul (thoughts).

Moreover, as D. W. Ross points out, in *De Interpretatione* we have a "frankly representative view of knowledge." The affections of the soul are characterized as "likenesses of things" and judgment then becomes the establishment of connections (or divisions) between these affections of the soul (thoughts, concepts)–not between connections in reality. Judgments, then, are syntheses or analyses of concepts, which are true only insofar as they are *like* the connections or separations of associated elements of reality. In essence, this is a correspondence view of truth, which is not, as Ross says, an example of Aristotle's best thinking.[12] The ultimate consequence is that things themselves are not involved in logical operations. Ernest Kapp points out that the case for basing the treatment of terms and logic on a consideration of ideas, which dominated logic from Descartes to Mill, has its origins here. Mill, however, opposed the mental representation theory of Aristotle:

> The notion that what is of primary importance to the logician in a proposition is the relation between two *ideas* corresponding to subject and predicate (instead of the relation between the two *phenomena* which things respectively express) seems to me to be one of the most fatal errors ever introduced into the philosophy of logic and the principal cause why the theory of science has made such inconsiderable progress during the last two centuries.[13]

Mill maintains that propositions are not assertions concerning our ideas of things, but assertions respecting the things themselves. And, as will be discussed later, Mill's critique draws him close to a Rabbinic view, wherein the relation between word and thing is far more intimate and crucial than it is in Greek and Western philosophy in general; Rabbinic logic can perhaps be seen as a model for the kind of logic Mill calls for.

Indeed, Aristotle goes so far as to separate the entire sphere of poetics and rhetoric (wherein words and things are intricately interrelated) from "true science" and logic. Dialectic, Aristotle tells us, is a method of critical investigation fundamentally different from demonstration. In dialectic, the principles are not necessary axioms, but are established only by consulting opinions and probabilities—in contrast to the scientific approach, which is a direct inquiry into the nature of things. Rhetoric is defined in the famous first passage of Aristotle's *Rhetorica* as the "counterpart of dialectic," belonging to no definite science. Aristotle's separation of poetics and rhetoric from science was a schism which had profound influence on the history of thought about language. Only recently has philosophy come to recognize the logic innate in language itself (and contemporary literary criticism now centers around this issue, having now become a religion of rhetoric). Gadamer puts it thus:

> Aristotle's measuring by the logical ideal of proof robs the logical achieve-
> ment of language of its scientific justification. . . . Whatever constituted the
> life of language, and made up its logical probability, the spontaneous and
> inventive seeking out of similarities by means of which it is possible to order
> things, is now pushed aside and instrumentalized into a rhetorical figure
> called metaphor.[14]

The struggle between philosophy and rhetoric in Greece ended in philosophy's conquest. (The Rabbis, we will find, never suffered this schism; their concepts of language and interpretation not only preserve but exalt the innate logic of language, for which reason Rabbinic logic was branded as unscientific.) Not only did a certain mode of philosophical thinking arise in this Greek conquest of the word, but also the fundamental methodology and logic of science, which has dominated Western culture until early in our century—a science predicated on an instrumental theory of language, wherein the word is merely a sign, and speech and thought are divided.

The consequences of the separation of science from rhetoric, and of logic from language, were far-reaching. With this in mind, we can further examine the concepts of meaning and truth underlying Aristotle's definition of the relation of written to spoken speech, and spoken speech to image or thought and to thing. The implication here again is that *truth* and *falsity* apply primarily to thoughts, not to words or things. Aristotle also follows Plato in the assumption that thoughts or parts of discourse are true or false only insofar as they are composite: "For falsity and truth have to do with combination and separation" (*Int.* 1.16a10). Names and verbs by themselves are neither true nor false, Aristotle continues. And when nouns and verbs are combined into sentences, of these only *declarative* sentences, or propositions, are true or false. A sentence is by definition "a significant spoken sound—some part of which is significant in separation—as an expression not as an affirmation" (16b26):

> Every sentence is significant (not as a tool but, as we said, by convention), but not every sentence is a statement-making sentence, but only those in which there is truth or falsity. There is not truth or falsity in all sentences: a prayer is neither true nor false. The present investigation deals with the statement-making sentence; the others we can dismiss, since consideration of them belongs rather to the study of rhetoric or poetry. [16b33-17a5.]

This text was as crucial to the history of semantics as that at the very beginning of *De Interpretatione,* "for nearly all logicians thereafter put such sentences aside and attended solely to the always true or false statement."[15]

Aristotle's concentration solely on declarative sentences was a mistake of major import, for, as we have seen, he suggested that there cannot be logical relations between other types of utterances, and this was a drastic delimitation of logic. Furthermore, Aristotle's schema of the four different kinds of general statements in *De Interpretatione* (affirmative, negative, universal, particular) again is determined by his interest in working out the forms of arguments that depend on the relations between *general* terms. His underlying assumption is that there is no difference between general and singular statements, and his problem is in trying to talk of the terms of all general statements in a way which is proper only for universal affirmative statements.[16] In the syllogism, for example, at least one premise must be universal and one affirmative. (In the next chapter, we shall discover how at the heart of the Rabbinic interpretive system is a stubborn particularization and an entirely different view of the relation between general and particular, wherein the particular is given the power to delimit the general in many cases.)

Hence, for Aristotle, both scientific and dialectic reasoning are for the most part about classes, not individuals, and the subject–predicate relation of the syllogism or declarative statement is largely quantitative, again revealing the influence of the mathematical model on Aristotle's thinking. The terms of Aristotle's statements and syllogisms in effect are not words and names as individuals. The very word for the syllogistic term, *horos,* initially denoted any of the members composing a mathematical proportion.

It is also noteworthy that Aristotle deals with the main questions of *De Interpretatione* through constructing contradictory pairs of statements based on a disjunction of the universal and particular (pairs of statements in which the same thing is asserted and denied of the same thing, wherein one must be true and the other false). The most important part of Aristotle's theory dealt with the *opposition* between universal and particular statements, and in his famous "square of opposition" he combined the distinction between universal and particular with that between affirmative and negative. The four classes of general statements are encompassed by the (1) universal affirmative ("Every man is white"), (2) universal negative ("No man is white"), (3) particular affirmative ("Some man is white"), and (4) particular negative ("Some man is not white"). The reductiveness of this schema led to what has been called a "straightjacketing of logic." (Rabbinic thought will relativize the concepts of "general" and "particular" and conceive their relationship in a more fluid way, as one of extension and limitation rather than opposition, and will substitute a contextual relationship for a proportional one.)

Aristotle further restricted his logic by making the parts of his arguments univocal terms; ambiguous or equivocal terms have no place in his science, and are relegated to the "inferior" sphere of rhetoric. As Aristotle bluntly puts it in the *Metaphysica* (1011.626f), "To say that what is is and what is not is not is the true definition of truth and falsehood conversely."

> If it be said that "man" has an infinite number of meanings, obviously there can be no discourse; for not to have one meaning is to have no meaning, and if words have no meaning there is an end of discourse with others, and even, strictly speaking with oneself; because it is impossible to think of anything if you do not think of one thing. [*Metaph.* Gamma 4. 1006b. 6–10.]

Every declarative statement, then, is either true or false. This is called the Principle of Bivalence: either P or not-P, and for Aristotle, the Law of Contradiction is "the firmest of all principles." "It is impossible for the same thing to belong and not belong to the same thing in the same respect" (*Metaph.* 1. 3. 1005b 1923).

The Law of Contradiction, of course, is a cornerstone of Western philosophy, but it is also dependent on certain unexamined ontological assumptions. In later chapters we will examine how Freud, for example, recognized the *logic* of an unconscious where the Law of Contradiction does not operate. Rabbinic thought can also at times suspend the Law of Contradiction. The same is true of poetry, rhetoric, metaphor, and so forth, all of which play with the equivocalness and ambiguity of words, and all of which Aristotle banished from the realm of pure science and logic. Yet, it should be noted, their "play" is no less serious than Aristotle's play with the forms of reasoning and statement. Aristotle, however, did not recognize any play within his system; he took his formulations of general statements as axiomatic rules of inference rather than as theses. For example, in the type of syllogism which is called *conditional,* where the formula is *"If* every M is L, and every S is M, then every S is L," the *if* becomes more or less forgotten, and statements are considered axioms. In fact, Aristotle does not examine conditional statements within his theory of logic, nor consider the kind of argument based on them as comparable to the syllogism. (Much of Rabbinic thought, in contrast, is oriented around conditional statements, where *if* becomes the key that opens the discourse to an almost endless play of argument based on all manner of seemingly unrelated conjecture. *If,* in literary terms, might also be said to correspond to the faculty of the imagination, the *what if* that opens and creates new and alternative visions of what *is*.) Aristotle, following Greek ontology, is more concerned with *what is* than *what if*. For Aristotle, all valid arguments involve syllogistic reasoning.

The history of interpretation nevertheless owes much to Aristotle, for according to his model, interpretation became saying something of something as a subject–predicate relation concerning general statements which are *either* true *or* false. There has obviously been an ongoing conflict between the claims of science as the true method of interpreting reality, and the claims of art, myth, and other systems where language, meaning, interpretation, and being are not patterned after mathematic and syllogistic ways of thinking. The effects of Aristotle are also evident in Christian theology, so dependent on Greek philosophy, where theology and Bible interpretation also became, in general, matters of affirming dogma, extracting general statements from texts, and disregarding the "letter," that play of equivocalness and multiplicity of interpretation in which the Rabbis delighted. Allegory was a favored method of the Church; it was passed over into literature by Christian poets, such as Dante, Spenser, and Milton. Allegory, of course, had also been popular among the Greeks, but there too as a particular approach to the problems of verbal discourse, wherein truth is achieved by discarding the "outer shell," the materiality of language for the inner thought, the universal general statement affirmed within the particular illogical word. (Such methods were applied, for example, to Homer by later generations offended by some seeming Homeric crudities.)

Of equal import for the history of interpretation was Aristotle's way of categorizing rhetoric and poetics; his texts on those topics became the manuals for all future work on those subjects. Aristotle's *separation* of rhetoric and poetics from "scientific logic" had as much impact on the study of these disciplines as what he actually wrote about them. In distinguishing between demonstrative (or apodeictic) reasoning and dialectical reasoning in the *Analytica Priora* (i 1. 24a22–23b12), Aristotle comments:

> The demonstrative premise differs from the dialectical because the demonstrative is the assumption of one of a pair of contradictory propositions (for the man who demonstrates assumes something and does not ask a question) but for the dialectical premise there is a question as to which of two contradictories are true. . . . [It is] demonstrative if it is true and accepted because deduced from basic assumptions, while a dialectical premise is for the enquirer a question as to which of two contradictories is true and for the reasoner the assumption of some plausible or generally held proposition.

In dialectical argument, premises are adopted for the sake of argument and need not necessarily be true. Dialectical reasoning is more of a process of criticism, conversation, and argument in which the premises are merely agreed upon. And rhetoric, as Aristotle had said, was in actuality the "counterpart of dialectic," not any science of itself.

Despite his separation of rhetoric from science, Aristotle did bring rhetoric within the sphere of philosophy. There had been, to be sure, a long-standing struggle between rhetoric and philosophy; rhetoric had originated in Sicily in the fifth century B.C.E. and was hence as old as philosophy. Its beginnings are attributed to Empedocles, his students Corax and Tisias, and later followers such as Gorgias, Lysias, and Isocrates. More specifically, the origin of rhetoric was in public oratory, where it was used as a powerful weapon for persuasion before tribunals, public assembly, and so forth (again, in contrast to Rabbinic argumentation, which arose from problems of a text). The art of persuasion can, of course, be used unscrupulously to support artifice as well as truth, and so rhetoric was perceived as a dangerous art. Plato condemned it as a lie in the *Protagoras, Gorgias,* and *Phaedrus.* Aristotle, however, did not go as far as Plato and connected rhetoric to philosophy through the logic of argumentation, as Paul Ricoeur points out.[17] Yet historically, as Ricoeur shows, rhetoric was reduced to a theory of style, and then even further to a theory of tropes, severing its connection to logic and philosophy.[18]

Despite his admission of a certain logic, albeit an inferior one, to rhetoric, Aristotle was responsible for rhetoric's ultimate demise:

> The more we try to make either dialectic or rhetoric not what they really are, practical faculties, but sciences, the more we shall inadvertently be destroying their true nature; for we shall be refashioning them and shall be passing into the region of sciences dealing with definite subjects rather than simply with words and forms of reasoning. [*Rh.* 1359b. 11–15.]

Only recently, however, has the advice of Aristotle been ignored. Literary critics and semioticians are ardently engaged in resurrecting and creating a *science* of rhetoric, indeed in constituting rhetoric as the *primary* science.*

The Contemporary Critique: Derrida and Ricoeur

One of Christianity's central interpretive axioms was the distinction between "spirit" and "letter." The severity of this differentiation justified the Church's overthrow of the authority of Rabbinic law, the divine text of the Jews, as mere "letter." For the Church, the true "spirit" was the New Testament through Jesus. In this attitude, the Church followed, in the main, a Hellenistic way of thinking, and a Greek metaphysic as well as metaphoric. Despite the separation of theology from hermeneutics in the eigh-

---

*Kenneth Burke led early in the field of rhetorical literary criticism. Jacques Derrida and the "Yale School"—Paul de Man, Geoffrey Hartman, J. Hillis Miller, Harold Bloom—are among the rhetorical school's foremost practitioners in America. In France, Tzvetan Todorov and Gerard Genette have led the field.

teenth and nineteenth centuries, interpretation theorists and especially literary critics have continued to think about literal and figurative language in a way that is still dependent on Greek ontology and its Christian extension.

Among recent thinkers attempting to articulate theories of language and interpretation appropriate to a twentieth century which has radically severed its ties with the Greco-Christian tradition are Paul Ricoeur, Hans-Georg Gadamer, and Jacques Derrida. The first two are, however, concerned to create a new hermeneutic based on a specifically Christian form of theology; the latter is intent on (Judaically) "deconstructing" the entire tradition of Western thought itself. Yet all are bound together in their debt to the thought of Heidegger. Though we must leave for later a more detailed examination of their contributions to hermeneutic theory, their critiques of Aristotle are most relevant here. Furthermore, the ideals they articulate for understanding language and interpreting texts will prepare us to understand Rabbinic thought.

Although Aristotle had separated poetics and rhetoric from metaphysics, Heidegger claimed in a famous statement, "The metaphorical exists only within the metaphysical," which meant, as Ricoeur explains, that "the transgressions of metaphor—and that of metaphysics are one and the same transfer."[19] In his well-known definition of metaphor in the *Poetica* (1457b), Aristotle had written: "Metaphor is the application of the name of a thing to something else, working either from genus to species, from species to genus, or from species to species, or by proportion." That is, metaphor is defined as a movement, a displacement, a transfer of name to an alien category, implying a deviation of sorts. This displacement involves the movement from a word's proper sense as constituted within the fixed order of genus and species, proportionality and coordination, to a figurative sense wherein the boundaries of these categories are transgressed, and one word is *substituted* for another from another category. Metaphor, in Ricoeur's apt phrases, is "calculated error," "aberrant attribution," "categorical transgression," and "semantic impertinence."[20]

This metaphorical transfer from the "proper" to the "figurative" sense, according to Heidegger and Derrida, is based on a metaphysical transfer from the "sensible" to the "nonsensible" realm, a transfer crucial for Western thought. The entire ontological tradition of Western metaphysics is based on the Platonic transfer of the soul from the visible to the invisible world. Sensible to nonsensible becomes literal to figurative, and then, in Christian thought, the letter versus the spirit. The distinction between literal and figurative, which became standard for the Western conception of language, also naturally leads to an allegorizing mode of interpretation, not only in theology but in literature as well. Rabbinic thought, we will find, developing its approaches to texts and words independently of Western metaphysics, has an entirely different approach to the meaning of the letter, and to the relations between various levels of meaning; they are conceived more as immanent aspects of one another than as elements in a hierarchically ordered progression. The entire tradition of transcending the word for the "unmediated vision" of being (to use the title of an early work of Geoffrey Hartman) inevitably left the letter behind.

The Hebrew God, however, though invisible, did not just statically exist, but *spoke*. His Being was apprehended through hearing, not seeing, through the text, the divine word. Rabbinic thought called for *more* intense concentration on the words and their relations, including even the physical shapes of the letters and even the text's punctuation. Behind the aspiration to the invisible, nonsensible world was the Greek desire to *see*, a concept of thought in terms of the image (*idea*, from the Greek *eidos, image*). Words were merely conventional signs, as Aristotle said, but thoughts were *likenesses* of things. Hence when the Christian deity was born in the cradle of the pagan world, he was, inevitably, a *physical* image of God, a mediator, and a *substitution*. He mediated the gap between sensible and nonsensible, thought and thing, by becoming both at once. The Rabbinic word became substantialized into flesh; the metaphorical transfer, which depended on the recognition of the tension between categories, the recognition that the metaphorical simultaneously "was" and "was not" what it "stood for," became itself literalized. As the first chapter of the Gospel of John puts it, "The Word became flesh and dwelt among us." While claiming to spiritualize Judaism, Christianity in effect literalized it with a vengeance.

Derrida, in his critique of Aristotle and the entire tradition of Western metaphysics, decries this literalization of metaphor as one of the most deadly sins. And herein, we might add, is one of the senses in which Derrida is most Rabbinic: Ricoeur and Gadamer will call for a restitution of metaphorical consciousness, of that preconceptual, spontaneous metaphorical conjunction of thoughts and images which is the primordial *iconicity* behind thought; Derrida will try to unmask the whole metaphysical basis upon which thought about metaphor takes place, and will label all of Western metaphysics a "white mythology"—a mythology which has "whitened," that is, blanked out the recognition of itself as mythology and taken itself for literal truth.

Writes Derrida,

> But if we turn the most critical and most properly Cartesian part of the critical process to the point of hyperbolic doubt . . . to the point at which doubt attacks not only ideas of sensible origin, but "clear and distinct" ideas, and the self-evident truths of mathematics. . . . the natural light and all the axioms which it enables us to see are never subjected to the most radical doubt.[21]

Quite true, for, as Aristotle had maintained, if one does not accept certain unquestioned, undemonstrated axioms, if a reason is asked for everything, then reasoning is destroyed (*Metaph.* 4. 4. 10006.a 5–11). Derrida is thus after the founding principle of Aristotelian ontology—the *ousia,* the ideal essence, the center of univocal being itself of which we always speak, but which is never totally contained in any subject or predicate, something which we must always abstract from language, sense, and thought to apprehend. "Abstract notions always conceal a sensible figure," he writes. What Greek thought split asunder—word and thing—Derrida seeks to rejoin, speaking of the "possibility of restoring or reconstituting beneath the metaphor which at once conceals and is concealed, what was orginally represented," the "primary concrete meaning."[22]

This primary meaning is always sensible, a kind of "transparent figure" which becomes metaphorical when put to philosophical use. In such cases the primary sensible meaning is not noticed, and the displacement into abstract meaning then becomes taken as the "proper" meaning. The philosophical concept cancels the original definiteness and determinacy, the sense of particular being, which was the essence of the original meaning. The expression of an abstract idea can only be an analogy, Derrida claims, based on metaphorical language. But philosophy masks the metaphorical nature of its concepts, detaches itself from their determinate and particular bases:

> By an odd fate, the very metaphysicians who think to escape the world of appearance are constrained to live perpetually in allegory. A sorry lot of poets, they dim the colors of the ancient fables, and they themselves but the garners of fables. They produce white mythology. . . . What is metaphysics?—a white mythology which assumes and reflects Western culture: the white man takes his own mythology (Indo-European mythology), his logos—that is, the mythos of his idiom, for the universal form of that which it is still his inescapable desire to call Reason. . . . White mythology, a metaphysics which has effaced in itself that fabulous science which brought it into being, and which yet remains, active and stirring, inscribed in white ink, an invisible drawing, covered over in the palimpsest.[23]

Derrida applauds Freud as one who was conscious of the metaphorical activity implicit in theoretical and philosophic discourse. Perhaps that was one of the reasons why Freud's method was attacked as unscientific. For, as Derrida contends, the problem of the sciences is that they are tempted to take the metaphor for the concept, to forget the fundamental metaphorical nature of abstraction. Like Christian thought, science literalizes the metaphor. As we have seen, the birth of science was due in part to the separation of word, concept, and thing in Greek thought, to a context where words could become mere empty signs pointing to concepts, with no life of their own. We will find in the next chapter how distinctive is Rabbinic thought in its faithfulness to the determinate and particular bases which underlie abstraction, and how skeptical of thought that seeks to abandon those bases.

The metaphor of the palimpsest is one Freud also uses for dream interpretation. Both he and Derrida—and the Rabbis—are probing for the original language, the concrete meaning behind the abstract concept, or dream image, or narrative. Lévi-Strauss is another of this school, whose fascination with "the savage mind" reveals the same desire to uncover a language, logic, and set of meanings which the tradition of Western thought has covered over. One of the most interesting aspects of Rabbinic thought is its development of a highly sophisticated system of interpretation based on uncovering and expanding the primary concrete meaning, and yet drawing a variety of logical inferences from these meanings without the abstracting, idealizing movement of Western thought.

Derrida especially proclaims the "superiority of the substantive," of "ideas of an object as superior to ideas of relations"; herein he shares Mill's and Hegel's attitude about the logical relation of subject and predicate, and the disappearance of the subject into the predicate in Aristotelian logic. It is precisely the whole Aristotelian apparatus of predicate and substance, of relating statements about a thing to what it *is,* that Derrida attacks. Ricoeur also notes that the operation of giving one thing's name to another in metaphor is intimately related to the predicative operation. *Proper* or *literal* meaning connotes *property,* the necessary inherence of a predicate in a subject, which for Aristotle is part of the nature of true definition. Ricoeur and Todorov try to rescue metaphor from the singular act of substituting one name for another, and place it on a *propositional* level instead. Metaphor is then defined as a preconceptual mode of ordering the world which does the groundwork, so to speak, for conceptual thought.

Derrida also condemns Aristotle for his "nominalization" of the whole field of metaphor, i.e., his defining metaphor solely as the transfer of a *noun* (*onoma*), thereby freezing the play of metaphor, restricting it to the role of independent significant apart from syntactic relations. (Rabbinic interpretation concentrates precisely on these syntactic relations not connected to substantive ideas.) And, Derrida claims, in an undisclosed way metaphor, *mimesis, logos, physis, phoné, onoma, semanein,* and *dianoia* are all linked, despite Aristotle's separation of science from rhetoric and of metaphysics from metaphor and mimesis. Derrida notes that the definition of metaphor in the *Poetica* is based on mimesis, on seeing likenesses, resemblances between disparate things: "To produce a good metaphor is to see a likeness" (*Poet.* 1459a. 7–8). But, Derrida maintains, the seeing of resemblances is also what makes metaphysics possible, and seeing resemblances is the power of truth, the unveiling of nature. Logos, mimesis, *alethea* (truth) are founded on one and the same movement, and lead to the same possibility: the "pleasure" in recognizing the same, the delight in seeing the picture, the representation. The *re*-cognition in catharsis is not only mimetic but metaphysical.

We recognize, we "know," by perceiving resemblance.* We see the

---

*See the interesting psychoanalytic interpretation of this in Marian Milner, "The Role of Illusion in Symbol Formation," in M. Klein et al., *New Directions in Psychoanalysis* (New York: Basic Books, 1957), pp. 82–107.

"same," implying the unchanging, static essence, the unmoving being which fixes for us a center of reference in the flux of phenomena, and without which there could be neither order, analogy, nor sense, nothing to determine whether the likeness was "correct" or "incorrect." The problem here, however, as Ricoeur points out, is the slippage of the language of analogy, the likeness of one term to another, over into the language of ontology, the *participation* of one thing in another. *To be like* then becomes *to be part of, to have partially*.

Hence Derrida asks that we concentrate not on the *be*-ing of nouns and predicates, but on what is *between* the significant members of speech, the conjunctions, articles, the joints of speech between the nouns, substantives, and verbs. For Aristotle, the minimal unit of signification is the noun, but Derrida (in good Rabbinic fashion) would have us leave the issues of being, predication, and participation for a nonontological, relational approach to language. An important consequence of such an approach, as Ricoeur notes, is that in overthrowing *ousia,* the primary central essence of Greek ontology, the metaphysical opposition between proper, or literal, meaning and figurative meaning is also undone. In sum, Derrida writes, "the sole thesis of philosophy" is "that the meaning aimed at through these figures is an essence rigorously independent of that which carries it over."[24] With the recognition that the metaphysical realm is at bottom metaphorical, and that there is no independent essence "beyond" (*meta*), the realm of language retains its *physis*, its concreteness, and is preserved. The claims of the letter are vindicated again.

(That is also the source of Derrida's dispute with Hegel in the latter's *Aesthetics*. Like Derrida, Hegel also observes that philosophical concepts are originally sensible meanings which have become transposed into the spiritual, nonsensible order. For Hegel, though, the effacement of the sensible aspect of the metaphor, the *Aufhebung* ("raising") of the sensible meaning into the spiritual meaning, which then becomes the proper expression, is an innovation. Derrida claims that this effacement of the original concreteness of the metaphor is a dissimulation, a masking of the true sensible and metaphorical origin of philosophy and a leap towards illusory idealization, and he attacks allegorized spiritual meanings and interpretive methods.)

With Derrida, the oppositions between what is the proper meaning and what is not, between essence and accident, intuition and discourse, thought and language, intelligible and sensible are overthrown. There is no nonmetaphorical realm to which one can aspire, or from which one can speak or think. The ideal of language is then no longer to allow the "thing-itself" to be known in its essential, proper truth. For Aristotle, the name can be said to be a proper name when it has only one sense. Derrida would free language from this univocity and open it up to an infinite plurality of meaning: "To be univocal is the essence, or rather the *telos* of language. This Aristotelian ideal has never been rejected by philosophy as such. It is philosophy."[25] Aristotle had written (*Metaph.* 4. 1006a. 34–b13) that although a word may have several senses, they must be limited, finite:

> If, however, they were not limited but if one were to say that the word has an infinite number of meanings, obviously reasoning [discourse, definition, logos] would be impossible; for not to have one meaning is to have no meaning, and if words have no meaning, reasoning with other people, and indeed with oneself, has been annihilated; for it is impossible to think anything if we do not think one thing; but if this is possible, one name might be assigned to *this* thing. Let it be assumed, then, as we said at the beginning, that the name has a meaning and has one meaning.

Hence, as Derrida comments, in Aristotle's view, man creates metaphors to express some one thing, and philosophy always has just one thing to say; those who manipulate the equivocalness of words and signs are to be dismissed as mere sophists.

As we will discover, the infinity of meaning and plurality of interpretation are as much the cardinal virtues, even divine imperatives, for Rabbinic thought as they are the cardinal sins for Greek thought. The movement of Rabbinic interpretation is not from one opposing sphere to another, from the sensible to the nonsensible, but rather "from sense to sense," a movement into the text, not out of it. Derrida complains that philosophy always attempts to conceal the sensible figures beneath its holy abstractions, and he speaks of the possibility of restoring or reconstructing, beneath the metaphor, what was originally represented, using the image of the palimpsest. (Derrida's aim should not be confused, however, with the finding of an originary "valid" level.) Freud, we noted, used the same figure to describe the way in which one must interpret the dream, and inveighed against the same allegorizing tendencies in "symbolic" dream interpretation; and Freud's reconstructive process, we will find, is clearly Rabbinic in methodology.

The Model of Metaphor

What such thinkers as Derrida, Freud, Ricoeur, Gadamer, and Lévi-Strauss are seeking is to recover the innate logic of language itself, to draw from language's own internal organization and energy the principles of thought that lie unacknowledged beneath the overlay of the conceptual framework with which we have hitherto approached words, things, and texts. Perhaps this is why a consideration of Rabbinic thought is so appropriate, for Rabbinic thought always gave primacy to the text, the word, and Greek thought to the mathematical figure. How does one discover, however, the inner living life of language without superimposing the conceptual framework which one seeks to penetrate? Ricoeur and Gadamer have looked to metaphor precisely for the reason that it represents the ordering act of language prior to the classifications of scientific logic, the seeing of resemblances where science had decreed separations.

Metaphorical seeing is an order of perceiving resemblances which transgresses the clear categories of rational logic. In Aristotelian terms, it is a "transfer": from species to genus, genus to species, and so forth. The transfer simultaneously recognizes and violates the logical structure of language, as Ricoeur notes.[26] In taking one thing for another, classifications are jumbled, the carefully constructed categories of thought transgressed, and the entire network disturbed. Ricoeur seeks to emphasize, in contrast to Aristotle, that this logical deviance is intimately related to the production of meaning, and that the essentially *discursive* nature of metaphor must be recognized. It is not merely the transfer of a *name* operating on one segment of discourse, but rather a production of meaning on the level of the *statement*.

We noted that when Aristotle defined metaphor solely in terms of the name, or noun, he determined its fate for centuries to come. It was relegated to the sphere of rhetoric and poetics and was banished from discourse and logic. Metaphor happened to the noun and not to discourse in general, and thus the theory of metaphor became a theory of tropes that one could classify taxonomically. Metaphor was treated rhetorically, not logically, and the same fault inherent in Plato's and Aristotle's theories of language in general—excessive emphasis on the noun or name as the axis of language—appears again in their theories of metaphor. Metaphor, however, has as much to do with proper predication as does metaphysics; moreover, as Derrida would have us believe, it is a truer, more open metaphysics than science or philosophy. The consequence of the Aristotelian definition for the history of rhetoric was that metaphor and rhetoric became, in general, theories of mere style, unrelated to argument and logic.

In the Aristotelian model, as explained by Ricoeur, certain names "properly" belong to certain kinds (species, genera) of things. Opposed to this "proper" meaning is the "metaphorical" or "figurative" meaning (which is "improper"). In the figurative meaning, one term is "borrowed" from another, "alien" realm and substituted for the "proper" term. This substitution is guided, according to the Aristotelian model, by a certain resemblance, which is generally a proportional relation between terms. One could, therefore, locate the "proper" terms for which the alien terms are substituted, and restore them. The figurative use of words, then, does not add or produce anything new, but cancels itself out. Figures of speech are thus merely ornaments and not generators of meaning.

(In not recognizing that metaphor operates on the semantic level of discourse, and in consigning it to the sphere of semiotics (signs), contemporary French linguistic theory, Ricoeur shows, follows the same hypothesis as classical rhetoric: that metaphor is a figure of one word only. The French theorists try to be somewhat more "scientific" than Aristotle in their cataloguing of the deviations and substitutions of metaphor within a general science of deviation, but they nevertheless do not conceive of metaphor as anything more than a one-word trope. English linguistics, on the other hand, has been influenced by propositional logic, and the British understand metaphor in terms of predication rather than substitution.)

In his critique, Ricoeur follows the line of those who fault Aristotle for not having developed a logic of propositions. Metaphorical movement is a "dis-ordering" of the classificatory scheme, which simultaneously destroys and creates a new order. In this sense, says Ricoeur, the category-mistake is the "complement of a logic of discovery,"[27] which "re-describes" reality. Metaphor belongs, then, to a heuristic of thought. But is not this process of disturbing the logical order the very same from which all classification itself originates? Is there not, asks Ricoeur, a metaphoric process at the very origin of all logical thought and classification?

Gadamer agrees. The dialectical capacity of discovering similarities and perceiving one quality common to the many, which is at the root of metaphor, the transpositions from one sphere to another, themselves have *logical* function, and the stylistic device of a metaphorical image is only the rhetorical form of this logical function. Metaphor, on this deeper level, is a generative principle of both logic and language. To see the similar in the disparate is what leads the mind to the universal. Aristotle's problem, says Gadamer, is that by

> measuring by the logical idea of proof, he robs the logical achievement of language of its scientific justification. . . . What originally constituted the life of a language and made up its logical productivity, the spontaneous and inventive seeking out of similarities by means of which it is possible to order things, is now pushed aside and instrumentalized into a rhetorical figure called metaphor.[28]

The similarities that metaphor discovers are not, however, absorbed into the universal. They are not the identity of a universal genus in which conceptual form is abstracted from particulars. In metaphor, to see the similar is to appreciate the "same" within and in spite of "difference"; "being as" simultaneously means both "being" and "not being," or what Ricoeur calls calls a "split reference." Metaphor exists within the tension of identity and difference, and metaphorical resemblance is at bottom a unity of identity and difference. This resemblance, furthermore, is not a pictorial one, as Aristotle would have it in his praise of the capacity of metaphor "to place things before your eyes," to make visible an abstraction. The resemblance, rather, is a tension between identity and difference, wherein the imagination does not merely produce physical images, pictures, but "sees as," perceives the similarity in dissimilarity. Hence, according to Ricoeur, "the 'place of metaphor' is neither the name, sentence nor discourse, but copula of the verb *to be*."[29] The metaphorical *is* means both *is not* and *is like,* and a central characteristic of metaphorical truth is that it preserves the *is not* within the *is.* Metaphor is, in this sense, a subversive element in the carefully constructed edifice of Greek ontology, and perhaps for this reason its unsettling ambiguities were relegated to the nonscientific realm of poetics. Thus tamed, metaphor became merely a type of figure of speech, a defused rhetorical trope.

Aristotle had strongly affirmed that the Law of Contradiction was the most certain of all principles, indeed that upon which his entire logic rested, but in Monroe Beardsley's apt words: "Metaphor is what forms a meaningful self-contradictory attribution."[30] Metaphor audaciously applies the predicate where it is "inapplicable." It is thus an agent of revelation, the same kind of revelation with which Derrida seeks to unmask the false abstraction inherent in the philosophic concept. Whereas the philosophic concept masks the "difference" in order to create a generic or universal identity out of dissimilar particulars, and an ideal essence abstracted from all, yet the sustaining unity of all, metaphor presents—in open form—the conflict and tension between identity and difference in any given concept. It juxtaposes but does not fuse. Metaphorical predication is based on relation, not substantive operation.

It is interesting to note that the principle of juxtaposition as a logical mechanism in the dream was recognized by Freud. In the dream, juxtaposition can indicate the relation of cause or that of identity; and in Rabbinic interpretation juxtaposition of passages or topics also provides one of the grounds for logical inference, technically called *smuchin*. For example, the Biblical text's juxtaposition of the description of the building of the Tabernacle (Exod. 25:8–31:12) with the commandment to observe the Sabbath (Exod. 31:13–17) is to teach, say the Rabbis, precisely which labors are forbidden on the Sabbath. They infer that the thirty-nine labors necessary to build the Tabernacle are the thirty-nine labors forbidden on the Sabbath. This type of inference based on juxaposition is quite obviously different from the predications of Greek thought. It is relational rather than ontological, dealing with propositions rather than predicates. In juxtaposition, two entities are related and applicable to one another, but not identical. There is similarity within difference, each retaining its own independent identity.

The relation of the structure of Semitic language to Rabbinic logic is an interesting question which we cannot, however, pursue here. It is important to note, though, that ancient Semitic did not have a verb "to be." The copula was not "is." As Emile Benveniste writes,

> It sufficed to juxtapose the nominal terms of the utterance in order to get a nominal sentence with the supplementary, feature—probable, though not graphemically represented—of a pause between the terms. . . . [This pause] is actually the sign of predication.[31]

If predicative utterances are linguistically constructed through the juxtaposition of nominal forms in a free order, one might speculate that this linguistic structure underlies–leads to the Rabbinic logical principle of predication by juxtaposition.

All this is a fitting prelude to my argument that the Rabbinic way of thinking is precisely that kind of linguistic-metaphorical hermeneutic which thinkers such as Gadamer, Ricoeur, Derrida, and others call for in their work. At the end of *The Rule of Metaphor,* Ricoeur speculates:

> One can imagine a hermeneutic style where interpretation conforms both to the notion of concept and to that of the constitutive intention of the experience seeking to be expressed in the metaphorical mode. . . . Interpretation is a mode of discourse that functions at the intersection of two domains, metaphorical and speculative, a composite discourse.[32]

Let us keep this definition in mind as we approach the discussion of Rabbinic thought.

2

Rabbinic Thought: The Divinity of the Text

> When Rabbi Meir came to Rabbi Ishmael and gave his profession as a scribe [of the Torah] the latter required of him the utmost care, "for if you leave out a single letter or write a single letter too much, you will be found as one who destroys the whole world."
>
> —*Eruv.* 13a

> In the days of King David innocent children could interpret the Torah in forty-nine ways positively and forty-nine ways negatively.
>
> —*Midrash Lev. Rab.* 26

> Ben Bag Bag said: Learn it and learn it [the Torah], for everything is in it.
>
> —*Avot* 5:21

> And God spoke to Moses "face to face" [Exod. 33:11]. The Holy One, blessed be He, said to Moses, "Moses, Let us, you and I, explain the various facets of the law."
>
> —*Ber.* 63b

With the deceptively simple words "In the beginning God created the heavens and the earth," the Hebrew Bible begins. In fact, however, this statement was (long before Derrida) a supreme challenge to the entire classical tradition of Western metaphysics: to assert that matter was not eternal, that the world had a temporal origin, that substance came into being through divine fiat, indeed through divine *speech* ("And God said, 'Let there be . . .' ") threatened the foundations of Greek ontology. As Hans Jonas puts it:

> There was an anti-metaphysical agent in the very nature of the Biblical position that led to the erosion of classical metaphysics, and changed the

whole character of philosophy. . . . The Biblical doctrine pitted contingency against necessity, particularity against universality, will against intellect. It secured a place for the contingent within philosophy, against the latter's original bias.[1]

In contemporary terms, we might say that the Biblical view was a kind of "deconstruction" of the classical idea; it posited an extreme negativity at the center of things.

For if the world was created through the arbitrary will of God, then it was contingent and had no necessary existence. This meant, furthermore, that there were no necessary *archai* (axioms), inherent in the nature of things, upon which one could construct logically necessary proofs in sound Aristotelian fasion.

Whereas Aristotle's "demonstrative" or "truly scientific" reasoning depended on the unquestioning acceptance of certain necessary premises, dialectical reasoning is based on premises which, according to Aristotle's definition, are not necessarily true; this form of reasoning is for Aristotle, therefore, an inferior mode of thought, such as that used in rhetoric. The man who lives in more intimate association with *natural* things is better able, says Aristotle, to lay down correct *archai* than one whose vision is narrowed by a profusion of words. And what this natural philosopher should seek in the pregiven matter upon which he focuses his attention are the universal forms imparted to creation by a Divinity whose essential function is to be the principle of form. True knowledge is of universals, not particulars.

In the Biblical view, however, all of creation was contingent, including all premises. Nothing was *necessary*: there were no *natural laws* that were logically deducible or rationally self-evident, and no unquestioned principles that formed the basis of reality.* Everything could have been otherwise; even reason itself was not necessary. An important consequence of this perspective was that reason, too, became subject to relentless probing in a way which was anathema to the Greeks. Perhaps the relentless skepticism of the Rabbis—manifested in the constant search for alternative explanations, an intense scrutiny of the most seemingly insignificant and mundane details, and the dialectical twists and turns of Rabbinic thought—can be viewed in part as a direct philosophic expression of creationist doctrine. (And, of course, it was applied to that which superseded nature's place in Greek thought: the divine speech, the Biblical text itself.) Jonas points out[2] that the divorce between mind and nature in the Biblical doctrine of creation was effected by a separation between God and the world

---

*Lev Shestov, the early twentieth-century Russian Jewish philosopher, passionately argues for the existential liberation which the Hebraic mind achieves in its undoing of the "Chains of Parmenides," the Principle of Necessity underlying Greek thought. His master-work, *Athens and Jerusalem*, trans. Bernard Martin (Athens, Ohio Univ. Press, 1966), expands upon some of the major themes of this chapter and is well worth reading. Shestov taught in Paris and had much influence on existential philosophy.

which also greatly diminished the status of nature. The hierarchical great chain of being was thereby also demolished. If all things were contingent, and must constantly be recreated from nothingness, all were then ontologically equal. Moreover, individual, particular existence now assumed supreme importance, for it was only God's constant creation and supervision of every particular thing that sustained and continually called it forth form nothingness. The universal was demoted, and the particular given primacy, in direct opposition to the status they had been allotted in Greek philosophy.

It is no wonder, then, that from a certain Greek point of view, the principle of contingency could be destructive of knowledge and philosophy. Precisely herein was one of Derrida's points of attack against Greek metaphysics. Derrida exhorts us to recognize the negativity at the heart of things, and in good Jewish prophetic fashion decries philosophy as "white mythology," a pagan making of images, an idol worship of being as a central, literal, present, and necessary essence. To Derrida, being has become the "graven image" of the Greeks and the philosophers, an idol insofar as it represents the *literalization* of the fundamental metaphoricity of things and substitutes presence for the negativity at the center of things. For Derrida, philosophy, like Christianity, is pagan because it literalizes the metaphor.

The Bible and the Greeks

In literary criticism, one of the most famous discussions of the contrast between Greek and Hebraic conceptions of reality is Erich Auerbach's classic essay, "Odysseus' Scar."[3] Auerbach's comparison of the Bible and Homer elucidates the way in which the *philosophic* differences Jonas points out are reflected in narrative structures.

Auerbach perceives, first of all, that the basic impulse of the Homeric style is "to represent phenomena in a fully externalized form, visible and palpable in all their parts, and completely fixed in their spatial and temporal relations . . . . nothing must remain hidden and unexpressed."[4] In Homer, everything takes place in a foreground in an absolute temporal present which is uniformly illuminated. By contrast, in Biblical narrative, such as the story of the sacrifice of Isaac, everything is indeterminate and contingent; time and space are undetermined, motives and purposes are unexpressed, and only what is minimally necessary for the narrative to proceed is externalized while the rest is left in obscurity. The account seems fragmentary, or in Auerbach's apt phrase, "fraught with background," full of lacunae. Speech here hides as much as it externalizes, and the narrative is entangled in layers of history, not at all entirely immersed in the present.

In Homer, psychic complexity is expressed through the alternation of emotional states, whereas in the Bible, consciousness extends into multilayered depths, which simultaneously exist and conflict. In Homer, there is no concealment, no secret hidden meaning, although later Greek allegorists tried to read him in this fashion. In Auerbach's felicitious words: "Homer can be analyzed . . . but he cannot be interpreted."[5] The Biblical text is oriented not towards "realism," but towards "truth." "Far from seeking, like Homer, merely to make us forget our own reality for a few hours, it seeks to overcome our reality: we are to fit our own life into its words, feel ourselves to be elements in its structure of universal history."[6] The Biblical narrative is not meant to "represent" simple reality or merely tell a story. It is intentionally mysterious, demanding subtle interpretation, imbedding doctrines within itself which are inextricably connected with the physical aspect of the narrative.* Indeed, Auerbach continues, the Biblical narrative claims an absolute authority which subsumes our own reality and everything that happens in our own world. The Homeric poems, on the other hand, are set in a particular space and time; events which come before and after them are not dependent upon them. But the Biblical narrative claims that it is the structure into which all of history fits, and everything that is known about the world becomes part of its sequence of events. Moreover, by interpretive extension, all new facts become fitted into its account. Hence, in the Hebraic view, as Auerbach perceives, "interpretation in a determined direction becomes a general method of comprehending reality."[7] And because of the text's claim to absolute authority, the method of interpretation spread to other non-Jewish traditions.

It is significant that Auerbach chose the essay "Odysseus' Scar" to begin his masterwork subtitled "The Representation of Reality in Western Literature." For we might say that the contrast between the Bible and Homer signifies two basic, though opposite, types of conceiving the world—and the word. In the contingent world of Hebrew thought, one must not look to nature for ultimate reality, but to the divine creative word which simultaneously reveals and conceals the hidden God, and He is not to be identified with nature, or any of its forms. The text claims an absolute authority in Hebraic thought which it could not possibly possess for the Greeks.

While it is true that Homer also became a religious text for the Greeks, Saul Lieberman shows that copies of Homer were handled with comparative levity.[8] Certain verses of Homer, for example, were eliminated, and

*A recent important addition to literary studies of the Bible is Robert Alter's *The Art of Biblical Narrative* (New York: Basic Books, Inc., 1981), published too late to be included here. Alter also writes: "An essential aim of the innovative technique of fiction worked out by the ancient Hebrew writers was to produce a certain indeterminacy of meaning, especially in regard to motive, moral character, and psychology. . . . Meaning, perhaps for the first time in narrative literature, was conceived as a *process*, requiring continual revision—both in the ordinary sense and in the etymological sense of seeing-again—continual suspension of judgment, weighing of multiple possibilities, brooding over gaps in the information provided" (p. 12).

corrections and emendations were made that have no parallel whatsoever in Rabbinic exegesis. According to Dilthey,[9] systematic exegesis in Greece arose out of the requirements of the educational system. To interpret Homer was originally a pastime for the intelligentsia. Exegesis acquired a more solid foundation with the rise of rhetoric among the Sophists, and of course with Aristotle's elaboration of the principles of literary composition, and with his *Rhetorica*. The Alexandrian grammarians and especially the Stoics deepened the process of interpretation, the latter by introducing the allegorical interpretation of Homer. They sought to read purely philosophical world views into his narratives. Allegory, of course, became a predominant mode of Christian Bible interpretation for a variety of reasons which will be discussed in the next chapter.

For the Greeks, Homer was an inspired text, but never attained the all-embracing authority that Scripture had for the Jews. The Rabbinic relation to the text was fundamentally different. Let us begin the attempt to define this relation by using Auerbach's perceptions, and then by considering the difference between the Greek *onoma*, analyzed in Chapter 1, and the Hebrew *davar*.

What Auerbach describes as a movement in the Homeric narrative towards fully illuminated, externalized form, toward realistic visibility, may be seen in light of our previous discussion of the function of the word in Greek thought: to be a sign which points beyond itself towards the *full vision* of the thing itself. The Biblical text, however, points not outwards towards images and forms, but inwards towards itself, its own network of relations, of verbal and temporal ambiguities. It calls for its own decipherment, not for a movement away from itself towards vision or abstraction; the word leads inwards into itself, not outwards towards the "thing." What is required is that one "listen" to or read it more intently. As we noted, the Hebrew term for word, *davar*, is also the term for *thing*.

Most writing about the "concept of the word" in Hebrew thought is concerned primarily with the Biblical, in contrast to the Rabbinic, context. (In general terms, we can define "Rabbinic" as the literature and attitudes that began to be formed in the time of the Second Temple—roughly, from the fourth century B.C.E. onwards—and that predominated after the destruction of the Second Temple in 70 C.E. until the redaction of the Babylonian Talmud in approximately the sixth century C.E. The development of this literature will be sketched in the next chapter.) Auerbach's perception of the Biblical text as fragmentary and obscure agrees well with the Rabbinic doctrine that the "Written Torah" (i.e., the Bible) is only a part of the total revelation of the divine word. According the Rabbinic view, the written Scriptures are intentionally incomplete and are meant to be accompanied and supplemented by the oral Torah, simultaneously given to Moses; this oral law explains, elaborates, and interprets the obscurities and ambiguities of the written text. The text and its interpretation, then, are not seen as two separate entities, but as twin aspects of the same revelation.

While this central concept will be examined in detail later, it is important to note it here, for one cannot truly grasp the Rabbinic concept of the word solely by considering the Biblical text, as does Auerbach and some of the writers whom we will presently discuss. (Moreover, this dispute about the validity of the "oral law" is at the heart of the conflict between Judaism and Christianity. Christianity rejected the oral law entirely, adhering to the written text alone, resolving many difficulties and obscurities of meaning through the belief in Jesus as the written law's "fulfillment.")

Though *davar* means both *thing* and *word* in Hebrew, it is crucial to point out that *thing* did not have the Greek connotations of *substance*. As I. Rabinowitz puts it, "the word is the reality in its most concentrated, compacted, essential form."[10] *Reality* is a far more appropriate word to use than *thing*, for it does not evoke the same connotations as do *substance* and *being*. Of course, the physical object itself was not considered to be identical to the word which designated it, but for the Hebrew mind, the essential reality of the table was the word of God, not any idea of the table as in the Platonic view, or some *ousia*.

The Hebrew word was not just an arbitrary designation, but an aspect of the continuous divine creative force itself. Each word, as Rabinowitz puts it, was the inner specific character or essence of its respective reality. Names are not conventional, but intrinsically connected to their referents; the name, indeed, is the real referent of the thing, its essential character— not the reverse, as in Greek thought. One does not pass beyond the name as an arbitrary sign towards a non verbal vision of the thing, but rather *from the thing to the word*, which creates, characterizes, and sustains it. Hence *davar* is not simply *thing* but also *action, efficacious fact, event, matter, process*. The *word of God* was more than the act of saying; it was a creative force, an instrument capable of enacting realities, a concentration of power—and in this sense a *thing*. The word possessed the properties of the reality, and was itself a palpable substance, but not in the manner of Greek being.

With the above in mind, one can see how Christianity took the Hebraic concept of the word as essential reality and combined it with Greek concepts of substance and being, and developed the idea of the incarnation— the word-become-flesh, *thing* in a literal sense. Then a distinction had to be made between the incarnate word, and the "old" word, which had merely prefigured in a symbolic way the "fulfilled" word: thus a distinction between the "Old" and "New" Testaments. In Christianity, the Hebrew Scriptures then acquired the status which words had in Greek thought— mere signs, figures, shadows pointing to the true word, the word of flesh. True reality became again for Christianity substantial being, not verbal pattern; the text was supplanted, the movement of interpretation now directed to the revelation of how all words point to and are fulfilled by the word of flesh. The opposition between literal and metaphorical is instituted, and allegory becomes a predominant mode of interpretation.

In the first verses of the Gospel of John, where the word-become-flesh idea is most fully articulated, the Greek term *logos* is used for *word*. Thorlief Boman devoted considerable attention to the contrast between *davar* and *logos* in his book *Hebrew Thought Compared with Greek*. Boman points out that the root of *logos* in Greek means *to gather, to put together in order, arrange,* and only gradually did *logos* come to designate *word, reckoning*. Originally, it had nothing to do with the function of speaking. *Logos*, the concept of *gathering together in an order* then came to be defined as *reasonable content, rational principle,* or *knowable governing law.* As Boman puts it:

> What is essential for a proper understanding of *logos* is the fact that various meanings could, for the Greeks, converge into one concept and thus into one comprehensive unity; accordingly logos expresses the mental function that is highest according to Greek understanding.[11]

The tendency to *gather* various meanings *into a one* is, as we have seen, characteristic of Greek thought in general: its movement towards the universal, the general, the univocal. The Rabbinic tendency, by contrast, is towards differentiation, metaphorical multiplicity, multiple meaning. One needs to search the forms, shapes, patterns of words, and their varying connections within an expansive text; there is no confinement of meaning within the ontology of substance. (This liberation from the ontology of substance is, of course, precisely Derrida's intent.)

Whereas for the Jews, God manifested Himself through words in a divine text, for the Greeks theophany was visual, not verbal—a direct, immediate appearance of the gods. Thus, in the Hellenistic era, the divine logos ultimately became, through the influences of Neoplatonism, Stoicism, and Christianity—visible theophany, a subject we will discuss in more detail in the next chapter.

Auerbach notes that the Homeric narrative pushes towards fully externalized form in an absolute present, whereas the Biblical text is abrupt, obscure, undefined. Boman also writes of the seeming lack of interest for the Hebrew mind in photographic appearances of things or persons, a lack of interest in representation as copy or plastic image. We have seen, too, how Aristotle's theory of knowledge was at bottom representative, how the image is at the heart of Greek thought. Boman agues that the Greeks experienced reality differently from the Hebrews. They considered reality to be "an objective, given quantity with which our own senses, particularly our sight, bring us into contact."[12] The Greeks recount and describe what they see, but show no inclination for verbose narration. Greek perception, he claims, has been of decisive significance for philosophy, for all our concepts are given through sight, even time. If sight is the predominant mode, then in the search for identity in knowledge, resemblance is bound to be defined in terms of copy, re-presentation, mirroring—and thought, therefore, is *spec*ulative. One seeks the reflection of true being in one's own consciousness.

Spectacle as the origin of *speculation* applies to Greek religion as well as to Greek philosophy and art. The Greek gods appear in order to observe and be observed; Zeus is the supreme spectator, or, as Boman puts it: "The standpoint of the spectator is for the Greeks already divine in itself."[13] One who participates in a cultic act or drama is also called a *spectator,* a word which is connected in the folk etymology to *god.*[14] Boman further argues that it was precisely this urge towards visualization that necessitated polytheism, for since it was impossible to gather together all the divine qualities and functions into a single image, they became distributed amongst several persons. (Rabbinic thought developed the doctrine of poly*semy* as opposed to poly*theism*: the multiple meanings that may be heard or read within the Word, rather than the many gods which may be seen.) Boman writes that for the Greeks, the *appearance* of the gods solved all difficulties in conception (this idea will be carried over into Christianity). *Image* as *copy* means also visibility as manifestation and substantiality; the image partakes of the essence of the thing itself, participates in its reality.

Perhaps one can also understand the Biblical ban on images in this light. The Jewish idea of the invisible God culminates in the confession of faith: "*Hear* O Israel." In the account of the revelation at Sinai, the Biblical text relates, "And all the people saw the thunderings and the lightnings, and the voice of the horn, and the mountain smoking" (Exod. 20:15). Comments Rashi, the famous Jewish medieval commentator, "They saw that which should be heard which is impossible to see in another place." The revelation was to see what is *heard*, a voice, not an image. The invisible is manifested through sound and the divine word does not become "fulfilled" or hypostatized into a present being. Revelation is not appearance.

Jean-François Lyotard, a contemporary critic belonging to the French school, delineates the difference between modern and Greek thought in the issue of fulfillment of the paternal word:

> What's in Hamlet that's not in Oedipus? There is non-fulfillment. This can be seen as the psychic dimension of neurosis or the tragic dimension of thought. It has quite another dimension. Oedipus fulfills his fate of desire; the fate of Hamlet is the non-fulfillment of desire; this chiasmus is the one that extends between what is Greek and what is Jewish, between the tragic and the ethical. . . . In Greek tragedy, traces of the figure in which we are dispossessed of origin are able to show themselves. There is no reconciliation, but a re-presentation. . . . In Hebraic ethics, representation is forbidden, the eye closes, the ear opens in order to hear the father's spoken word. The image figure is rejected because of its fulfillment of desire and delusion; its function of truth is denied.[15]

In Lyotard's analysis, the God who speaks dispossesses, so to speak, the subject. Just as Oedipus is dispossessed of his origin, so too is the ethical subject dispossessed by being chosen through the imperative of the divine word. The difference between himself and the other remains; it does not collapse into an erotic drive to bring the other back to the same

(Hamlet's unfulfilled wish). In Jewish thought, the difference between the father and son is irrevocable. There is no fulfillment of the word in an ontological return to the sameness of son and father, as there is for Christianity. In the language of contemporary literary theory, the writing, the text as a gift, is the father's presence-in-absence. Through the text, the subject is taken and possessed: the son is possessed by the voice of the father.

Lyotard reads Hamlet within this framework. Hamlet has been displaced and is not able to fulfill his desire in identifying with Claudius.

> Hamlet's displacement by his uncle is the displacement of the subject in his relation to desire. Oedipus fulfills his desire in non-recognition; Hamlet unfulfills his desire in representation. The complex function of representation in Shakespearean tragedy must be tied to the dimension of non-fulfillment, that is to say, the properly Judaic contribution.[16]

In Lyotard's view, the difference between Greek fate and Jewish *kerygma* is the difference between Oedipus and Hamlet: the representation of desire fulfilling itself in nonrecognition, and desire nonfulfilling itself in compulsive representation,[17] by which Lyotard presumably means the process of continual hearing as interpretation, not imagistic representation. And, of course, *Hamlet* is indeed permeated with references to the *ear*—poison in the ears, ears assailed both literally and metaphorically.

This tension between presence and absence is expressed more readily through voice than vision. Vision, appearance, is fullness, complete presence of the thing; sound is a more subtle mode of presence, a moving vibration that both is and is not there. Sound creates patterns but not static presences, themes but not theophanies. Stability is attained through repetition, recognition of recurring patterns in a structure of inner relationships. In Lévi-Strauss, for example, musical pattern provides the most accurate model for the logical structure of myth (see the "overture" to *The Raw and the Cooked*).[18] Indeed, the entire movement of modern thought is away from classical metaphysics and ontology towards a structural or processual rather than substantial approach to reality.

Perhaps it could be said that Western literature has always been plagued by the appearance–reality conundrum because of the conflict between the foundational world view of Greek philosophy and the insights of art. The delusions of appearance, the ambiguities of being, the contradictory rather than solidly logical and substantial nature of being and time, are issues in art from its earliest beginnings to the present—and Shakespeare, of course, is one who examined these issues most penetratingly. One of the reasons, no doubt, why we are at present witnessing the coronation of metaphor as the new philosophical idol is because the metaphorical view of reality, as delineated in the last chapter, celebrates ambiguity, contradiction, and occurs precisely on the borderlines of ontology when something simultaneously both is and is not. Metaphor is alternative metaphysics.

Rabbinic thought is also an alternative metaphysics, in sharp contrast to our entire Western conceptual framework, which Boman claims developed from Greek dependence on the visual faculty.* Boman makes much of von Dobschutz's assertion that Hebrew thinking moves in time while the Greeks take space as their dominant thought form.[19] The Greco-European concept of time is "rectilinear": time is conceived as a straight line, a series in succession. Western time is determined by the solar cycle, whereas the Jewish year is based on a lunar cycle, time rhythms rather than time cycles or time lines. Instead of conceiving time in terms of the circle, based on solar movement, Hebrew time is conceived in terms of rhythmic alternation, based on the phases of the moon. "For us, the turn of the year is the time when the annual cycle is at an end; in Hebraic time, it is when the beginning of the year returns. . . . Time is a rhythm which is a ceaseless return of the same time-content."[20] Hence time is something qualitative defined by its content.

Although the characterization of the contrast between Greek and Hebrew thought as spatial versus temporal is too facile, it is worth examining the idea somewhat further. According to Boman, space is the predominant mode of thought for us, functioning somewhat like a vast container holding everything together. For the Hebrews, time plays this role and consciousness is the great container of life. Furthermore, the unity of time consciousness is not divisible. Any event is a coherent whole. Again, melody is a most accurate representation of this concept. In melody, past, present, and future are simultaneously bound together in rhythmic alternation and an indivisible whole. Modern literature has many parallels to this type of time consciousness, most obviously in the stream-of-consciousness technique.

In temporal consciousness, events are not things, but abiding facts, and historical events are indestructible. In Boman's words, "The consequences of events can be altered, but the events themselves can never be altered. They are the permanent stock of a people's life. The difference between past and present is less important than the qualitative distinction between events. A decisive event of antiquity can balance many current events in evaluation of the present."[21]

(One need not strain too hard to see the relation of psychoanalysis to the kind of temporal consciousness Boman describes as Hebraic. Past events are continuously present in the unconscious, the past indeed is indestructible, and its consequences subsume the present.)

The space–time polarity may be compared to our previous distinction between Greek and Hebrew thought in terms of seeing and hearing. The spatial is what is seen; time is a function of inner hearing. Hebraic time is an epistemological mode. Inevitably, the Jews are the people of *history*, of time—wanderers in space, exiled from place, but rooted in time, a time in

*Derrida agrees with this claim; see his "White Mythology," pp. 47–61.

which linear chronology is overcome by contemporaneity. This capacity for experiencing contemporaneity with the action under discussion will be important for understanding Rabbinic hermeneutics and its seeming anachronisms. Boman points out that contemporaneity is a kind of psychological time with its own laws: "Strict contemporaneity is therefore the same as psychic identity. Two psychological contents coalesce into one. . . . It corresponds to the geometric congruence of Greek thought which expresses the spatial identity of two quantities."[22] The multifarious patterns of identity in Rabbinic interpretation could be seen in this light. In fact, it is one of the fundamental principles of Scriptural interpretation that "There is no chronological sequence in Scripture" (*Pes.* 6b). The Biblical text, that is, is not considered to be in temporal order. Events which happened earlier are often placed after events which transpired later, and are interpreted accordingly.

The Greek *present* is defined by the place where the action takes place, and we are there as spectators and witnesses. The Hebrew present, however, is fluid, containing both past and future simultaneously.[23] One can see, therefore, how multiple meanings could be derived from and are inherent in every event, for every event is full of reverberations, references, and patterns of identity that can be infinitely extended. In the Christian reading of the Biblical text, though, events are seen on a sequential time line, as predictive of the fulfillment that would later come with Jesus: they attain their meaning as signs pointing towards him. This view of the text uses a more Greek sense of time.

The Text

Boman's analysis of the Hebraic mind, however, does not at all touch upon the concept of the *text* itself and the Jewish relation to it. At this point we can move on to the Rabbinic concept of language and meaning which has at its center the concept of the divinity of the text. The Biblical text is not, according to the Rabbinic view, a material thing located in a single space and circumscribed by a quantifiable time. The text ultimately is not even that authoritative and divine document which was given to Moses at a particular time and place, but, claims the Talmud, "The Torah preceded the world" (*Shab.* 88b). If the world of space and time had not yet been created, then in what manner did the Torah exist? "It was written with letters of black fire upon a background of white fire" (Yer, *Shek.* 13b; Rashi on Deut. 33:2). The material ink and parchment are seen as the garments for the divine wisdom enclothed therein.

In other words, in the Rabbinic view the Torah is not an artifact of nature, a product of the universe; the universe, on the contrary, is the product of the Torah. According to the famous midrash on the first verses of Genesis:

It is customary that when a human being builds a palace, he does not build it according to his own widsom, but according to the wisdom of a craftsman. And the craftsman does not build according to his own wisdom, rather he has plans and records in order to know how to make rooms and corridors. The Holy One, blessed be He did the same. He looked into the Torah and created the world. [*Ber. Rab.* 1:1]

Far from being a physical book, the Torah, in the Rabbinic view, is the blueprint of creation and, therefore, there is a direct correlation between the world and Torah. The Torah is not seen as speculation *about* the world, but part of its very essence. Where ought one look to fathom the secrets of creation, to comprehend the laws of nature? To the Text.

Nachmanides (1195–1270 c.e.) writes in the introduction to his classic commentary on the Torah that God explained all the secrets of creation to Moses, and, as the Talmud says, all of it was written into the Torah either explicitly or implicitly—in words, in the numerical value of the letters, or in the form of the letters, whether written normally or with some change in forms (such as bent or crooked letters), or in the tips of letters and their crownlets. He cites the well-known passage from the Talmud (*Men.* 29b) which relates that when Moses ascended to heaven he found God attaching crownlets to certain letters of the Torah. Moses asked Him what they were for, and God answered, "One man is destined to interpret mountains of laws on their basis." When Moses asked to be shown this man, he saw Rabbi Akiba (second century c.e.) teaching his disciples a lesson which Moses was not able to follow, and Moses felt very grieved. Then he heard the disciples ask R. Akiba, "How do you know this?" and R. Akiba answer: "This is a law given to Moses on Mt. Sinai." Nachmanides explains that these hints can only be understood from an oral tradition traceable to Moses, who received it on Sinai.

Hence the written text is not only the enclothing of the fiery preexistent letters in which are contained the secrets of creation, but with the proper methods of interpretation, one can unlock the mysteries of all being. Every crownlet of every letter is filled with significance, and even the forms of letters are hints to profound meanings. To understand creation, one looks not to nature but to the Torah; the world can be read out of the Torah, and the Torah read from the world.

The material text, then, is the embodiment or enclothing of this non-material original Torah, and the parameters of the text are, to begin with, infinite. The name *Torah* also expresses this concept. It comes from a root meaning not *book* or *law*, but *teaching, instruction* in its most comprehensive sense. Thus while Torah is considered to be a blueprint of the universe, it is also a guide to the most minute and mundane details of daily life. There is a well-known story in the Talmud concerning a disciple who concealed himself under the bed of his great teacher in order to discover how he behaved with his wife. When asked the reasons for his behavior the disciple answered, "It is Torah and deserves to be studied" (*Ber.* 62a). The story illuminates a crucial concept—the all-embracing unity of Torah as the underlying structure of reality; all aspects of existence can be seen as ramifications of and connected to the Torah. Nothing is allowed to be "irrelevant" or outside its scope. (As Derrida or Barthes would say: "There is nothing outside the Text.")

Perhaps we can further understand, this concept through our previous discussion of the consequences of the creation-*ex-nihilo* doctrine. This doctrine was a blow to the hierarchical order of being, and it meant that *all* things, from the most minute to the most metaphysical, are equal in relation to the nothingness from which they emerged and from which they must be constantly created. Hence the relation of general to particular, abstract to concrete, and so forth, is necessarily different from that in Greek philosophy. In Rabbinic thought, as we will find, it is often the obverse—the particular and concrete take precedence over the general and abstract. With the doctrine of monotheism, there is also a unified force behind all things, all is interconnected and interrelated. Every minute particular connects somehow to the whole. And we shall also discover that, in the hermeneutic rules of Rabbinic interpretation, the relation between general and particular is not formulated in terms of *classes*, as in Greek logic. General and particular are interdependent, are seen as different aspects of propositions and defined more in terms of extension and limitation of the textual process and its provisions. The general is not an abstracted rule, but more of an extension of the particular, never losing its grounding in the particular; there is no fundamental opposition between them. These extensions and limitations are also never fixed, but fluid within the textual context.

Process, a term much in vogue to describe contemporary philosophic and scientific models of reality, can aptly be applied to Rabbinic thought. As creation is considered to be a continuous and unified process, so is the Torah and so its interpretation. The world of time and space is connected to realms beyond time and space through Torah, and every verse, letter, and so on contains, therefore, a plurality of meanings and references, applicable not only to Biblical time and place, but to all time and place. Through proper interpretation, then, the application and meaning appropriate for any contingency is revealed. Thus interpretation is not essentially separate from the text itself—an external act intruded upon it—but rather the *extension* of the text, the uncovering of the connective network of relations, a part of the continuous revelation of the text itself: at bottom, another aspect of the text.

Hence one of the fundamental doctrines of Rabbinic Judaism is that the written Torah is accompanied by an oral Torah, without which the written is incomplete and incomprehensible. The relation of the oral to the written is not that of inferior to superior. Since the oral Torah is the revelation of the deeper aspects of the written, it also has divine status. More accurately, one could say that the Torah has two parts: written and unwritten. We have noted Auerbach's perception that the Biblical accounts are fragmentary, ambiguous, that they intimate concealed depths, unspoken events, that they are "fraught with background." For the Rabbis, the oral Torah is precisely what lies between the lines, so to speak: the explanations, the filling in of the lacunae, the elucidations of the enigmas, and the probing into what was not explicitly written: It is the text within the text. The written Torah is something like a notebook in which every jotting condenses a whole train of thought[24] (the same conception as Freud's treatment of the dream text). Louis Finkelstein writes:

> That the text is at once perfect and perpetually incomplete; that like the universe itself it was created to be a process rather than a system—a method of inquiry into the right, rather than a codified collection of answers; that to discover possible situations with which it might deal and to analyze their moral implications in the light of its teachings is to share the labour of Divinity—these are inherent elements of Rabbinic thought, dominating the manner of life it recommends.[24]

Thus in speaking of *Torah*, the act of interpretation is included and integral. Say the Rabbis: "Words were given orally and words were given in writing, and we know not which of the two sets is the more valuable. However, from the verse 'According to these words [*al-pi ha-dvarim ha-ellah*] have I made a covenant with thee' [Exod. 34:27] we learn that those that were transmitted orally are the more valuable" (Yer. *Peah* 3; *Hag.* 1; *Meg.* 4). This inference is characteristically drawn from a play on words: *Al-pi* means *according to* and also, more literally, *of the mouth*. The Hebrew designation for the oral Torah, *Torah she-be-al-pi*, is based on the two words quoted in this verse.

At the same time that the Rabbis declare, "All that a faithful disciple will expound in the future in front of his master was already disclosed to Moses at Sinai" (Yer. *Peah* 6:2) they also assert, "The Torah is not in Heaven," but is revealed through the decisions of the judges and sages of every generation. A famous story in the Talmud makes this point in a most striking way. R. Eliezer was disputing with the sages on the question whether a certain oven was ritually clean or unclean:

> On that day R. Eliezer brought forth every imaginable argument, but they did not accept them. Said he to them: "If the law agrees with me, let this carob-tree prove it!" Thereupon the carob-tree was torn a hundred cubits out of its place—others affirm four hundred cubits. "No proof can be brought from a carob-tree" they retorted. Again he said to them: "If the law agrees with me, let the stream of water prove it!" Whereupon the stream of water flowed backwards. "No proof can be brought from a stream of water" they rejoined. . . . Again he said to them: "If the law agrees with me, let it be proved from Heaven!" Whereupon a Heavenly Voice cried out: "Why do you dispute with R. Eliezer, seeing that in all matters the law agrees with him!" But R. Joshua arose and exclaimed: "It is not in heaven." What did he mean by this? Said R. Jeremiah: That the Torah had already been given at Mt.

Sinai; we pay no attention to a Heavenly Voice, because Thou hast long since written in the Torah at Mt. Sinai, *After the majority must one incline*.

R. Nathan met Elijah and asked him: What did the Holy One, Blessed be He, do in that hour?—He laughed, he replied, saying, "My sons have defeated Me, My sons have defeated Me." [*B. Metzia* 59a, 59b.]

Thus, while "all was already given at Sinai," the revelation was ongoing and mediated by the interpreters.

According to Rabbinic tradition, even principles of interpretation were given at Sinai, and whatever is drawn from the text by application of these principles is not an addition, but a latent aspect of the text which is revealed in its relevant time and place. Moreover, whatever is deduced by common human reasoning is given the same authority and status as that which is derived from the divinely given hermeneutic principles. Says the Talmud, "It is either a matter of reason, or based on Scriptures" (*Zev.* beg.). For example, the question is asked: "How do we know that one should expose himself to death rather than commit murder?" (*Pes.* 25a; *Sanh.* 74a.) The Rabbis answer, "This is common sense: who knows that your blood is redder; perhaps his blood is redder" (i.e., his life may be more valuable than yours. In the case where one is ordered by the authorities to murder, or else oneself be killed, one should face the threat rather than commit the murder). A ruling derived from common sense is thus also included in the "words of the Torah," and is as authoritative as if it were based on the written text.

The boundaries between text and interpretation are fluid in a way which is difficult for us to imagine for a sacred text, but this fluidity is a central tenet of much contemporary literary theory. The elevation of later commentary to the status of earlier primary text is one of the extraordinary characteristics of Rabbinic interpretation, and involves a not so subtle power struggle. Interpretation as a species of will-to-power will be investigated in Chapter 8, on Harold Bloom, whose literary theory focuses on the Oedipal conflict between belated interpreter and canonical precursor.

Suffice it to add here the comments of one of the few scholars in the field of Judaic studies to recognize and admit the radical nature of Rabbinic revisionist interpretation, Simon Rawidowicz. In Rawidowicz's view, the Rabbis of the period from Ezra to the completion of the Babylonian Talmud created, in effect, a "revolution from within," and sought to reshape their home. The oral law they created should not be seen as a secondary commentary that simply explains, particularizes, and clarifies the written law. The oral law, or *Bayit Sheni* (*Second House*) as he terms it, is

> not just a continuation or a development but a new act of weaving undertaken by master weavers of rare power. . . . an *interpretatio* of the highest order. *Bayit Sheni* is second only in time; it is first in essence, in its own particular essence. I dare say *Bayit Rishon* [the *First House*, the inherited written scriptures] and *Bayit Sheni* are two beginnings of a system of thought and mode of life. This means that Israel has two beginnings. The second begin-

ning or *interpretatio* achieved by the *Bayit Sheni* may serve as a model for *interpretatio* in the sphere of thought at large.[25]

The Rabbis of the Second House, that is, freely reshaped and recreated the materials they had inherited from the First House, the written scriptures, in an interpretive battle born of the tension between continuation and rebellion, tradition and innovation, attachment to the text and alienation from it. Their work, he asserts, is a model for all interpreting because it teaches man how to "uproot and stabilize simultaneously; to reject and preserve in one breath; to break up and build—inside, from within, casting a new layer on a previous layer and welding them into one mold (which became later the great problem of Jewish thought and being)."[26] We shall find that the modern Jewish thinkers discussed in Part II share the same dilemma, and the same solution—*interpretatio*—as the Rabbis.

The Rabbis of the Second House, as part of this struggle, sought to elevate their interpretation to the same status of the text they came to interpret by asserting it had the same origin. (Everything a student in the future will innovate was already given to Moses at Sinai, they said; and Moses, worrying that he could not understand Rabbi Akiba's interpretations, heard Rabbi Akiba claim that all his insights came from Moses at Sinai). The God of the Rabbis, furthermore, became a learner of their interpretations of the Torah He had given—a concept which seemed blasphemous to outsiders. The Rabbis' interpretation subtly takes primacy over the text in a way unprecedented in the history of religion: human interpretation becomes divine. "What," asks Rawidowicz, "did God give to Moses and Moses bring to Israel? A 'text' for *interpretatio*; not a finished, independent, self-sufficient text, but one which is open and has to remain open to *interpretatio*."[27] Interpretation is the great imperative of Israel, and the secret of its history.

The Development of the Oral Law

Before analyzing in depth the methodology of Rabbinic hermeneutics, though, we need to briefly sketch the historical development of the oral law, keeping in mind the insights of Rawidowicz. The oral interpretations that accompanied the written text fell into several categories. Not only were there oral interpretations which were derived from the given exegetical rules, there were also interpretations handed down independently of exegesis, though some support could be found for them in Scripture. Then there were laws received by tradition for which no support could be found in Scripture. And there were also enactments (*takkanot*) and decrees (*gezerot*) instituted by the Rabbis to "make a fence around the Torah" (*Avot* 1:1) i.e., protect the laws in accordance with the passage, "And you shall safeguard my safeguards" (Lev. 18:30).

For example, the famous phrase "hand for hand, eye for eye, tooth for

tooth" was never taken in its literal sense to mean actual physical retaliation in kind. The oral law had always maintained that it meant monetary
recompense (Exod. 21:24). Or the vagueness of the phrase, "you shall take
the fruit of the glorious [*hadar*] tree" (Lev. 23:40) is clarified in the oral law
as referring specifically to an *etrog* (*citron*). About these clarifications there
is no dispute—they are considered to be given from Sinai—but when the
Rabbis attempt to then find *proofs* from the text itself to support these
traditional interpretations, the whole play of interpretation opens. One
Rabbi says that the phrase means that the fruit must be of a tree whose bark
tastes the same as its fruit (the citron); another says it means "the fruit
which dwells by all bodies of water" (*hadar* is related to the Greek word for
water), which is again the citron.

The search process here concerns not the *validity* of the law, but its
supporting *proof*. Laws deduced *solely* through the methods of exegesis,
on the other hand, were subject to dispute and settled by majority rule, as
indicated in the story of R. Eliezer. Until the time of Ezra (fifth century
C.E.), however, the search process, the elaboration and argumentation
over meanings, was more or less in a nascent stage. However, it is difficult
to know just how much of this activity had always gone on orally: in effect,
the activity of searching and interpreting Scripture is as old as Scripture
itself.

The destruction of the first Temple in Jerusalem in 586 B.C.E. and the
exile to Babylon were traumatic events in Jewish history and threatened
the continued existence of Judaism. The Temple had been the religious and
political center of Judaism. Upon his return from Babylon, Ezra determined to reconstruct the life of the Jews, and renew, so to speak, the
convenant with the Book that was in danger of being forgotten. Ezra's great
accomplishment was to finally reestablish the centrality of the Book, the
written Torah, as the basis for the entire life of the people. Ezra is described
as "a ready *sofer* [*bookman, student, scribe*] of the law of Moses which the
Lord had given" (Ezra 7:6). "For Ezra had set his heart to seek the Law of
the Lord" (Ezra 7:10).

In 444 B.C.E., he called a convocation of the people and secured their
acceptance of the Torah as the constitution for the new community in
Judea. He commemorated this occasion, a turning point in Jewish history,
with a public reading of the law. As he read, others stoody by and "gave the
sense": "And they read in the book, in the Torah of God, distinctly; and
they gave the sense, and caused them to understand the reading" (Neh.
8:8).* Ezra's "search" and this "giving of the sense" of the Torah to the

---

*This "giving the sense" can also mean a "translation" to an Aramaic-speaking people.
Here arises the complicated issue of the relation of this interpretive translation, or *targum,*
and midrash . . . a problem which we cannot pursue here. The Septuagint, for example, the
translation of the Bible into Greek, is clearly an interpretive, not literal, translation. See John
Bowker, *Targums and Rabbinic Literature* (Cambridge: Cambridge Univ. Press, 1969);
Martin McNamara, *Targum and Testament* (Irish Academic Press, 1972); and Geza Vermes,
Scripture and Tradition in Judaism (Leiden: Brill, 1961).

people are often cited as the beginnings of the exegetical tradition of *midrash*. The verb used for search in Ezra 7:10 is *drash*, from which the word *midrash* is derived. Ezra and his school, the *soferim*, developed the exegesis of Scripture, the *search, inquiry, investigation* into the meaning of the Torah in order to apply it to contemporary needs and problems. It was Ezra who preserved the idea of the book as the central concept of Judaism. Says the Talmud, "When the Torah had been forgotten by Israel, Ezra came up from Babylon and re-established it" (*Suk.* 209).*

The period of the *soferim* lasted approximately two hundred years, until the second century B.C.E., whereupon it was followed by the era of the "Men of the Great Assembly," a legislative body about which not too much is known, but whose activities were linked to those of the *soferim*. The Men of the Great Assembly were responsible for collecting all the Holy Writings, deciding which were to be canonized in the Bible, and giving the Bible its definitive form. During this period, Palestine was conquered by the Greeks, and another century and a half passed until the Maccabbees freed the Jews from Greek rule. The work of the *soferim* was fundamental in preventing the incursion of foreign influence and combating its allure. Midrash during this time was applied to all aspects of the Torah, to both legal and nonlegal matters. The search applied to the legal portions of the Torah was called *midrash halacha*, and that applied to the nonlegal portions was called *midrash aggadah*. *Aggadah*, from a verbal root meaning *to narrate, tell*, dealt with philosophy, ethics, legend, and so forth. An important characteristic of midrash is that its interpretations are always tied to the Biblical text itself.

As the bulk of commentary and interpretation grew, a method for organizing and remembering it became of increasing importance. Many areas of the oral law had developed far beyond the original verses which had served to substantiate them, and the need for classification into more general categories became more pressing. The process of organization and classification took place in the era of the *Tannaim (Teachers, Repeaters)*, beginning with Hillel and Shammai (10–220 C.E.). During this time, the *Mishnah*, the code of oral law, was composed. In essence, the difference between the *Midrash* and the *Mishnah* is that the *Mishnah* is concerned with the oral law *apart from* its ties to the written text.†

*Scholars such as Geza Vermes and Renée Bloch have stressed that midrash is *not* essentially a post-Biblical phenomenon. Scripture itself emphasizes the necessity to ponder and meditate upon it, and Vermes hypothesizes that the Deuteronomic corpus and more recent Biblical legal codes and apocrypha are themselves products of the midrashic process. See Vermes' book *Scripture and Tradition in Judaism* (Leiden: Brill, 1961) and article "Bible and Midrash: Early Old Testament Exegesis," in the *Cambridge History of the Bible*, Vol. 1 (Cambridge: Cambridge Univ. Press, 1970), pp. 199–231. See also Renée Bloch, "Midrash," trans. M. Callaway, in W. S. Green, ed., *Approaches to Ancient Judaism* (Missoula: Scholars Press, 1978), pp. 27–50; and her "Methodological Note for the Study of Rabbinic Literature," pp. 51–76 in the same volume.

†Perhaps the major scholar in mishnaic studies is Jacob Neusner. For further explanation, consult his many works, including *The Modern Study of the Mishnah* (Leiden: Brill,

The systematization of the Mishnah began with Hillel and was continued by R. Akiba (d. 132 C.E.), who subdivided the subject matter into homogeneous parts and arranged the laws according to their interconnections and mnemonical considerations. R. Judah the Prince, who is credited with the final edition and compilation of the Mishnah in 220 C.E., had the following to say of R. Akiba:

> R. Akiba he called a "well-stocked storehouse." To what might R. Akiba be likened? To a laborer who took his basket and went forth. When he found wheat, he put some in the basket; when he found barley, he put that in; spelt, he put that in; lentils, he put them in. Upon returning home he sorted out the wheat by itself, the barley by itself, the beans by themselves, the lentils by themselves. This is how R. Akiba acted, and he arranged the whole Torah in rings. [*Av. R. Nat.*, ch. 18]

The system which R. Akiba arranged was the foundation for the final codification by R. Judah the Prince.

During the period of the composition of the Mishnah, (approximately the first two centuries C.E.) the Jews suffered the catastrophe of the destruction of the Second Temple and severe oppression by the Romans. Indeed, the weakening of the nation, the exiles, and wars led to the permission for the oral Torah to be written down. This final compilation of the Mishnah in the second century was not meant, however, to fix the law, but to organize, facilitate, and preserve its study. Like the written Torah, the Mishnah was also to be a kind of notebook that would serve as a basic text for generations to come. And as with the written Torah, every phrase had to encompass a whole world, serve as an indication and reference to an entire argument, train of thought, and series of meanings. The Mishnah often includes the methods and disputes through which laws were deduced, and even retains (because of their aid in understanding the issue, and for their comparative value) controversial methods not accepted as law.

(As finally codified, the Mishnah had "Six Orders," or basic categories, which were then subdivided into a number of tractates [*massichtot*— from the word *massechta*, "the loom on which cloth is woven"], and the tractates were further divided into chapters [523 in all] and paragraphs. The "Orders" of the Mishnah are not abstract theological categories, but are divided as follows: (1) Seeds [*Zeraim*]—laws concerning agriculture, blessings, and prayers; (2) Festivals [*Moed*]; (3) Women [*Nashim*]—laws of marriage and divorce; (4) Damages [*Nezikin*]—civil and criminal law; (5)

1973) and *A History of the Mishnaic Law of Purities* (Leiden: Brill, 1974–77). For a view of mishnaic logic, see "Form and Meaning in Mishnah," *Journal of the American Academy of Religion* 45 (1977): 27–54. See also his dissenting opinion that the oral law is not a product of organic historical development from the written text but an entirely autonomous coexistent body of thought correlative to but independent of the written scriptures in his essay, "The Meaning of *Torah She be'al Peh* with Special Reference to *Kelim* and *Ohalot*," *Association for Jewish Studies Review*, Vol. 1 (Cambridge, Mass: Association for Jewish Studies, 1976), pp. 151–170.

Sacred Things [*Kodoshim*]—sacrifices and the Temple service; and (6) Purifications [*Toharot*]—laws regarding ritual purity and impurity.)

The disciples of R. Judah continued the work of compiling and editing the source material of previous generations for study and comparative purposes and engaged in the interpretation of the Mishnah itself. The sages of the period approximately 200–500 C.E. were known as *Amoraim* (*Expounders*) and produced, in effect, a Mishnah on the Mishnah debating its meanings, commenting, citing other evidence. The record and compilations of their debates was called the *Gemara*. These studies were carried on in two centers, Palestine and Babylonia. The same cause that led to the creation of the Mishnah, the need for providing a coherent framework for the mass of material and discussion, led also to the creation of the *Talmud* (*the Study*), which is the Mishnah plus the Gemara. Two Talmuds were redacted in the two centers of scholarship, and became known as the Babylonian and Jerusalem Talmuds, completed in approximately the fifth century C.E.

For another two hundred years, scholars known as the *Savoraim* (*Expositers*) studied the Talmud, making amendments and adjustments. No single scholar is named as officially having completed the editing and writing of the Talmud, and the activity of interpreting and commenting upon it continues to this day. Hence the saying, "The Talmud was never completed." Likewise, each one of the twenty volumes of the Talmud begins with page two—to teach, as one interpretation has it, that no matter how much one has learned, one hasn't begun to fathom its depths.

The Talmud is the source book which itself became the basis of interpretation, commentary, and codification. With the decline of the center of learning in Babylonia in the eleventh century, two new Jewish centers arose—one in North Africa and Spain, and one in Europe—ultimately leading to the two traditions of Sephardic and Ashkenazic thought, which differed in their exegetical approaches to texts (an issue beyond the scope of the present discussion). One of the European school's many luminaries was R. Shlomo Yitzhaki of Troyes, known more familiarly by the acronym Rashi, who lived in the eleventh century C.E. Rashi is still considered the greatest Biblical and Talmudic commentator; the exegetical methods he introduced remain valid. Rashi's work was continued by his sons-in-law and grandsons, who completed and critically commented upon his work. They were known as the *ba'alei tosafot* (from *tosafot: additions*). The work of the tosafists was, in fact, a Talmud on the Talmud, and a collective effort spanning two centuries.

The Crusades and expulsions of the Jews from France and Germany destroyed the European center. Though new methods of study and research developed, no new commentaries were written until the sixteenth century, when intensive and comprehensive exegesis developed in the new Jewish center of learning in Poland. Among the techniques developed in the sixteenth century was the method of *pilpul* (*dialectical casuistic*).

Pilpul was a method of complex dialectics attempting to create harmony between incongruent matters, often in the form of question, answer, and retort between two sages. This method had its basis in Talmudic debate, but was herein developed to an extreme.

Until 1520, there was no standard format for the page of the Talmud. Manuscripts and copies of the 2½ million words were until then difficult to obtain, and large portions of the Talmud were memorized and transmitted orally. Persecution of the Jews, and banning and burning of the Talmud, frequently by the Church itself in the Middle Ages, hindered dissemination of the Talmud. The edition of the Talmud printed in 1520 in Venice became, however, the standard format followed in all successive versions. In the standard edition of the Talmud, a brief part of the Mishnah is set in the center of the page, followed by the Gemara's discussion and commentary. The commentary of Rashi is printed to one side and that of the tosafists on the other side. Bordering these columns are additional notes, cross-references, glosses, emendations, and comments by later authorities. This text has been aptly described as "graphological goldsmithery, the jewel of the text set in a surrounding expanse of commentary."[28] The central pattern of the text surrounded by commentary was followed in other basic works of Rabbinic thought. (This is also the format of Derrida's *Glas*, which is examined in Chapter 7.)

This mode of arrangement expresses an attitude towards the text and its interpretation which is fundamental to Jewish thought. The Rabbinic world is, to use a contemporary term, one of *intertextuality*. Texts echo, interact, and interpenetrate. In the world of the text, rigid temporal and spatial distinctions collapse. The elements of the text are treated as much as objective reality for its students as empirical facts are by scientific observers. The Talmud student of today engages in a debate between Hillel and Shammai (teachers of the first century) as if they were his contemporaries, checks the opinion of another Rabbi from the seventeenth century in support of one side, and draws his own conclusions. There is no linear chronology in the Talmud.

Moreover, it was the cohesiveness of the *text* that was the binding force of a people dispersed geographically. The unity of the text overcame all breaks in physical and temporal continuity. All begins with the text of the Torah given to Moses, and consummates with the text of the Torah that the redeeming Messiah will teach. And what is the world to come, but a great yeshiva on high, where one studies Torah on deeper and deeper levels. Indeed, the Talmud is never completed.

The Talmud is not only a great repository of law, ritual, and debate. It is an encyclopedic work encompassing the entire fund of Jewish wisdom, learning, experience accumulated through the centuries. It is significant as much for its methods of analysis and research as for its conclusions themselves. The Talmud is also not simply the record of the discussions and interpretations of the sages, but is a reconstruction by later students and

Sample page (7a) of the tractate *Makkot* (of the fourth order, *Neziqin*) of the Vilna edition of the Babylonian Talmud, first printed in 1880–86. It discusses the fate of a man who was convicted and escaped and how he is to be judged. Code numbers, a box surrounding the Mishna, and brackets indicating the extent of comments (3-a) and (3-b) have been superimposed onto the original page. (1) End of the Gemara to the previous Mishna. (2) Mishna. (3) Gemara. (3-a) Halakhic Midrash supporting the Mishna. (3-b) Three short comments from Palestine, Sura, and Pumbedita. (4) Mark indicating the end of the chapter. (5) Mishna of the next chapter. (6) Commentary of Rashi (1040–1105). (7) *Tosafot,* discussing special points in the Gemara and Rashi. (8) Cross-reference notes to other Talmudic and Rabbinic sources and textual variants. (9) Notes by Joel Sirkes (1561–1640). (10) References to the codes of Maimonides, Moses of Concy, The Tur, and the *Shulhan 'arukh.* (11) Commentary of Hananel of North Africa, early 11th century. (12) References to scripture. (13) Notes by Elijah Gaon of Vilna (1720–97).

generations. It has, hence, a form unlike any other literature. The reconstruction presents itself as a mélange of voices from different times and countries brought together within the perimeters of the text. The style is often freely associative and laconic. It is not at all a flowing prose, and to those not familiar with its special vocabulary it is cryptic.

Since the Torah was considered to be all-embracing, Talmudic discussions are likewise expansive, often shifting from sphere to sphere and issue to issue without clear demarcation. Any subject may be related by association: a legalistic discussion of a detail of ritual may blossom into a discussion of ethics or metaphysics. Though it is the most important legal source for Judaism, the Talmud itself is not a law book. It provides the basis for discussion and decision, but rulings are always part of an ongoing process, which needs to be determined according to individual instances.

We have taken this brief excursus through the history of the oral law in order to provide the background for our discussion of the hermeneutical principles used by the Rabbis in their incessant activity of interpretation and commentary. One needs to approach Rabbinic thought from within, for the elaboration of abstract rules is not a process which for the Rabbis was separate from the concrete instance which gives them rise. The text which gives rise to the interpretation is so intertwined with the interpretation that one cannot really separate the description of the process, the rules which govern the process, from the process itself.

This is one of the major problems in attempting to describe the oral Torah and its exegetical procedures. The nature of historical description, and the setting forth of hermeneutic rules, assume a standpoint outside the textual event itself. That is, the elaboration of abstract rules or chronological order is a secondary process separate from the concrete instances which given them rise. There is a whole set of philosophical assumptions inherent in this very process of abstraction which recent literary critics such as Barthes and Derrida have uncovered. (The nature of the "higher Biblical criticism" as based on the mode of historical understanding of the nineteenth century is, in this sense, most unfaithful to the true nature of Rabbinic thinking.) This is not to say that the Rabbis did not elaborate and abstract their methods of interpretation from the text itself, or that they were unaware of chronology. They did engage in systematization and historical ordering. But these processes remained *secondary*, not primary. Primary was the direct engagement in the continuing process of the text. The elaboration of the hermeneutic rules and so forth were tools through which the primary process of intertextual interplay could be carried even deeper. There is, then, no ultimate outside point of view. The text continues to develop each time it is studied, with each new interpretation, for the interpretation is an uncovering of what was latent in the text, and thus only an extension of it; the text is a self-regenerating process. This aspect of Rabbinic thought, we shall find, has parallels with psychoanalysis, which uses the secondary process to uncover the primary process. The secondary process of the interpreting mind must partake of the language of the unconscious, adopt methods of free association and so forth in order to decipher the text of the dream.

Throughout our discussion of the various hermeneutic rules elaborated by the Rabbis, therefore, we must keep in mind, that in constrast to Greek thinking, these rules arose not in a process of abstraction from the text, which could then be separated and manipulated independently of the text—as in the case of any pure symbol system—but they form part of the mesh and interweave of the text itself, never separated from the concrete situation to which they apply. This manner of concrete thinking and the ability to carry on a highly abstract discussion without the use of abstract symbols is one of the distinguishing features of Rabbinic thought, a point to which we will later return. Roland Barthes, in an essay defining the nature of the contemporary post-structuralist "Text" (and also inadvertently Rabbinic sensibility), sums up this position as follows:

> . . . A theory of the Text cannot be fully satisfied by a metalinguistic exposition. The destruction of metalanguage, or at least (since it may become necessary to return to it provisionally) the questioning of it, is part of the theory itself. Discourse on the Text should itself be only "text," search, and textual toil, since the Text is that *social* space that . . . allows no enunciative subject to hold the position of judge, teacher, analyst, confessor, or decoder. The theory of the text can coincide only with the activity of writing.[29]

The Rabbis enunciated, judged, and analyzed—but in an ongoing communal process that disseminated authority. In their case, this textual toil, this writing became the endlessly proliferating commentaries and super-commentaries of Talmud.

3

Some Philosophic Aspects of the Rabbinic Interpretive System

"For it is no empty thing from you" [Deut. 32:47], and if it is empty it is on your account, because you do not know how to interpret it.
—R. Akiba, *Ber. Rab.* 22:2

Despite the exhortations at the end of the last chapter about the danger of separating hermeneutic rules from their textual basis, precisely that is done in this chapter. The Talmud is a set of massive tomes; every verse of Scripture is accompanied by thousands of years of midrash, commentary, and debate by countless Rabbis. How can we enter this textual maze, which has no beginning and no end, innumerable detours, and endless pathways? The thread I have chosen to guide our way is the "philosophic concept of interpretation" in Rabbinic thought. In this chapter, we shall concentrate not on examples of practical exegesis, but on the main hermeneutic rules with which the Rabbis engaged the text. It should be clear from the outset, though, that the few rules examined here are by no means comprehensive; there are hundreds of others. Nor can one say that one "understands" the Talmud merely by study of these rules. The rules can, however, serve as examples to illuminate underlying Rabbinic attitudes towards texts, language, and meaning.*

*My concern in this chapter is to articulate the *structural differences* between Rabbinic and Greek thought. I do not venture into the ongoing scholarly debate about how one might have influenced the other. For this, see, for example, the works of David Daube, W. D. Davies, Henry Fischel, Martin Hengel, and Saul Lieberman, listed in the bibliography.

The core of the Rabbinic interpretive system is the "Thirteen Middot of R. Ishmael." *Middah* means *measure* or *rule*, and R. Ishmael was a teacher in the first and second centuries. Hillel (first century B.C.E.) had already articulated seven rules prior to R. Ishmael, some of which R. Ishmael amplified. Hillel's elaboration of the seven Middot (see Tos. *San.* 7; *Av. R. Nat.* 37) represented a compilation of the main kinds of evidence customary at the time and were not invented by him. (In addition, there were many other rules in use at the time, not specifically codified.)

The Thirteen Middot of R. Ishmael expanded upon Hillel's rules, and were held in such high esteem that they were incorporated into the daily morning prayers (interpretation as devotion!). And, as mentioned previously, according to many ancient authorities, these Middot were considered to have been handed down from Sinai. R. Nachum of Gimzo also introduced certain exegetical methods which were followed and expanded by R. Akiba. A disciple of R. Akiba, R. Eliezer ben Jose ha-Galili further elaborated thirty-two rules of exegesis for the *aggadah* (found in the introduction to the *Sifra*.) Though the Thirteen Middot of R. Ishmael were the core of midrash halacha and are the heart of the interpretive system, they are also used in the aggadah, and some of the thirty-two rules of R. Eliezer are, conversely, used for halacha as well. The thirty-two were primarily aggadic, but they were as prominent as the thirteen. The Talmud says, "Wherever you hear the words of R. Eliezer b. Jose in the aggadah, incline your ear into a funnel" (*Chul.* 89a).

Kal Ve-Chomer

Let us begin, then, with an examination of the Thirteen Middot.[1] The first rule in the systems of both Hillel and R. Ishmael is called the *kal ve-chomer*, literally "from the light in weight to the heavy." This rule is often confused with the Aristotelian syllogism because it is an argument a fortiori, which draws a conclusion from a minor premise or more lenient condition, to a major, or stricter, one, and vice versa. When the kal ve-chomer is examined in depth, however, its difference from the syllogism can be seen as a model for the general differences between Rabbinic and Greek thought.

The prototype of the kal ve-chomer is found in the Bible; according to the midrash there are ten kal ve-chomer arguments in the text of Scripture. In Exod. 6:12, for example, God tells Moses to go to Pharoah and tell him to release the Jews. "And Moses spoke before the Lord saying: 'Behold, the children of Israel have not hearkened to me; how then shall Pharoah hear me, who am of uncircumcised lips.' " Or, in Deut. 31:27, Moses says when he gives the scrolls of the Torah to the Levites to put with the ark of the covenant, "that it may be there for a witness against thee. For I know thy rebellion, and thy stiff neck; behold while I am yet alive with you this day, ye have been rebellious against me; and how much more after my death?"

These are forms of simple kal ve-chomer where the argument is a plain *de minore ad majus*. The severity of the major is self-evident. In Louis Jacobs' formula,[2] the simple kal ve-chomer would be, "If A has X, then B certainly has X." In complex form, it becomes, "If A, which lacks Y, has X, then B, which has Y, certainly has X."

In its legalistic usage, the inference is a transference of a restriction or permission in the law. For example, the traditional interpretation of Exod. 21:24—that the phrase "eye for an eye" means monetary compensation and not actual physical retaliation—was suported by many arguments, among which is a kal ve-chomer from major to minor. Exod. 21:29–30 contains a law concerning certain circumstances where a beast which is known as dangerous has killed someone. The owner is judged liable to the death penalty, but the punishment could be redeemed through monetary compensation. The *Mekilta* to Exodus on this passage argues kal ve-chomer that if the law expressly allows for monetary compensation in a case where the guilty person deserves capital punishment, *how much more so* is monetary compensation admissible in our case, where it does not even concern capital punishment.

According to both Louis Jacobs and Arnold Kunst, the kal ve-chomer has no true similarity to the syllogism. For one thing, the element of *de minore ad majus*, the *how much more so* is absent in the syllogism. And where the syllogism deals with names and predicates which are the genus of the species or subject, the kal ve-chomer deals with sentences. It is not concerned with the relations of *classes*.[3] We noted at length in Chapter 1 that the syllogism, following the trends of Greek thought about language, concentrates on and is limited to names, to the relations between subject and predicate; the relation of major and minor is that of species to genus. Because of this limitation, modern logicians have criticized the syllogism as tautologous. The terms of the syllogism are also restricted by the classes of "all," "every," and so forth. The kal ve-chomer, however, is based on a principle of juxtaposition: the minor is raised by juxtaposing it with the major. Kunst writes, "The strength of the juxtaposition rests on the powers of two confronted objects, both of which lead in spite of their differing positions to equal consequences."[4] Here, we might say, is the "logic of metaphor" which Ricoeur articulated, wherein the logical action takes place in a "transgression" of ontology—in the positing that something is and is not, existing on the boundary of the same and the different. This movement is not so much a transference as a juxtaposition which avoids any positing of identities and predicates.

In the classical example of the syllogism, "All men are mortal, Socrates is a man; therefore, Socrates is mortal," the important step is to show that Socrates belongs to the *class* (the general species) man. In the kal ve-chomer, the important intermediate step is not to show that Y belongs to class X, but that Y is like X (only more so), and therefore if X has Z, then Y *has* Z also, not that Y is X *is* Z. The *how much more so* depends on perception of resemblance despite difference (not a collapse of difference) and leads not to statements of predication, where the copula is *is,* but to inclusion without identity. As we will see, the logical principle of juxtaposition is important in much of Rabbinic hermeneutics; and *difference* will be one of the key Derridean terms.

Tzvetan Todorov, in an article entitled, "On Linguistic Symbolism,"[5] is one of the few contemporary linguists to take note of the kal ve-chomer and its relation to Greek and Christian modes of exegesis. Todorov distinguishes between what he terms *propositional* and *lexical* symbolism. As an example of the first type, he uses a kal ve-chomer, presumably from a midrash. In the Bible it is said that God will reward even animals. The Rabbis comment, "Can it not be reasoned a fortiori if it is thus for a beast, for men it is all the more certain that God will not withhold His reward?" A single proposition in the text, "animals will be rewarded," indicates a secondary interpretation, "men will be rewarded." If, however, we took the term *animals* as a metaphor to designate, for example, *the humble of spirit,* the segment gearing the linguistic process would be a word, not a proposition. Todorov writes:

> I will call the first kind of linguistic symbolism in which one proceeds from a proposition with its meaning intact, propositional *symbolism;* and the second kind, in which one proceeds from a word, having cancelled the meaning of the initial proposition, *lexical symbolism.* The opposition between *lexical* (or predicational) and *propositional* symbolism is continuous with the one that allows logic to be divided into two great divisions, the calculus of predicates (or functions) and the calculus of propositions.[6]

Though Todorov contends that Christian allegory belongs to propositional symbolism, and pagan allegory to lexical symbolism, a point on which I differ, it is clear that lexical symbolism is a direct continuation of the Aristotelian mode of thinking about language and metaphor, wherein the axis is the name or word, not sentence. In lexical symbolism, the movement is from the literal to the figurative or metaphorical. The figurative meaning substitutes for and cancels the literal meaning of the word.

We remember that in the *Poetica,* Aristotle identified four varieties of metaphor, "either transferred from the genus and applied to the species or from the species and applied to the genus, or from one species to another or else by analogy" (*Poet.* 1457b). Todorov notes that genus-to-species is equivalent to what in current terminology would be called particularizing synecdoche; species-to-genus is generalizing synecdoche; species-to-species is metaphor; and the missing variation, genus-to-genus, is metonymy; "for while metaphor implies two terms (species) having a property (genus) in common, for example 'love' and 'flame' both 'burning,' metonymy requires that one term (species) be liable to be qualified by two independent properties . . . 'didactic' and 'false' both considered as properties, we might say, of 'textbooks.' "[7] Todorov also notes Aristotle's lack of the category genus-to-genus, and adds that this category is really put forth by Aristotle in his discussion of the *sign* and the *example* in the *Rhetorica,* conceived as an inferior form of syllogism. Propositional symbolism of the kal ve-chomer type belongs to movement from general to general (or genus-to-genus).

In his definition of the sign, Aristotle writes, "That which coexists with something else, or before or after whose happening something else has happened, is a sign of that something's having happened or being" (*An. Pr.* 70a). The standard example, "a woman has milk," is the sign that "a woman has given birth." Todorov criticizes Aristotle for not realizing the propositional nature of this relation and for placing it in the sphere of classical syllogism—the logic of classes, not propositions. Modifying Aristotle's terminology, Todorov terms this relation *allusion,* which he notes is the sense in which Freud at times uses this term. Also important here for our purposes is that what Todorov calls *allusion,* this movement from general to general, proposition to proposition, is a metonymical mode in which two predicates coexist simultaneously, both retaining their differences within the same subject. There is no cancellation or substitution of one by the other, nor a postulation of a relation of identity where the copula is *is;* the copula could just as well be *and* as Todorov notes.

However, I would maintain that Christian thought is predominantly lexical and metaphorical, whereas the Rabbinic mode may be characterized as metonymical and propositional. Not only is there an entirely different concept of *literal* and *metaphorical* in each tradition, but the idea of multiple meaning within the text is different. Furthermore, the coexistence of different interpretations and the proliferation of meanings can be seen as an extension of the propositional mode of thought, which allows for the coexistence of two different predicates simultaneously, and for the retention of differences on a semantic level. In Greco-Christian thought, metaphor is what happens to a word or name and depends on a relation of resemblance where there is a transfer of one word or name or idea for another. Resemblance here passes over into substitution, election, identification, cancellation, and the differences underlying the transfer are effaced ("white mythology"). As we have seen, in Rabbinic thought, the relation of the word to the thing is not a relation of substitution to begin with. Rather, the relationships underlying the logic of Rabbinic (or propositional) interpretation—and psychoanalysis—are contiguity, juxtaposition, and association. Here resemblance never effaces difference, *as if* never becomes *is,* the literal is never cancelled. Say the Rabbis, "No text ever loses its plain meaning" (*Shab.* 63a; *Yev.* 24a), even though every word of Scripture has many interpretations on many levels. The cancellation of the literal meaning of the "Old Testament" was, in fact, one of the major points of dispute between Jews and Christians in the interpretation of Scripture.

In sum, the heart of the issue is again the problem of predication. Since Aristotelian logic is a logic of classes, describing the relation of predicates that make up the proposition and not the relations between the propositions themselves, it is no wonder that Aristotle ignores this fourth category of movement from general to general (or proposition to proposition), and that he defines metaphor as predicative substitution and equivalence. In kal ve-chomer, however, the relation of juxtaposition allows for multiple predication. The *how much more so* is a relation of likeness which depends on an *if*, not an *is*, and therefore conclusions are always relative and are subject to further interpretation and application. There are no categorical statements or proofs in a demonstration which preclude further discussion. The *if* always remains apparent, and subject to further revision and extension.

The kal ve-chomer, like all Rabbinic thought, does not present us with *Q.E.D.*, but with a relative conclusion based on a hypothesis and subject to continual testing and scrutiny. Hence the paradox that while the Torah represents absolute and ultimate truth, this truth is never simple and single, but is always subject to interpretation; and the interpretation, while also divine, is to a certain degree a provisional and relative *process*. Interpretation generates further interpretation and further scrutiny of different aspects, possibilities, and situations. With the recognition of the *if*, the difference, the coexisting predicates retain their independence and do not cancel each other out, thus generating further interpretation. Rabbinic thinking presents us with a process, not a product.

This agrees well with Ricoeur's description of the fundamental metaphoric of thought:

> A family resemblance first brings individuals together before the rule of logical class dominates them. Metaphor, a figure of speech present in the genesis of concepts through similarity presents in an open fashion, by means of a conflict *between* identity and difference, the process that in a *covert* manner, generates semantic grids by fusion of differences *into* identity . . . . the rhetorical trope is an agent of revelation.[8]

In general we can characterize Rabbinic thought as *metaphorical* in these specific terms, that is, in its open revelation of this conflict. For Aristotelian and much of Christian thought in general, it is the fusion of these differences, not their conflict, that generates the process of interpretation. (Derrida's critique of these fusions and the forgetting of difference reveals him again as Rabbinic; his emphasis, above all, is on difference.)

A well-known Talmudic passage relates: "For three years Beit Shammai and Beit Hillel were disputing, the former asserting, "The law is in accord with our views," while the latter contended, "The law is in agreement with our views!" A heavenly voice answered, "Both statements are the words of the living God, but the law is according to Beit Hillel." (*Eruv.* 13b). In the actual decision concerning which law to follow in practice, the law follows the House of Hillel, but both opinions, even the refuted one, are "the words of the living God," and both are recorded and studied; both are Torah. There is room for difference, conflict, and contradiction, and Rabbinic thought discourages easy generalizations.

Indeed, the use of the kal ve-chomer itself depended on certain conditions and restrictions. It is not a universal principle or an apodictic premise. In legal application, for instance, the restrictive principle is called *dayyo— it is sufficient.* This principle means that the legal conclusion drawn from an inference cannot surpass in severity the original law. As Jacobs puts it, "It must not be argued that if A has x, then B has x plus y. The *kal ve-chomer* suffices only to prove that B has x, and it is beyond the evidence to say that it also has y."[9] Another restriction was that one cannot apply the inference from minor to major in penal law; a penalty cannot be inflicted when based on an inference, because the inference might have been mistaken, and the penalty then unjustified. A third restriction was, "No inferences must be made from traditional laws to establish a new law" (*Shab.* 132; *Naz.* 57), although R. Akiba did not accept this rule. In the nonlegal realm, however, the kal ve-chomer could be far more freely applied, especially in the teaching of ethical lessons.

The Other Twelve Middot: The Relations of General and Particular

Gezerah Shava

The second of R. Ishmael's Thirteen Middot, *gezerah shava,* is even more overtly linguistic. The gezerah shava is an analogy between two laws based on identical *expressions* in the Biblical text. Literally, the words mean *similar injunction* or *a comparison with the equal,* they connote *philological measure.* In this case, the analogy between two different laws is dependent not on the inner content of the laws themselves, but on purely linguistic similarities, on the analogous expressions in two different passages of Scripture. Through the gezerah shava one tries to prove that the provisions of one law may also apply to another, based solely on identity of expression.

The most well-known example comes from Hillel's answer to the question whether it is permitted to sacrifice the Paschal lamb on a Sabbath. Normally, such an act would be considered in the category of a forbidden labor, but in this instance, the eve of Passover (when this sacrifice was supposed to take place) fell on the Sabbath. Hillel argued that it was permissible by citing the law referring to the daily offering *(tamid),* where it is said that the daily offering was brought *in its appointed season (b'moadoh,* Num. 23:2). In the law concerning the Paschal lamb, the same expression, *b'moadoh,* is used: the children of Israel shall keep the Passover *b'moadoh—in its appointed season.* There is an express provision that the daily offering also be brought on the Sabbath (Num. 28:10). Hillel therefore makes the analogy that in the same way that *b'moadoh* includes the Sabbath in the case of the daily offering, *b'moadoh* here also means that the Paschal sacrifice is permitted on a Sabbath (*Pes.* 66a).

(Hillel also used kal ve-chomer to support his view: if the daily offering, which does not carry the punishment of *corat* [*cutting off*] for not sacrificing it, does take precedence over the Sabbath, the Paschal lamb, which carries the punishment of *corat* for not sacrificing it, should certainly take precedence over the Sabbath.)

The gezerah shava can also be used to supply an omission in the law, or to clarify ambiguities in the text. An example may be found in the *Mekilta* on Exod. 21:27, where the Biblical text says, "And if a man smite the eye of his bondman, or the eye of his bondwoman, and destroy it, he shall let him go free for his eye's sake." The verb used here is *shallach, to send out, to let go.* The *Mekilta* comments: "Eliezer said: Here we meet with the verb *shallach*, and so also further below [Deut. 24:1]. As further below a bill [a *get*, the bill of divorcement which a man is required to give his wife upon separation] is spoken of, so here also a bill is intended." That a bill of manumission is also meant in the first case is derived solely from the use of *shallach* in both places in Scripture.

Obviously, the use of gezerah shava could easily be abused, and for the purpose of making legal inferences, there were restrictions (though, again, these restrictions did not apply for aggadah. In deducing *laws*, the gezerah shava is accepted only if it can be proved that the key word used in both passages is superfluous to the text—pleonastic. If no pleonasm can be recognized in either of the two passages, then no analogy can be formed on the basis of identical expressions (*B. Kamma* 25b; *Yev.* 70a; *Nid.* 22b; *Shab.* 13a). Furthermore, one may not deduce a new law by means of a gezerah shava unless he learned it from his teacher (*Pes.* 66; *Nid.* 19b). New laws, that is, may not be deduced without the authority of tradition, but such analogies are acceptable to offer Biblical support to an already existing law.

(There is another type of analogy called *hekkesh*, similar to the gezerah shava but not listed among the Thirteen Rules of R. Ishmael. The difference may be put thus: whereas the gezerah shava deals with similarities in two passages, hekkesh is an analogy based on the close connection of two subjects in one and the same passage.)

Binyan Av: Constructing a General Principle

The third of R. Ishmael's rules is called the *binyan av,* literally, *constructing a general rule.* In binyan av, a general principle derived from one Biblical text, or from two related texts, is applicable to all similar cases, though they are not specified in detail. That is, from a single, special provision in one passage, a general principle is constructed which is applicable to other related passages. A simple example is found in the interpretation of Deut. 24:6: "No man shall take the mill or the upper millstone as a pledge; for he takes a man's life to pledge." In this case, the law is particular, referring to certain utensils, the hand mill and the millstone. However, a general reason is given: pledging those specific utensils deprives the pledger's family of the means of preparing food. Hence the Rabbis generalized this law to mean, "Everything which is used for preparing food is forbidden to be taken as a pledge" (*Mishnah B. Metzia* 9:13). The underlying concept is that any law in Scripture may be applicable to similar or analogous cases. Only where Scripture itself indicates that the law in question is specifically limited to the case mentioned can one not generalize therefrom. In the binyan av the particular case is regarded as an illustrative example for its general application; in essence, it is a mode of induction. It should be noted that the general rule is not abstracted from its original base in the special provision.

(There is also a variant of binyan av not found in R. Ishmael's rules, called *ma matzinu* [*as we find concerning . . . so here*]. This method is used not to raise a special provision to a generalization applicable for all similar cases, but only for one similar case.)

The binyan av may also be deduced from two Biblical passages, instead of from only one special provision. The text in Exod. 21:6 and 27 provides: "If a man smite the eye of his servant and destroy it, he shall let him go free for his eye's sake. And if he smite out his servant's tooth, he shall let him go free for his tooth's sake." The specific members here mentioned are eye and tooth, no other organs. Though eye and tooth are different members of the body, they share the common characteristic of being essential parts of the body, whose loss cannot be restored. From these two special provisions, the Rabbis deduce the general law that mutilation of any member of the servant's body by the master causes the servant's immediate manumission.

The interpretive text may be found in the *Mekilta* on the passage Exod. 21:27:

> "He shall let him go free for his tooth's sake." One might infer therefrom that the master is obligated to let him go free on account of a milk-tooth. For that reason "eye" is placed by the side thereof. Just as the eye does not grow again, so also a tooth is meant which does not grow again. One might still think the manumission results only on account of the two specifically mentioned members, the eye and the tooth. Whence the proof that an injury of other members (which do not grow again) leads to manumission? Join both verses and apply the rule binyan av. The tooth is not like the eye, and the eye is not like the tooth; but they resemble each other in that when they are injured no restitution is possible and they are principal members which do not grow again. Hence just as the slave is let free on account of them, so also on account of all principal members which do not grow again.

The question of generalization again raises the issue of the nature of abstraction in Rabbinic thought, and its difference from Greek and Patristic modes of abstraction and generalizing. Adin Steinsaltz has written at some length about this issue and comments:

In the Talmud, as in most areas of original Jewish thought, there is deliberate evasion of abstract thinking based on abstract concepts. Even matters that could be easily discussed through abstraction are analyzed sometimes cumbersomely, by other methods, based mostly on unique logical systems aided by models. The Talmud employs models in place of abstract concepts.[10]

Let us here paraphrase Steinsaltz's analysis from the laws of damages in the first mishnah of the tractate *Bava Kamma* (the tractate dealing with direct or indirect injury inflicted by one man on another). In this mishnah, reference is made to the four principal damages *(avot: principal categories)* provided for in the law: (1) the damage caused by a goring beast (Exod. 21:28; 35–36); (2) the damage caused by an uncovered pit (Exod. 31:33–34); (3) the damage caused by depasturing foreign fields (Exod. 22:4); (4) damage caused by unguarded fire (Exod. 22:5). A binyan av is constructed from these four provisions that a man is responsible and has to make restitution for any damage caused by property for which he is responsible. (These four principles do not include directly inflicted injury.) For our purposes it is important to recognize that the mishnah's four categories— ox, cistern, grazing, and conflagration—are themselves the technical symbols which abstract concepts. As one sage put it, "He who believes that the ox in the Talmud is a real ox has not even begun to understand the halacha."

In another classification of injuries, the four *avot* are denoted as "horn, tooth, pit, and fire." *Horn (keren)* is based on Biblical texts which describe the "butting ox" that injures other humans or oxen. *Horn* becomes the classificatory category in the Talmud under which falls the specific case of a dog biting a man, or a cockerel pecking another bird to death. *Tooth (shen)* becomes the classificatory category whereby a man is responsible for damage caused by his animal through its eating or any other act that causes it satisfaction, and covers for example, the case in which an animal rubs against a wall and causes it to collapse.

This classificatory logic is unusual because its general principles are not abstract symbols detached from the concrete bases (especially the textual bases) which give them rise, nor are they examples or parables. They operate, claims Steinsaltz, "like modern mathematic or scientific models,"[11] though the model is utilized according to steps provided by the tradition. Steinsaltz writes that though such methods of demonstration are used in our own century, they are not usually applied to everyday matters. The Rabbis, however, applied them to all and every manner of phenomena. Furthermore, he adds,

> The great value of employing such models, as opposed to abstract concepts lies, *inter alia,* in the ability to constantly supervise the validity of methods of demonstration. The elementary and relatively simple model serves as the basis for examination and enables us to draw inferences or examine whether we have diverged from the fundamental issue through abstract thinking on unclear issues. The weakness of all abstract thought lies in the fact that it is constantly creating new terms and concepts, and since

they cannot be defined except through use of similarly abstract terms, we can never know whether they constitute a departure from the subject or are still relevant. Therefore we almost never find abstract terms in the Talmud even when they would seem to be vital to the discussion and when any other legal system would have introduced them. Words such as "authority," "discipline," "framework," and "spirituality," have only been recently translated into Hebrew from other languages and philosophies.[12]

We can hear echoes here of Derrida's critique of the process of abstraction and of Lévi-Strauss's work concerning the "logic of the concrete." As Steinsaltz argues, the Rabbinic avoidance of abstraction is not due to its antiquity, nor to a more "primitive" way of thinking. Rabbinic thought constitutes a distinct and unique logical structure, differing from the central trends of thought in Western philosophy. However, it does deal with abstractions and has its own highly technical logic. But the concepts are, as Steinsaltz puts it, "plastic and depictive, and they communicate their meaning rather like a metaphor or a visual representation. In other words, Jewish thought uses pictorial or imagery concepts instead of abstract concepts."[13]

It is somewhat curious to find "imagery" resurfacing in the thought of those severely banned images. But "Rabbinic imagery" is vastly different from Greek *icon*. This "imagery concept" or model is derived from the commonplace, from everyday life and work, or from a specific textual reference, not abstracted from it. As Steinsaltz explains, the phrase, "the blow of a hammer," for example, is used to encompass those activities which in abstract formula would be termed "the completion of a task." In Jewish law, a man who makes a collar for a garment on the Sabbath is culpable because of "the blow of a hammer."[14]

The imagery concept, Steinsaltz emphasizes, is not a symbol, a metaphor, a circumscription, or a Jewish substitute for an abstract concept, but a unique mode with its own nature. Nor does the abstract equivalent, for example, "the completion of a task," exhaust the full meaning of "the blow of a hammer." "Its particular, detailed representation is included within, and is part of, the generalized abstraction or category it is expressing. Perhaps the best definition is that the imagery concept is a special case, a concrete and characteristic example, of a certain category of abstraction."[15] (This category we will later define as a metonymical mode.) In legal discussion, a characteristic activity—one which is highly specific and concrete—can be selected from the totality and become the key imagery word for the concept: a person who milks a cow on the Sabbath can be said to have transgressed the law against "threshing." Since the image is never far removed from the abstraction, it is always possible to make the transformation from the general to the particular and back with facility.[16]

General and particular, then, are not seen as independent categories; they are aspects of each other, extensions or limitations. The "imagery concept" is representative of a category, but at the same time partakes of the entire class of things it represents. And the general category is pro-scribed by the nature of the representative thing.

The use of the word *representation* here, however, sharply contrasts with the notion of representation as it is usually conceived in Western thought. The question of representation and mimesis is too vast to be examined here, but as we noted in the beginning of Chapter 2, representa-tion for the Greeks connotes imitation, copy, plastic image, visualization. (Derrida and the deconstructionist school of critics have focused their attack on this very notion of representation.) This concept is a corollary of the view of language as a *sign,* which represents by abstracting from the particular and pointing towards the invisible. The highest order of repre-sentation then becomes a semiotic system, an abstract "seeing" of the invisible remote from the particular, and imaging the inner relations and resemblances of a purer world. Today, this desire to flee from content also motivates contemporary linguistic theory; the sign is posited as arbitrary, having no necessary relation to the signified. The sign, like the word, is separate from the thing.

This is not the case, as we noted, with Hebraic thought, where word and thing are intimately interconnected; the relation of word to thing is not the relation of abstract to concrete, but rather the characterization of the inner specific reality of the thing. In place of *representation* is *grasped reality.* Because there is no absolute division between word and thing, the general mode of Rabbinic thought ties the generalization to the particular, or rather "embeds" it within the particular. Perhaps it could be said that the *imagery concept* is to the *represented category* as the *word* is to the *thing* in the meaning of *davar.* To use the linguist Jakobson's terms, the relation is not one of substitution (metaphor) but contiguity (metonymy).

The link between *tooth* and *rubbing against the wall* lies perhaps in a kind of quasi-verbal and quasi-sensible association which might be equated with "productive imagination" in the Kantian sense, in contrast to "repro-ductive imagination."[17] *Tooth* becomes a verbal image, and the iconic aspect of this verbal image helps us to grasp the identity-in-difference in a preconceptual pattern. One of the main functions of metaphor, as Aristotle had defined it, was "to set before the eyes," or image abstract relation-ships. The "imagery concept" in Rabbinic thought, however, is not repro-ductive or imitative (mimetic). There is no one-to-one substitutive or proportional relationship between *tooth* and *rubbing against the wall.* That is, the visual aspect is not directly mimetic but requires some indirect, nonproportional, contiguous association. Aristotelian metaphorical re-semblance is based on a notion of mathematical equivalence; Rabbinic metonymical equivalence is based on a contiguous narrative, on a textual interweave.

Boman, we noted, made much of the seeing–hearing polarity as the predominant contrasting modes of Greek and Hebrew thought. The para-dox here is that the freedom from the compulsion to see allows Rabbinic thought to be more freely and playfully visual and imagistic, whereas Greek thought tends to generate logical categories as far removed from concrete image as possible. With the perspective of *spectator* as divine, there remains a gap between see-er and seen, mode of perception and object perceived; the object of knowledge must be presented, re-presented, imaged, or signified. With the *text* divine, there is no gap between word and thing, and vision is hearing the word. As Rashi commented on the nature of Sinaitic revelation, "they saw that which should be heard"; the object of knowledge must be interpreted, respoken, heard again, and again.

In sum, the relation between general and particular in the binyan av is much more fluid than in Western logic. This fluidity also characterizes Rules Four through Eleven of R. Ishmael's system, which all have to do with the relations between *clal (general)* and *prat (particular)*. Clal, however, can mean not only a general rule but also a simple term, noun, or verb. The clal applies to a number of things which have a certain point in common; prat is that which singles out an individual from a class or number. (In Exod. 21:12, "He that smites a man, so that he dies, shall be put to death," the terms are *general;* in Exod. 23:19, "Thou shalt not seethe a kid in his mother's milk," the terms are *particular*.) The inferences drawn from the interpretation of the text depend on whether the use of particular terms is seen as referring exclusively to the single objects mentioned, or also to others of a similar nature; and how, in the case of both terms being used together in Scripture, the general and particular modify each other. The method of *clal u-frat* assumes that it is possible to draw conclusions from the way in which the passage is written, whether (1) the general is followed by the particulars, (2) the particulars are followed by the general, or (3) there is one term *preceding* and another *following* the particulars. The contents of either the general or the particular are modified in some way by the order in the text. See the Appendix to this chapter for a detailed discussion.

These rules of inference might seem artificially contrived, but they are based on an attitude underlying all of Rabbinic interpretation: the unity (and reversibility) of the text. The exegetical rules are also logical principles. Louis Jacobs clearly reveals this logic behind the principle of the binyan av:

> The principle underlying the method of *binyan av* in Talmudic literature is the belief in the unity of Torah, just as the principle behind the method of agreement is the belief in the unity of nature. To the rational mind it appears inconceivable that the different characteristics of the instances examined should result in the same effect rather than the characteristic they have in common. In the same way it appeared impossible to the Rabbis that a principle found in a number of instances of the Torah laws should be attributed to diverse factors rather than to a common factor.[18]

Jacobs is referring here to J. S. Mill's "Method of Agreement": "If two or more instances of the phenomenon under investigation have one circumstance in common, the circumstance in which alone all the instances agree is the cause (or effect) of the phenomenon." In this sense, says Jacobs, Rabbinic examination of Scripture parallels the investigation of the natural order in modern science.[19] Steinsaltz, among others, also notes the similarity between Rabbinic logic and scientific method. The Rabbis, he writes, "anticipated modern science while endeavoring to employ an empirical approach without having recourse to theoretical structures that did not derive from tested facts."[20] The obvious difference is that the Rabbis applied these methods to a text, to already given linguistic patterns, rather than to already given natural objects: for them the text *was* nature; it was the very constitution of the natural order.

Perhaps this attitude can help us understand the seemingly severe mishnaic statement, "R. Yaakov said: One who walks on the road and studies [Torah], and interrupts his study and remarks, "How beautiful is this tree! How beautiful is this plowed field! Scripture considers it as if he were guilty of a mortal sin" (*Avot* 3:8). Nature is to be studied only in order to supplement Torah, not vice versa; or rather, nature is an aspect of Torah. The Rabbis studied medicine, astronomy, mathematics, and so forth, in the same manner: they speculated on these disciplines not for their own sake but for the ultimate purpose of clarifying the Text. The laws dealing with ritual impurity, for example, required an extensive knowledge of anatomy and physiology, and the Rabbis conducted their own experiments in addition to using the scientific knowledge of their day. In interpreting the laws of defilement, it was necessary to determine the number of bones in the human body, and for this purpose R. Ishmael's disciples examined the corpses of women sentenced to death and executed by the authorities.

Yet this discourse always remained tied to the text and to its own terminology.* Perhaps what Steinsaltz calls the "image concept" is not a "representation" of a class, nor even a particular instance of a general, but a "concrete construction." The construction of any general rule is built from the text and avoids any secondary system of discourse, or other order of signs. Max Kadushin points out that conceptualization in Rabbinic thought is always tied to and relies upon the verbal symbols of the text; they are the constants. In scientific thought, though, the verbal symbols are variable and replaceable: it is the definition that abstracts and classifies the elements, and the verbal symbols may be redefined, replaced, or exchanged. The scientific concept always consists of a definition and statement because it is always a *conclusion,* an idea which is the final result of speculation or observation. In Rabbinic thinking, by contrast, no verbal concept or symbol can be delimited, defined, or considered as a finalized statement. New conceptual terms are not introduced, and thought depends on a play of all the concepts in an integrated manner.[21]

Moreover, the concepts, the verbal symbols, are themselves, in my

---

*This was indicated in the discussion of the laws of damages, where the categories used include *tooth* and *horn.*

term, *constructive*. From them the Rabbis build, extend, elaborate, modify, and relate to other provisions, interpretations, and texts. They are not merely descriptive but are themselves generative; re-productive instead of re-presentative. The concepts are always embedded within the textual matrix, or its extension; the general is embedded within the particular.

The rules for the relations of *general* and *particular* illustrate quite clearly this mode of thinking. In contrast to their use in Aristotelian logic, *general* and *particular* are above all semantic and predicative categories. They are, therefore, relativized, as that which is *more general* or *more particular,* and not predicates preceded by the words *all* or *some.* The general is constructed from a number of situations in the text and cannot be detached from those instances, as the rules of R. Ishamel amply show. In fact, the scope of the general, for the most part, is restricted by R. Ishmael's rules and made dependent on the mode of linguistic expression, textual sequence, and so forth. *The "general" does not have the power of predicating an essence beyond the particular.* And this precludes any hierarchy in interpretation. The extraction of a general application is not logically superior to the particular instance. The hermeneutic rules set up no hierarchy of interpretation, but call for a horizontal interplay; for since the text is a unity, all elements are potentially equal in the interpretive process. Hence, instead of geometrical organized patterns, the Talmud is composed of a cacophony of voices, arranged in a seemingly freely associative way. There is no special privilege given to general statements.

One of the rules which is applicable solely to interpreting the Talmud (as distinct from interpreting Scripture) is, "We may not infer from general rules" *(ain lomdin min ha-clal).* That is, when a law is stated in general terms, introduced by such words as *all, whatever,* and so forth, other laws cannot be inferred from it, as there might be exceptions. The term *all* as used in the Talmud (again not to be confused with its use in Scripture) means *majority* or *most*—and one cannot infer from a general rule. (For example, the Mishnah (*Kid.* 29a) states that every positive precept determined by time is binding on men, but women are exempt; and every positive precept not determined by time is binding on both men and women. Yet this rule is not absolute: some positive precepts determined by time are binding on women, and some undetermined by time are not.) Moreover, even when *except* is added, the general still cannot be used for inference, even though the exception is expressly mentioned; there are still other exceptions. And the principle that we must not infer from a general rule itself has exceptions. It holds good only when it is shown by a Mishnah, Baraitha, or the Gemara, but not where there is no such indication; otherwise, one could not rely on any clear statement in the Talmud.[22]

The "general rule" on general rules illustrates this cautious attitude towards generalization. The Talmud also states that one may not base a legal decision on a halachic statement, unless that statement was applied to an actual incident. Hence a lesson derived from a story where the principle was applied has greater substantiality than a direct statement of the principle! That a lesson or law derived from a *story* in the Talmud has greater validity than a law directly stated in the Talmud firmly underscores the priority of the concrete embodiment of a thought over its abstract representation.

Thus, the general is subject to constant scrutiny, to a search for exceptions, variations, instances that might contradict it, and alternative explanations. A Torah law is never a statistical mean. In their description of the effect of Talmudic thought on Eastern European culture, Zborowski and Herzog write,

> Since Truth has so many aspects and so many levels, each situation must be analyzed in its own terms. By using repeated if's, but's and but if's, all possible pros and cons must be weighed before an answer is accepted. . . . The relativistic and provisional view discourages the classic opposition between "yes" and "no," for everything contains elements of both. . . . According to this tradition it is the business of the thinker to recognize and reconcile incompatible opposites, in the realm of the spirit and the practical world, realms which are themselves inseparable. Moreover, overtones and undertones of implication or assumption are a proper part of the question and the response.[23]

Steinsaltz adds that the Talmud does not consider its subjects as "law in the socio-legal meaning of the term, but the clarification of facts and actual situations of intrinsic importance."[24] There is, then, no differentiation between important and minor issues, the irrelevant and the useful, nor is importance attached to the practical value or significance of a problem. There are implausible and bizarre discussions of utterly no historical relevance. Long after the Temple was destroyed, the Rabbis earnestly discussed the intricate laws of sacrifice, which were no longer applicable. As they said about certain laws that no longer existed, or "never did exist and never will" because so many restrictions were imposed upon them (for example, the case of the punishment meted out to a rebellious son), "Why were they written? Study and you will be rewarded" (*Sot.* 44a; *Sanh.* 51b).

Midrash

This openness to hypotheses, to all aspects of a problem, this relativization of generalization and conclusion, and this search for alternative explanations, all lead to the multiplicity of interpretation and diversity of opinion found in Rabbinic thought. So far, we have discussed the rules for halachic or legalistic interpretation. Many of the restrictions applied to these rules were necessary in order to arrive at authoritative decisions for practical situations; they did not apply, however, to the interpretation of the non-legal aspects of Scripture. And here, especially, interpretive play flourishes.

Since the aggadah is not concerned with halachic inference, nor is there any practical need for a determinative opinion, multiple meaning and proliferating interpretation are even more untamed. (It should be noted, though, that aggadic interpretations cannot be used to make halachic inferences.) As usual, though, the Rabbis had to justify this interpretive multiplicity through appeal to the Text. The principle that one verse of Scripture may have many meanings was deduced from the verse in Ps. 62:12, "Once hath God spoken, twice have I heard this." Upon citing this verse, the Talmud goes on to explain, "This was in accord with the school of R. Ishmael which taught that the verse 'Is not my word like fire, says the Lord, and like a hammer that breaks the rock in pieces' [Jer. 23:29] means that just as the hammer splits the rock into many fragments, so may one verse be split into many meanings" (*Sanh.* 34a). As another source has it, each word has at least seventy meanings (*Ot. R. Akiba*) and "seventy" in Rabbinic usage is an epithet for "an endless number." The Midrash Aggadah, as finally collected, often follows a format of extracting verse-by-verse sections from the Scripture, and then compiling all manner of possible interpretation together, the only connective link between them being the words "Another Interpretation."

Since the Midrash Aggadah is not as technical as the Talmud, and since one cannot truly comprehend the hermeneutical principles in abstraction from their textual matrix, let us examine some typical aggadic texts, and then proceed to discuss the exegetical principles.

The very first words of the Bible, "In the beginning God created," have been subjected, needless to say, to endless interpretation and commentary. The *Midrash Rabbah* on Genesis opens as follows:

> R. Oshaya commences: " 'Then I was by Him as a nursling [*amon*]; and I was daily all His delight' [Prov. 8:30]. *Amon* means tutor; *amon* means covered; *amon* means hidden; and some say *amon* means great. *Amon* is a tutor as you read, 'As an *omen* [nursing-father] carrieth the suckling child' [Num. 11:12]. *Amon* means covered, as in the verse, '*Ha-emunim* [they that were clad—i.e. covered] in scarlet' [Lam. 4:5]. *Amon* means hidden, as in the verse, 'And he concealed [*omen*] Haddassah' [Est. 2:7]. *Amon* means great as in the verse, 'Art thou better than *no-amon*' [Neh. 3:8] which is rendered, Art thou better than Alexandria the great that is situate among the rivers? Another interpretation: *amon* is a working man [*uman*]. The Torah declares: 'I was the working tool of the Holy One blessed be He.' In human practice, when a mortal king builds a palace, he builds it not with his own skill but with the skill of an architect. The architect, moreover, does not build it out of his head, but employs plans and diagrams to know how to arrange the chambers and the wicket doors. Thus God consulted the Torah and created the world, while the Torah declares, 'In the beginning God created.' 'Beginning' referring to the Torah, as in the verse, 'The Lord made me at the beginning of His way' [Prov. 8:22]."

The speaker here is Torah (Wisdom) personified, and the reference is to the era before creation when the Torah was, so to speak, tutored by God, brought up by Him, so to speak, like a child, though it was yet covered and hidden, not revealed. This midrash is the source of the idea that the Torah preceded the world as the blueprint of creation. This concept begins from a lively wordplay on a verse from the Book of Psalms, and the varied meanings of *amon* are elaborated from their contextual use in other books of the Bible.

There are midrashim which seek to clarify ambiguities in the text by filling in the lacunae. For instance, the Biblical text never specifies what kind of tree it was from which Adam and Eve ate. Comments the midrash (*Ber. Rab.* 15:7):

> What was the tree whereof Adam and Eve ate? R. Meir said: It was wheat, for when a person lacks knowledge people say, "That man has never eaten bread of wheat." R. Samuel b. Isaac asked R. Ze'ra: "Is it possible that it was wheat?" "Yes," replied he. "But surely tree is written?" he argued. "It grew lofty like the cedars of Lebanon," replied he. . . . R. Judah b. R. Ilai said: It was grapes, for it says, "their grapes are grapes of gall, they have clusters of bitterness" [Deut. 32:32]; those clusters brought bitterness into the world. R. Abba of Acco said: It was the etrog [citron] as it was written, "And when the woman saw that the tree was good for food" [Gen. 3:6]. Consider: go forth and see, what tree is it whose wood can be eaten just like its fruit, and you will find none but the etrog. [In Hebrew the word for *wood* and the word for *tree* are the same—*etz;* the verse is interpreted to mean that the tree itself, i.e., the wood, was good for food.] R. Jose said: They were figs. He learns the obscure from the implicit and [the meaning of] a statement from its context, thus: This may be compared to a royal prince who sinned with a slave girl, and the king on learning of it expelled him from court. He went from door to door of the slaves, but they would not receive him; but she who had sinned with him opened her door and received him. So when Adam ate of that tree, He expelled him and cast him out of the garden of Eden; and he appealed to all the trees but they would not receive him . . . But because he had eaten of its fruit, the fig-tree opened its door and received him, as it is written, "And they sewed fig leaves together" [Gen. 3:7]. . . . R. Azariah and R. Judah b. R. Simeon in the name of R. Joshua b. Levi said: Heaven forfend [that we should conjecture what the tree was]! The Holy One, blessed be He, did not and will not reveal to man what that tree was. For see what is written: "And if a woman approach unto any beast, and lie down thereto, thou shalt kill the woman and the beast" [Lev. 20:16]. Now if man has sinned, how did the animal sin? But [it is killed] lest when it stands in the market place people should say, "Through this animal so-and-so was stoned." Then if the Holy One blessed be He, was anxious to safeguard the honor of his [Adam's] descendents, how much more his own honor. [I.e., God did not reveal the nature of the tree so that it might not be said "Through this tree Adam brought death into the world."]

Concerning this entire incident, the midrash supplies many other details. It asks, quite straightforwardly, "Now where was Adam during this conversation [of the snake and the woman]? Abba b. Koriah said: He had engaged in his natural functions [intercourse] and then fallen asleep."

The midrash also supplies us with the serpent's motive. There is an exegetical principle that the *juxtaposition* of one verse next to another means that there is an inference to be drawn from one verse to the next. The midrash notes the continuity between verses 2:25 and 3:1 in Genesis; the previous verse describes how Adam and Eve were naked and not ashamed, and the next verse begins, "Now the serpent was cunning beyond any beast," and proceeds with the story of Eve's temptation. This juxtaposition indicates, the midrash says, the reason why the serpent tempted Eve: he had seen them engaging in sexual intercourse before the eyes of all, and he desired Eve for himself! The midrash also supplies the technique the serpent used; in case anyone wondered. Since Eve had added words to the original prohibition—God had only warned them not to eat from the tree, but she told the serpent in the Genesis text, "God said you shall neither eat of it nor touch it"—the serpent cleverly pushed her against the tree and said: "Just as you did not die from touching it, so you will not die from eating it!" His own species of kal ve-chomer.

Another typical midrash is that which discusses what the quarrel between Cain and Abel was all about, as the text does not explicitly tell us:

> "And Cain spoke unto Abel his brother . . . " [Gen. 4:8]. About what did they quarrel? "Come," said they, "let us divide the world." One took the land and the other took the moveables. The former said, "The land you are standing on is mine," while the latter retorted, "What you are wearing is mine." One said "Strip"; the other retorted "Fly" [off the ground]. Out of this quarrel, "Cain rose up against his brother Abel. . . . " R. Joshua of Siknin said in R. Levi's name: Both took land and both took moveables, but about what did they quarrel? One said, "The Temple must be built in my area," while the other claimed, "It must be built in mine." For it is written, "and it came to pass when they were in the field": now field refers to naught but the Temple, as you read, "Zion [i.e., the Temple] shall be plowed as a field" [Mic. 3:12]. Out of this argument, "Cain rose up against his brother Abel. . . . " Judah b. Rabbi said: Their quarrel was about the first Eve. Said R. Aibu: The first Eve had returned to dust. Then about what was their quarrel? Said R. Huna: An additional twin was born with Abel, and each claimed her. The one claimed: "I will have her, because I am the firstborn"; while the other maintained: "I must have her, because she was born with me." [*Ber. Rab.* 22:7]

The midrash proceeds to speculate about what instrument the deed was done with, and so forth. The last interpretation in the preceding text refers to Gen. 4:1–3, "And the man knew his wife; and she conceived, and she bore Cain; and she said: I have gotten a man with [the help of] God." In Hebrew, the grammatical particle *et* is used before the words *Cain, God, his brother,* and *Abel. Et* has no direct equivalent in English, but is the sign of the accusative. Among the thirty-two rules of R. Eliezer for the interpretation of the aggadah are those which draw inferences from the use of certain particles and conjunctions. They are interpreted to indicate the exclusion or limitations of provisions in the text. In technical terms, these rules are in the category of *ribbuyin u-mi'yutin* (*inclusion* and *exclusion*).

R. Akiba especially favored this method, which is the counterpart of R. Ishmael's clal and prat. R. Akiba had learned these principles from his teacher Nachum of Gimzo (first century c.e.). According to the principle of *rabbui*, the particles of *af* and *gam (even, also)* and *et* indicate an extension or amplification of the text. According to *mi'yut*, the particles *ak, rak* (*only*), *min (from)* indicate a limitation or exclusion. Though *et* is a sign for the direct objective case in Hebrew, it agrees in form with the preposition *with*. Hence in the text under consideration here in Genesis, the use of the particle *et* in all the above instances indicates augmentation, teaching that a twin sister was born with (*et* read here as *with*) Cain, and with Abel there were born two others:

> . . . R. Joshua b. Karhah said: Only two entered the bed, and seven left it: Cain and his twin sister, Abel and his twin-sisters.
>
> "And she said: I have gotten a man. . . . " R. Isaac said: When a woman sees that she has a child she exclaims, "Behold, my husband is now in my possession"[i.e., a child binds a man to his wife—R. Isaac reads the text as "I now have a man (Adam) in my possession through having given birth to Cain"].
>
> "With the help of [*et*] the Lord." R. Ishmael asked R. Akiba: "Since you have served Nachum of Gimzo for twenty-two years, [and he taught] Every *ak* and *rak* is a limitation, while every *et* and *gam* is an extension, tell me what is the purpose of the *et* written here?" "If it had said, 'I have gotten a man the Lord,' " he replied, "it would have been difficult [to interpret]; hence *et* [*with the help of*] the Lord is required." Thereupon he quoted to him: "For it is no empty thing from you" [Deut. 32:47], and if it is empty it is on your account, because you do not know how to interpret it. Rather *et* the Lord [teaches this]: In the past, Adam was created from the ground, and Eve from Adam; but henceforth it shall be, "In our image, after our likeness" [Gen. 1:26] neither man without woman nor woman without man, nor both of them without the Shechinah [the Divine Presence]. [*Ber. Rab.* 22:2]

This midrash hints at a certain dispute between R. Akiba and R. Ishmael over the validity of inference through the method of *ribbui u-mi'yut*. In fact, R. Akiba extended the method of Nachum of Gimzo from referring just to certain particles and conjunctions, to *any* word or part thereof in the text which is not absolutely indispensable to express the meaning. Although in human language there may be rhetorical flourishes, superfluous words, and so forth, according to R. Akiba every syllable of Torah is vital and hints at deeper meanings. R. Ishmael countered with the famous statement, "The Torah speaks in human language" (*Sifre* Num. 112), and in his view such inferences are inappropriate. Akiba and his school, however, made inferences from the repetition of a word, from the use of an absolute infinitive, from the conjunction *and,* from pronominal suffixes, and so forth.

Drawing inferences from particles of speech is, of course, alien to

Aristotle's way of thinking about logic and language. In the *Poetica* (1456b) he enumerates eight parts of speech: letter, syllable, conjunction, noun, verb, article, inflection, utterance. For Aristotle, a letter is nothing more than an indivisible sound, and to investigate what constitutes it "is the job of the metrician." A syllable is defined as "a nonmeaningful composite sound"; a conjunction or article is also a "nonmeaningful sound." Characteristically, the first unit of meaning is the noun, defined as "a meaningful composite sound without tense, no part of which is meaningful by itself." Only the utterance can be said to be "a complete meaningful sound, some parts of which mean something by themselves." Directly following this passage, Aristotle gives his famous definition of metaphor as "the application of a name to something else," a definition that naturally follows from his definition of the noun as the first unit of significance.

According to Rabbinic thinking about language, even a vowel is in the category of Aristotle's "utterance." Every vowel and letter is a meaningful sound, subject to inference and interpretation. This concept stemmed both from belief in the divinity of the text, and belief in the divinity of the Hebrew language. Language was not conventional; even the smallest detail of expression and punctuation was not fortuitous. Innumerable interpretations, therefore, were based on a seeming pleonasm, or even an unusual spelling of a word. An extra letter *yud* in the spelling of the word *va-yitzer* (*and he formed* man) in Gen. 2:7 leads the midrash to a series of speculations on why two *yuds* here are used instead of the usual one, and in the course of interpretation to a play with Greek letters as well.

> This connotes two formations, viz. that of Adam and that of Eve. [Another interpretation:] There is a viable birth at nine [months] and a viable birth at seven. R. Huna said: When the foetus is formed as to be born at seven months, and it is born either at seven or nine months, it is viable; if it is born at eight months, it cannot live. When it is formed so as to be born at nine but yet it is born at seven months, it cannot live, and all the more so if it is born at eight months. R. Abbahu was asked: "How do we know that when the foetus is fully developed at seven months it is viable?" "From your own [language] I will prove it to you," replied he: "Live seven; go eight." [*Ber. Rab.* 14:2.]

The Greek letter *zeta* had the numerical value of seven and is phonetically like *zeto,* meaning *let it live; eita,* whose numerical value is eight, sounds like *ito, let it go* (i.e., die). Among other explanations, the midrash notes that the two *yuds* connote the good inclination and the evil inclination, the earthly beings and the celestial being, life in this world and in the world to come, etc.

The single letter is a condensed cipher of other meanings, itself a miniature inner discourse. Consonant with this view are the hermeneutic rules called *gematria, notarikon,* and *al tikrei.* Gematria is the computation of the numerical values of letters, or the use of secret alphabets or methods of substituting one letter for another. For example, the numerical value of the name of Eliezer, Abraham's servant, is 318, which is the same number of soldiers the Genesis account tells us that Abraham sent out to battle (Gen. 14:14). The midrash states, therefore, that Abraham sent only Eliezer into battle (*Ber. Rab.* 43:2). In the verse, "Thus shall Aron come into the Holy Place," the word *thus* (*zot*) has the numerical value of 410, and the text is taken to hint that the first Temple was to last 410 years. The Book of Lamentations begins with the word *eichah* (*woe, alas*), which is composed of the letters *alef, yud, chaf, hay.* "Ben Azzai said, By the first word *eichah* of Lamentations, it is implied that the Israelites were not carried into captivity until they denied the One (*alef*) God, the ten (*yud*) commandments, the law of circumcision given after twenty (*chaf*) generations, and the five (*hay*) books of the Torah" (*Eichah Rab.* beg.)

In the method of notarikon, one word is broken up into two or more, and its single letters are interpreted as standing for just as many words which commence with them. In Gen. 17:5, God changes Abraham's name from Abram to Abraham, "for a father of a multitude of nations have I made thee" (*av hamon goyim*). Rashi cites the midrash on this verse:

> This is a notarikon of his name [av-r-ham] And the [letter] *reish* which was in it from the beginning [Avram] when he was a father only to Aram which was his place [Av-Aram—father of Aram] even now when he became father of the entire world [Av-Ham] nevertheless the *reish* did not move from its place [was not deleted]. For even the letter *yud* of Sarai complained against the Divine Presence [when it was removed from Sarah's name] until it was added to Joshua, as it is stated [Num. 13:16] And Moses called Hoshea the son of Nun, Joshua [Yehoshua]. [*Ber. Rab.* 46:7]

The letters of the alphabet here are personified—they speak and complain against God. This personification is meant to indicate that they are not arbitrary signs, but have a life-force of their own, a life-force which expresses and is an instrument of a divine creative power. Since in the Jewish view, God created the world through utterance, the letters of the Holy Tongue are perforce special powers. The midrash interprets Gen. 2:4 in this vein. In the verse, "These are the generations of the heaven and the earth when they were created," the phrase "when they were created" is written in Hebrew as one word *be'hibarram:*

> R. Abbahu said in R. Yohanan's name: He created them with the letter *heh* [reading *be'hibbaram* as two words—*b'heh baram*, with *heh*, He created them]. All letters demand an effort to pronounce them, whereas the *heh* demands no effort [*heh* is a mere aspirate]; similarly, not with labour or wearying toil did the Holy One, blessed be He, create His world, but "*By the word of the Lord*" [Ps. 33:6] and "The heavens were made" [ibid.].
>
> R. Judah the Nasi asked R. Samuel b. Nahman: "As I have heard that you are a master of *haggadah,* tell me the meaning of, 'Extol Him that rideth upon the skies, be-Jah is his name' " [Ps. 68:5]. Said he to him: "There is not a single place which has not someone appointed to rule over it: thus a commissioner in a province is appointed to its governship; a magistrate is appointed to its governorship. Similarly, who is appointed to the governor-

ship of His world? The Holy One, blessed be He: '*Be-Jah* is His name' means *biyah* [governorship] is His name." . . . . "I asked R. Eleazar, and he did not explain it thus. But the verse, 'Trust ye in the Lord for ever, for the Lord *be-Jah* is an everlasting rock' [Isa. 26:4] means: By these two letters did the Lord create His world." Now we do not know whether this world was created with a *heh* or the next world with a *yud,* but from what R. Abbahu said in R. Johanan's name, viz. "*be'hibbaram* means, with a *heh* created He them," it follows that this world was created by means of a *heh.* Now the *heh* is closed on all sides [   ] and open underneath: that is an indication that all the dead descend into *she'ol';* its upper hook is an indication that they are destined to ascend thence; the opening at the side is a hint to penitents. The next world was created with a *yud:* [   ] as the *yud* has a bent back, so are the wicked: their erectness shall be bent and their faces blackened in the Messianic future, as it is written, "And the loftiness of man shall be bowed down" [Isa. 2:17]. What will he [the wicked] say? "And the idols shall utterly pass away" [Isa. 18]. [*Ber. Rab.* 12:10.]

The concept of creation through the letters of speech was taken even further in the mystical tradition, which we will discuss further in the last chapter. For example, according to the great Kabbalist R. Isaac Luria, there is a spiritual force even in completely inanimate matter, which is constituted by the "enclothing" of the Letters of Speech of the Ten Utterances (the "And God said, 'Let there be' " of Genesis). These Letters of Speech vivify and create matter *ex nihilo.* The Hebrew names of all created things are the letters of speech that descend from the Ten Utterances, and through various substitutions and transpositions, become invested in the thing to vivify it.[25] (These combinations of letters are explained in Kabbalah, the esoteric writings, and refer to different arrangements of the letters of the Hebrew alphabet. The immediate contrast with Greek thought is obvious: in Rabbinic thought, letters play the role of numbers; instead of a mathematical reality, there is a linguistic one.)

The variation in letter combinations also extends to a play of variant readings of words. Because of the structure of Hebrew, and the nonvocalized text of Scripture, it is possible to read words in several ways. All manner of intentional misreadings were codified in the exegetical principle *al tikrei* ("Do not read it thus, but thus"). For instance: "It was taught by Elijah: Whoever studies Torah laws every day is assured of life in the World to Come, for it is said: *Halichot* [the ways of] the world are his. Do not read *halichot,* but *halachot* [Torah laws]" (*Tan. El. Zut.* ch. 2; *Meg.* 28b; *Nid.* 73a). Or, "If one dreams he has intercourse with a betrothed maiden, he may expect to obtain knowledge of Torah, since it says, 'Moses commanded us a law, an inheritance of the congregation of Jacob' [Deut. 33:4] Read not *morosha* [inheritance] but *me-orosah* [betrothed]" (*Ber.* 57a). A third example: " 'And thou shalt have a paddle *[azeneka]* among thy weapons' [Deut. 23:4]: read not *azeneka* but *ozeneka* [thy ears]—if a man hears a thing that is not proper, let him put his finger in his ears" (*Ket.* 5a-b). Alternative readings also apply to the construction of clauses and sentences. There are in the Torah, neither vowel punctuations nor punctuation marks to separate verse from verse. (However, there are six types of spacing used in writing the Torah scroll: the separation between the Five Books, between portions, between words, between letters—and between lines only in two specific instances the Song of the Sea and the Song of *Ha'azinu*. The division of the Bible into chapters and verse is of entirely non-Jewish origin, and these divisons became used in the printed Bible of the Jews only during the Middle Ages, when Christians forced theological debates upon the Jews.) Indeed, the exegetical principle of *smuchin* (contiguous passages, or the analogy made from the juxtaposition of laws or verses in Scripture) depends on this lack of punctuation between verses. As mentioned previously, the derivation of the nature of those labors which are forbidden on the Sabbath is based on the juxtaposition of the Sabbath law with the description of the building of the Tabernacle in Exod. 31:1–17; 35:1 ff. (*Shab*. 49b). Smuchin allowed the interpreter to separate the final part of a clause or sentence and, conjoining it with the following clause, to form a new sentence. Lev. 23:22 states, "And the gleaning of thy harvest thou shalt not gather; unto the poor and the stranger thou shalt leave them." By doing away with the semicolon, the new clause "thou shalt not gather unto the poor" is formed, intimating that the owner of a field may not gather the gleaning on behalf of a certain poor, and deprive the others of their rights to the gleaning (*Git*. 12a).

There were, however, restrictions on the use of al tikrei and smuchin, especially in regard to legal inference. For example, the following inference was made from the juxtaposition of the verse, "Whoever lies with a beast shall be put to death," after, "Thou shalt not suffer a sorceress to live" (Exod. 22:17, 18): just as a beast is put to death by stoning, so too a sorceress is put to death by stoning (*Ber*. 21b). R. Judah retorts: "Just because the two statements are juxtaposed are we to take this one out to be stoned?" According to his view, one may apply the principle only to the Book of Deuteronomy. And though the text was unpunctuated in writing, the correct pronunciation was fixed in the oral tradition. In certain cases, there are variations between the *kri,* the traditional oral reading, and the *ktiv,* the traditional written form, leading, as one might expect, to varying interpretations.

Although there were marked differences between the application of these interpretive methods to legal and nonlegal material, in general, *midrash* as *inquiry* into the meaning of the text presents us with a way of thinking that contrasts sharply with Greek thought. Henry Slonimsky has written that midrash is the "most authentic and mature thinking on all the main topics of life. . . . it is present in an atmosphere or medium of freedom and unconstraint, not as a set of propositions to be soberly argued in the schools; but rather as a set of themes and images to guide and influence the listener in all the workings of his mind, and still to retain the fluidity of a story."[26] Midrash is a curious intermingling of logic and narrative, concept and image, fact and speculation, wherein the data and the interpretation cannot be distinguished. This merging of the language of interpretation with the language of the object described is, of course, a distinguishing feature of recent radical literary theory.

These characteristics follow, of course, a general idea of Rabbinic interpretation—that the interpretation is only an uncovering of what was concealed or latent in the text and therefore is part of the text itself. Although we have seen that the Rabbis formulated various hermeneutic principles with much precision, they did not articulate a set of meta-principles governing these hermeneutic rules. Presumably, any further abstraction from the text is suspect. Further definition seems to be sought not through further reductive abstraction, or the search for more general symbols to express abstract relations, but through further instances of proliferating interpretation, further readings into rather than out of the text. There are no final statements of definition, but rather an expanding, continuous process of interpretation, an accumulation of concrete instances in new combinations. The central movement is not away from the concrete and the multiplicity of meaning towards a singular definition or final determinative rule.

Moreover, the midrash always reveals its sequence of thought—never omits the steps in its chain of reasoning, and is always at pains to retain its links to the textual situation which is its basis. As Jacob Neusner puts it, "The creative force of Midrash depends on stubborn particularization."[27] And he comes to the same conclusion as Steinsaltz, that midrash is "speculation in terms of the concrete on the inner nature of reality," or "thought in concrete images."[28] In midrash, concepts exist only in particular forms, and this is one of the aspects in which midrash may be distinguished from allegory or figurative interpretation. The concept uncovered through interpretation never dispenses with the particular form in which it is clothed, nor does the midrashic meaning take any precedence over the plain, simple meaning. Furthermore, there is never any one single interpretation to which all understanding of the text aims, but a continuous production of multiple meaning. In midrash, one Rabbi can interpret a verse in several different ways, and conflicting interpretations are placed side by side with no concern for reconciling them (this is not the case with Talmud). There is no hierarchical scheme in midrash; no interpretation has more authority than any other.

Moreover, as far as aggadah was concerned (in contrast to halacha), the Rabbis did not demand belief. In Kadushin's phrase, aggadah is "serious play"[29] involving an indeterminacy of belief; or perhaps one could use Coleridge's phrase, "suspension of disbelief." In aggadah, Kadushin asserts, the text is a "non-determining stimulus" for aggadic interpretation; and belief can become determinate in aggadah only when it is concretized in a specific situation, idea, or law. Since the text acts as a new stimulus each time it is interpreted, it therefore requires different determinate meanings by different personalities at different times, or even at the same time.

There is an even deeper relation of the aggadah to the Biblical text. The

Biblical text, we noted, is not conceived as a linear, chronological, propositional narrative, but as an elliptical, truncated, nonchronological system of
signs; the principles of contiguity, juxtaposition, and the like make up its
fabric. In this sense, the midrash is itself conceptually akin to the Bible, an
imitation, reconstruction, or, perhaps better, continuation of the text itself,
and thus it can be said to represent a text's simple meaning.

Metaphor and Metonymy in Interpretation

In trying to understand further the underlying notions governing Rabbinic
thought, let us return to the proposition that Rabbinic thought may be
considered as fundamentally *metonymic,* in contract to Greek and Patristic
thought, which is essentially *metaphoric.* I use these terms as they are
defined by the linguistic structuralist Roman Jakobson in his well-known
essay, "Two Aspects of Language: Metaphor and Metonymy." According
to Jakobson, there are two kinds of arrangements in any linguistic sign:
combination and selection. Combination is based on two or more terms
which are present in actual series:

> Any sign is made up of constituent signs and/or occurs only in combination
> with other signs. This means that any linguistic unit at one and the same time
> serves as a context for simpler units and/or finds its own context in a more
> complex linguistic unit. Hence any actual grouping of linguistic units binds
> them into a superior unit. Combination and contexture are two faces of the
> same operation.[30]

The essential relations are contexture and contiguity.

In the arrangement of the sign through selection, however, a connection is made between terms in absentia. "A selection between alternatives
implies the possibility of substituting one for another, equivalent to the
former in one respect and different from it in another. Actually, selection
and substitution are two faces of the same operation."[31] These two operations give the sign two sets of interpretants, the context and the code,

> and in each of these ways the sign is related to another set of linguistic signs,
> through an alternation in the former case and through an alignment in the
> latter. A given significative unit may be replaced by other, more explicit signs
> of the same code, whereby its general meaning is revealed, while its contex-
> tual meaning is determined by its connection with other signs, within the
> same sequence. . . . The constituents of any message are necessarily linked
> with the code by an internal relation and with the message by an external
> relation.[32]

Important for our purposes here is the way Jakobson extends his
definition of these aspects of the sign to more general patterns of discourse,
and even further to nonverbal art. This, of course, is the modern structuralist project. Metaphor and metonymy become the two "gravitational poles"

within any sign system. In romantic and symbolic poetry, for example, the metaphorical process predominates, whereas in the realistic novel, metonymy predominates. In painting, metonymy is dominant in cubism, metaphor in surrealism. As Jakobson points out, however, there is a conspicuous neglect of the study of metonymy in favor of the study of metaphor. He reasons that since in metaphor, the principle of similarity connects the metaphorical term with the term for which it is substituted, the construction of the meta-language to interpret tropes is much more easily handled by the researcher. Metonymy, since it is not based on a principle of similarity, is much more difficult to handle and defies interpretation. And tropes and figures have been studied mainly as poetic devices because poetry focuses on the sign, and its underlying principle is similarity. Prose, however, is essentially constructed through contiguity, but has been studied metaphorically.

We might expand Jakobson's distinction to include modes of Biblical interpretation as well, and say that the narrative of the Biblical text is considered, in general, *metonymically* by the Rabbis and *metaphorically* by the Church Fathers. We could then characterize R. Ishmael's principles as a kind of methodology of metonymy. Needless to say, the principle of similarity operates in Rabbinic thought as well, as in the gezerah shavah; substitution is the order in techniques such as gematria, and so forth. However, our study of the philosophical concept of similarity underlying metaphor has shown that within *similarity* itself, one needs to make a further and finer distinction than does Jakobson. There is, on the one hand, similarity as substitutive identity within a logic of classes and predicates; and on the other, similarity through juxtaposition without any predicative identity, a similarity which seeks to openly retain differences on the boundary of is–is not. And though Jakobson classifies poetry as basically metaphoric and prose as metonymic, within prose itself there are different arrangements. There is a linear, progressive prose, for example, and a cubist prose. And there is a vast difference between the example of prose which Jakobson presents, *War and Peace,* and, say, *To the Lighthouse.*

In his book *Beginnings,* Edward Said considers the question of narrative and the history of the novel in light of the question of language. He points out that the late nineteenth- and early twentieth-century novelists had reached an impasse, and because of their "disillusionment with mimetic attempts to represent man in language"[33] turned to new techniques that overthrew the classical canon of prose making. These novelistic techniques had their analogue in what Freud accomplished in *The Interpretation of Dreams.* We shall consider the relation of that work to Rabbinic thought in another chapter, but some of Said's insights about twentieth-century prose and critical theory may be used here to provide a descriptive model of the Rabbinic thought which we have been discussing (though the deeper relation of Rabbinic thought to contemporary trends in criticism must wait until the final chapters).

Mimesis, of course, is the concept so central to Aristotle; as we have seen, it reflects the over-all structure of Greek thought. According to Said, what Freud accomplished in the *Interpretation of Dreams* was the construction of a text which consciously avoided certain specific textual conventions which the classical novel had employed. We can use Said's analysis as a way of contrasting Rabbinic concepts of narrative and interpretation with classical notions. The first convention, according to Said is *supplementarity,* whereby the text is temporally and spatially separated from the events it is describing. The events are taken to be material and the succeeding text, verbal. We have seen that the Rabbinic view also inverts this convention and treats the text as prior, and the verbal as material. As Auerbach noted, the Biblical narrative claims an absolute authority that subsumes our reality, and we are to fit ourselves into its structure of universal history; all new facts become fitted into its account. The text is only superficially a description of the past.

Said's second category of textual convention abandoned by Freud and the modern novel was the "adoption of a logic of structure and argument based on temporal and forward spatial movement, a sequential movement leading to some conclusion."[34] Basic to Rabbinic interpretation was the assumption that the text is not in chronological sequence; the Midrash and Talmud are organized even less historically, and have an entirely different structural logic, not based on temporal or spatial forward movement.

The abandonment of what Said calls *adequacy*—the assumption that the text is equal to the task of realizing its intention and meaning—does not, however, exactly apply to Rabbinic thought, save in the sense that the text always exceeds any meaning which can be given it, and hence does not provide an *adequate* meaning that can be finalized or completely fulfilled. (This concept of the Torah was one of the critical points of dispute between Judaism and Christianity. As we shall see in the next chapter, one of Christianity's central tenets was that the Old Testament text was now superseded and fulfilled with the messiahship of Jesus.)

The fourth convention, *finality,* is the assumption that each portion of the text is a discrete unit, firmly established in its place, precluding consideration of what precedes and follows it at any given moment. This convention obviously never applied to Rabbinic interpretation. There, not only is contextual reading an exegetical principle, but all units are so closely interwoven and simultaneously present that none can be considered in separation from any other at any given moment; it is a world of "intertextuality," to use a contemporary literary term.

Said's fifth category, *finality,* is the maintenance of the unity of the text through genealogical connections, such as author–text, beginning–middle–end, text–meaning, and reader–interpretation. These distinctions are blurred in Rabbinic thought: the text has a divine author, but is continuously created by its readers–interpreters.

As Said also notes, one of the strategies important to Freud's construction of his text is the avoidance of images, the transformation of dream image into words. Again, this is a nonmimetic approach that does not follow linear progression but leads to multiple and endless interpretation. The movement from image to language is also the movement of the twentieth-century novel, which turns around the problems of its own articulation in a space and time which are preeminently verbal, not visual. Needless to say, the same is true of Rabbinic interpretation. Said notes Foucault's insight at the end of *The Order of Things* that after such writers as De Sade, Mallarmé, and Nietzsche, mimetic representation could no longer be an appropriate mode for authors to express their desires or psychological discoveries. Concurrently, there was an assault on the logic of syntax and the linear sequence of printed language, a desire to express nonsyntactic, nonsequential thought. Marx, Saussure, and Freud, together with these writers, invented systems of thought which also undermined mimetic representation.

> Thus writing could no longer exhibit a predictive form like that of the classical realistic novel or the simple biographical continuum, formally based either upon biological growth or a representative governing image. Instead, writing sought to constitute its own realm, inhabited from the beginning entirely by words and the spaces between them. In turn, the relationships between this realm and empirical reality were established according to particular strategies and enunciative functions.[35]

In Freud, the relation between dreamer and interpreter replaces the univocity of the author. The same is true of the colloquy of voices in the Midrash or Talmud; the interpretive process is collective. And the modern writer, like Freud and the Rabbis, yields up any notion of the finality or completeness of the text. The modern writer's work, says Said,

> intentionally begins moving away from the traditional continuities of form and towards projects whose trajectory must be created, in Merleau-Ponty's phrase, as a constant experience, without distinctive form, without authorizing imagery, without predetermined "progress toward a goal". . . . for the sake of a type of indeterminacy. . . . the text yields up its formal completeness to a constantly reforged discursivity or productivity.[36]

The notion of the text as an unending process of meaning has been extended to the extreme in much of contemporary critical theory, especially in the work of Barthes and Derrida. The *Text* has become, in fact, as divine an object, as authoritative a source of meaning—indeed the very field of existence itself—as was the Torah for the Rabbis. Whether called *Text* or *Écriture,* the text today is the Holy Scripture for its critics, or perhaps we should say "worshippers." As Barthes plainly puts it in his *The Pleasure of the Text,* a work which expresses this attitude as none other, "The text is a fetish object, and *this fetish desires me."*[37]

In fact, says Barthes, there really is no "me" independent of the text; " 'I' is itself a plurality of other texts."[38] Nothing exists outside the text, asserts Derrida. The crucial recognitions here are that the text is a "production" and not a "representation" of meaning, and that the goal of literature is to make the reader a producer of texts, to give him "access to the magic of the signifier."[39] "To interpret a text is not to give it a meaning (more or less justified, more or less free), but on the contrary to appreciate what *plural* constitutes it."[40] Reading must be a "metonymic labor" of a text which is a network with a thousand entrances. In Barthes's view, reading should be in the nature of a step-by-step commentary, a process of "decomposition" of the text, a "systematic use of digression," a cutting up the text into contiguous fragments, "manhandling the text, interrupting it": that is to say, playing with its infinite possibilities. Barthes's *S/Z,* a reading of a story by Balzac, embodies these critical principles, and is a pure form of secular midrash. The text

> practices the infinite deferment of the signified, is dilatory. . . . the *infinity* of the signifier refers not to some idea of the ineffable (the unnameable signified) but to that of *playing:* the generation of the perpetual signifier . . . according to a serial movement of disconnections, overlappings, variations. The logic regulating the text is not comprehensive . . . but metonymic; the activity of associations, contiguities, carryings-over coincides with a liberation of symbolic energy.[41]*

In all this we have a most apt description of midrash, even of the Rabbinic process in general; and as we have seen, the Jew is the devotee of Scripture, the text, par excellence.

Derrida notes this fact with much insight in his essay on the French Jewish author Edmond Jabès. (We will return to this essay again in the last chapter.) Derrida there speaks of a Judaism

> as the birth and passion of writing. The passion *of* writing, the love and endurance of the letter itself whose subject is not decidedly the Jew or the Letter itself. Perhaps the common root of a people and of writing. In any event, the incommensurable destiny which grafts the history of a "race born of the book" onto the radical origin of meaning as literality, that is, onto

---

*In this essay of Barthes, he defines seven characteristics that distinguish the Text from the work. They are worth adding here because they articulate, I think, the Rabbinic mentality as well:

1. The Text, as opposed to the work, is not a defined object, but a methodological field which exists in discourse and is experienced only in an activity, a production.

2. The Text subverts old hierarchical classifications of genres, and is paradoxical.

3. The Text is experienced in relation to the sign, *not* the signified; it infinitely defers the signified. It is radically symbolic, without closure. Its play of signifiers is not a process of deepening, but a serial movement of metonymic dislocations.

4. The Text is irreducibly plural, intertextual.

5. The Text is read without the father's signature.

6. The work is an object of consumption; the Text abolishes the distinction between reading and writing. Reading is playing the Text, and the Text demands the reader's collaboration.

7. The Text is its own Social utopia; a sphere of pleasure.

historicity itself, for there could be no history without the gravity and labor of literality.[42]

The Jew, says Derrida, chooses Scripture (Writing–Écriture), which chooses the Jew. Jabès is correct in perceiving that the difficulty of being a Jew is confused with the difficulty of writing, for Judaism and Scripture (or Writing) are nothing but the same expectation, the same hope.[43] This exchange between the Jew and Scripture makes the book a "long metonymy," wherein, writes Derrida, the Jewish situation becomes exemplary of the situation of the poet, the man of the word and of writing. The poet, too, is *chosen,* selected by words, and engages in an arduous labor of deliverance by the poem of which he is the father. The poet is also a *subject* of the book, its substance and its master, its servant and its theme"; and the book is the subject of the poet.[44] For both the Jew and the poet, the book becomes a subject in itself and for itself, reflecting on itself. The poet and the Jew, Derrida continues, are not rooted in any empirical, natural present; they are never *here,* but always *there,* where the immemorial past is the future. They are natives only to the word and to Scripture, sons of a land to come. The home of the Jews is a sacred text in the middle of commentaries. Barthes would probably substitute the word *critic* for *poet* here. In his (Rabbinic) words, "The book creates meaning; the meaning creates life."[45]

As both Barthes and Derrida are well aware, this conception of text, commentary and Scripture, of the plurality and infinite play of signifiers, is most disturbing to monist philosophy. Writes Barthes:

> For such a philosophy, plural is the Evil. Against the work, therefore, the text could well take as its motto the words of the man possessed by demons (Mark 5:9): "My name is Legion: for we are many." The plural of demoniacal texture which opposes text to work can bring with it fundamental changes in reading, and precisely in areas where monologism appears to be the Law: certain of the "texts" of Holy Scripture traditionally recuperated by theological monism (historical or anagogical) will perhaps offer themselves to a diffraction of meaning.[46]

This diffracted reading was the special province of the Rabbis and in this light, it is little wonder that Rabbinic interpretation has often been stigmatized as a species of demonism by Western Christian culture. (The Talmud was actually "tried" and burned several times in the Middle Ages.)

> In the non-Jewish literature it [the Talmud] was often decried as "one of the most repulsive books that exist," as a "confused medley of perverted logic, absurd subtleties, foolish tales and fables, and full of profanity, superstition and even obscenity," or at the most, as "an immense heap of rubbish at the bottom of which some stray pearls of Eastern wisdom are hidden.[47]

Monologic reading of Scripture was the province of the Church Fathers, recently converted from monist pagan philosophy to a faith in a savior who was the absolute and ultimate signified, who exorcized the demons of the text, its unmanageable pluralism, and centered it in himself as fulfillment. The text as process, plural, all-encompassing field of existence, became reduced to what Barthes calls "a work." Instead of the ceaseless play of interpretation, the Church Fathers needed to articulate dogma, and did not tolerate plurality and difference lightly. Scripture remained, however, a basis for proofs of the new messiah.

Harry Wolfson writes, "We all have a feeling that between ancient Greek philosophy which knew not Scripture, and the philosophy which ever since the seventeenth century has tried to free itself from the influence of Scripture there was a philosophy which placed itself at the service of Scripture."[48] He is referring, of course, to medieval philosophy, beginning with the Church Fathers, but which in his view is ultimately the philosophy of the Alexandrian Jew Philo. And it is to this era that we now turn in order to understand why today criticism, bereft of its original master, seeks another Holy Scripture.

4

Escape from Textuality: The Fulfiller of Signs

"Christ, thief of energies," according to Rimbaud. For a while he was a different kind of sacred monster. He stole texts or eased the burden of the letter. With him interpretation seems so assured. Verily, verily, I say unto you. Take comfort . . . His immediacy to events is fatal to no one but himself.
—Geoffrey Hartman[1]

If Jesus is the father of the Christian community, every instance of writing signifies his death, or at least the transfer of spoken words to a written document and the community's ambivalent reaction to it. In either case, his presence is transmuted into or sacrificed for word, just as, conversely, he was the Word made flesh. . . .
Everything about Jesus . . . resists textuality. . . .
—Edward Said[2]

For the written code kills, but the Spirit gives life.
—2 Cor. 3:6

The Jews are the most deranged of all men. They have carried impiety to its limit, and their mania exceeds even that of the Greeks. They read the Scriptures and do not understand what they read. Although they had heavenly light from above, they preferred to walk in darkness. They are like people who had neither their mind nor their thinking faculty. Accordingly, they were seized by the darkness and live as in the night. They were deprived completely of the divine splendour and did not have the divine light.
—Cyril of Alexandria[3]

What could so enrage the Church Father Cyril about the Jews? Of course, the Jewish refusal to accept the Christian principle of salvation was irritating and threatening. At the bottom of the great dispute was, however, a life-and-death reading controversy. The Greeks, too, had their conflicts with Jewish texts and interpretations, but never did their disdain for Jewish modes of thought and behavior reach the intensity of the Christian antipathy.

For the Greeks, the culmination of theology was a wordless vision of divine being; for the Jews it was commentary on the divine word, deeper immersion in the text, further interpretation of Scripture. When the apostle Paul began to preach his doctrine of the new savior Jesus to Greeks and Jews alike, he confronted two opposing cultures. "For the Jews," he complains, "demand signs and the Greeks seek wisdom, but we preach Christ crucified, a stumbling block to Jews and folly to Gentiles" (1 Cor. 1:22–23). His message that Jesus was the long-awaited Messiah prophesied in the Hebrew Scriptures was of little import to the Greeks, and was heresy to the Jews. And so, in order to persuade both Jews and Greeks of the truth of his new creed, Paul needed to speak the language of both:

> To the Jews I became as a Jew, in order to win Jews; to those under the law I became as one under the law—though not being myself under the law—that I might win those under the law. To those outside the law I became as one outside the law—not being without law toward God but under the law of Christ—that I might win those outside the law. . . . I have become all things to all men. . . . [1 Cor. 9:20–22.]

Paul, who before his conversion had been Saul, the Jew of Tarsus and a persecutor of the new cult of Christians, desperately sought to reconcile his newly adopted faith with that of his forefathers, and to extend it further to "those outside the law," the Gentiles—especially after he had been so bitterly stung by the Jews' rejection of him. The oppositions which he so painfully lived and experienced inevitably were expressed in the contents of his preaching. Above all, his Jesus is a *mediator* of irreconcilable oppositions: between Jews and Gentiles, righteousness and sin, God and the world, soul and flesh, faith and works, the spirit and the letter, life and death. In place now of textual mediation is personal mediation through the figure of the new redeemer, whose presence has ended the long metonymy of Jewish history, which Paul calls the "curse" of the law: "For Christ is the end of the law, that everyone who has faith may be justified" (Rom. 10:4).

But how could Paul explain to the Jews this heretical abrogation of their Sacred text, and to the Gentiles the metaphysical importance of the miserable Jew Jesus who had been so ignobly put to death as a criminal? Paul had to make both Jews and Greeks perceive that the Scriptures in fact spoke of something quite other than what appeared to be the case. He had to speak, that is, a double language. For this task, the most suitable interpretive methods were, of course, typology and allegory.

In the classical rhetoric with which Paul was so familiar, *allegory* essentially meant *saying one thing to mean another*. Cicero had equated *allegory* with *translation* "the connection of many metaphors so that one thing may be said and another understood." Quintillian identified *allegory* with *inversion*—to mean something other than what the words of a statement suggest, or to mean something which is opposite to what the words convey.[4] The method of interpreting one system of thought in terms of another actually goes back further than the Latin writers, originating around the sixth century B.C.E. in Greece. For the Greeks, Homer and Hesiod had come to have the status of divinely inspired texts. To harmonize Homer's accounts and their inherited popular religious beliefs and sometimes crudities with Greek philosophy, Theagenes of Rhegium introduced formal allegorical interpretation into his works, and the method was followed by Heraclitus, Anaxagoras, Metrodorus, Diogenes, and Democritus. The Stoics continued the application of the allegorical method to Homer and Hesiod, and it was especially cultivated by philosophers such as Zeno, Cleanthes, Chrysippus, and Diogenes.[5] Through this method, for example, Heraclitus was able to vindicate Homer from the charge of impiety.

Allegory survived as a literary form long after its original purpose had failed. It was pervasive in the Middle Ages, indeed up until the eighteenth century. Much of its popularity was due to the fact that it became a central technique of the Church in interpreting Scripture and was passed over into literature through such Christian poets as Dante and Spenser. Our concepts of "literal" and "figurative" meaning today, and our ways of "reading into" our secular scripture "other" meanings arc decply rooted in the uses of allegorical interpretaton in Paul and the Church Fathers. And it is to this formative period of Western thought that we must now turn in order to understand how both this method, and the reaction to it in the Reformation, have profoundly influenced all our ways of treating texts.

We should note here that although Paul's Epistles make much use of the allegorical and typological methods, they do not provide any systematic application or theoretical basis for the principles of allegorical interpretation. Interestingly enough, allegory as a systematically developed exegetic method came to the Church Fathers through Alexandrian Judaism, particularly through Philo; from Philo Origen learned it and passed it on to Clement and others. It was ultimately perfected in the work of Augustine. Before examining these crucial figures in the history of interpretation, though, let us first consider the primitive Christian community as it began to break away from the synagogue and as Paul took up his "mission to the Gentiles."

The Letter and the Spirit

Paul faced opposition both from Jews, to whom Jesus did not appear to fulfill the criteria designated by Scripture for the Messiah, and from

Greeks, to whom the entire canon of Hebrew Scripture was distasteful, barbarous, and crude. James Shiel writes,

> Ancient philosophy was wedded to a literary style, supremely exemplified by Plato, alongside which the Semitic type of expression seemed barbarous. Antiquity had fostered dramatic beauty of dialogue and had also developed a scientific prose, both of which were foreign to the idiom of the Scriptures. It is true that when we come to the fourth century, Christian writers like Gregory of Nazianzus and John Chrysostom can emulate the pagan stylists. But their studied emulation of the Attic writers is an admission of victory for the pagan intellect in this respect. Their philosophic style meant the adoption of images and examples of myth and poetry stored in the magazine of pagan philosophy. . . .
>
> The thought world of Judaism with its Oriental apocalyptic, ritual, blood sacrifice, and tortuous legislation, was foreign to the Greek philosophic mind. This tension between "Jew" and "Greek" was deep-rooted and has remained in the European tradition.[6]

There were, furthermore, all manner of accusations made in the Roman world against the Christians—that they were disloyal to the state, practiced cannibalism and incest, and so forth. It was thus most necessary for Paul and those who followed him to represent the new faith as respectable, to somehow take the sting out of the offending passages, and reconcile them with what had been taught among the best and most respected pagan philosophers (Philo's use of allegory as an apologetic technique, we shall find, arose in similar circumstances in Alexandria, where he sought to harmonize Judaism with pagan philosophy). Through the use of allegory, Paul and the Church Fathers tried to show that behind the crude and offensive letter of Scripture were hidden spiritual and philosophic truths acceptable and appealing to the Greeks. And, furthermore, that when read correctly, i.e., spiritually, these same Scriptural prophecies about the Messiah which the Jews claimed had not been literally fulfilled, could be proven to have been spiritually fulfilled; the Jews were wrong in their interpretation of Scriptures because they failed to have the "light of the Spirit" to illumine them to the truth.

Hence the distinction between *letter* and *spirit* became crucial to the articulation and continued justification of the Christian faith. The contrast of letter and spirit antedated Paul by quite some time and can be traced back to Protagoras (481–411 B.C.E.).[7] Paul was quite obviously familiar with the techniques of the rhetoricians and much influenced by the culture of his day. Tarsus, his birthplace, was the home of a university that taught Stoic philosophy and Roman law, and from the style of his Epistles, it is quite apparent that Paul artfully used all the techniques of the rhetoricians and advocates in the law courts. Putting all his Greek and Jewish learning to the task of discrediting Jewish law, he radicalized the antithesis of letter and spirit and applied it to Scripture in an unprecedented way.

As we have seen in the previous chapter, however, Rabbinic interpretation was anything but *literal* in the derisive sense in which Paul and his successors used the term. According to Harry Wolfson, Paul's allegorical interpretations of Scripture were not so much of the philosophical kind as patterned after a certain variety of midrash that Wolfson calls "predictive midrash."[8] In Wolfson's schema, the New Testament contains four kinds of nonliteral interpretations of the Old Testament: (1) interpretive predictions of the first coming of Jesus; (2) interpretive predictions of his second coming; (3) proofs of his preexistence; and (4) nonliteral interpretations of legal and moral matters.[9] In Wolfson's view, the first category coincides with the Rabbinic genre of predictive midrashim, wherein the text is taken to hint of certain future events. Paul's reading of the Old Testament centered around proving how the text allegorically predicted Jesus. As Louis Ginzberg writes, "He learned the art of destroying the law by the law . . . from his Jewish masters. . . . Israel's history and legal enactments were construed (by Paul) as being in reality intimations of the realities of the faith, concealing the spirit in the letter and reducing the Old Testament to mere shadows."[10] Among terms Paul uses are *allegory* (Gal. 4:24), *type* (Rom. 5:14; 1 Cor. 10:11), and *shadow* (Col. 2:16–17). Paul's predictive type of interpretation, known as *typological allegory,* is considered one of his major innovations.[11]

In his letter to the Galatians, Paul argues with those who continue to want to observe the law of circumcision literally, articulates his doctrine of justification-by-faith versus justification-by-works, and calls the law a "curse":

> Tell them who desire to be under the law, do you not hear the law? For it is written that Abraham had two sons, one by a slave and one by a free woman. But the son of the slave was born according to the flesh, the son of the free woman through promise. Now this is an allegory: these women are two covenants. One is from Mt. Sinai bearing children for slavery; she is Hagar. Now Hagar is Mount Sinai in Arabia; she corresponds to the present Jerusalem, for she is in slavery with her children. But the Jerusalem above is free and she is our mother. . . . Now we, brethren, like Isaac are children of promise. . . . But what does the scripture say? "Cast out the slave and her son; for the son of the slave shall not inherit with the son of the free woman." So, brethren, we are not children of the slave but of the free woman. [Gal. 4:21–31.]

Paul's antinomianism is perfectly evident here in his identification of the law with Ishmael, the disinherited son of Abraham's concubine, and the New Testament with Isaac, the promised child. The passage is also characteristic in its setting up of rigid oppositions. Paul continues: "Did you receive the Spirit by the works of the law, or by hearing with faith? Are you so foolish? Having begun with the Spirit, are you now ending with the flesh? . . . For the desires of the flesh are against the Spirit and the desires of the Spirit are against the flesh; for these are opposed to each other, to prevent you from doing what you would" (Gal. 3:2–3.); "But if you are led by the Spirit you are not under the law" (Gal. 5:17–18).

For Paul, the spiritual meaning utterly nullifies the literal meaning, and allegory becomes the technique through which he uses the law to destroy the law. "For I through the law died to the law, that I might live to God" (Gal. 2:19). Typological reading accomplished the same end. All the acts, laws, narratives of the Old Testament are considered only as *figures, types,* and *shadows* of the truer realities now revealed: "Therefore let no one pass judgment on you in questions of food and drink or with regard to a festival or a new moon or a Sabbath. These are only a shadow of what is to come; but the substance belongs to Christ" (Col. 2:16–17). The shadow–substance distinction is, of course, an inheritance from Greek philosophy, and is connected with our previous discussion of the manner in which certain metaphysical presuppositions determined the classical theory of language. The figurative meaning of metaphor was seen as a sort of transfer, a deviation from the proper meaning, for which it was substituted. The ultimate determinant of the proper was the true predicate of all things, the foundational principle of Greek metaphysics, the central *ousia,* the univocal being beyond language, which nevertheless allows the entire system of words and things to operate. The restoration of the proper meaning in effect cancels the figurative meaning, considered as merely an ornament, an alien deviation which by virtue of a certain resemblance with the proper meaning acts as a substitute for it.

In Paul's schema, the law or written code is the temporary *figure* or *type;* the spiritual interpretation returns the proper meaning to the text, making all that had come before a mere shadow compared to the substance (literally) that Jesus represents for him. Jesus becomes the true predicate of all statements, the singular and ultimate referent, a referent beyond language entirely, whose appearance nullifies the written text—which is now considered as a long deviation, a detour, an exile. With the restoration of the substance, the shadow disappears, the figures of the text are cancelled, and direct union with the presence of Jesus is left. Paul is not only antinomian, he is also antitextual. He is impatient and frustrated with the Jews because they cling to the letter still; that is, they will not read the text Christocentrically: "But their minds were hardened; for to this day whenever Moses is read a veil lies over their minds; but when a man turns to the Lord the veil is removed" (2 Cor. 14–17).

We have characterized Rabbinic reading of texts as *metonymical*—as retaining differences within identity, stressing relationships of contiguity rather than substitution, preferring multivocal as opposed to univocal meanings, the play of *as if* over the assertions of *is,* juxtapositions over equivalencies, concrete images over abstractions. Rabbinic interpretation never dispenses with the particular form in which the idea is enclothed. The text, for the Rabbis, is a continuous generator of meaning, which arises from the innate logic of the divine language, the letter itself, and is not sought in a nonlinguistic realm external to the text. Language and the text are, to use a contemporary term, the space of *differences,* and truth as conceived by the Rabbis was not an instantaneous unveiling of the One, but a continuous sequential process of interpretation. For the Jew, God's presence is inscribed or traced within a text, not a body. Divinity is located in language, not person.

Paul and the Church Fathers after him replaced this prolonged meditation on and mediation of the text with the pure unmediated presence of Jesus, who resolves all oppositions, stabilizes all meaning, provides ultimate identity, and collapses differentiation. Paul writes, "There is neither Jew nor Greek, there is neither slave nor free, there is neither male nor female; for you are all one in Christ Jesus" (Gal. 3:28).

The Christian desire, then, is to escape the deferral and mediation of the text and language for a communion with pure presence. Language, interpretation, argument, and play of difference hinder the immediacy of direct union. For the Christian, the fact that language involves the absence of its referent is an unbearable circumlocution. Paul seeks to rend the veil of the text, attain the pure presence of the ultimate referent, collapse differentiation, bridge the gap between all signs and the ultimate signified. Jesus, as the word-become-flesh, redeems language, returns substance to shadows, collapses the text, time, history, and the distance between man and God. And absolute presence means the end of language, the text, the law.

In an essay on Augustine's theory of language, to which we shall later return, Margaret Ferguson discusses these aspects of Christian thought in relation to Derrida's critique of metaphysics and his insights into the way the ontological assumptions of Greek metaphysics affect attitudes towards language. When language is seen as an external imitation (mimesis) of things, there is an extralinguistic standard of correctness posited for discourse. This standard becomes the true inside of signification, and language itself (as in the theories of Aristotle and Plato) becomes externalized. "Mimetic theories of language traditionally privileged proper over figurative language because the latter is seen as erring from the norm whereby each word points (univocally) to its referent," she writes.[12] As we have seen, Derrida traces the very distinction between proper and figurative language to the idea of a source of signification utterly removed from the words which reflect it. In this sense, Paul and the Church Fathers perceive language as represented by the law, the written text, primarily from a Greek point of view. In the Rabbinic view, by contrast, there is no mimetic conception of language, no radical separation of word and thing, signifier and signified. Consequently, there was no need for a mediator, no sense of language as loss, exile, detour, or the text as a curse. The movement *out* of the text was, instead, an exile and detour. The letter was never discarded, for the radical distinction between proper and figurative does not apply.

Jesus, however, saw himself as literally *fulfilling signs* with his body.

In this regard, it would be especially appropriate to remember Lyotard's pointing to *nonfulfillment* as a characteristically Jewish mode. Judaism is not, as he writes, a religion of reconciliation of son and father, where the other (father) is returned to the same.[13] In Judaism, there is between father and son what Lyotard calls an "alliance, a preconciliation" because the son is possessed by the father's voice, through the gift of the text. Christianity is "Oedipal" in the sense that it fulfills the desire of the son to take the place of the father; and Oedipus' desire and his fate coincide. In this view Jesus, in representing the desire to replace the father, bears the guilt of the desire through his death, but simultaneously is transformed into father. In Judaism, however, there is no such conciliatory dialectic. Lyotard quotes Emmanuel Levinas, the French Jewish philosopher who greatly influenced Derrida: "Jews remain particularly insensitive to Jesus. . . . The Bible furnishes the symbols, but the Talmud does not fulfill the Bible in the sense that the New Testament claims to fulfill and also prolong the Old."[14] The letter for the Jew does not press for fulfillment and transcendence; it refers, instead, to another sign.

Jesus, however, transgresses the linear chain of signification and makes himself the ultimate fulfilled sign. As Edward Said notes, "In the Christian West, the central text, the New Testament, has formally existed as a Gospel whose physical existence commemorates the communal guilt and redemption,"[15] and Jesus is the "textless original" claiming a "Sonship" with God that supersedes the previous text. His death results in a new set of texts that are linked to his absence. His sacrifice, his substitution of himself results in another substitution for him—the Gospels, which generate an ambivalent reaction on the part of the new community. The New Testament, it should be emphasized, was not considered a commentary on the Old, but as an entirely new Scripture, taking the place of the Old. Furthermore, for the early Christian community, the end of history—the time of unfulfilled desire—was thought to be imminent with the second coming of Jesus; the New Testament became written down in the prolonged interval of waiting. It gained importance as the interval lengthened and it had to now provide a kind of substitute. At its extreme, the new attitude towards Scripture led Marcion, for example, to reject the Old Testament completely, as unfit for Christianity.

Similarly, the central pattern of the new Christian text is not interpretation, but imitation: imitation of Jesus ("Do this is remembrance of me"), and also imitation as a mixture of styles, of *figura,* mimetic representation, allegory, and form.[16] The ability of language to imitate is at the furthest remove from the presence of the textless original, and language becomes identified in the Christian mind with loss, guilt, death, sacrifice, unsatisfactory substitution. It is little wonder, then, that Paul, himself so torn by feelings of sinfulness, blames the text, the written law. Immediately after the text in Rom. 7:6 where he describes the new freedom from the law "which held us captive" "so that we serve not under the old written code but in the new life of the Spirit," Paul writes:

> If it had not been for the law, I should not have known sin. I should not have known what it is to covet if the law had not said "You shall not covet." But sin finding an opportunity in the commandment, wrought in me all kinds of covetousness. Apart from the law sin lies dead. I was once alive apart from the law, but when the commandment came, sin revived and I died; the very commandment which promised life proved death to me. [Rom. 7:7-11.]

> For the law of the Spirit of life in Jesus Christ . . . has done what the law, weakened by the flesh, could not do: sending his own Son in the likeness of sinful flesh and for sin he condemned sin in the flesh. [Rom. 8: 2–4.]

In order to set up these rigid oppositions, Paul literalizes the law, the written code, opposing it to the Spirit. The literal meaning can only be overcome by an equally literal cancellation of it, for there is no common ground between the two. Inevitably, then, Christianity would center around substitutive sacrifice. Lévi-Strauss writes that sacrifice is a scandalous collapse of differentiation, wherein the intermediary effects a contiguity between two polar terms "between which there is essentially no homology nor even any sort of relation. For the object of sacrifice is to establish a relation not of resemblance but of contiguity, by means of a series of successive identifications."[17] It was thus necessary that Jesus share the substance of both the divine and the human, that he literally be incarnated into the sinful flesh, in order to cancel it entirely—as in the cancellation of the figurative term by its proper meaning. Thus Paul's claim that Jesus is the end of the law, a law that is fulfilled in its destruction.

The attempt to transcend the literal, we will remember, to discard the sensuous basis of metaphor for a transcendent spiritual referent which represents pure presence, is the sin which Derrida locates at the basis of philosophy. It is precisely this antithesis of literal and figurative, this inability to exist within the tension of absence-in-presence characterizing the linguistic realm, and this search for immediate union with the presence of being that Derrida ridicules, and here we can again see his Rabbinic slant. (And as Paul uses the law to destroy the law, Derrida uses philosophy to destroy philosophy.)

It is also interesting to note that much of Derrida's discussion of Hegel in *Glas* centers around Hegel's early, overlooked text, *The Spirit of Christianity,* in which Hegel discusses Christianity as the religion of the holy family par excellence. According to Gayatri Spivak's reading of *Glas,* Derrida claims that precisely what the Jew cannot understand is the relation between the Christian and the Divine Father, especially in its combination of finite and infinite: ". . . what he does not understand . . . [is] the commensurability of the passage between the two, the presence of the immense in the determinate, the beauty and immanence in the finite."[18] Spivak adds that in the process, the Jew is perhaps denied an understanding of the philosophical proposition. Writes Derrida,

> In every proposition, the binding, agglutinating, ligamenting position of the copula *is* conciliates the subject and predicate, interlaces one around the

other to form one sole being. . . . Now this conciliation which supposes—
déjà—a reconciliation, which produces in a way the ontological proposition
in general, is also the reconciliation of the infinite with itself, of God with
Himself, of man with God as a unity of father-to-son.[19]

Despite the rather slippery leaps of thought in this passage, its connection
of the classical philosophic proposition with the Christian reconciliation of
father and son is illuminating, bearing in mind our previous discussion of
metaphor and predication, and the modes of rhetoric adopted by Christianity. One of the distinguishing features of Rabbinic thought, we have argued,
was its development of a logic not bound by the inferential modes of the
subject–predicate relation in the classical syllogism. Ricoeur had said that
true metaphorical consciousness centers precisely on the copula, on the
recognition that something *is* and *is not* and *is like* simultaneously, retaining
the difference within identity. Such a metaphysical consciousness operates
on a propositional rather than substitutive level. What we have called the
literalized metaphors of Christianity collapse these differences, a movement paralleling the collapse of differentiation between son and father,
subject and predicate.

Lévi-Strauss, who defined the logic of sacrifice as exactly this "scandalous" collapse of differentiation, this attempt to establish a relation
between two opposite terms, writes in a characteristically Jewish manner
about the sense of distance, of unbridgeable difference:

> This casual attitude to the supernatural was all the more surprising to me
> . . . I lived during the First World War with my grandfather, who was Rabbi of
> Versailles. The house was attached to the synagogue by a long passage, along
> which it was difficult to venture without a feeling of anguish, and which in
> itself formed an impassable frontier between the profane world and the other
> which was lacking precisely in the human warmth that was a necessary
> precondition to its being experienced as sacred.[20]

Lévi-Straussian antinomies are not resolved in scandalous sacrifices, but
by his own supremely ingenious interpretive dialectics. Nevertheless, we
find earlier in *Tristes Tropiques* the startling statement that the existence of
the anthropologist "is incomprehensible except as an attempt at redemption: he is the symbol of atonement."[21] And this from the man who wrote
that the system of sacrifice "represents a private discourse wanting in all
good sense for all that it may frequently be pronounced."[22] In Rabbinic
fashion, Lévi-Strauss's solution is to become an anthropologist as a replacement for actual, literal atonement, to *study* the laws, the logic of
primitive totemic and sacrificial systems. When the Temple in Jerusalem
was destroyed by the Romans, the Rabbis offered the same solution: "He
who studies the laws of sacrifices, it is accounted to him as if he actually
offered them" (*Men.* 110a). Study and interpretation are the realm of *as if*,
wherein difference is recognized and retained and not collapsed into *is*,
literalized in physical presence.

Philo

Paul was thus driven by both internal and external necessities to his doctrine of the sacrificial substitute of Jesus, which cancelled the law and gave the believer immediate union via faith with the presence of the deity. And the allegorical method, we have seen, was the interpretive device that helped him accomplish this end. He did not, however, provide a systematic basis for its use. This theoretical basis had been developing elsewhere during Paul's time and in the preceding two centuries in the city of Alexandria. There, the large Jewish community, threatened by the challenge of Hellenism, had to defend its faith, and there philosophy was united to Scripture. Paul's methods of interpreting Scripture and his arguments against the letter, however, were based more on rhetorical techniques and personal imperatives than upon any fully worked out philosophical system. Paul, moreover, was reserved about the entire value of philosophy: "See to it that no one makes a prey of you by philosophy and empty deceit, according to human tradition" (Col. 2:8), for "Has not God made foolish the wisdom of the world?" (1 Cor. 1:20). The question whether philosophy could be united with revelation was one long fought over by the Church Fathers. It was the Alexandrian school of Christian exegesis, including Clement and Origen, which attempted after the model of Philo to unite them. Tertullian and Iraeneus, however, were much opposed to this endeavor.

Philo, the Alexandrian Jew, was the first to wed philosophy and Scripture, and for this reason Harry Wolfson labels him the founder of medieval philosophy:[23]

> Ostensibly, Philo is only the interpreter of the Hebrew Scriptures in terms of Greek philosophy. But actually he is more than that. He is the interpreter of Greek philosophy in terms of certain fundamental teachings of Hebrew Scripture, whereby he revolutionized philosophy and remade it into what became the common philosophy of the three religions with cognate Scripture, Judaism, Christianity, and Islam. This triple scriptural religious philosophy, which was built up by Philo, reigned supreme as a homogeneous if not a thoroughly unified system of thought until the seventeenth century, when it was pulled down by Spinoza.[24]

In this endeavor, maintains Wolfson, Philo and his school were unique. The other peoples whom Alexander had conquered, mastered and taught Greek philosophy, but none made any radical attempts to change or remake it in terms of an entirely different tradition.[25] In Wolfson's view, Philo not only formulated the principles of allegorical exegesis as an apologetic tactic to defend Judaism to the Hellenistic world; what is more important, he also intended a revision of Greek philosophy in light of Scripture. In so doing he inadvertently opened the way for the Church Fathers (many of whom were pagan philosophers who had recently been converted), to articulate the dogmas of Christianity in terms of philosophy, and to simultaneously Christianize their philosophic tradition.

Jews had settled in Alexandria from the time of its founding in 332 B.C.E. by Alexander the Great, and comprised a significant part of the population. By the time of Philo, in the first century C.E., Jews numbered close to one million and were quite prominent and influential. The first and second centuries, however, saw the Roman wars against the Jews. The Alexandrian community also suffered considerable persecution; by the time of Hadrian it had been almost completely destroyed.

Before the time of Philo, as we have noted, Judaism appeared to the Greeks as a crude and barbaric religion; and the Jews reciprocated, condemning the Greek gods as heathen idols. There were, however, some similar teachings concerning ethics, virtue, justice, and so forth. In the fragments of Aristobulus and the letter of Aristeas, both Alexandrian Jews of the second century B.C.E., the origins of the allegoric method and the attempt to harmonize philosophy with Scripture can be found. Aristobulus tried to show that the Greek philosophers had borrowed from Moses, and that indeed all the tenets of Greek philosophy, especially those of Aristotle, could be found in Moses if one used the proper method of inquiry—that nonliteral method already familiar to the Greeks from its application to the poems of Homer and its use by the Stoics. Philo and these other writers maintained that just as in Homer there were concealed the hidden teachings of philosophy, an "underlying meaning," so Scripture too possessed an underlying meaning, which Philo described by the term *allegory*.

Nevertheless, there were several marked differences between Philo's treatment of the subject and that of the pagan interpreters. Wolfson says that Philo was actually the first to use the term *allegory* exegetically in combination with the nonliteral interpretation of Scripture.[26] Before Philo, it had been used only rhetorically, where it meant a continuous succession of metaphors. Philo applied the term *allegory* even to single terms. Furthermore, in contrast to the exclusively nonliteral interpretation of myths by the Greek philosophers, Philo used the allegorical interpretation of Scripture in reference to texts wherein the literal meaning was not rejected.[27] Philo also used other terms for the underlying meaning of the text, such as *inner meaning, mystery, secret, unintelligible,* and *unseen,* as well as *type, outward symbol, parable,* and so forth.

There were other important differences between the attitudes of the pagan allegorists to the texts they were interpreting and Philo's attitudes towards Scripture. The very concept of *Scripture,* as we have seen, was foreign to the Greek mind. Despite their respect for Homer and other poets, the interpreters of these works never considered them to be divine revelations in the same sense in which Philo considered the text of Scripture to be so. The popular beliefs found in the poets and myths were generally regarded as inferior and primitive modes of knowledge, far beneath that which could be obtained through the philosophic use of reason. Nor did the

Greek philosophers regard the popular forms of religious worship as divinely ordained, or as having any intrinsic worth. For Philo, in contrast, the Pentateuch, and all its prescriptions, rules, modes of worship, as well as the other parts of Scripture, was a divine document, perfect, utterly authoritative and true. Philo clearly did not consider the Greek myths to be so, and he did not claim that they, too, had an inner meaning. In this respect, he differed markedly with the Greek philosophers; he did not accept the idea that the man-made myths of the Greeks contained certain philosophic truths discoverable by allegory.[28] Whereas for the Greeks, myths are subordinate to philosophy, Philo's accomplishment was to make philosophy the "handmaid of Scripture." He expressed this in his famous allegory of the two wives of Abraham, Sarah and Hagar, who are taken to represent this relationship (Paul, as we will remember, also interpreted this passage allegorically to refer to the "Old" and "New" Covenants).

Philo, (as Wolfson shows,) tried to combine traditional methods of Rabbinic interpretation of the Palestinian midrashic variety with the exigencies of Alexandrian Hellenism. He did not by any means, view Scripture as a myth, and affirmed that every Scriptural story has an underlying meaning, whether literally true or not. Moreover, he criticized those who entirely rejected the literal meaning of the law, and maintained that actual observance of its precepts was crucial to understanding its inner meaning. He would have completely opposed Paul's use of allegorical interpretation to abrogate the law. Allegorical interpretation for Philo did not mean the rejection of the factuality or historicity of the narrative.*

Philo well recognized the dangers of overly free allegorical interpretation, and claimed that the method was something into which one had to be initiated; only those possessing unusual natural abilities and moral character could be instructed in it. In his book on dreams, *De Somniis,* he does give certain hermeneutic principles, among which one finds the following: the literal sense must be excluded when anything is stated that appears "unworthy" of God; when a contradiction would otherwise be involved; when Scripture itself is allegorizing. Other principles are similar to those found in midrash, such as the use of allegory when expressions are doubled, when superfluous words are used, when there is a repetition of facts already known, when synonyms are employed, when a play of words is

---

*Rosemary Reuther, in her admirable work, *Faith and Fratricide: The Theological Roots of Anti-Semitism,* shows how Christianity's assertion that it had been freed from the literal outward observance of the Law by being given the inward symbolic, spiritual meaning "depended on the spiritualizing exegesis of Hellenistic Judaism. But the Christians interpret the relationship of outward form and inward meaning antithetically, while Philo interpreted it sacramentally" (p. 154): "Originally, Philo understood the allegorical meaning not as antithetical to the outward commandment. When Christianity fused the Philonic dualism of letter and spirit with the messianic dualism of the historical age and the messianic age, this made the relationship of letter and spirit antithetical and supersessionary" (p. 160.) What was dialectical in Philo became dualistic in Christianity.

possible; when the expression is unusual or the words allow slight alteration, or when there is any marked abnormality in grammar.[29]

To interpret the text in a nonliteral manner was an integral part of
Rabbinic tradition, but Philo gave the native Jewish midrashic method a
Greek philosophical turn. This meant the adoption of an entirely different
way of thinking about meaning, truth, being, and inference, which implicitly had, as we have seen, an antilinguistic (and anti-Scriptural) attitude at
its center. Philo was trying, moreover, to illumine the truths of Greek
philosophy within the text of Scripture. It was natural, then, that his
methods were opposed, in the main, by the Palestinian Rabbis who did not
favor his brand of philosophic allegorizing. The truths of Scripture were,
for them, of a different and higher order than the ontological truths of
philosophy.

Origen

Philo, in fact, has been of almost no signficance for Rabbinic tradition,
but of absolutely central importance for Christian thought. (In the libraries,
one finds his works shelved with the Church Fathers, not the Midrash.) The
two greatest Christian teachers of Alexandria, Clement (d. 216 C.E.) and
Origen (d. 254 C.E.) were deeply influenced by Philo, and the importance of
the groundwork laid by Clement and Origen cannot be overemphasized:
they were the founders of Christian philosophy. As Beryl Smalley writes,
"To write a history of Origenist influence on the West would be tantamount
to writing a history of Western exegesis."[30] Through the work of Clement
and Origen, the allegorical method became firmly established in the Church
and in Western thought in general.

In effect, the problems encountered by Philo in his attempts to reconcile philosophy and Scripture became the central problems faced by the
Church Fathers as they tried to recast Christian beliefs in the form of
philosophy. Despite the wariness of Paul and the early Apostles towards
philosophy (the Apostolic Era may be dated from the death of Jesus to
approximately 160 C.E.), the attitude changes with the rise of the Apolo-
gists in the second century C.E., when Christianity began to be presented
the same way Philo had presented Judaism. Wolfson cites three reasons for
the rise of a philosophical Christianity: (1) the conversion to Christianity of
pagans who had been trained in philosophy, from Aristedes and Clement to
Justin Martyr, Tatian, Theopolis, and Augustine; (2) the usefulness of
philosophy in helping Christianity defend itself against various accusations
to which it was subject in the Roman Empire, by showing its teachings to be
in harmony with the best of pagan philosophy; and (3) the usefulness of the
philosophy introduced by these pagan converts in the various doctrinal
disputes and debates with other competing sects, such as the Gnostics.[31]

We have noted that although nonliteral interpretation of Scripture was important for earlier writers such as Paul, most of these interpretations were in the nature of predictive midrashim and were called *typological, parables, symbols,* and so forth. The first Church Father to introduce nonliteral interpretations of a philosophical kind to the text of both the Old and New Testament was Clement of Alexandria, and henceforth this manner of philosophical allegoric reading would be used along with the typological and predictive kinds. In sum, Wolfson writes, "Allegorical interpretation did not come to the fathers directly from Greek philosophy; it came to them from Philo, partly through the Pauline writings, though in the course of its use by them it came into direct contact with the allegorical method, as used in Greek philosophy, and was affected by it."[32]

Philo, however, had dealt in the main with the Pentateuch, while the early Christian writers applied the method mostly to the prophets and other books. The early Church Fathers were also particularly concerned to show through the use of allegorical interpretation that the Hebrew Scriptures implicitly contained Christian doctrine, and further extended Philo's method to include the New Testament.

Philo had posited a twofold meaning to Scripture: a literal, obvious meaning, and an underlying meaning. He then subdivided the nonliteral into two categories, *physical* and *ethical.* In Clement, this subdivision was expanded to a threefold way of interpreting the Scriptures: the mystic *(symbol),* the moral *(precepts for right conduct),* and the prophetic *(prophetic utterance),* all of which were Christocentric.

Origen was heavily indebted to Philo. Philo is quoted by name in several places in Origen's works, often with the term "one of our predecessors." It appears that Origen regarded Philo as part of the Church's heritage. He also refers to Philo in stating his basic position on the sense of Scripture: "The law has a twofold sense, one according to a literal meaning and the other according to an inner meaning as has also been shown by some before us," and he identifies this twofold sense with Paul's contrast of the *letter* and *spirit* of the law *(Contra Celsus* 7. 20). In many other passages, he explicitly approves of Philo's interpretation.

Origen's work, in fact, was an amalgamation of many sources and ideas. He also saw himself as a successor to and follower of Paul, and furthermore was familiar with varieties of interpretation in the Palestinian school of Rabbinic exegesis. It is known that he consulted Rabbinic authorities for clarifications of textual problems, especially in the work he undertook of completing the *Hexapla,* a text of the Old Testament with different versions placed side by side for comparison, the aim of which was to ascertain the true text of the Septuagint. After his departure from Alexandria in 231 C.E., he settled in Palestine at Caesarea. Caesarea was at the time an important administrative center and also housed a well-known academy of Rabbis, including the famous R. Hoshaya who is often mentioned as the compiler of the *Midrash Rabbah* on Genesis. In sum, as N. R.

M. de Lange writes, "With the exception of Jerome, no other Church Father knew the Jews so well as Origen."[33]

The work in which he sets forth his systematic theory of the interpretation of Scriptures was written, however, before he left Alexandria. This treatise, *On First Principles,* was a comprehensive investigation of Christian doctrine on a hitherto unprecedented scale, and it is in the Fourth Book of that work that Origen lays down his principles for the interpretation of Scripture. Here he also argues against the misinterpretations of Scripture by Jews and "heretics," by which he presumably means Gnostics. Those erring interpretations exist, claims Origen,

> because the method by which we should approach the interpretation of the divine writings is unknown to the multitude. For the Jews, owing to the hardness of their heart and their desire to appear wise in their own sight, have refused to believe in our Lord and Saviour because they suppose that the prophecies that relate to him must be understood literally, that is, he ought literally and visibly to have "proclaimed release to the captives," and that he ought to have at once built a city such as they think the "city of God" really is. . . . Now the reason why those we have mentioned above have a false apprehension of all these matters is nothing else but this, that the holy scripture is not understood by them in its spiritual sense, but according to the sound of the letter.[34]

Origen then proceeds to postulate a threefold meaning to Scripture, basing his view on a verse from Prov. 22:20–21: "Do thou portray these things to thyself in threefold counsel and knowledge, so that thou may answer words of truth to those who question thee." Origen postulates what he calls the *body* of the Scriptures (the literal interpretation), the *soul* of Scripture (referring to a mortal sense), and the *spiritual sense* (referring to the mysteries and secrets hidden therein). The first sense, he says, is for the simple believer, the second for initiates, and the third for the Christian Gnostics. Just as a man is said to consist of body, soul, and spirit, says Origen, so Scripture has the same three aspects. Following Paul, whom he also here quotes at length, Origen believes that certain narratives described in the Old Testament cannot be taken literally, and that the law as a whole is a shadow and figure of Christian realities. While he believed that the whole of Scripture had a spiritual meaning, he did not admit that it all had a literal meaning, as he writes in Chapter 3: "For our contention with the regard to the whole of the divine scripture is, that it all has a spiritual meaning, but not all a bodily meaning; for the bodily meaning is often proved to be an impossibility."[35] Though he provides no clear guidance on how to interpret the letter, he does claim that the literal sense should be rejected when the account is irrational and impossible. And on this basis, he rejected certain historical narratives as well as laws in both the Old and New Testaments.

Origen was thus an inheritor of Pauline antinomianism and the Christian teaching that the Old Testament merely prefigures or foreshadows the

New. Pursuing this line of thought, Origen located four general types in the Old Testament: (1) prophecies of the Coming of Jesus; (2) prophecies of the Church and its sacraments; (3) eschatological prophecies of Last Things and the Kingdom of Heaven; and (4) mystical figures of the relation of God and the individual soul, as exemplified in the history of the chosen people. And despite his familiarity with and dependence upon Jewish sources, Origen castigated the Jews as literalists. It is quite evident that he knew and made use of various nonliteral methods employed by the Jews, but the source of his accusation was that the Jews refused to interpret the Old Testament as predicting and referring to Jesus. This stigma of literalism passed into the subsequent history of Christian thought as a general condemnation of Jewish exegesis. Without a philosophic allegorical exegesis, the Hellenistic mind simply could not tolerate the letter of Scripture; it was too crude, irrational, and alien. Rabbinic attempts to reveal the rationality of this realm of unreason without "sacrificing the body" of the text were condemned as far-fetched and equally irrational. (And—to look ahead somewhat—when Freud used similar methodology to interpret the language of the unconscious, to show the "logic of the illogical kingdom," he confronted the opposition of a mentality conditioned by over a thousand years of Christian allegorizing, and was accused of being crude and irrational as well. Perhaps we can say that he reconnected the meaning to the "body of the text" in an unprecedented way, giving life once more to the letter.)

Origen's influence over the subsequent history of interpretation was immense. With his work and that of Clement, the allegorical method became firmly established, was systematically explained, and reached its culmination. Nothing radically new happened thereafter in the Church Fathers with regard to the classification and approach to Scriptural interpretation. The threefold meaning was extended to what became the famous fourfold method in the Middle Ages, when the last category of "spiritual" or "secret" meaning was further subdivided into the "allegorical" and "analogical."

(There was, however, some significant opposition to what was considered an overemphasis on the allegorical method in the Church, and an attempt was made to give more importance to the literal and historical meanings of Scripture. This opposition centered in Antioch. The Antiochene teachers and those who leaned towards their views, such as Jerome, were, as might be expected, heavily influenced by Jewish teachers and the influential Jewish community in Antioch. Among other things, the school of Antioch insisted on the historical reality of the Biblical revelation. Such writers as Chrysostom, Theodore, and Theodoret tried to found typological reading on the literal sense, though their interpretations were, of course, essentially Christological. The Antiochan tradition, however, did not gain any general acceptance, and it has been the school of Alexandria that has determined Western thinking.)

The Logos and the Letter

In addition to providing Christianity with the basis for the allegorical approach to Scripture, Philo made another important contribution: the doctrine of the logos.[36] *Logos* was a term familar in Greek philosophy, and in using it Philo combined two precedents. From Aristotle, Philo took the idea of *nous*, the thinking soul or mind, which Aristotle defines as the *place of forms* (*De An.* 3. 4. 429a27–28) and substituted for it the term *logos* (*word, reason, explanation,* etc.), thus making *logos* something identical with the essence of God. From Plato, he took the idea that all things are created by a *logos* (i.e., a reason) and a divine knowledge which comes from God, thus making *logos* something equivalent to the divine mind, and a first principle, or instrument of creation. This interpretation harmonized with Scriptural statements such as Ps. 33:6, that "by the word of God the heavens were established" (see also Pss. 147:18, and 148:18, and similar uses of the figure of *wisdom* in Scripture in Prov. 3:19, Ps. 104:24, and others). Furthermore, for Philo, the logos has two stages: one in which it existed within God and was identifiable with Him, and another in which it was a created incorporeal being, existing outside of God and immanent in the world.

Wolfson also notes that "Philo, who, on the basis of Scripture supplemented by Jewish tradition, believed that, before the creation of the world, God created certain incorporeal things after the pattern of which He subsequently created corporeal things in this created world, identified this belief of his with the Platonic Theory of Ideas."[37] In fact, these very elements of Jewish tradition led Paul to his doctrine of the preexistent Christ as an instrument of creation. In Wolfson's analysis, the Gospel of John adopted the Philonic term *logos* as a description of Paul's preexistent Christ in its famous statement that "in the beginning was the logos and the logos became flesh." But John does not describe the logos as the place of the intelligible world of ideas, as does Philo. The Church Fathers developed John's ideas of the logos by adding certain Philonic conceptions, but then departed from Philo in other crucial respects. Let us try to trace this process a little more clearly.

In Jewish tradition, there were references made in the aggadah to the preexistence of the Messiah and to a personified figure of wisdom. Paul then identified the preexistent wisdom with the preexistent Messiah and claimed that the revelation of the law of Moses and the birth of Jesus were two stages in the earthly revelation of the preexistent wisdom.[38] The first stage was the written Torah, the second the body of Jesus: again the displacement of text or word to a literal body, a person. Paul even goes so far as to call Jesus "the image of the invisible God" (Col. 1:15; Heb. 1:3). But in Paul, John, and the Church Fathers, the logos attained a state of existence that Philo and the Jewish tradition had never allowed. For Philo, the logos was immanent in the world as a guiding principle or instrument of divine providence; it was that through which the laws of nature operate, and the career of the logos ends there. For the Church Fathers, the logos had another stage of existence: it actually and literally became flesh (John 1:14). And from the earliest times, the Church Fathers took John's statement to mean that the logos was literally begotten out of the essence of God, and was God.

In making the logos begotten rather than created by God, too, the Church Fathers radically departed from Philo and Jewish ideas, as Wolfson shows.[39] In popular Greek religion, the gods were anthropomorphically envisioned as producers of things after the analogy of animal procreation. The divinity begot other gods. Jewish thought was strikingly different. The God of Scripture was a creator of the world, not as begetter but as artisan (as in the famous midrash, "God looked into the Torah and created the world," after the manner of an architect). A begetter begets something out of his own essence, like himself; whereas an artisan creates something different from and unlike himself. (Again the theme of difference seems to be typically Jewish, from the Bible to Derrida.) Indeed, the problem of the one and the many, so central to Greek philosophy, reflects the dilemma of how—if creation is modelled after the pattern of natural generation—God could create something unlike himself: how indeed there could be multiplicity. In any case, in Christianity, God was seen as the begetter of the earthly Jesus, and the preexistent logos was no longer seen as something created, but rather something generated in the literal sense. (The influence of Neoplatonism and Gnosticism are readily evident here.) In the Creed of Nicaea, "begotten of the father" meant "of the substance of" the father, not "created from nothing."

In sum, as Wolfson[40] traces this process, with the Epistles of Paul and the Gospel of John, the Christian God became the begetter of the earthly Jesus and the preexistent Christ. The preexistent Christ was not created after the analogy of the handiwork of an artisan, but generated by God after the analogy of the offspring of a human father. Paul's declaration that Christ was equal with God and John's statement that the logos was God were taken literally. The preexistent Christ was not only identified with the logos, was not merely divine; he was God.

One can see here the beginnings of the doctrine of the Trinity, the formulation of which involved the Church Fathers in so many agonizing and passionate debates. Wolfson writes, "The problem of the mystery of the Trinity arose only when Paul's description of the pre-existent Christ as being 'equal with God' and John's description of the logos as 'being God' began to be taken literally. The starting point of all the discussion of the problem of the Trinity was the rejection of the concept of absolute unity of God as defined on behalf of Judaism by Philo."[41]

Here was another critical departure of the Church Fathers from Philo and Jewish thought; they relativized the concept of the unity of God. Yet, at the same time, they tried to defend their concept of the Trinity from becoming a pagan polytheism to which they were also opposed. In essence, their doctrine was a combination of both ideas. Gregory of Nyssa writes, "Truth passes in the mean between these two concepts. . . . The Jewish dogma is destroyed by acceptance of the Word and by belief in the Spirit, while the polytheism of the Greek school is made to vanish by the unity of nature abrogating the imagination of plurality."[42] Gregory's association of the overthrow of Judaism specifically by the doctrine of the "Word" and "Spirit" indicates how crucial the idea of the word-become-flesh was for Christian thought.

Unity, Trinity
Literal, Figurative

Most important for us here is how the problem of the Three-in-One God influenced the problem of interpretation and attitudes towards language. That is, since the unity of God in Jewish thought was absolute, unknowable, and ultimately beyond definition (and different from the conception of unity the Church Fathers inherited from Greek ontology, especially from Aristotle), the Jewish concept of unity gave rise to a different notion of multiplicity. It was not a unity defined in terms of *ousia,* being, substance, or *res.* It was a unity that underlay everything, but not as substance; and therefore the problems of how different substances could be one, the problem of the one and the many which so plagued Greek philosophy, was not a central issue in Jewish thought. The world was not generated but created. And we have seen at the beginning of Chapter 2 how the creationist doctrine was a challenge to the entire tradition of classical Western metaphysics. The artist creates difference, he does not beget likeness. Hans Jonas wrote that the Biblical doctrine placed contingency against necessity, and particularity against universality.[43] It secured a place for the contingent within philosophy and diminished the status of nature.

In an essay on the relation of the Biblical exegesis of Maimonides to literary criticism, Kenneth Stein[44] shows how it was, in fact, the creationist doctrine that served to preserve the literal sense of Scripture. Maimonides (1135–1204 C.E.), as is well known, wrote his *Guide to the Perplexed* in answer to the problems about Scripture raised by the philosophy and science of his day, and was well aware of the objections of the medieval Christian exegetes to Rabbinic interpretation. Maimonides proposed that Scripture should be taken figuratively when reason requires it. For example, Scripture speaks in concrete terms about God's body and emotion, but since reason requires an understanding of God as incorporeal, such passages cannot be taken literally (and Scripture also hints at this fact). On the other hand (and this is what is distinctively Jewish in Maimonides), when reason cannot demonstrate the teaching of Scripture—for example, reason cannot prove the eternity of the universe—precisely then the text should be taken literally. Interestingly, Origen and the Christian writers followed Maimonides specifically on this basis, rejecting the literal meaning of many of the Old Testament narratives; they thought they were rationally impossible. Maimonides, however, maintains, "The Law has given us knowledge of a matter the grasp of which is not within our power, and the miracle attests to the correctness of our claims. Know that with a belief in the creation of the world in time, all the miracles become possible and the Law thus becomes possible, and all questions that may be asked on this subject vanish."[45]

The connection of the literal meaning to the concept of creation *ex nihilo* is crucial here. To assume that the universe is eternal destroys the possibility of revelation, and of the letter:

> If, however, someone says that the world is as it is in virtue of necessity, it would be a necessary obligation to ask all those questions; and there would be no way out of them except through a recourse to unseemly answers in which there would be combined the giving the lie to, and the annulment of, all extenal meanings of the Law with regard to which no intelligent man has any doubt that they are to be taken in their external meanings.[46]

Stein explains Maimonides' idea as follows: The fact that Scripture does teach the doctrine of creation *ex nihilo,* a doctrine which reason cannot prove, shows that the text does have a literal sense—an existential and historical meaning. Without this doctrine, Scripture would become an analogical (symbolic) system. Creation *ex nihilo,* however, saves the text from a complete spiritualizing, a conception in which the historical and existential meanings would only be parts or phases of a larger whole. Because the doctrine of creation *ex nihilo* asserts a complete difference between the Creator and the creation, the literal sense cannot be subsumed under the spiritual.[47]

Stein further shows that therefore Maimonides' exegesis of different meanings of Scripture was not a multiple-layered hierarchy in which the spirit rules the letter. We have also previously noted that the absence of hierarchical interpretation in Rabbinic thought may be connected to the absence of the concept of the hierarchy of being. In the great chain of Aristotelian being, certain things had an ontological priority over others. In the Jewish view, every particular had equal status with every other: the literal had as much importance as the spiritual; there was no hierarchy of interpretation. Interpretation was a horizontal process, where many meanings simultaneously existed together, and there could be no end to the law. As the differences between particulars were retained, because every particular was a creation *ex nihilo,* so the differences in interpretation were retained, indeed multiplied, by the Rabbis.

When the Church tried to negate the literal meanings of the Torah and subsume them into the spiritual meaning, the Jews reacted violently. To the

Jews, the Christians were improperly taking things for signs, and signs for things. Moreover, the Christian definition of sign and thing was entirely alien to Jewish thought, for the Christian ideas came from Greek ontology. Perhaps one of the most crucial moves was Philo's use of *logos* in place of *nous,* his compounding *word* with the Greek principles *thought* and *being.* This was the Jewish *davar* (*word thing*) transposed into Greek ontology. The Hebrew *davar* was not, as we have seen, a *res,* a *being* in the Greek sense. The essential contrast for the Jews was not between sign and thing or spiritual and literal, God and the word—but between God and the world. The Jews did not need a mediator between signs and things, words and being. Reality was already divinely verbal, not silently ontological. What the Jews did consider as idol worship, however, was the reification of signs—image making—and this is what the Christians were doing, literalizing Jewish metaphors, taking signs for things, and applying the whole of Greek ontology to Scripture and God, thus determining His absolute unity and difference. For the Jews, this unity transcended even the unities that can be conceived of in terms of substance. In trying to make God absolutely present within the being of nature as a substance, it was inevitable that the Christians would also reify words, and make incarnation the central doctrine. The play of interpretation (and difference) was similarly frozen into attempts to solidify words into substance, with singular referents, instead of allowing for multiplication of meaning, as difference became subsumed into the concept of the Trinity, a relative unity of three-in-one.

Wolfson analyzes the problem of unity in the Trinity as follows.[48] In Aristotle's discussion of unity in the *Metaphysica* (5. 6. 1016a, b), he claims that the term *one* is relative to the term *indivisible.* Even though things may be indivisible in one respect, they might be divisible in another. Aristotle postulates five types of unity: (1) by *accident*—the inherence of an accident in a subject; (2) by *continuity*—the combination of objects in a single collection; (3) of *substratum*—the existence in two different elements of a common underlying element, such as oil and water, which have water in common; (4) of *genus*—the unity of different species; and (5) *relative unity of genus*—the sense in which two individuals of the same species are one because they belong to the same species; one formula states their essence. The Church Fathers, in trying to work out the problem of the relation of the persons of God and the logos to the actual flesh, excluded the first two modes of unity—accident and continuity—and used the models of unity of substratum, genus, and species. Each member of the Trinity was seen as an individual species, unified after the anology of Aristotle's last three categories.

In determining how logos could actually unite with flesh, the Fathers also used the idea of union *by predominance.* That is, in contrast to the unity of things by juxtaposition or aggregation, wherein their individual species remained unchanged, or wherein each of the constituents changed towards the other into a *tertium quid* (some intermediate and common element), the mode of unity the Fathers used to describe the union of body to logos was a union of predominance. In this case, one of the elements changes into another which predominates, and not into a third intermediary element. An example given is the drop of wine put into thousands of gallons of water.[49]

The development and details of the doctrine of the Trinity are far beyond the scope of this discussion, but the dependence of the Church Fathers on Aristotelian categories of substance and species to describe the Trinity is most relevant. We have seen in Chapter 1 how Greek ontology drastically affected concepts of meaning, inference, language, and metaphor. And we can connect these issues to the moment at which the Church Fathers split with the Rabbis over the interpretation of Scripture.

Ricoeur, Derrida, and others criticized the Aristotelian theory of metaphor because it postulated an opposition between literal and figurative, proper and improper meanings. The concept of *proper* as *univocally belonging* or *necessarily inhering* is based on an ontology of sameness, which Derrida claims creates an illusory logic of generic, universal, unequivocal identities. These types of identities, as just noted, were used by the Church Fathers to describe the unity of the Trinity and furthermore to negate literal meanings and the modes of differential multiple interpretation of the Rabbis, who often posited unities of contiguity and juxtaposition and not substance. Rabbinic thought, because it was not committed to an ontology of substance and sameness, retained differences within resemblance, and it did not negate the letter or abstract into universals.

There is perhaps another interesting parallel between Aristotle's logic of oppositions (the dogma of the law of contradiction, the absolute difference between affirmation and negation, universal and particular, etc.) and Paul's absolute opposition between letter and spirit, old law and new law, etc. The Aristotelian opposition of proper and figurative meaning becomes the opposition of letter and spirit in Paul.* The contemporary theorists of metaphor point out, however, that in truth metaphor is an irritant, something that confuses these categories, mixes up these oppositions, and yet

---

*Rosemary Reuther, in *Faith and Fratricide*, incisively examines the schism between Jews and Christians over the proper interpretation of Scripture in the context of the Church's growing anti-Judaic tradition. See, especially, Chapter 2 of her work. Reuther asserts that Christology and anti-Judaism are two sides of the same exegetical tradition in Christianity (pp. 64–65). She traces the violence of Paul's attitudes not only to a dualistic Gnostic influence, but also to Christianity's "illegitimate historicizing of the eschatological. This is a false reifying [sic] of the experience of the eschatological in history" (p. 248):

> Realized eschatology converts each of the dialectics we have examined—judgment and promise, particularism and universalism, letter and spirit, history and eschatology—into dualisms, applying one side to "the new messianic people," the Christians, and the negative side to the "old people," the Jews. The message of messianic expectation is imported into history and reified as a historical event in a way that makes it a reality-denying, rather than a reality-discerning principle. [P. 246.]

retains the tension of their differences. True "metaphorical consciousness," in Ricoeur's sense, refuses to allow us the comforts of a clear and simple opposition between literal and figurative. Ricoeur and Derrida want to tell us that not only can we not believe in the literal, literally, but we also cannot believe in the purely figurative, literally.

If we may disgress slightly, this insight into the dialectical nature of literal and figurative meaning takes the broader form of the dialectic between illusion and reality, and Shakespeare, for example, is one who constantly plays on it. A character like Bottom in *A Midsummer Night's Dream* is ludicrous because he takes things literally; he cannot play with the illusions of art; and yet there is an equally literal mentality in the aesthete (or playgoer) who also takes his art literally, believing too much in the figures of the imagination. Certain modes of tragedy and comedy focus on the problem of literalism. Macbeth's tragedy might be seen, for example, in part as an attempt to literalize the figures of his imagination, embody prophecies.

In the substitution theory of metaphor, where the opposition is established between literal and figurative, one is necessarily led to the death either of the letter or of the figure—or to the destruction either of reality for art, or of art for reality. In an essay subtly probing the relations of literal and metaphorical, Michael McCanles aptly defines a literalist "as one who both takes metaphors too seriously and does not take metaphors seriously enough."[50] A literalist is also one who gives precedence to one lexicon of terms, calling it "true" as opposed to all others, this lexicon alone referring to objective reality, which the other "false" ones do not. This kind of literalism, he notes, depends upon a copy theory of language that assumes some kind of mirrorlike or isomorphic relation between word and object. Hence the literalist cannot recognize when his own lexicon is being used literally and when it is being used metaphorically; he may treat his own metaphorical statements as literal, and the literal statements of others as metaphorical (i.e., ambiguous or false). For him the literal and metaphorical are in a state of what McCanles calls "interchange," by which he means opposition, mutual cancellation. The *Cratylus,* McCanles notes, propounds this literalist position on language, and one finds it even more pronounced in the literalism of the seventeenth century, beginning with Bacon's attacks on terms that have more than one definition or referent. This mode of thinking also forms the basis of classical science, of course.

McCanles argues against this definition of the literal–metaphorical relation in favor of what he calls the "literal–metaphorical dialectic," the recognition that both terms are dependent upon and define one another; they do not cancel each other out. The difference between nonfictive and fictive discourse, in his view, is that fiction deliberately and openly exploits the dialectical tension between literal and metaphorical meaning, whereas nonfiction—assuming a direct word–object correspondence—is subject to an interchange between literal and metaphorical:

A) nonfictive discourse treats its language "as if" it were literal; B) fictive discourse treats its language "as if" it were literal. This first "as if" means that the language is not literal at all but metaphorical. Because of theoretical blinders obscuring this fact (e.g., scientific objectivity, precision in definitions, etc.) the writers are often unaware of this. Nonfictive discourse may treat the metaphors latent in its putatively literal grammar as if they did not exist, opening itself up to covert, and therefore uncontrolled, interchange between literal and metaphorical meanings. The second "as if" means that fictional discourse overtly displays itself exploiting the literal meanings of its words in order to turn them into metaphors. To this extent, fictive writing exercises the greater control over its own structures and meanings. In it the "as if" is open and palpable, part of the "let's pretend" presentation of itself to a reader or an audience.[51]

McCanles's insights can be used to characterize some of the disputes about literalism in Biblical interpretation. Christian writers, following Greek categories of a copy language (and all that that implies for the theory of metaphor) treat spiritual allegorical interpretations as if they were literal, i.e., the proper meanings, the correct interpretations; the word literally becomes flesh. Rabbinic thought, in its insistence on the letter, nevertheless plays with and exposes the as-if nature of the literal, especially in midrash and aggadah. It holds the literal and metaphorical in a dialectical tension, wherein neither cancels the other because "the recognition of either literal or metaphorical meanings depends radically on our recognizing at the same time the one, the other, and both." In McCanles's apt words, "One might say that the 'moral' of *A Midsummer Night's Dream,* like that of *Don Quixote,* is that those who misunderstand poetic fictions are condemned to act our poetic fictions."[52] We may perhaps extend this insight to the literal acting out of the Hebrew concept of the *davar,* the *word thing,* in Christianity's doctrine of the word-become-flesh, and then the literal cancellation of this fleshly embodiment through the crucifixion.

Discussing these problems is not a digression, for they are really extensions of problems inherited from Greek philosophy and the Patristic tradition of interpretation. The paradox of the literal–metaphorical interchange in the Christian tradition is that the new spiritual meaning becomes another variety of letter.

Augustine

We have shown at length how the radical distinction between letter and spirit formed an important polemical basis for the Church in the era of the Greek Fathers. The allegorical method went on to captivate the Latin world and the Latin Fathers as well. Hilary and Ambrose continued it, Ambrose going so far as to make Philo the basis of his commentary on Genesis. Augustine (d. 430), whose elaborate treatment of the principles of exegesis in *On Christian Doctrine* became a central text for all medieval aesthetics, writes in his *Confessions* that it was only through Ambrose's allegorical interpretations of Scripture that he was able to accept Catholicism:

> I began to believe that the Catholic faith, which I had thought impossible to defend against the objections of the Manichees, might fairly be maintained, especially since I had heard one passage after another in the Old Testament figuratively explained. These passages had been death to me when I took them literally, but once I heard them explained in their spiritual meaning I began to blame myself for my despair, at least insofar as it had led me to suppose that it was quite impossible to counter people who hated and derided the law and the prophets. [*Confessions* V:14.]

> I was glad too that at last I had been shown how to interpret the ancient Scriptures of the law and the prophets in a different light from that which had previously made them seem absurd, when I used to criticize your saints for holding beliefs which they had never really held at all. I was pleased to hear that in his sermons to the people Ambrose often repeated the text: *The written law inflicts death, whereas the spiritual law brings life,* as though this were a rule upon which he wished to insist most carefully. And when he lifted the veil of mystery and disclosed the spiritual meaning of texts which, taken literally, appeared to contain the most unlikely doctrines, I was not aggrieved by what he said, although I did not know whether it was true. [*Confessions* VI:4.]

Nevertheless, there was no consensus in the Patristic tradition about the meaning of *literal*. Origen's proposal that there were three senses to Scripture—literal, moral, and spiritual—was adopted by Jerome and Augustine and expanded into the famous "fourfold sense" of Scripture so pervasive in medieval thought. This doctrine is first found expressly laid out in the *Collationes* of John Cassian (370–435 C.E.). The use made of it by Eucherius of Lyons (d. 449) set the style for the Middle Ages. The spiritual sense was subdivided into "allegorical" and "anagogical" meanings. The example of the fourfold meaning, which became standard for the Middle Ages as found in Cassian, was based on Paul's allegorical interpretation of Abraham's two wives in Gal. 4:21 ff. (Sarah and the concubine Hagar, writes Paul, represent the two covenants: "One is from Mount Sinai, bearing children for slavery; she is Hagar. Now Hagar is Mount Sinai in Arabia; she corresponds to the present Jerusalem, for she is in slavery with her children. But the Jerusalem above is free, and she is our mother.") The literal meaning of Jerusalem in the fourfold schema is the city by that name; the allegorical meaning is the Church; the moral, or *tropological* meaning is the human soul; and the anagogical or *mystical* meaning is the Heavenly City.

There were also varying definitions of the exact meanings of the above four categories. Augustine formulated them as *history* (literal); *etiology* (a consideration of causes, and of difficult passages for a Christian); *anagogia* (typology, or considerations of congruence between the Old and New Testaments); and *allegoria* (figurative interpretation, also usually typology). Aquinas, for example, placed the first three of Augustine's categories under the first, and insisted, furthermore, that the literal meaning should be the basis for the other three; while Dante considered them all to be equal.

In any case, neither Augustine, Gregory, nor Bede considered the text to have a continuous, simultaneous fourfold meaning in every aspect. It was thought, rather, that the nature of a given particular text determined the level at which it should be read. (This attitude was in marked contrast to Rabbinic thought about the multiple meaning of Scripture, where the text was considered to be continuously and simultaneously multileveled in every detail.) It can be generally asserted that for medieval thought, the literal meaning was devalued. When one does find special attention given to the letter, in thinkers such as Aquinas, one also often finds a Rabbinic influence. (Aquinas's familiarity with and interest in the works of Maimonides is well known.) Jewish influence is traced in depth in Beryl Smalley's *The Study of the Bible in the Middle Ages.* Smalley emphasizes that for the Middle Ages Bible study represented the highest branch of learning, and shows the great extent to which the language and content of Scripture permeated medieval thought. Christian scholars, in their eagerness to study the text, frequently sought contact with Jews:

> Far from avoiding the Jews, the Latin scholars asked them for information on rabbinics as well as for guidance in the Hebrew tongue. Jews of Northern France and the Rhineland, from Rashi onward, supplemented their traditional lore by an original method of exegesis. Hence Christians of the 12th and 13th centuries, who consulted the rabbis would get two types of answers to their questions: collections of old traditions and specimens of the traditional interpretations, and they would make the acquaintance of a living contemporary scholarship, which could influence their own approach. Christian knowledge of rabbinics in the Middle Ages used to be underestimated.[53]

Rashi (Rabbi Shlomo Yitzhaki, the foremost Jewish medieval commentator) was a major influence on Nicholas of Lyra (fourteenth century), and through Nicholas on Luther and the Reformation. Nicholas studied Rashi so closely that he was called *Simia Solomonis* (after Rashi's name, *Solomon*). Nicholas followed Aquinas in placing more emphasis on the literal sense, and he bases the mystical sense exclusively on the letter. To Nicholas is attributed the famous saying: *Littera gesta docet, quid credas Allegoria, / Moralis quid agas, quo tendas Anagogia* ("The letter shows us what God and our fathers did; The allegory shows us where our faith is hid; The moral meaning gives us rules of daily life; The anagogy shows us where we end our strife").

Nicholas did more than any other to break down the authority of ecclesiastical tradition.[54] As the famous saying had it, *Si Lyra non lyrasset, Lutherus non saltasset.* ("If [Nicholus of] Lyra didn't play the lyre, Luther would not dance.") Luther's Reformation, which we shall discuss presently, was an attempt to reject the authority of the Church and return to the authority of Scripture, and moreover, to reject the doctrine of the fourfold meaning and return Scripture to its literal sense. Luther made extensive use of Lyra. The influence of Jews on Christian exegesis in the Middle Ages is a topic which needs investigation in its own right, but it is appropriate to add here that, as Smalley shows, besides Nicholas, there was much Rabbinic influence in the school of Saint Victor, in the circle of scholars surrounding Thomas of Canterbury, on Bernard of Clairvaux, and of course on Aquinas. Nevertheless, the most influential Patristic mode for aesthetics and literature was allegorical interpretation, not the interest of these scholars in the letter.

D. W. Robertson, discussing medieval aesthetics in his *A Preface to Chaucer,* writes that "the idea that the letter is 'old,' 'sterile,' 'unprofitable' is constantly reiterated by medieval commentators,"[55] and he also explains at length how the development of literary allegory in the Middle Ages was closely bound up with the allegorical interpretation of Scripture. Dante, Boccaccio, and Petrarch, as well as other medieval exegetes and critics, did not miss the connection between the allegories of poetry and those of Scripture, and how, indeed, poetry might be treated as a sort of Scripture. Dante in his famous letter to Can Grande della Scala explained how the fourfold method of Biblical interpretation could be applied to his masterwork, and one can see the influence of Scriptural exegesis in his conceptions of literary analysis in the *Convivio* as well.[56] The defense of poetry through allegory was a technique as common to Christian humanists as it had been to the Greeks. Boccaccio in his *Genealogy of the Gods* (XV:8), a work which became a standard manual for poets and painters, illustrated how the fourfold method of interpreting Scripture might be applied even to pagan fictions. He qualified this, however, by referring it only to pagan fictions used in Christian writings to illumine Christine truths; pagan fictions in pagan writings could only be interpreted according to their literal and moral meanings.

Beryl Smalley also points to the parallel between the conceptions of reality in medieval painting and conceptions of the text in medieval exegesis. She uses a description of Carolingian art to show the relation:

> "It is as though we were invited to focus our eyes not on the physical surface of the object, but on infinity as seen through the lattice . . . the object exists—as it were—merely to define and detach a certain portion of infinite space, and make it more manageable and apprehensible."
>
> This description of the "pierced technique" in Early Northern Art is also an exact description of exegesis as understood by Claudius—if we substitute "text" for the "physical surface" of the artist's material and "truth" for the "infinite" space, we are invited to look not at the text but through it.[57]

This attitude towards the text is a direct continuation of the fundamental suppositions of Christianity as we have traced them from the beginnings with Paul; and the substitution of a higher reality for the realm of words was also the primary trend of Greek thought. It is not difficult, then, to see why the tendency to think in allegorical terms pervaded medieval philosophy, literature, and art.

In his discussion of New Testament style, Erich Auerbach also finds this tendency of Christian thought. Writing of Paul's attempt to adapt the message of the Gospels to the preconceptions of the Gentile world, Auerbach notes,

> Its detachment from the special preconceptions of the Jewish world, became a necessity and was effected by a method rooted in Jewish tradition but now applied with incomparably greater boldness, the method of revisional interpretation. The Old Testament was played down . . . and assumed the appearance of a series of "figures," that is of prophetic announcements and anticipations of the coming of Jesus and the concomitant events. . . . The total content of the sacred writings was placed in an exegetic context which often removed the thing told very far from its sensory base, in that the reader was forced to turn his attention away from the sensory occurrence and toward its meaning. . . . the antagonism between sensory appearance and meaning . . . permeates the early, and indeed the whole, Christian view of reality.[58]

Henri de Lubac, the authoritative expositor of medieval exegesis, notes further that it was "not Scripture as text [sic] but, as sacred history as contained in Scripture, which offers a spiritual meaning, since spiritual meaning is not the meaning of words but the meaning of things."[59] This schism between the meaning of words and the meaning of things also has its roots in Greek thought about the relation between word and thing, and is crucial in the work of Augustine. Again, one sees the central tendency of Christian thought from its beginnings to displace meaning away from text and word.

The most important figure for medieval aesthetics is without question Augustine, whom Robertson calls "the most profound and influential spiritual exegete in the history of the Church."[60] Augustine's *On Christian Doctrine* was the single most important work on exegesis for the Middle Ages. Moreover, Robertson writes, the philosophy propounded by Augustine in that work "had a large share in creating the pattern of a culture which endured in the West throughout the thousand years we rather unjustly call 'the Middle Ages.' It formulates an approach to the Scriptures whose principles determined the character of education during that period; and . . . . [which] was still an important part of Christian humanism in the Renaissance."[61] Let us first examine those aspects of *On Christian Doctrine* which were significant for aesthetics, and then proceed to the important theory of signs found in this work.

Augustine was a Latin Church Father who had to deal with the same problems faced by the Greek Fathers—the educated intellectuals' distaste for the crude character of Scripture. As a professor of rhetoric himself, Augustine was eminently qualified for his task, and brought to his work a blend of insights from Aristotle, Plato, and Cicero. (When writing in the *Confessions* [III:5] about his first examination of Scripture, Augustine says, "To me they seemed quite unworthy of comparison with the stately prose of Cicero because I had too much conceit to accept their simplicity and not enough to penetrate their depths.") In explaining the obscurity of Scripture, Augustine formulated an aesthetic principle that had far-ranging influence on the Middle Ages and on the character of early Western art and literature.*

In Book II, Chapter 6 of *On Christian Doctrine,* Augustine propounds a theory of the "aesthetics of obscurity." First, he claims, parts of Scripture are intentionally obscure in order to conquer men's pride and their disdain for that which is easily acquired. Moreover, by some strange psychological twist which Augustine does not propose to explain, men delight much more in ideas which are expressed through similitudes than statements which are directly expressed. In a famous passage, Augustine writes,

> But why is it, I ask, that if anyone says this he delights his hearers less than if he had said the same thing in expounding that place in the Canticles of Canticles where it is said of the church, as she is being praised as a beautiful woman, "Thy teeth are as flocks of sheep, that are shorn, which come up from the washing, all with twins, and there is none barren among them?" Does one learn anything else besides that which he learns when he hears the same thought expressed in plain words without this similitude. Nevertheless, in a strange way, I contemplate the saints more pleasantly when I envisage them as the teeth of the Church cutting men off from their errors and transferring them to her body after their hardness has been softened as if by being bitten and chewed. I recognize them most pleasantly as shorn sheep having put aside the burden of the world so much like fleece, and as ascending from the washing, which is baptism, all to create twins, which are the two precepts of love, and I see no one of them sterile of this holy fruit.
>
> But why it seems sweeter to me than if no such similitude were offered in the divine books, since the thing perceived is the same, is difficult to say and is a problem for another discussion.[62]

Significantly, Augustine does not connect obscurity with the possibility of multiple meaning, as do the Rabbis. Nor does he infer the meaning through the play of verbal equivocation, of configuration, but rather seeks an abstract pattern, or symbolic one-to-one equivalent of meaning to the figures. The notion that the function of figurative language was to arouse the observer to seek an underlying abstract pattern of philosophical

---

*Kevin Dungey defines a medieval literary tradition of the aesthetics of obscurity based on Christian hermeneutic styles of reading the Bible. He characterizes this Christian hermeneutic style as: intellectual, erudite, esoteric, allegorical, and contemplative. Dungey holds that one can explain much of the medieval use of etymology, paronomasia, opaque vocabulary, and verbal play through the tradition of esoteric Scriptural interpretation in such exegetes as Philo, Clement, Origen, and Augustine. See Dungey's "Christian Hermeneutic Styles" (Ph.D. diss., Stanford University, 1980).

significance became important in medieval art and literature, especially in Petrarch and Boccaccio, and intentional obscurity has of course been cultivated by many contemporary authors. (Needless to say, many contemporary critics have adopted this concept as well.)

The modern reader, however, might find Augustine's "pleasure" in the above figure difficult to understand. The image of holy men as the teeth of a woman, which chew up evil from men, who in turn are digested and who then become sheep, is rather awkward. (I shall resist the temptation to apply the insights of psychoanalysis to the nature of Augustine's pleasure here.) It is evident, as D. W. Robertson explains, that

> for Augustine figurative expression is not of any value in itself; it is valuable only as an adjunct to the intellectual search for truth. . . . It is important to understand that the affective value of this figurative language lies in what is found beneath the language and not in the concrete materials of the figures. . . . It is obvious that St. Augustine was not concerned with any spontaneous associations his experience may have led him to have with teeth and sheep.[63]

Again one sees the devaluation of the concrete aspects of language for an abstract sense removed from the matrix of words themselves. For the Middle Ages and the Renaissance, in both literary and visual art, the idea dominating aesthetics was that the function of figurative language was to lead the mind to a higher spiritual understanding. As Beryl Smalley emphasized, the aim is to look through the surface of the text. An important corollary of this concept for Augustine was that one needed to look not at the words themselves but at the truth "in" the word, or "pointed to" by the words.

Augustine wrote much about the nature of signs, and it has been said that his originality lay specifically in applying traditional sign theory to the new task of interpreting Scripture: "Augustine's application consists in using the technical terms of semantics to make distinctions and definitions which delineate clearly the problems faced by the interpreter of Scripture. The detailed application of an explicit semantics would seem to be an innovation in the history of Christian hermeneutics."[64] While Origen, in *On First Principles,* and Tyconius, in his *Liber Regularem,* also discussed the signification of Scripture, they did not reflect on the problems of semantics in any systematic way.

Augustine's Theory of Signs

Ralph Markus writes that prior to Augustine—in Hellenistic reflection about signs, Roman rhetoric, and Christian theology—the theory of signs was considered in an essentially nonlinguistic context primarily in terms of theories of inference.[65] That words signify was incidental. The theory of signs was not the theory of language. Augustine, however, discussed the theory of language in terms of the theory of signs, and this probably because of his interest in the nature of Scriptural signs. It is most significant that this crucial move—the recognition that the theory of signs was the theory of language—was stimulated by the problems of divine scripture.

In Aristotle, anything which involved in its *being* the being of something else, either at the same time or before, is defined as a *sign* of that thing or event. Aristotle elaborated a rudimentary theory of signs *(Rh.* 1. 1357a-b36) in which the sign is considered a means of inference from the empirically given to the nonapparent, as in one of Aristotle's examples, "The fact that she is giving milk is a sign that she has lately borne a child." Signs are considered a class of argument, and Cicero and Quintillian follow Aristotle, but place the inferential theory of signs in an even more forensic context. In all these definitions, there is no concern with words. The focus of sign theory, rather, is the meaning of events and how they might be used to establish a point. Prior to Augustine, the earlier ecclesiastical writers used *sign* in the same classical sense; they read the Old Testament figuratively and typologically, as signs of the New Testament.

In the Stoic and Peripatetic schools, however, signs do occur in semantic contexts, and some see Stoic influence on Augustine's theory of signs and deduction. The three major components in the Stoic theory of the signs were: (1) that which is signified—the thing revealed by it which subsists with our thought; (2) that which signifies—speech; and (3) the object—that which exists outside.[66] Like the Stoics, Augustine postulates a triadic formula of the sign, but with some important differences. In the beginning of his discussin on this topic in the first book, second chapter, of *On Christian Doctrine,* he writes:

> All doctrine concerns either things or signs, but things are learned by signs. Strictly speaking I have here called a "thing" that which is not used to signify something else, like wood, stone, cattle, and so on: but not that wood concerning which we read that Moses cast it onto bitter waters that their bitterness might be dispelled, nor that stone which Jacob placed at his head, nor that beast which Abraham sacrificed in place of his son. For these are things in such a way that they are also signs of other things. There are other signs whose whole use is in signifying, like words. For no one uses words except for the purpose of signifying something. From this it may be understood that what we call "signs"; they are things used to signify something. Thus every sign is also a thing, for that which is not a thing is nothing at all; but not every thing is also a sign.[67]

In the rest of this first book, Augustine proceeds to discuss things, and reserves signs for later.

Distinguishing between words and things, he then subdivides the category of things (or realities) into two categories: final goals to be enjoyed for their own sake, and means to be used for achieving goals. Only God is the final end; words and lesser realities are only means to that end, he claims. The major object of enjoyment and love is the Trinity—not the text.

And the principle of love becomes one of his major *exegetical* principles. If an understanding of Scripture does not contribute to the love of God and neighbor, Augustine says it is not valid (I:36). At the end of the first book, he makes the following statement: "Thus a man supported by faith, hope, and charity, with an unshaken hold upon them, does not need Scripture except for the instruction of others. And many live by these three things in solitude without books."[68] Such a statement would be unthinkable in Rabbinic tradition, but Augustine is rearticulating the displacement and escape from textuality that permeates Christian thought.

It is also significant that he states this principle in his discussion of "things" before he even embarks on his discussion of signs in the second book. Obviously, the apprehension and enjoyment of things is a process considered apart from words. What, then, are signs? Book II, chapter 1 begins by Augustine's telling us that "A sign is a thing which causes us to think of something beyond the impression the thing itself makes upon the senses. Thus if we see a track, we think of the animal that made the track. . . ." He then differentiates between what he calls *natural* and *conventional* signs. Natural signs are those that signify without intention, like smoke, which signifies fire. Conventional signs are those used by living creatures with the direct intention of conveying something they have sensed or understood. "Nor is there any other reason for signifying, or for giving signs, except for bringing forth and transferring to another mind the action on the mind in the person who makes the sign" (II:2).

In this second category, Augustine places the signs given by God and contained in Scripture. What Augustine adds, though, is a significantly psychological dimension to the concept of the sign, and this definition of the sign was to become classic for the Middle Ages: a sign was something that also brings something else to mind. The structure of the sign, then, was triadic, relating the following three terms: (1) the object of signification for which the sign stands; (2) the sign itself; and (3) the subject to whom the sign stands for the object signified. Prior to Augustine there was no stress on the subject or interpreter of the sign. His important contribution to sign theory was precisely the interpreting subject.

For Augustine, letters are signs of words, and written words signify spoken words, which in turn signify things. The parallel with Aristotle's formulation of this relation at the beginning of *De Interpretatione* is readily apparent. Aristotle there said that spoken sounds are symbols of affections in the soul, and written marks are symbols of spoken sounds. Neither written nor spoken sounds in Aristotle's view were the same for all men, but that which they are signs of—affections in the soul—are universal, as are the things of which these affections are likenesses. There are, however, some important differences between Aristotle and Augustine, as B. Jackson points out.[69] For Augustine, the thing is more important than the word chosen to designate it. And Augustine does not say that words are signs of movements of the soul, nor does he see a relation of likeness between the mind and things, as does Aristotle. The gap between word and thing becomes even more exacerbated here in Christian thought, and *On Christian Doctrine* finally turns out to be a laudation of the eloquence not of words, but of things. The crucial movement for Augustine in the interpretation of Scripture is the movement from the sign to the thing, and then to the divine silence. As Joseph Mazzeo puts it: "Thus true rhetoric culminates in silence, in which the mind is in immediate contact with reality. . . . Whether or not the text was obscure, the movement of thought was through words to the realities themselves, from temporal realities to eternal realities, from talk to silence, from discourse to vision." And Mazzeo notes that "the movement from words to silence, from signs to realities, is the fundamental presupposition of Augustinian allegorical exegesis."[70]

In this context, Augustine makes another distinction within the class of conventional signs. When written things are not understood, he says, it is because they are obscured either by "unknown" or by "ambiguous" signs:

> For signs are either literal or figurative. They are called literal when they are used to designate those things on account of which they were instituted; thus we say *bos [ox]* when we mean an animal of a herd because all men using the Latin language call it by that name just as we do. Figurative signs occur when that thing which we designate by a literal sign is used to signify something else; thus we say "ox" and by that syllable understand the animal which is ordinarily designated by that word, but again by that animal we understand an evangelist, as is signified in the Scripture. [II:10.]

To understand unknown literal signs, one needs, says Augustine, an understanding of languages; it is simply a question of translation. To understand difficult figurative signs, one needs to refer partly to a knowledge of language and partly to a knowledge of things (II:16).

This schism between words and things is further developed in Book III, where Augustine discusses the nature of literal and figurative meaning in more detail. He does not consider ambiguity as an occasion for a multiple play of interpretation, as do the Rabbis, but rather as a problem that requires finding a solution, i.e., the singular equivalent, the real referent of the difficult expression. We have seen an example of this approach in Augustine's discussion of a difficult passage in the Song of Songs. Here in Book III, Augustine also proposes that to understand figurative language one needs only to find that "thing" which is signified by the "sign." That is, as in the above quoted passage, there is a one-to-one relationship between sign and referent, a relation of nominal substitution. In the case of a literal sign, it is a matter of common agreement as to what "thing" the word refers to; in the case of figurative language it is a question of one more substitution of "thing" for another "thing." When we remember the description of metaphor in Aristotle as a transfer of the name of one thing to another, we can clearly see how directly in line Augustine is with Aristotle's mode of thought. The "proper" meaning has to do with proper predication, discovering that thing to which the figure refers. In allegorical interpretation—the reference is to yet another "thing," and this is then construed as the "spiritual" meaning.

Augustine warns that one must be very careful not to take the figurative expressions literally, for the letter kills. "He who follows the letter takes figurative expressions as though they were literal and does not refer the things signified to anything else" (III:5). And that, he claims, is the servitude and blindness of the Jews: they took signs of spiritual things for the things themselves, not knowing what they referred to; they stubbornly adhered to signs as things, and they did not believe in Jesus, "since he did not treat the signs in accordance with Jewish observance" (III:6). In saying that the Jews adhered to signs, Augustine begins to articulate what may be called a semiotics of idolatry. To him, idolatry is in essence semiotic: the Jews adhere to the sign instead of to the thing it was designed to signify— this he brands as literalism, being a slave to the sign. Christian liberty, he says, is freedom from signs, and interpreting them, i.e., elevating them to the things they represent (III:8). Hence Christian liberty leads to a destruction of these servile signs. And now, since the Resurrection, "we are not heavily burdened with the use of certain signs whose meaning we understand; rather we have few in place of many, which the teaching of the Lord and the Apostles has transmitted to us, and these are very easy to perform. . . . Such are the sacrament of Baptism and the celebration of the Body and Blood of the Lord" (III:9). Signs here are not linguistic but sacraments, i.e., the invocation of the presence of that which the sign points to, the fulfillment in the present thing which thus cancels out the empty word.

But it is precisely this reification of signs that is idolatry to the Jews. Since Augustine makes such an absolute distinction between word or sign and thing, they become two mutually exclusive realms (as in literal and metaphorical interchange). Jews adhere to signs not because they take the sign for the thing as *res* in the Greek philosophical sense, but because there is no primal division between word and thing in Jewish thought, and no conception of reality in terms of Greek metaphysics, or of truth as a totally self-identical present being. Jews adhere to signs because reality innately is constituted as linguistic for them. For the Jew it is precisely the cancellation of the sign or word for thing that is idolatrous. John Freccero adds to the discussion Yehezkel Kaufmann's insight:

> The Jewish concept of idolatry was of a kind of fetishism, the worship of reified signs devoid of significance. The gods of the Gentiles were co-existensive with their representations, as though they dwelt not on Olympus or in skies, but within a golden calf, or stone or piece of wood. Signs point to an absence or a signification yet to come, they are in this sense allegorical. Idols, as the Jews understood them, like fetishes, were a desperate attempt to render *presence*, a reified sign, one might almost say a metaphor. It is almost as if the gentiles, in the Jews' reading, sought to evade the temporality inherent in the human condition by reifying their signs and thereby eternalizing significance in the here and now.[71]

The semiological meaning of idolatry as Freccero defines it is the "reification of the sign in an attempt to create poetic presence,"[72] and an attempt to "short-circuit the referentiality of signs." Freccero connects this insight about Augustine's sign theory with the poetics of Dante and Petrarch, and preceptively points out how the thematics of idolatry become transferred in their work into the poetics of presence. He also refers, of course, to the roots of this tendency in Paul's metaphor of lifting the veil of the letter.

Freccero's analysis is influenced by Derrida, and Augustine doubtless would view Derrida more than anyone else as a slave of the sign, a stubborn adherent of word play who refuses to recognize any proper referents whatsoever. And Derrida's critique of philosophy is an indictment of the idolatry of literalized metaphors, of a thought process that mistook signs for things, reifying them into spurious abstract meanings which were then posited as the "proper" sense. Let us allow Derrida to speak for himself here. The very concept of the sign, and the distinction between signifying and signified—even in contemporary thinkers such as Saussure—remain "committed to the history of classical ontology":

> That this distinction, first appearing in Stoic logic, was necessary for the coherence of a scholastic thematics dominated by infinitist theology, forbids us to treat today's debt to it as a contingency or convenience. . . . The *signatum* always referred, as to its referent, to a *res*, to an entity created or at any rate first thought and spoken, thinkable and speakable, in the eternal present of the divine logos and especially in its breath. If it came to relate to the speech of a finite being . . . through the *intermediary* of a *signans*, the *signatum* had an *immediate* relationship with the divine logos which thought it within presence and for which it was not a trace. And for modern linguistics, if the signifier is a trace, the signified is a meaning thinkable in principle within the full presence of an intuitive consciousness. . . . This reference to a meaning of a signified thinkable and possible outside of all signifiers remains dependent upon the onto-theology that I have just evoked.[73]

One of Freccero's most important insights is that with Augustine the issue of idolatry becomes explicitly semiological; poetics is defined as the attempt to make words convey an idolatrous presence. One can observe this not only in the poetics of the Middle Ages but indeed as an underlying trend in all of Western poetics. The doctrine of the incarnation expresses this semiological idolatry more than any other aspect of Christian thought. For the only solution for the gap between word and thing is the incarnation, which thereby provides "unmediated vision," a mode far more attractive than the mediations of the text.[74] The assumption is that the single word is superior to any multivocity of words. Hence the only important signs, as Augustine conceives them, are, inevitably, the sacraments—signs literally become flesh. Margaret Ferguson puts it aptly in her discussion of Augustine: "Incarnation does not redeem language itself; rather, the Incarnation guarantees the end of language because it promises the possibility of an ultimate transcendence of time."[75] The end of language is precisely this end of the sign "stubbornly adhered to by the Jews," now replaced by its referent, the incarnate divinity. Freccero also demonstrates that for Augustine, the end of language represents the end of desire, language and desire being indistinguishable insofar as they are founded on the absence of the referent or object. The theology of the word is the end of signification and the consummation of desire in complete presence, and thus the word becomes literally flesh, the word that is a silence transcending the entire system of discourse.

Augustine speaks of this silent word in several passages. In Book XI of the *Confessions,* which takes the form of a commentary on Genesis, he discusses the meaning of creation by divine speech. In Chapter 6 he says that there is a linear, syllabic speech that is sounded and dies away, a speech expressed through the motion of some created thing subject to the laws of time:

> These words, which you had caused to sound in time, were reported by the bodily ear of the hearer to the mind, which has intelligence and inward hearing responsive to your eternal Word. The mind compared these words, which it heard sounding in time, with your Word, which is silent and eternal, and said, "God's eternal Word is far, far different from these words which sound in time. They are far beneath me; in fact they are not at all, because they die away and are lost. But the Word of my God is above me and endures forever."[76]

According to this view, the creation of heaven and earth could not have come about via sounded linear syllables, without some prior created material thing to serve as a mouthpiece through which the words could be temporally spoken. But such a thing did not exist, Augustine says. The word, he therefore concludes, is something that is God and coeternal with God. It is not a sequential, linear pattern of syllables: "For your Word is not speech in which each part comes to an end when it has been spoken, giving place to the next, so that finally the whole may be uttered. In our Word all is uttered at one and the same time, yet eternally" (XI:7). As Ferguson points out, Augustine links language and time with spatial metaphors of linear distance and difference, which leads him to thereby postulate the innate failure of language to express truth literally: "That failure stems from the linear temporality which makes any linguistic unit exist in a synecdochic relation to the truth Augustine conceives as a 'whole.' Indeed he uses human discourse as the prime illustration of his belief that the fundamental flaw of earthly epistemology consists in the necessity of synecdoche, of substituting the part for the whole."[77]

As we argued in Chapters 2 and 3, metonymy and synecdoche are underlying modes of Rabbinic hermeneutics. Augustine, however, associates a synecdochic mode of knowing with the fall, and considers human language, which he so radically separates from the divine word, to be indicative of imprisonment in temporality. Reading and interpreting as an endless horizontal sequence of knowing-by-part can never render the simultaneous whole presence that Augustine seeks. Because language cannot express this essence of perfect sameness, and because there is such an irremediable gap between this simultaneous apprehension of truth and man's nature, the incarnation becomes the bridge of an otherwise unfathomable abyss. God descends into human language, into human time and history: the word becomes flesh. And this doctrine becomes the only possible escape from man's exile into language. Jesus is the essential link between signifier and signified because with the doctrine of the incarnation, the substance and its representation are one and the same.[78]

In sum, for Augustine linguistic multiplicity is a condition of the fall. The loss of a stable referent that grounds the literal and proper meaning of words is a manner of exile. Ferguson perceives that the classical definition of metaphor—the transfer or substitution of an alien term for the proper term—likewise implies that metaphor is another mode of exile. She demonstrates how in Augustine's thought, as well, this conception of language is considered to be an aspect of human exile: exile from the atemporal essence, the presence of God. What Augustine, following the Greek metaphysicians, particularly Plato, seeks is the mode of knowing as being-and-having—not the endlessness of interpretation, but the absoluteness of presence. Words for the Greek and Christian are at best only imitations of things; and Derrida stresses that all mimetic theories of language postulate an extralinguistic standard of correctness that privileges proper over figurative language, for figurative language is a departure from the (proper) norm whereby each word points univocally to its referent.[79] Hence for Augustine, as for Christian thought in general, language is only a detour from the goal, from the atemporal union with God, the immediate vision of the whole.

From this point of view, the "play of difference" advocated by Derrida is the torment of the Christian thinker, the unacceptable exile. How is it, the Christian wonders, that Jews so stubbornly adhere to the sign, refuse the consolations of instantaneous unveiling of presence, can exist so well within the realm of temporality? Jews are so strangely at home in exile, in the play of signs, in the wanderings of figurative language, and in their own constant physical wanderings: strange literalists who take figures for things, refusing to acknowledge their real referents, remaining under the curse of the original sin by refusing to believe in the incarnate word. What collusion with Satan enables them to exist so well in the realm of difference, in the infinite regression of signs, in the cacophony of words and interpretations, in the endless referentiality of the letter, without the redeeming ultimate referent of the word?

II.

THE SLAYERS OF MOSES

FREUD, LACAN, DERRIDA, BLOOM, AND THE DARK SIDE OF DISPLACEMENT

Prologue:
The Book of Books
and the Book of Nature

The elaborate edifice of Patristic interpretation constructed over fifteen hundred years was pulled down by the Reformation of the fifteenth century, and with the Reformation begins the modern science of hermeneutics. As Hans-Georg Gadamer explains:

> Insofar as scriptural hermeneutics is regarded as the prehistory of the hermeneutics of the modern human sciences, it is based on the scriptural principle of the Reformation. Luther's position is more or less the following: Scripture is *sui ipsus interpres*. We do not need tradition to reach the proper understanding of it, nor do we need an art of interpretation in the style of the ancient teaching of the fourfold meaning of Scripture, but the text of Scripture has a clear sense that can be derived from itself, the *sensus literalis*.[1]

> Modern hermeneutics, as a protestant discipline of the art of interpreting Scripture, is clearly related in a polemical way to the dogmatic tradition of the Catholic church. It has itself a dogmatic denominational significance.[2]

Luther aimed his attack at the very foundation of the Church's claim to authority. He insisted, above all, that Scripture was self-interpreting and self-sufficient, that one needed no outside authority, nor any doctrine of a fourfold meaning, nor even a commentary. The literal sense of Scripture alone was for Luther the essence of Christian faith and theology, or as he more bluntly put it: "Origen's allegories are not worth so much dirt," they are the "scum of Scripture."[3]

Although as we have mentioned previously, Luther was influenced to some extent by Rabbinic thought in his insistence on the letter of Scripture, the Protestant Reformation was by no means a return to the text in the Rabbinic sense. It was, instead, an attempt to return to the direct unmediated word of God independent of interpretation—to return to and recapture the direct presence of Jesus as the interior teacher: "Allegories were not what Christ meant, but what Christ was."[4] Luther and the Reformers did not at all regard the word of God as absolutely identical with Holy Scripture. *Letter* meant essentially the absolute singular referent—Jesus; and Jesus alone, not the various books that comprised Scripture, was to Luther the essential word of God.

The Reformation is often accused of Bibliolatry, but in truth, Luther's insistence on Scripture was an insistence on a direct unmediated presence that could be independent of Scripture, and available to the mind of every individual worshipper. As we shall see, this challenge to Church authority ultimately led to a challenge of the divine authority of the Holy Book itself. Luther's view of divine inspiration was neither verbal nor textual. He did not conceive of Scripture as dictated by the holy spirit, but rather as written by men whose minds were illumined by the divine and who expressed these divine truths in human form; the text was by no means considered divine in the Rabbinic sense.

The ultimate canon of interpretation was Jesus, whom Luther and his followers considered to be the sole meaning of both the Old and New Testaments. Ultimately, this meaning could be conceived as entirely independent of Scripture, as expressed in Zwingli's statement, "He who is born of the spirit is no longer solely dependent on a book."[5] Hence the Reformation, despite its proclaimed rebellion against Patristic thought, shared with it a fundamental tendency to circumvent language, and to collapse time and textuality. The rejection of allegory, of Church authority, and so forth, was another attempt to render direct presence—the thing itself behind the word.[6] As Hans Frei sums up the attitude of the Reformation, ultimately, it is "the *reader,* not the text, who is to be illumined by the internal or inspiring testimony of the Spirit, so that he may discover the written biblical word to be God's own word for his own and the Church's edification. . . . For both Calvin and Luther, if one has to choose between the subject matter and the words of the biblical text, one opts for the former."[7] (Contemporary reader-response theories of criticism might be seen as direct descendents of this line of Protestant thought.)

More important are the consequences of Luther's Reformation not only for theology and the development of the modern science of hermeneutics but for the entire Western philosophical and scientific tradition. The Reformation, in its overthrow of medieval attitudes towards the *Book of Books* and the *Book of Nature,* opened the way for the development of classical science. Sigurd Burckhardt's analysis of this development is worth examining in some detail. As he summarizes it,

> Let us assume that God created the world, and that he did so in such a way as to instruct and enable men to understand it. The world, then, would be an object of interpretation from which the Creator's design and thus probably also his "meaning" could be known and understood. Our assumption describes the concept of nature held by the West for the greatest part of its history. From the natural philosopher of the Middle Ages to the scientist of

the nineteenth century, men have regarded it as their task to interpret the "Book of Nature" and thus reveal the meaning of creation. . . .

To the medieval mind, it seemed that the Creator had manifested His will in two books: in the "Book of Books" and in the "Book of Nature" . . . . the Bible was actually and literally a book, a statement, whereas the "Book of Nature" had to be "read" metaphorically.[8]

Burckhardt proposes that the radical difference between medieval natural philosophy and classical science was the assumption basic to science that the only reliable method for interpreting the Book of Nature was what he calls the *intrinsic method* (*werkimmanente Deutung*), i.e., empiricism. By *intrinsic,* he means the ability to deduce from the phenomena under study their authorized agent of interpretation. In the Middle Ages, the Book of Books had unquestioned precedence over the Book of Nature. The Book of Books was unique in being itself a source of ultimately valid interpretation. The Book of Nature, however, had to be interpreted in light of the Book of Books, that is, as only allegorical, illustrative of the actual direct text—the word of God. Nature, to the medieval mind, could in no way be interpreted intrinsically.

The Reformation, in Burckhardt's view, was a critical turning point, for it was then that the Bible lost its status as the Book of Books, precisely at the point when the authority of those who claimed divine sanctions from the text—the Catholic Church—was challenged. The passages on which Rome based its claim to authority were disputed and differently interpreted: thereby the Bible became a book like any other. From this point, it was not far to the assertion that every book could become a Bible.

The Bible, having lost the grounds of authority for its own interpretation, was now seen as extraordinarily inconsistent. What now took the place of the Book of Books was the Book of Nature. All the assumptions guiding the interpretation of the Bible—that it was totally consistent, infallible, the source of its own interpretation—were now transferred to the other Book, the Book of Nature, which henceforth acquired unprecedented authority and significance.

> For the intrinsic interpretation of the other divine book, on the other hand, a truly intrinsic method was necessary and prescribed. As soon as nature became more than just an illustration for the now ambiguous word of God, the principle of infallibility—that is of a totally consistent, perfect creation—led to certain inferences, which may confidently be called the foundations of science. In the "Book of Nature" God did not speak directly, but rather exclusively through metaphors of the sensory world. Here, therefore, there could be no assertions which derived their ultimate interpretive authority from a specific institution. It also no longer sufficed to explain individual phenomena as edifying annotations to God's word. Interpretation now meant a proof of necessary connection and harmony with other phenomena—i.e., the recognition of ever more general laws.[9]

The interpretive method of science depended on the assumption of utterly consistent laws in nature, but the new and crucial idea was that the formulation of these laws was now only a *human attempt* at interpretation, a hypothesis; there was no longer any direct divine pronouncement, only human formulations of divine meanings. There had to be, therefore, proof of the hypotheses in terms of the phenomena themselves. If a discrepancy were to be found, one could not look to an outside authority for its resolution, nor could one assume an inconsistency in creation. Rather, one had to prove that the hypothesis could account for the inconsistency, that the disparate elements were somehow interdependent. The hypothesis, in any case, was subordinate to the authority of the phenomena. The scientific method, then, is based on the two elements of discrepancy and infallibility. (As Burckhardt notes, he is describing classical and not contemporary science, with the latter's "uncertainty principle" and completely altered concept of natural "law.")

According to Burckhardt's view, then, it was only when the Book of Nature was no longer read allegorically that modern science could arise. (For the Rabbis, however, this distinction between the Book of Books and the Book of Nature never occurred; nature was seen as an extension of the text, and not any challenge to the authority of the Text, except when reified as an independent existence. As we have seen in Chapters 2 and 3, the Rabbis approached the text as the modern scientist approaches nature: as phenomena subject to empirical interpretation. It is also interesting to note that Burckhardt's concept of apparent discrepancy as one of the essential elements of scientific interpretation is also one of the essential aspects of Rabbinic interpretation. The text is approached in terms of its problems: seeming contradictions in language, meaning, and logic.)

It took an overthrow of the concept of the book dominant from the Middle Ages in order to clear the path for Bacon and the rise of science—in our terms, an overthrow of the attempt to escape from textuality. Unfortunately, it is beyond the scope of the present discussion to trace this path in detail.[10] Suffice it to say that the breakdown of the Greco-Christian world view after the Enlightenment cleared a space for alternate visions, and for the reemergence of hitherto neglected currents of Western thought.

When classical reason and classical faith came in doubt, the search for an alternate metaphysics began, and the theory of interpretation had to adjust accordingly. Nietzsche, for example (Derrida's forefather in deconstruction), is the man of radical new doubt and radical new faith. The apostate son of a Lutheran pastor, Nietzsche had to grapple with a still powerful, though disintegrating, Christian tradition: thus his *Twilight of the Idols, Anti-Christ,* and revision of our conception of the Greeks.

But an alternate metaphysics and anti-Christian tradition had existed all along in Rabbinic thought. As the Jews were emancipated from their ghettoes beginning with the Enlightenment, became secularized, and attempted to assimilate into modern culture, Rabbinic modes of thinking commingled with, altered, and became altered by an abrupt confrontation with the disintegrating Greco-Christian culture. Many strange hybrids were produced.

Freud's case is paradigmatic. He is a figure who exists at the crossroads—the crossroads of the Victorian and modern eras, of science and art, physiology and psychology, mind and myth, Jewish and Gentile worlds. Freud is also one of the creators of modern thought; and he has lately been embraced by the most fashionable literary critics, philosophers, and aestheticians. It is to psychoanalysis, then, as eminently an art of interpretation, that we now turn in order to uncover the Rabbinics underlying so much of contemporary thought.

Athens and Jerusalem are reintroduced.

5

Solomon-Sigmund, the Son of Jakob

Rabbi Hisda said: A dream which is not interpreted is like a letter which is not read.

—Ber. 55b

Rabbi Bana'ah said: There were twenty-four interpreters of dreams in Jerusalem. Once I dreamt a dream and I went around to all of them and they all gave different interpretations, and all were fulfilled, thus confirming that which is said: All dreams follow the mouth [a dream follows its interpretation].

—Ber. 55b

But there remained enough other things to make the attraction of Judaism and Jews irresistible—many dark emotional forces, all the more potent for being so hard to group in words, as well as the clear consciousness of our inner identity, the intimacy that comes from the same psychic structure.

—Sigmund Freud in a speech to the
B'nai Brith Lodge in Vienna on
his seventieth birthday

We have attached no less importance in interpreting dreams to every shade of the form of words in which they were laid before us. . . . In short, we treated as Holy Writ what previous writers have regarded as an arbitrary improvisation. . . .

—Freud, *The Interpretation of Dreams*

And lastly, it is not attractive to be classed with scholastics and Talmudists who are satisfied to exercise their ingenuity, unconcerned how far removed their conclusions may be from the truth.

—Freud, *Moses and Monotheism*

129

The German philosophic tradition—from Schleiermacher, Fichte, Hegel, and Feuerbach to Dilthey, Heidegger, and Gadamer—is deeply rooted in the matrix of Protestant hermeneutics; it culminates in an existential mode of understanding independent of any scientific method.[1] Freud has often been analyzed in relation to the German philosophy and science of the late nineteenth century, to German romanticism, to Nietzsche, and so forth. The founder of psychoanalysis did share, as we have said, the intellectual dilemmas of his day. It is part of my thesis, however, that the German school of philosophic hermeneutics, because its prehistory and foundation is the tradition of Protestant and Christian Biblical hermeneutics, cannot fully, adequately, and insightfully illuminate the specific nature of Freud's contribution, which was an extension of the line of Jewish Rabbinic hermeneutics and differs decisively from the German Protestant tradition that culminates in the phenomenology of Heidegger and Gadamer.

The neglect, displacement, or censorship of the Jewish hermeneutic tradition by the philosophers of interpretation is not accidental. Of course, the continental philosophies of hermeneutics arose in a milieu that had excluded Jews from participating in its intellectual, mercantile, and general cultural life since the Middle Ages. And yet, this exclusion of the Jews ultimately goes back to the great debate precisely over the issue of interpretation—interpretation of the Bible. This original conflict of interpretation, we may say, led to the rejection of the Jewish interpretive science of psychoanalysis two thousand years later. As we have seen, when the Christians' claims were rejected by the Jews, they in turn rejected the validity of the Jewish tradition of interpretation—the oral law which had been handed down side by side with the written Scriptures—and tried, through the Christian claim of a new covenant, to make obsolete and unnecessary all the commentary, explanation, and interpretation of the Rabbis. They reread and reinterpreted the Scriptures in terms of the figures of Jesus, with Luther arguing for a similar kind of rejection of traditional interpretation by the body of the church in favor of immediate, individual inspiration; this opened the way for Schleiermacher, Dilthey, Heidegger, etc.

From one perspective, this Protestant antitraditionalism in favor of individualistic personal interpretation on the literal level, which stemmed from Luther's rejection of the fourfold meaning of Scriptures, was a blow to the whole theory and *science* of interpretation. It was no longer a question of methodological rules, mediated traditions, dialectics with the past. Luther's Reformation culminated in the idea of interpretation not as a set of rules but as a condition of one's being, as the *Dasein* of Heidegger and the demythologized text of Bultman, and as Gadamer's definition of hermeneutics as "not a problem of method . . . not concerned with a method of understanding by means of which texts are subjected to scientific understanding like all other objects of experience."[2]

Freud, however, wanted to claim that indeed interpretation is scientific, that the existential, engaged mode of the interpreting psychoanalyst ought to be subject to scientific procedures and methods that can lead to valid theoretical, objective scientific knowledge of the psyche—and, moreover, of history and culture in general. In the first paragraph of Chapter 1 of *The Interpretation of Dreams,* Freud writes:

> In the pages that follow I shall bring forth proof that there is a psycholog-ical technique which makes it possible to interpret dreams, and that, if that procedure is employed, every dream reveals itself as a psychical structure which has a meaning and which can be inserted at an assignable part in the mental activities of waking life. I shall further endeavor to elucidate the processes to which the strangeness and obscurity of dreams are due and to deduce from those processes the nature of the psychical forces by whose concurrent or mutually opposing action dreams are generated.[3]

In the apt phrase of W. W. Meissner, psychoanalysis is the "science of subjectivity."[4] This hybrid nature of psychoanalysis makes it an anomaly for both the human and the natural sciences.

Psychoanalysis, it might be said, owes its hybrid character in the history of Western thought to its continuation of the Jewish exegetic tradition in contrast to late nineteenth-century German Protestant herme-neutics. We have seen that the effects of Protestant literalism were to collapse and cancel the endless multiple meanings which the Rabbinic tradition ascribed to each word and letter of the Torah, and to make all the words subordinate to and embodied in the single word-become-flesh in a literal person; the consequence was a theology and hermeneutics of imma-nence, grace, and univocal meaning, and a finality to the free play of interpretation. The entire past history of interpretation was seen to only prefigure the final and complete interpretation, which abrogates all that came before and stands as the absolute signifier and signified together. The priority then is belief in (as opposed to continuous interpretation of) this singular figure for individual salvation. All of this was in direct conflict with the entire body of Jewish thought not only insofar as the identity of the messiah was concerned, but also the whole traditional method of interpre-tation of Scripture, which affirmed the principle of multiple meaning, the necessity of continuous interpretation, historical understanding and ad-justment, and the application of specific hermeneutic procedures them-selves considered to be of divine origin. The text was inseparable from its interpretation and commentary; interpretation is not a provisional prelude to a final understanding but part of the divine revelation itself.

As Freud wrote, the uniqueness of his approach to the dream and his success in revealing its secret (and thereby the secrets of psychic life) was that he treated it as Holy Writ, as would a Rabbi, searching for hidden significance in every word and detail, and applying ingenious methods of symbolic and linguistic interpretation which to his contemporaries were unorthodox, unscientific madness. Being classed with Talmudists was also painful to Freud, as he tried to make his way in a secular European culture, which was with difficulty just beginning to accept Jews. It was not only the method in Freud's madness, and the stunning revelations of psychoanalysis concerning the hidden and less savory side of man's life, which were offensive, but also, as Freud knew, Freud's own religious identity. Psychoanalysis was the Jewish science. In 1908, writing to Abraham concerning difficulties with Jung, Freud asked Abraham to be "tolerant" and recognize that Jung, unlike Abraham, did not share what Freud calls "my intellectual constitution because of racial kinship . . . [he] as a Christian and a pastor's son finds his way to me only against great inner resistance. His association with us is the more valuable for that. I nearly said that it was only by his appearance on the scene that psychoanalysis escaped the danger of becoming a Jewish national affair."[5] Responded Abraham: "I freely admit that I find it easier to go along with you rather than with Jung. I, too, have always felt this intellectual kinship. After all, our Talmudic way of thinking cannot disappear just like that."[6]

It is my thesis, though, that psychoanalysis was the Jewish science in a far deeper way than has been recognized. Its founder, who affirmed a "common psychic structure" with the Jews, created what might be called a secular version of Talmud, and an interpretive science whose methodology was in its finest details deeply Rabbinic. Freud displaced Rabbinic hermeneutics from the text of the Holy Writ to the text of the dream, the speaking psyche of the person.

Undoing Moses

"Displacement" was one of the techniques Freud discovered as fundamental to the formation of the dream. It figured greatly in his interpretation of the Bible and of the person of Moses in *Moses and Monotheism,* an interpretation which is itself a kind of dreamlike representation and fantasy reconstruction. The displacement he detects in the Bible concerns the intentional distortion of the text in order to cover up Freud's hypothesized murder of Moses by the Jews; but as with all murders, Freud claims, one can always find the traces, the hidden material altered in shape and torn from its original connection, and recognizable only with difficulty.[7] We will examine psychoanalysis as Freud's own Talmudic Rabbinism, altered in shape and torn from its original connection as a result of Freud's own deeply ambivalent relationship to his father and the Jews, a relationship epitomized in his treatment of the father figure of Moses, whom he needed simultaneously to murder, identify with, and replace. Psychoanalysis was, like the dream, a compromise formation, mediating between Freud the Jewish Talmudist and Freud the German doctor.[8] A serious consideration of the relation of psychoanalytic hermeneutics to Rabbinic hermeneutics may not only account for the anomalous nature of psychoanalysis in the history of Western European thought, but also answer Freud's own question in his letter to Pastor Oskar Pfister: ". . . by the way, how comes it that none of the godly ever devised psychoanalysis and that one had to wait for a godless Jew?"[9]

In a sense, the lack of recognition and omission ("displacement") of Rabbinic hermeneutics in Freud's thought is similar to one of those gaps in consciousness that psychoanalysis tries to discover. The analogy is not incidental. One of the main themes of psychoanalysis is the recovery of the past, reconstruction of lost fragments (as in so many of Freud's archeological metaphors), and reappropriation of one's life history. What the analyst reconstructs, the patient remembers, and comes to accept as his own life history, restoring the link between himself and his past by overcoming his resistance and repression. And yet, at the same time, psychoanalysis is a ruthless rational critique of that which it brings to light. When Freud writes *Moses and Monotheism,* analogously working through to his own Jewish past, his interpretation makes Moses into an Egyptian, as if both to deny and affirm Freud's link to the covenant of his forefathers: to restore Judaism and demolish it; to affirm himself as a Jew and deny it, to destroy the giver of the Law, and then himself give the new law of psychoanalysis.

Freud's fascination with the figure of Moses is well known. In his essay on Michelangelo's famous statue of Moses he wrote:

> No piece of statuary has ever made a stronger impression on me than this. How often have I mounted the steep steps of the unlovely Corso Cavour to the lonely place where the deserted church stands, and have essayed to support the angry scorn of the hero's glance! Sometimes I have crept cautiously out of the half-gloom of the interior as though I myself belong to the mob upon whom his eye is turned—the mob which can hold fast no conviction, which has neither faith nor patience and rejoices when it regains its illusory idols.[10]

The ambivalence of Freud's feelings is quite apparent: he was one of the faithless mob, one of the recalcitrant Jews, who with his illusory idols of Western civilization had betrayed his heritage. (As photographs of Freud's apartment in Vienna reveal, he also literally surrounded himself with all kinds of figurines and idols of various ancient Mediterranean religions.) And yet he was also Moses, giving the law of psychoanalysis, restraining his wrath in the face of the unbelievers who attacked him from all spheres of the Gentile academic society to which he so desperately desired to belong. Psychoanalysis then becomes, at the same time, an unveiling of the illusory idols of the Gentiles, an undoing of their culture, and an attack on the presumptuousness and hypocrisy of the anti-Semitic society that excluded and humiliated him.*

In *The Interpretation of Dreams,* Freud writes of his identification

---

*John Murray Cuddihy has examined this aspect of psychoanalysis at length in his *The Ordeal of Civility: Freud, Marx, Lévi-Strauss and the Jewish Struggle with Modernity* (New York: Basic Books, 1974). He also interprets psychoanalysis as reflective of the ambivalent Jewish identity of its founder, but takes a sociology-of-knowledge approach; his concern is not interpretation theory. Nevertheless, this book is filled with important insights about the relation of Jewish sensibility to modernity.

with the Semitic general Hannibal, in a passage preceded by a joke about an impecunious, intrusive, and abused Jew, and followed by an account of his father's humiliation when a Gentile anti-Semite had knocked off his cap and pushed him off the street. Freud writes: "To my youthful mind Hannibal and Rome symbolized the conflict between the tenacity of Jewry and the organization of the Catholic Church. And the increasing importance of the anti-Semitic movement upon our emotional life helped to fix the thoughts and feelings of those early days."[11] Freud contrasts these memories with the scene in which Hannibal's father makes him swear to take vengeance on the Romans; like Hannibal, Freud too would have his vengeance on Rome.

But there is another twist to the story. Freud writes in a footnote, added to *The Interpretation of Dreams* in 1909, that in the first edition of the text he had mistakenly named Hannibal's father "Hasdrubal" instead of "Hamilcar Barca." He later tried to account for the error in *The Psycho-pathology of Everyday Life*. Hasdrubal was the name not of Hannibal's father, but of his brother, and of his brother-in-law and predecessor in command. There were other generational errors of this type in *The Interpretation of Dreams,* including one in which Freud asserted that it was Zeus who emasculated his father Kronos, when in fact it was Kronos who had committed this act on his father Uranos. In discussing these errors, Freud maintains that he had to break off some of his analyses in *The Interpretation of Dreams* before they were complete, for the sake of "discretion" and also because of the "difficulty" in making the repressed thoughts become conscious. Nevertheless, he continues, that which he wished to repress obtruded itself anyway against his will, appearing in the unnoticed errors: "Indeed, each of the three examples given is based on the same theme: the errors are the results of repressed thoughts which have to do with my deceased father."[12] These repressed thoughts, Freud adds, have to do with "unfavorable criticism of my father" and express Freud's desire to have been born the son of his half-brother rather than the son of his father.[13]

It is further significant that *The Interpretation of Dreams* was written, as Freud says in his preface to the second edition, as "a portion of my own self-analysis, my reaction to my father's death—that is to say, to the most important event, the most poignant loss of a man's life."[14] Marthe Robert, in her admirable book *From Oedipus to Moses: Freud's Jewish Identity,* claims that Freud's conflicts with and ambivalence towards his own father—especially the Judaism of his father—are the key to the origin of psychoanalysis, and the central link to all of Freud's work, from *The Interpretation of Dreams* to *Moses and Monotheism:*

> To Sigmund Freud, the primordial murdered father was Jakob Freud, the Galician Jew, and not a legendary Greek King. . . . For Freud's unique work . . . does not develop in a continuous straight line, but describes an enormous

circle around one and the same motif that is constantly reconsidered. Beginning with *The Interpretation of Dreams* where the real person of Jakob Freud scarcely figures in the Oedipean drama inspired by his recent death but conceived as the constituent factor of the human psche at all times and places, the circle closes in *Moses and Monotheism* with a grandiose vision of the Jewish parricide, that is, a return to the very act whose horror Freud had long ago to surmount, but which he re-embraces on the eve of his death and now calls by its right name, considering it as the act that initiated an entire civilization.[15]

Freud, that is, began by naming the "father-complex" he had discovered after the Greek King who represented the glories of that culture to which Freud so intensely aspired, but which he was prevented from entering by the "stain" of his birth as a Jew. He ended by unmasking the Jewish parricide which lay behind the Greek, the supposed parricide of Moses by the Jews—which was in fact Freud's own parricide. His attempt to remake Moses into an Egytian was at bottom a project to rewrite the identity of Freud's own father Jakob and thus to remake his own origins.

In her analysis of Freud, Robert adopts Kafka's insight into the particular father-complex of German-Jewish writers of his generation, and their revolt against their fathers. The father-complex, Kafka wrote to Max Brod, from which so many Jews drew their spiritual nourishment, related not to the innocent father, but to the father's Judaism. The German Jewish writers wanted to break with Judaism, with the vague approval of their fathers, but as Kafka puts it, "their hind legs were bogged down in their father's Judaism, and their front legs could find no new ground. The resulting despair was their inspiration.[16] The Jewish father of Jakob Freud's generation neither made a full break with the past, nor was he able to transmit any authentic sense of Jewish existence to his children, thus leaving his sons doomed to struggle unsuccessfully between two mutually irreconcilable worlds. In additon, of course, were all the difficulties and humiliations caused by the anti-Semitism of the period, to which Freud, a man of much ambition, was acutely sensitive.

Robert, then, reads *The Interpretation of Dreams* as the first part of Freud's "family novel," wherein one can everywhere locate the themes of disavowal and imaginary filiation. At the same time, however, psychoanalysis was a subversive critique of authority, of the powerful prevailing Gentile culture of Freud's time, and enabled Freud to remain faithful to his own poor, humble father. Jakob Freud, Robert claims, is the real hero of *The Interpretation of Dreams*, a hero both cherished and despised, loved and hated. As a result of his father's death, and Freud's need to free himself from this ghost through his own self-analysis, psychoanalysis was born. The crucial turning point was Freud's realization that the stories his hysterical female patients had told him of seductions by their fathers were fantasies, not facts—fantasies, Robert says, in which Freud had believed for so long because of his need to justify his animosity towards his own father. When Freud relocated the cause as a fantasy emanating from the patient, psychoanalysis could be born, and Freud, too, could be born as his own man, finally laying to rest the ghost of his father, disentangling the mythical monstrous parent from the real one.

And yet, there is the curiosity of Freud's return to a belief in the existence of a real primal father, murdered by the horde of sons, expressed in *Totem and Taboo,* and his belief in the actual murder of Moses by the Jews, expressed in his last work, *Moses and Monotheism.* Robert claims, "As his late work shows, he had not gained peace; to the very end he remained the transgressor, the tormented, tormenting, haunted son, whose only surcease lay in continually renewing the mystery of his remorse. . . . his confessions were in a sense impersonal, implied in the obsessive recurrence of certain themes—revolt of the sons, murder of the father, the needless chain of crime and expiation.[17]" Freud, in fact, kept delaying the complete publication of *Moses and Monotheism* and would only publish the essay on "The Moses of Michelangelo" anonymously.* Freud in effect replaced the infantile fantasy of murder of the father with a theory of its historical reality. Little wonder then that he felt himself cowering under the glance of the statue of Moses, as if he were part of the faithless mob.

To Robert, *Moses and Monotheism* was the last chapter of Freud's "family novel," an attempt to disavow his father and rewrite his own origins. Depriving the founder of Jewish nationhood of his identity was, in her words, "a ruthless act of dispossession," a making of an entire people "illegitimate." In this act, Freud attempted to legitimize himself, recreate his own genealogy. As Robert writes, in *Moses and Monotheism* Freud once again gave himself over to the unreality of his dreams, his dream of breaking the chain of generations and freeing himself forever from all fathers and ancestors— from "the return of the repressed," from his own dissolution and death, and from return to "the bosom of his forefathers." He tried, in this last work, to deny himself both as Solomon the son of Jakob and as Sigmund the rebellious son, both as Jew and as German, and affirm himself only as the son of his own work.[18]

Robert's analysis of Freud's Jewish identity is penetrating and insightful. She is not willing, however, to discuss the relation of the substance of psychoanalysis, and more particularly its interpretive techniques, to the tradition of Jewish hermeneutics. Though she does admit that parallels can be drawn between Rabbinic ideas and methods and Freudian symbols and theories of words and numbers, she maintains, "All this, to be sure, makes it possible to draw ingenious correspondences, but amounts to little more than doubtful speculation."[19] My thesis, however, is that Freud's methodology was not so very different from the Rabbis', and that the neglect or displacement of the tradition of Rabbinic hermeneutics in considering

---

*See Freud's discussion of this delay in the "Prefatory Notes" to Part III of *Moses and Monotheism* and the "Summary" to Section II.

Freud's thought can be seen as part of the general conflict of interpretation which we have been tracing from Aristotle through the Church Fathers.

Heretic Hermeneutics: Re-writing Origins

Displacement is a key term in the characterization of Freud's own psyche, in the theory of the Oedipus complex (displacement of the father by the son), and in Freud's own interpretive technique. More importantly, *displacement* may be taken as a key term for Jewish hermeneutics in general, and more specifically for a unique brand of Jewish heretical hermeneutics. *Displacement*, first of all, may be considered in terms of metonymy and metaphor: as a metonymical repositioning in the manner of contiguity, or as a metaphorical mode of cancellation in substitution. We have maintained that metonymy is a characteristic mode of Rabbinic hermeneutics, and metaphor, of Christian thought. We may now read Jesus, Paul, Freud, and Freud's most recent interpreters, Derrida, Lacan, and Bloom as all sharing in a particular mode of Jewish interpretive heresy: a distorted displacement, an aspect of which is the conversion of metonymy into metaphor, or displacement pretending to substitution. This mode is directly connected to Robert's insight about Freud's need to rewrite origins, usurp the father, and break the chain of generations.

Jesus, for example, claimed that he came "not to destroy but to fulfill the law" (Matt. 5:17), but his interpretation of fulfillment was ultimately usurpation, a destruction of the endless chain of Rabbinic interpretation. He claimed to make an end to absence and exile, by virtue of his special relation to the Father and his own substitutive sacrifice. This religion of the Son was organized, articulated, and propounded by none other than another apostate Jew—Paul, who made the cancellation of the law and the invalidation of Rabbinic interpretation the decisive cornerstone of the new faith. With Paul, the Son becomes identified with the Father, the metonymical distance between man and God, desire and fulfillment, is collapsed. The Son's New Gospel displaces the "Old" Testament in a new manifestation of the logos. Through Philo, another Jew with suspicious Greek leanings, the Church Fathers were able to elaborate this usurpation through a philosophical system founded on allegorical reading and the logos theology, where the logos now is equivalent to God. Displacement, usurpation, substitution.

Freud, the assimilated Jew struggling with two cultures, Hebrew and Hellene, reenacts the drama of displacement in his psyche and his work, combining Rabbinism and German science in a project to murder and usurp Moses with the new gospel of psychoanalysis. Derrida much more unabashedly proclaims his intention to "deconstruct" the entire Western tradition of "onto-theology" and "logocentrism" by crucifying the word and sending it into the dissemination of exile, gleefully proclaiming a new liberation in this overthrow of the idols. Lacan, we shall find in the next chapter, points to the "insistence of the letter" in the unconscious, a letter which is a polysemous endless chain of signification, in a "symbolic Order" governed by what Lacan calls the "Name-of-the-Father."

The problems of generation, succession, the "chain of signifiers," the belatedness of consciousness, and of the interpreter are all central issues here. Harold Bloom, perhaps our most overtly Hebraic contemporary critic, has elaborated an entire poetics of belatedness, "anxiety of influence" in which poets engage in a dialectical–historical struggle, each making room for himself by manipulating the tradition he has inherited, claiming to revise and purify it from error while in fact covertly overthrowing his predecessors. Through this revisionist interpretation, the poet can see himself as his own father, redeemed from error, thus making the father only a prefiguraton of the son. Bloom's description of the poetic process well describes the heretic Jewish hermeneutic I have been trying to articulate and we shall examine his theory in depth in the last chapter.

This heretic hermeneutic is a complex dialectic of identification and displacement. Whether Moses comes to be read as a prefiguration of Jesus, as in Christian interpretation, or as a prefiguration of the heroic secular prophecy of Freud, the dynamic is the same. The dead father in *Totem and Taboo* or *Moses and Monotheism* or *The Interpretation of Dreams*, or the Name-of-the-Father in Lacan, or all the fathers of philosophy in Derrida: all enforce upon the living sons a certain contract of guilt and a desire to be free of that burden. And freedom comes in a characteristically Rabbinic mode—through interpretation, but here purposeful misinterpretation, "misprision," in Bloom's term.[20] Under the guise of a new interpretation, the metonymic chain of succession is breached. The new interpreter usurps the place of the predecessor. Christianity as Jewish heresy leads to the literal usurpation by the Son (now himself become divine) of the Father's place—as does psychoanalysis. As Cynthia Ozick describes Bloom's system, it all centers on the single idea of discontinuity: "What Bloom means by 'revisionism,' is a breaking off with the precursor; a violation of what has been transmitted; a deliberate offense against the given, against the hallowed: an unhallowing of the old great gods; the usurpation of an inheritance by the inheritor himself; displacement. Above all, the theft of power."[21] Freud's misprisions of the psyche gave him the key to the unconscious in the power struggle within man for control of himself and his history. The language of the unconscious could be deciphered only when it was recognized that desire itself speaks through displacement, condensation, suppression, and subversion. Then could Freud master the dream, the "royal road to the unconscious"—"Where it was there shall I be."

Jean-François Lyotard, mentioned in Chapter 2, discusses the theme of displacement-as-truth in Freud in relation to Hamlet and Oedipus, two characters who figured almost as prominently in Freud's psyche as Moses. Both Hamlet and Oedipus struggle with the problem of paternal displacement, parricide, and usurpation, but it is "Hamlet's *non-fulfillment* of the paternal word which marks the modern's difference from the Greek." "Oedipus fulfills his fate of desire; the fate of Hamlet is the non-fulfillment of desire: this chiasmus is the one that extends between what is Greek and what is Jewish, between the tragic and the ethical."[22] Lyotard claims that in Hebraic ethics representation is forbidden precisely because the image fulfills desire. Greek representation, on the other hand, welcomes the play of the primary process within the secondary process; discourse becomes desire. In Hebraic ethics, by contrast, the subject is possessed by an other, dispossessed of origin in a passive filiation; there is no fulfillment of desire. As with Hamlet, the *difference* between the dead voice of the father and the living son is an irrevocable one. (The Derrideanism of Lyotard's analysis, his emphasis on non-fulfillment, absence, difference, possession by the other, are all the most Rabbinic aspects of Derrida's thought.) There is no reconciliation as in Christianity.

In Lyotard's reading of *Moses and Monotheism,* the essential thesis is not the Egyptian identity of Moses, but his assassination, for it is in this acting out of "the compulsive murder of the paternal figure, repeating in nonrecognition that of the primal father, thematized in *Totem and Taboo* in 1913 that the Jews escape the general movement of the first murder's recognition and the religion of reconciliation, Christianity."[23] Like Hamlet, who does not recognize his fate or fulfill his desire, who remains dispossessed and does not recognize his own parricidal desire, the Jewish murder of Moses is, in Lyotard's view, an acting out which foregoes recognizing itself as the father's murder.

Lyotard, however, like Freud, takes this mythical murder for actual reality. He forgets that it is in effect *Freud's* acting out of parricide—as a matter of interpretive construction of a text, not as actual deed; as Freud, too, forgets that there is no literal reality to the primal seductive father. It would be better to say that Freud's Moses myth is his own attempt not to recognize his parricidal desire, and at the same time an ambivalent act of identification with the father. Freud's parricide was a fantasy—interpretive, not actual—and interpretation was as much an attempt to identify with his father as to destroy him, to affirm—in a distorted and displaced way— his links to the Jewish tradition. Moreover, it is the *nonfulfillment* of the interpretation that is crucial here. It is in Christianity that the murderous deed actually occurred; there was the actual sacrifice of the Incarnate Father–Son that ended the succession of Jewish fathers, Jewish law, and Rabbinic tradition.

Freud, however, never had any illusions about freeing himself from the exile of interpretation or about the redemptive fulfillment of desire. His goal was to replace repetition with remembrance. As Murray Schwartz writes,

> Freud, as interpreter, saw himself engaged in a heroic battle against the
> patient's repetitions of infantile experience. The essence of the interpretive
> process was to convert repetition into remembering "reproduction in the

mind". . . . The end of analysis, in this model, is the reconstruction of historical truth, the "real life" that was unconsciously enacted in the present and that the analyst relegates once more to the past, its proper place.[24]

It is the displaced repetition of infantile experience in the present that Freud seeks to cure by the process of interpretation: to convert the hysterical symptoms that manifested themselves in the actual bodies of his patients (the word-become-flesh) back into words. Instead of Incarnation is Interpretation; this stance is eminently Judaic. That Freud himself, however, repeats in nonrecognition, through his own interpretations, his own infantile desires, is a displacement of this Judaic bent, a heretical hermeneutics. Paradoxically, it is precisely this repetition which Freud most sought to avoid.

Barbara Johnson clarifies this issue most brilliantly in her discussion of Derrida and Lacan, noting that the "act of (psycho) analysis has no identity *apart from* its status as a repetition of the structure it seeks to analyze. . . . Psychoanalysis is in fact *itself* the primal scene it is seeking."[25]

> Psychoanalysis is not itself the *interpretation* of repetition; it is the repetition of a *trauma of interpretation*—called "castration" or "parental coitus" or "the Oedipus complex" or even "sexuality"—the traumatic deferred interpretation not *of* an event, but *as* an event which never took place as such. The "primal scene" is not a scene but an *interpretive infelicity* whose result was to situate the interpreter in an intolerable position. And psychoanalysis is the reconstruction of that interpretive infelicity not as *its* interpretation, but as its first and last *act*.[26]

The merging of the language of interpretation with the discourse of that which it interprets characterizes a Rabbinic relation to the text (and much of contemporary literary theory). Moreover, we might say that classical Rabbinic interpretation-as-repetition means in linguistic terms the succession of links on the chain of metonymic signification, a chain where signified and signifier do not coalesce; one approaches the other only by interpretive approximation, and one's identity is constituted by positioning oneself along this chain within the play of its polysemy. Heretic Rabbinic interpretation, as in Christianity for example, is interpretation-as-repetition as breakage of the successive links, and replacement via metaphoric substitution, a union of signifier and signified, same and other, desire and fulfillment, literal sacrifice, the word-become-flesh.

Whereas Freud tried to replace repetition by remembrance to cure his patients, he could not, it would seem, cure himself, and turned his own interpretive methodology to the service of repetition. In an essay on Freud, Derrida points precisely to this maneuver in *Beyond the Pleasure Principle*. Derrida points out that as in *The Interpretation of Dreams,* the central passages in *Beyond the Pleasure Principle* are autobiographical and domestic, and focus on an important moment in Freud's own genealogy, although claiming "to be nothing less than a genealogy of objectivity in general." According to Derrida, Freud is "producing the institution of his desire, making it the start of his own genealogy." *In Beyond the Pleasure Principle,* Freud describes at length the game of his grandson, who, in the absence of the mother, throws and retrieves a wooden spool, exclaiming, *"Fort–da"* (*gone–here*). Derrida claims that this is a game of "self-engen-dering of self-repetition" and, at the same time, the game that Freud himself is playing in his earnest speculations in writing *Beyond the Pleasure Principle* itself, a book wherein Freud "repeats repetition compulsively, but it all never advances by a single step." The *PP (pleasure principle),* and *Pepe (Grandfather*—Freud himself) are endlessly dispatched only to end-lessly return and retain total authority. The grandson's game is an autobi-ography of Freud.[27]

The *PP (grandfather–pleasure principle),* says Derrida, is not thwarted by repetition; on the contrary, it therein asserts its mastery. In fact, the *PP* is mastery in general "that *leaves* itself only to reappropriate itself, to *come* into its own (self)—a tautology. . ." The game of the *fort–da* is playing with oneself as one's own object, involving self-representation and re-presentation, self-return. Freud plays with his text precisely as Grandson Ernest does with his wooden spool: "He is doing what he describes." Just as Ernest recalls *himself* in recalling the object (mother, toy, etc.), Freud in his speculations and descriptions recalls *himself* and produces his text, "making a contract with himself so as to be left holding all the strings of his line, descendents and ascendents, in an incontestable ascendancy," all of which amounts to a "teleological self-institution." In this, Derrida claims, Freud writes autobiography in a new way, opening up a domain in which the inscription of the subject in his text is the necessary condition for the pertinence and worth of that text, beyond empirical subjectivity, and beyond ordinary notions of subjective and objective truth.[28]

Derrida's insights about the movements of Freud's autobiographical self-substitution in *Beyond the Pleasure Principle* bring into relief the general problem of origins we have been discussing as a central theme in Freud's work. We have mentioned previously the connection of the ques-tion of origins to the movement of displacement. The manner in which the problems Freud describes become the very structure of his methodology remains to be seen. Autobiographical inscription in the text, a new truth value beyond the traditional subject–object split, the displacement of fa-thers, and Rabbinic methodology underlying a heretic hermeneutic are all connected issues.

Freud's Methodology: New Arrangements, Hidden Gaps

Let us begin with some of Edward Said's insights about the way in which Freud's methodology provided an entirely new textual dynamic which closely paralleled developments in late nineteenth-and early twentieth-century literature. Freud's "family novel" followed the same course as the late nineteenth-century novel, and in both science and fiction became inextricably intermingled. We have discussed in Chapter 3 how Said's description of the textual conventions consciously avoided by Freud in *The Interpretation of Dreams* has striking parallels to Rabbinic thought. Among these were the avoidance of "supplementarity," i.e., the defensive spatial and temporal separation of the text from the events it is describing; the avoidance of a spatial and temporal logic of structure that is essentially linear and sequential; the rejection of the notion of the finality of each discrete portion of the text; and the destruction of the unity or integrity of the text as maintained by a series of genealogical connections (author–text, beginning–middle–end, reader–interpretation). Underlying the rejection of these conventions lies the overthrow of the imagery of succession, paternity, and hierarchy.[29] Said also recognizes in Freud's overthrow of the "paternal authority" of the text a link to his obsession with the role of the father.

> Freud's displacement and qualification in his psychology of the father's role—a role which is always complex and, despite radical qualifications upon it, highly ambivalent— is accompanied by parallel displacements and qualifications made in those genealogical, hierarchical, and consecutive conventions to be found in the idea of a text. Perhaps it is too glib to see in this Freud's interest in substituting brothers for fathers, co-presence for consecutiveness, temporal and spatial simultaneity for the (relative) family sequence. None of these displacements comes about by assertion, however; rather each is concomitant with Freud's special sort of analytical reasoning, in which a healthy respect for what he calls the wisdom of the ancients is combined with daring insolence in advancing novel hypotheses. Another way of stating this is to call Freud's writing an amalgam of scientific and "traditional" wisdom.[30]

This "wisdom of the ancients" is Rabbinic. Said notes that Freud's method is consistently antivisual and antimimetic. The dream images must be transferred to language: "The difficulty of this method is that it does not imitate nature, but rather displaces it."[31] This displacement from image to word, nature to verbal text, although new for the nineteenth century, was the Rabbinic construction of reality, emanating from the Hebraic ban on images and the concept of the divine Scripture as the creator of nature. (Derrida's *Écriture* and his attempt to describe Freud's view of the psyche as a "writing machine" carry the implications of this concept to their fullest extreme.)

The displacement of nature is, at the same time, the destruction of the logic of biological succession, and filiation. In place of father and son is the brother, or in place of the author's univocity is the relation between dreamer and interpreter, as the analyst becomes the brother interlocutor. (Perhaps this is why so many of the early Biblical texts deal with conflicts between *brothers*: Cain and Abel, Ishmael and Isaac, Esau and Jacob. The underlying theme of the usurping brother counters the strong narrative geneologies. The Rabbis assume, in a sense, the role of brother interlocuter to God through their interpretive powers.) In place of image, genesis, and story are discontinuous concepts, paragenesis, and constructions. Complementarity and adjacency prevail over a dynastic and mimetic model.[32] The text is no longer an object but a dynamic producing structure whose effect is to constantly multiply instead of fix meaning. *The Interpretation of Dreams* in its structure as a book repeats the very structure of understanding which it describes, as Said shows at length.

It is our contention that this strange structure, while undoing the classical canons of the novel, autobiography, science, mimesis, and representation, was not only a revolt against the paternal authority these traditions represented—as part of Freud's displacement of the father—but at the same time a return to and identification with a kind of Jewish paternity that stood opposed to and repressed by the classical Western, Greco-Christian tradition. As we have seen, by overthrowing the Hellenistic Gentile culture and uncovering its dark side, Freud could at the same time defend both himself and his father. Perhaps it was also the return of Freud's own Rabbinic repressed, something of which he himself was unconscious and which he repeated in nonrecognition in the textual structure of his work and thought. As Johnson and Derrida point out, psychoanalysis repeats what it describes not only in content but in its very methodology. They do not, however, connect this "unconscious repetition" with Freud's Jewish background.

It is curious that although proud of his heritage, Freud pretended to forget anything having to do with knowledge of its more religious aspects. In writing to a correspondent who had questioned him about his religious background, Freud answered, "My education was so un-Jewish that today I cannot even read your dedication, which is evidently written in Hebrew." Marthe Robert notes that Freud was so close to his old Hebrew teacher Samuel Hammerschlag that he named his second daughter Sophie after Sophie Schwab, Hammerschlag's niece. Robert furthermore speculates that the "Irma" of Freud's famous dream was Anna Hammerschlag, Samuel's daughter.[33] Freud's father had also given him a Bible for his thirty-fifth birthday with a dedication written in Hebrew, which would have been strange had Freud not known how to read it. (There are a number of examples such as these of Freud's "forgetting" of certain aspects of his background. For instance, the famous incident of Freud's forgetting the word *Signor* in the name of the painter *Signorelli*, about which he wrote in *The Psychopathology of Everyday Life*, may be read as an attempt to repress the *Signor—master* or, as Lacan would put it, "Name-of-the-Father," which in Jewish tradition represents God, whose name is not pronounced but who is referred to as "the Name." Likewise, in writing to Fliess of his father's death, Freud could not even refer to his father by name, or as "my father," but instead refers to him as "the old man.")[34]

Freud's description of Biblical interpretation in *Moses and Monotheism* is a revealing key. He claims that the Biblical account of Moses is actually a product of a struggle between two opposing forces: one sought to transform and falsify the text, turn it into its opposite; the other sought piously to maintain the story as it stood. Hence there are striking omissions, repetitions, and contradictions in the text. The distortion of a text, says Freud, is like a murder, the difficulty being not with the deed itself, but in doing away with the traces. One might find these two processes working within Freud and standing as a model for the interpretive act in general, aside from their particular relation to Freud's Judaism, psychoanalysis, and the displacements of heretic hermeneutics. Repression is unconscious textual distortion, as is interpretation. In this sense, interpretation is analogous to the dream-work as it operates on the latent content—reaffirming Barbara Johnson's insight that psychoanalytic interpretation repeats the structure it seeks to analyze. As Freud writes a little further on in *Moses and Monotheism*, distortion means "to put in another place," describing it as metonymical displacement: "That is why in so many textual distortions we may count on finding the suppressed and abnegated material hidden away somewhere, though in an altered shape and torn out of its original connection. Only it is not always easy to recognize it."[35] Just as the dream-work effects a compromise formation, simultaneously revealing and concealing, satisfying and suppressing, so interpretation represses and transgresses.

We may take Freud at his word and say that in his own textual distortions we may count on finding the suppressed material hidden away somewhere though in an altered shape, torn out of its original connection. Psychoanalysis, like the dream, is a compromise formation, simultaneously revealing and concealing, satisfying and suppressing, an interpretation that represses and transgresses.

Repression and textual distortion occur, then, not only in the realm of the unconscious, the patient, and even in the analyst, but on the broader level of culture as well. Hence Freud reconnected the deepest layers of his own psyche to broadest neuroses of civilization in general. In a stunning remark:

> But none the less I have not been able to resist the seduction of an analogy. The delusions of patients appear to me to be the equivalents of the constructions which we build up in the course of an analytic treatment—attempts at explanation and cure, though it is true that these, under the conditions of a pyschosis, can do no more than replace the fragment of reality that is being disavowed in the present by another fragment that had already been disavowed in the remote past. . . . If we consider mankind as a whole and substitute it for the single human individual, we discover that it too has developed delusions which are inaccessible to logical criticism and which contradict reality.[36]

Psychoanalysis as the interpretive method of illuminating the hidden gaps of consciousness is not only directly connected to the question of

Freud's relation to the Jews, insofar as they are part of the hidden gaps of his past, but also because the Jews themselves bear projections of some of the deepest repressed fantasies and guilts of civilization. The conscious gaps and lacunae, the off-centered and neglected phenomena to which psychoanalysis directs its attention, are also extended by Freud to a general theory of culture: to the evasions, repressions, and omissions of truth underlying our most exalted achievements. Freud's explanation of anti-Semitism, in his own project of recovering his past, is intimately connected with his analysis of civilization and its discontents.

With *Moses and Monotheism*, however, the Jewish science reaches both its culmination and its undoing; it undid the Jews as the murderers of Moses; it undid Moses as an Egyptian; and it undid Freud's whole careful scientific facade. It is his least respected and accepted book, often held up to point to the absurdities of psychoanalysis—psychoanalysis, indeed, as delusion. For it is precisely around the nature of psychoanalysis as a specific technique of interpretation and hermeneutics that the controversy concerning its status as a science rages to this day. The question is whether the validity of science depends on the achievement of a completely objective, noninvolved, nonprejudicial point of view, or whether the acknowledgement of the necessary relativity, subjectivity, and prejudice involved in any act of perception is, in fact, a truer and more scientific approach to knowledge. Under Freud's scrutiny, the precious achievement of Western European man, the conscious thinking ego—its theorems, reasons, constructions, science, objectivity—became suspect and was dispossessed. In Freud's famous phrase, "The ego is not master in its own house."[37] But once this territory was dispossessed, Freud could conquer Canaan. As he wrote to Jung: "If I am Moses, then you are Joshua and will take possession of the promised land of psychoanalysis, which I shall be able to glimpse only from afar."[38]

Behind the Cartesian cogito lay another order, a hidden order of reality impelling, distorting, and determining the character of consciousness. Observation must be shifted off-center, so to speak, to what is hidden in the gaps of consciousness. The problem in psychoanalysis is to make consciousness transparent to itself, but to do so involves using the suspect surface rational consciousness itself to understand that which it conceals. The analyst must become his own patient, displace the center of his rational consciousness, and partake of the very thought processes that are the objects of his observation; he is an engaged, not an impartial, observer.

The Hybrid Science

The argument between interpretation and fact, objectivity and subjectivity, psychoanalysis and science, takes place on the old grounds of the battle between the human sciences and the natural sciences. Psychoanalysis, however, to use Paul Ricoeur's word, is a "hybrid" because "it arrives at its energy concepts solely by way of interpretation. Because of this mixed nature, analytic interpretation will always seem an anomaly in the human sciences." That is to say, Freud operates both within the schemas of scientific mechanism and symbolic meaning. His work is an interplay between economics and hermeneutics. Ricoeur explains, "The speculative hypotheses are verified by their capacity to inter-relate hermeneutic concepts—such as apparent meaning and hidden meaning, symptom and fantasy, instinctual representation, ideas, and affects—with economic concepts, such as cathexis, displacement, substitution, projection, introjection, etc."[39]

Ricoeur is in agreement with many other contemporary interpretation theorists, who have stressed that Freud's specific contribution to psychology in particular, and the natural sciences in general, was a hermeneutic one. Gerard Radnitzky, for example, has written:

> It is generally agreed that Freud made us see parapraxes, dreams, and neurotic behavior as "meaningful." However, "meaningful," in this context is often construed—from the point of view of naturalism—as:
> He enabled us to *explain* the occurrence of such phenomena in a satisfactory way (hence we understood them). What Freud de facto did was to produce a shift in the tradition of psychology by introducing a new way of studying these phenomena which is *primarily* hermeneutic.[40]

We have maintained, however, that Freud's innovative hermeneutic was a particularly Judaic one, which accounts in part for its peculiar hybrid nature. We remember that for Aristotle, interpretation had to do with declarative, logical discourse, not with rhetoric and poetics. Interpretation was concerned with the truth or falsity of logical propositions, not with the multiple meanings of semantics. The univocity of meaning, and the concept of hermeneutics as ascertaining the truth or falsehood of a logic of oppositions, were connected to the Christian logos. In the Jewish concept of interpretation, in contrast to the Greco-Christian tradition, interpretation is multivocal, indeterminate, rhetorical and poetic, as well as logical (as is Freud's), concerned with the affirmation of truth or falsehood in terms of uncovering deeper meanings. Instead of a logic of oppositions, the Talmud, we saw, uses a dialectical model of reasoning that presents and encourages opposing opinions. Often the pattern is to record a mishnah, follow it with the Gemara's debate and discussion analyzing the mishnah, then cite another, unrecorded, text, analyze it and subject it to opposing statements. The connections between arguments, citations, and traditions may take the discussion seemingly far from its original subject and expand into explanations of other statements, which in turn may invoke aggadic interpolations, stories, proverbs, etc. before the original halachic question is returned to. Like a good Talmudist, Freud claims that in the dream:

> Each train of thought is almost invariably accompanied by its contradictory counterpart, linked to it by antithetical association. The different portions of

this complicated structure stand, of course, in the most manifold logical relations to one another. They can represent foreground and background, digressions and illustrations, conditions, chains of evidence and counter-argument. . . . The restoration of the connections which the dream-work has destroyed is a task which has to be performed by the interpretive process.[41]

The Talmudic mode of thought became the ingrained model of the Jewish psyche, the intimacy and identity with which Freud so keenly felt. Like psychoanalysis, Talmudic thought is an evolutionary record not just of laws and concepts, but of the processes by which those judgments are reached, linking the entire historical past with the present and tying the most abstract discussions to the most ordinary details of life.

We have seen, moreover, how Freud's concept of the relation of the dream text to interpretation parallels the Rabbinic concept of the relation of the written to the oral Torah. The written Scripture was a product of condensation, a coded shorthand that needed elucidation and interpretation; externally it appeared fragmentary, disjointed, and illogical, each letter compressing many meanings hinted and implied. These meanings are latent, concealed within the text. One of Freud's most contested assertions was that beneath the seeming fragments and illogical manifest content of the dream was a latent content, a locus of entirely rational and comprehensible dream thoughts. All other interpreters of dreams, Freud wrote, dealt only with the manifest content:

> We are almost alone in taking something else into account. We have introduced a new class of psychical material between the manifest content of the dreams and the conclusions of our enquiry: namely, their *latent* content, or (as we say) the dream-thoughts, arrived at by means of our procedure. It is from these dream-thoughts and not from a dream's manifest content that we disentangle its meaning.[42]

This concept of latent content that needs to be uncovered through hermeneutical procedure, which places both Freud and the Rabbis in direct opposition to the tradition of Protestant literalism, rejects any attempt to define meaning by a reduction of the manifest to any one single latent referent. Freud added in a 1925 footnote to *The Interpretation of Dreams* that after overcoming the initial difficulty of persuading his readers to accept the idea of latent content, he then faced the problem that

> They seek to find the essence of dreams in their latent content and in doing so overlook the distinction between the latent dream-thoughts and the dream-work. At bottom, dreams are nothing other than a particular *form* of thinking, made possible by the condition of the state of sleep. It is the *dream-work* which creates that form, and it alone is the essence of dreaming—the explanation of its peculiar nature.[43]

To reify the concept of latent content is, in a sense, a product of the same kind of literalist thought that at first refused to look beyond manifest content, and that disallowed the possibility of meaning as a continuous process, of content as "convergence" (or in Freud's word "nodal point") of many thoughts in an endless interpretability. In addition to the "navel point" of the dream, as Freud calls it, which reaches to the unknown, secret, and ultimately uninterpretable level of the dream, Freud writes that

> A dream never tells us whether its elements are to be interpreted literally, or in a figurative sense, or whether they are to be connected with the material of the dream-thoughts directly or through the intermediary of some interpolated phraseology. . . . whether it is to be interpreted in a positive or negative sense (antithetical relation), whether it is to be interpreted historically, whether it is to be interpreted symbolically, or whether its interpretation is to depend on its wording.[44]

The interpretive process is the dream-work in reverse; the interpreter's own procedures must correspond to the procedures of the unconscious in forming and representing the dream. By the interpreter's own condensations, associations, displacements, reversals, wordplays, multiple meanings, dramatic representations, etc., he can uncover the dream thoughts, and "construct" the meaning, a meaning which was latent in and not arbitrarily read into the dream—and that precisely was the technique of the Rabbis as well.

And like the Rabbis, Freud insisted that he was not creating new meanings, only uncovering, like an archaeologist, what lay buried beneath. Everything is connected under the surface; the interpreter's job is to reveal, elucidate, and construct for conscious awareness those hidden unities that contain a core of definite historical truth.

Interpretation is not, in the Aristotelian sense, the distinguishing of truth from falsehood, but the relationship of hidden to shown: not appearance to reality, but manifest to latent. The idiom is disguise, displacement, censorship of the superego. A dream cannot be true or false, but can only have a more or less deep meaning. Everything that logical consciousness rejects as nonsensical, useless, disconnnected, contradictory, and impossible has, in fact, a meaning; and to say that dreams indeed have a meaning, Freud recognized, put him in opposition to every ruling theory. As Ricoeur puts it, Freud was the "exegete who rediscovers the logic of the illogical kingdom."[45] For Freud, what looked illogical was only so (as in the case of the written Torah) because the text is truncated, lacunary, but nothing in it is arbitrary, senseless, or out of place:

> The most trivial elements of a dream are indispensable to its interpretation. . . . We have attached no less importance in interpreting dreams to every shade of the form of words in which they were laid down before us. And even when it happened that the text of the dream as we had it was meaningless or inadequate—we had taken this defect into acount as well. In short, we have treated as Holy Writ what previous writers have regarded as an arbitrary improvisation, hurriedly patched together in the embarassment of the moment.[46]

Many of Freud's methods of approaching this "Holy Writ" bear striking similarity to some of the Rabbinic hermeneutic rules discussed in

Chapter 3. Freud writes, for example, that the logical relation most favored by the mechanism of dream formation is "the relation of similarity, consonance, or approximation—the relation of 'just as'. . .": "Parallels or instances of 'just as' inherent in the material of the dream-thoughts constitute the first foundation for the construction of a dream. . . . The representation of the relation of similarity is assisted by the tendency of the dream-work towards condensation, similarity, consonance, the possession of common attributes—all these are represented in dreams by unification."[47] In Rabbinic interpretation we found many corresponding principles concerning the relation and placing of words, verses, sections, or laws next to each other (*semuchin* and *hekkesh*), inferring that what is true of one is also true of the other. Moreover, we have seen in our analysis of the kal ve-chomer mode of argument (*how much more so*) an underlying logical principle of juxtaposition allowing for multiple predication; this principle is fundamental to much of Rabbinic thought and distinguishes it from logic based on Greek ontology and reason.

The assumption of a hidden all-pervasive unity of the text—not as ontological sameness but as a simultaneous coexistence of various related and constantly proliferating meanings—accounts for some of the strangeness of Rabbinic and psychoanalytic technique, especially the use of plays on words and numbers. Freud uses methods exactly equivalent to the Rabbinic notarikon and gematria. He finds the meaningless compound word *Maistollmutz* in a woman's dream, for instance, and breaks it down by analysis into *Mais (maize), toll (mad), mannstol (mad for men),* and *Olmutz* (a town in Moravia), and derives a whole chain of thoughts and associations from each syllable. Freud calls this phenomenon "syllabic chemistry."[48] One of Freud's most well-known uses of number play (gematria) was his analysis of one of his own seemingly arbitrary statements that he would not make any further changes in *The Interpretation of Dreams* even if it contained 2,467 mistakes. He calculates that twenty-four represented his twenty-fourth birthday and coming of age, which added to his then present age of forty-three equalled sixty-seven; the number 2,467 therefore expresses his wish to be able to work another twenty-four years. And so Freud writes, one cannot underestimate

> the extent to which psychical events are determined. There is nothing arbitrary about them. It can be shown quite generally that if an element is left undetermined by one train of thought, its determination is immediately effected by a second one. For instance, I may try to think of a number arbitrarily. But this is impossible: the number that occurs to me will be unambiguously and necessarily determined by thoughts of mine though they may be remote from my immediate intention.[49]

There is in Freud's world of the dream—which is the model of the psyche and of culture itself—nothing arbitrary; nor is there anything arbitrary in the world of the interpreter. Behind the irrationalities and trivialities is an all-embracing unity of meaning achieved through condensations, displacements, over-determinations; and even the most far-fetched associations are pathways that follow concealed circuits back to the dream thoughts. Writes Freud,

> These new connections are only set up between thoughts which were already linked in some way in the dream-thoughts. The new connections are, as it were, looplines or short-circuits, made possible by the existence of other and deeper lying connecting paths. It must be allowed that the great bulk of the thoughts which are revealed in analysis were already active during the process of forming the dream.[50]

Everything is already connected under the surface; the interpreter reveals these connections and applies them to the continuous developing life of the present. But the character of that ongoing life itself is formed by these already laid-down materials. Interpretation thus becomes part of the dream-work. In the assumption of a hidden unity behind all the disparate phenomena, both the psychoanalyst and the Rabbi assume a hidden meaning which in its manifestation is multiple—and is not so much found *in* the text, as a reified essence, but *in* the *process* of interpretation. What Freud analyzed were not so much the mechanisms *in* the dream, or latent content, as the *arrangements of* the dream-work, which become indistinguishable from the arrangements of the interpreter's own psyche, his method of making sense of the dream-work. The dream is the form of thinking called the dream-work, which is manifested through its interpretation, with which it becomes one.

For the Rabbis, while interpretation was from Sinai, "the Torah is not in heaven" but is decided in the ongoing process of debate on earth. This idea of interpretation is a curious hybrid between the belief in an absolute origin and authority and the belief in man's ability to alter and overcome it—a hybrid in the same way that Freud's theories combined, on the one hand, concepts of absolute origins (complexes, primal crimes, desires, and traumas), determining mechanisms which operated from the earliest periods and controlled the formation of character, with, on the other hand, the affirmation of the amendment, alteration, and susceptibility to change of these absolute origins through interpretation and insight. In the same way that the holy Scripture is itself the speaking subject, speaking to men, instituting laws, shaping the norms of life and behavior, and yet at the same time an object of analysis shaped by its interpreters—for Freud, the dream as the royal road to the unconscious is the psyche speaking to men, and yet an object of and subject to their interpretations. The interpreter stands in a passive-aggressive role, engaged and detached, determined by and determining the associations and thoughts of the unconscious, which ultimately lead to the mysterious unknown, beyond reason, explanation, and understanding. Freud writes, "There is at least one spot in every dream at which it is unfathomable—a navel, as it were, that is part of its contact with the unknown."[51]

For both Freud and the Rabbis, interpretation was the preeminent mode of knowing, applicable in every context and to every idea. Both subjected their respective holy writs to interpretation after interpretation, to an exhaustive search of every word, letter, and detail—and not just for the purpose of deriving law, or better understanding the text, but for a key to the ultimate source of wisdom and knowledge of the universe. Both valued constant study and scrutiny of the text in the search for ever deeper meanings, connections, convergences. Perhaps Freud's Jewish bias has something to do with the intellectuality, verbosity, and agonistic relation of patient and analyst, the long-drawn-out nature of therapy: know the truth and it will make you free.

Study is the solution to and consolation for present disaster. As Freud prepared to leave Vienna in flight from the Nazis, as he disbanded the Vienna Psychoanalytical Society, he said: "After the destruction of the temple in Jerusalem by Titus, Rabbi Jochanan ben Zakkai asked for permission to open a school at Yavneh for the study of the Torah. We are going to do the same. We, after all, are accustomed to our history and tradition, and some of us by our personal experience, to being persecuted."[52] Even though the Temple had been destroyed and the people decimated, in Yavneh all the intricate laws dealing with the Temple and its sacrifices were not abandoned, but intensively studied and interpreted—as they are to this day. Nothing was lost, so to speak . . . in the same way in which Freud, the archaeologist of the psyche in exile, returns to build its Temple from the ground up through interpretation and study of dreams and the dialectical theories of psychoanalysis. Or as Freud himself put it, "It is typically Jewish not to renounce anything and to replace what has been lost."[53] Through devotion to study and learning, one will survive the rigors of exile.

Freud's combination of therapy and theory, finally, contains an uncanny resemblance to Rabbinic thought. When Freud writes of his feeling of inner identity, and of sharing a common psychic structure with the Jews, he uses, as David Bakan notes, the German word for *the uncanny*—*Heimlichkeit,* a word upon which he had written an entire essay, "The Uncanny," and which Bakan perceptively says, sums up Freud's entire relation to Judaism.[54] Freud defines *the uncanny* to mean something terrifying that leads back to something familiar and long known, which has undergone repression and has later reemerged. Thus psychoanalysis, in its project of uncovering the secret repression and making reemerge what was long forgotten, is itself uncanny. And psychoanalysis is an uncanny version of Rabbinic hermeneutics. At the end of his life, Freud sat in exile, like the Rabbis, meditating about Moses, searching for the original crime that had caused his own, and man's, expulsion from Eden, in a book where interpretation is likened to concealed transgression.[55]

The whole of Freud's ambivalent attempts to, on the one hand, block out and, on the other, uncover his relation to his Jewish past, to be part of modern science, non-Jewish Vienna, and yet maintain his sense of inner identity with the Jews, might to some degree account for his heavy emphasis on the ideas of concealment, distortion, disguise, and censorship . . . on representation as a compromise between censorship and desire. Recent psychoanalytic theory has criticized Freud for his lack of a deeper understanding of symbolic and semantic functioning in conscious representation, and for his deterministic scheme of unconscious causality and censorship. Perhaps this theme of censorship had, again, deeply to do with Freud's Jewish identity. And psychoanalysis itself might be seen as a compromise formation between Freud the Talmudic dialectician and midrashic commentator, scrutinizer of texts, pursuer of secrets, and believer in hidden unities, and Freud the German scientist, materialist, atheist, skeptical professor, and dispassionate observer. Psychoanalysis intimately shares Freud's peculiar hybrid character, and his position as a kind of pariah in both the human and natural sciences.

Perhaps only one who belonged to and felt himself to be a part of a people in exile could have transformed the hermeneutics of historical understanding from the cool philosophical abstractions of Dilthey and the Protestant nineteenth-century schools of historicism to a passionate confrontation with the inner lost and pained self and its suffering. *Remember* is the theme that permeates both the Bible and Jewish history. In place of what is lost . . . the Temple, the land, the glory of the nation . . . is study, analysis, interpretation—and, as for Freud, no immediate grace, but only a continuing narrative.

6

The Analyst as Scribe: Jacques Lacan and the Return of the Father's Name

For the letter kills, but the spirit gives life.

—2 Cor. 3:6

Of course, as it is said, the letter killeth while the spirit giveth life . . . but we should like to know, also, how the spirit could live without the letter. Even so, the claims of the spirit would remain unassailable if the letter had not in fact shown us that it can produce all the effects of truth in man without involving the spirit at all.

It is none other than Freud who had this revelation, and he called his discovery the Unconscious.

—Jacques Lacan[1]

To what were the words of the Law to be compared before the time of Solomon? To a well the waters of which are at a great depth, and this cool and fresh, yet no man could drink of them. A clever man joined cord with cord and rope with rope and drew up and drank. So Solomon went from figure to figure, and from subject to subject, until he obtained the true sense of the Law.

—*Midrash Rabbah* on Song of Songs I.1:8

If Freud was Moses, he had more than one aspiring Joshua. The disciples of his academy in exile preserved and continued the teaching—not, however, without much acrimonious debate and several schisms. Jung, the pastor's son, who had found his way to Freud with such difficulty, also found his way out; and their dispute had much to do with their religious differences.

153

In France, another aspirant to the mantle of Joshua has arisen: Jacques Lacan. Lacan split from the mainline, orthodox international psychoanalytic association in the early 1950s. He has asserted that his "return to Freud" through the modern science of linguistics is the true path to the promised land. And since the 1960s Lacan has been one of the most influential intellectual figures in France and America.* More or less neglected by American psychoanalysts, Lacan, because of his profound sensitivity to poetics and language, has been embraced by many influential American critics. Those who do not embrace him find it hard, however, to ignore him.

Lacan has perceptively recognized the relation of Freud to Rabbinic thought. He directly situates Freud within the exegetic tradition of midrash, about which he writes:

> In effect, for this people who have the Book, alone among all to affirm itself as historical, in never propagating myth, midrash represents a primary mode of which modern historical criticism could well be only the bastardization. For if it takes the Book perfectly literally, it is not in order to make it the bearer of more or less patent intentions, but because of its signifying collusion taken in its materiality . . . to draw another statement from the text: nay, to imply in the text what it itself neglected. [Translation mine.][2]

Lacan, too, views the Jews as the interpretive people par excellence, developing their hermeneutic skills particularly in the crush of exile: " . . . ever since the return from Babylon, the Jew is he who knows how to read. This means he withdraws from his literal utterance so as to find an interval which then allows the game of interpretation."[3]

Lacan's rereading of Freud in terms of linguistics, however, is another displacement. As Jeffrey Mehlman comments, "It is as if the side of Freud most resonant for Lacan is not his gaze at a hidden center, but his displacement of center into the margins."[4] Repeating Freud's own methodology of displaced readings, Lacan focuses on the underside of Freud's text; it is not psychoanalysis as a search for latent content, an ultimate signified, that intrigues Lacan, but as a midrashic interpolation of lacunae, of the play possible within the gaps of the letter. The "full word" into which Lacan claims he wants to restore his patients is, for all its theological resonance, not in any way a word that transcends the letter for the spirit. The Lacanian unconscious is neither primordial nor instinctual. It is, in Lacan's famous phrases, "structured like a language," "the discourse of the Other," a *linguistic* entity defined by Saussure's formula for the sign:

*For the best sociological study of the phenomenon of Lacanianism, and a very basic introduction to Lacan's thought, see Sherry Turkle, *Psychoanalytic Politics: Freud's French Revolution* (New York: Basic Books, 1978). The most lucid exposition of Lacanian theory I have seen is the work of John P. Muller and William J. Richardson, who have written an outline and commentary to the major essays of the *Écrits*. They published successive chapters in the journal *Psychoanalysis and Contemporary Thought* 1 (1978): 323–353, 503–529; 2 (1979): 199–252, 345–375, 377–435. These are to be collectively published in a forthcoming book.

$$\frac{S}{s} \quad \text{(signifier/signified).}$$

"The dream-work only follows the laws of the signifier."[5]

Lacan asserts that Freud's description of the dream as a rebus validates Lacan's central thesis that the dream "must be understood literally": "This derives from the persistence in the dream of that same literal (or phonematic) structure through which the signifier in ordinary discourse is articulated and analyzed."[6] In Lacan's view, the structure of language will provide us with the correct way to read the dream, and he takes to their utmost extreme the antivisual and antimimetic aspects of Freud's thought in order to write his literal commentary.

One of Lacan's central maneuvers is to translate Freud's dream mechanisms of *condensation* and *displacement* into Roman Jakobson's linguistic categories—*metaphor* and *metonymy,* which we defined in Chapter 3. Condensation, for Lacan, becomes the "superimposition of signifiers." And this precisely is metaphor, here defined as "one word for another," which springs from "two signifiers, one of which has taken the place of the other in the signifying chain."[7] Displacement is retranslated as the metonymical "veering off of meaning." This method enables the unconscious to get around censorship, and is a mode particularly suited, according to Lacan, to the expression of truth under conditions of oppression.

More interesting is Lacan's connection of the mechanism of metaphor, in which the subject disappears and is "cancelled" by the figure of speech (as in the classical Aristotelian theory of the cancellation of the proper name for the metaphorical one), with Freud's theory of the murder of the primordial father in *Totem and Taboo.* "So, it is between the signifier in the form of the proper name of a man, and the signifier which metaphorically abolishes him that the poetic spark is produced, and it is in this case all the more effective in realizing the meaning of paternity in that it reproduces the mythic event in terms of which Freud reconstructed the progress, in the individual unconsciousness, of the mystery of the father."[8] The proper name, or "father," disappears in metaphor "only in order to rise again in what surrounds this figure by which he was annihilated."[9] It would seem that Lacan is saying that just as the father is abolished by his sons, who then reinstitute him in a bond of collective guilt—so the proper name is reinstituted, affirmed in its paternity through the metaphorical movement and reappropriation—a movement we traced in our discussion of metaphor in Chapter 1.

In Lacan's view, metaphor, furthermore, is the agent of the psychoanalytic symptom "in which the flesh or function are taken as signifying elements."[10] Metonymy, by contrast, is the eternal desire for something else, the chain reproducing itself in dread desire, man's lack of being. Desire is manifest in an endless chain of signifiers, or endless play of interpretation. As Lacan linguistically, mathematically (and obscurely) formulates the metonymic structure, $f(S \ldots S')\,S \sim S\,(-)$ where "The sign — placed between ( ) represents here the retention of the line — which in the original formula marked the irreducibility in which, in the relations between signifier and signified, the resistance of meaning is constituted."[11] In linguistic terms, the inadequacy of signifier to signified constitutes a "resistance of meaning." That is, the line that divides the signifier from the signified in Saussure's formula for the sign, $\frac{S}{s}$, indicates the predetermined inability of the signifier to merge, to become *one* with the signified. Hence also, the desiring subject and meaningful object are barred from each other. On a larger scale—subject and object, consciousness and other are irrevocably separated. There can be metonymical multiplication of signifiers, but no true coincidence, no crossing the line, breaking the barrier between signifier and signified.

In a metaphoric structure, however, as opposed to a metonymic one, there is a certain collapse and crossing over, identification of signifier and signified; metaphor postulates more of an identity between the two terms. The leap over the bar is how Lacan formulates metaphor, in contrast to metonymy:

$$f\frac{S'}{(S)}S \sim S\,(\,+\,)s.$$

In the metaphorical structure, "it is in the substitution of signifier for signifier that an effect of signification is produced. . . . The sign + between ( ) represents here the leap over the line — . . . . This leap is an expression of the condition of passage of the signifier into the signified . . . confusing it with the place of the subject."[12]

We have stressed that one of the main points of contention between Judaism and Christianity was Christianity's "literalized" metaphor, its replacing of Interpretation with Incarnation. In Lacanian terms, Paul, in making the crucifixion of Jesus the substitutive sacrifice, saw his new faith as effecting a kind of leap over the bar, a vertical slash across the linear chain of Rabbinic interpretation (+). "To this day whenever Moses is read a veil lies over their minds, but when a man turns to the Lord the veil is removed" (2 Cor. 3:15). Within the metaphorical relation the gap of desire is crossed: word becomes for Paul the full logos. The text is no longer linear, interpretive, written, but the body and personhood of Jesus, with which the believer unites as an immediate member.

Paul and the New Testament writers make predominant use of allegory as a mode of interpretation because it posits a one-to-one relationship between the manifest and latent meanings. The latent meaning is Jesus, who is a determined fixed center, a mediator and resolver of oppositions, the ultimate sign, the referent for every other signifier. In Rabbinic interpretation, however, the central word, the name of God, is not pronounceable. This unpronounceable name translates as "I am what I am," a power that cannot be incarnated as a man. The relation between man and God in Judaism is contiguous, not substitutive—man is in God's image, but God is not of man's substance. Rabbinic interpretation, therefore, predicates statements about the subject but never collapses the sentence, the linear collective historical experience, into the subject, the word, the timeless son.

Lacan's own notion of truth may also be categorized as "metonymical." In his famous seminar on Poe's story "The Purloined Letter," to be discussed later in the next chapter, Lacan elaborates the course of the letter's displacements in the story, but emphasizes that its contents are never revealed. Similarly, the letter of the Lacanian unconscious is not found in any singular deep meaning, but in the course of its continuous displacements along the chain of signification—without any recourse to a signified. "No meaning," writes Lacan, "is sustained by anything other than reference to another meaning. . . . [we must get rid of] the illusion that the signifier answers to the function of representing the signified, or better, that the signifier has to answer for its existence in the name of any signification whatever. . . ."[13]

More striking is such a coincidence of this metonymical doctrine of truth with a Rabbinic mode that Lacan chooses to characterize his version of the normalized stage of the Oedipus complex or mature psychic identity (the symbolic realm) as "the Name-of-the-Father," using a term filled with Rabbinic echoes. In the Lacanian scheme of psychological development, the child moves from a nonverbal narcissistic mirror stage (the "empty word") into the realm of language—from specular to symbolic identification. As Anthony Wilden explains, in the specular identification of the boy with the father, he is placed in the *position* of the real father and thus in an impossible rivalry. In moving to symbolic identification with the father, the boy takes over the *function* of the father, thus normalizing the Oedipus complex. The father whom the child identifies with in this stage is neither real nor imaginary, but symbolic, and is none other than the figure of the Law.[14] The Name-of-the-Father is the signifier of the function of the father, and as Lacan notes, this term is a "religious invocation." There is little doubt to which religion Lacan refers when he writes,

> The Symbolic father is to be distinguished from the Imaginary father . . . to whom is related the whole dialectic of aggressivity and identification. In all strictness the Symbolic father is to be conceived as "transcendent," as an irreducible given of the signifier. The Symbolic father—he who is ultimately capable of saying "I am who I am"—can only be imperfectly incarnate in the real father. He is nowhere.[15]

Or as he puts it more directly in the *Four Fundamental Concepts of Psycho-Analysis*:

> I don't know whether you have noticed—you would have been much more capable of doing so if this year I had done the seminar I had intended doing on

the Name-of-the-Father—but the Lord with the unpronounceable name is precisely he who sends children to barren women and old men. The fundamentally transbiological character of paternity, introduced by the tradition of the destiny of the chosen people, has something that is intrinsically repressed there.[16]

The symbolic father also corresponds to Freud's mythical primordial father of *Totem and Taboo,* who is linked to the authority of the law—and the guilt of the sons whose murder of him institutes the debt wherein the subject binds himself for life to the Law. In Lacanian terms, the rejection of the Name-of-the-Father is the rejection of the entire symbolic order, the order of psychic health and maturity. In such a case, signifier and signified coalesce to the point of psychotic delusion where one cannot tell the symbol from the thing symbolized, the word from the thing–presentation.

It is interesting that Lacan associates rejection of the law and Name-of-the-Father with neurotic metaphorical coalescence, for that rejection is precisely the movement we have traced as predominant in Patristic thought, which rejects the father's law for the incarnate son, a word wherein symbol and thing symbolized become one. Perhaps this might be seen as a reversion back to Lacan's "imaginary stage," where the son places himself in the position of the father; he substitutes for him in a metaphorical cancellation. In this situation, the movement of substitution is frozen, and the "paternal proper name" is never regained: Christianity focuses on the actual moment of substitution and sacrifice. In the fullness of that moment, the sons avoid reaffirming the father and his law.

Geoffrey Hartman also reads Lacan in terms of the "scandal of theological survivals in even the most secular thinkers,"[17] and notes a connection between Lacan's definition of the *mirror phase* and the concept of word as logos. The specular image in the mirror phase provides a fixative, unifying effect that corresponds to the concept of a magical logos, which is *the* singular word in whose image all signification occurs.[18] This is the logos Derrida will seek to overthrow. This phase, according to Hartman, is also the realm of belief in the ultimately "proper" name, the "scene of nomination," and the principle of self-identity against which Derrida argues. The desire for a fixed image or defining word is also the Christian scandal of the "presence of the word." The logos reifies metaphor in its reappropriation of presence and suppresses the fertility of language. The logos Derrida will call for is one not based on any principle of self-identity, representation, or presence, and it does not pretend to an ultimate signified.

Metonymy, however, suffers the unending nature of desire and nonfulfillment, endlessly multiplying the chain of signifiers. Freud, with his tragic view of life and his stern recognition of the reality principle, remains firmly within the metonymical interpretive tradition of the Jews, for whom the great "I am" was unspeakable and an object of desire. If content is ungraspable and God is not to be imaged, one must approach indirectly: through covenant, law, interpretation, and analysis, all of which might be seen as compromise formations—as Freud said dreams were compromise formations by which one tried simultaneously to satisfy and renounce the claims of the id. As Freud also recognized, the separation from the object of desire engenders ambivalence. The impossibility of fulfilled desire initiates a countermovement aimed at both destruction of the object (and the giving of a new law) and an interpretive recovery.

Metonymy can also be a mode of displacement, from signifier to signifier, without any reference to a signified. Metonymy could be characterized as the predominantly Jewish mode of displacing (and approaching) the Father, in contrast to the Christian mode of metaphorical substitution described above. Metonymy as eternal desire produces eternal interpretation, and constantly reproduces itself in interpretation after interpretation, each of which is an attempt to approach the unreachable object (the transcendent Name-of-the-Father). Each new interpretation repeats the desire and is but another link on the chain. And we may add, each new Jewish hermeneutic—Freud, Bloom, Derrida—metonymically repeats, displaces, multiplies the links in the chain of Rabbinic interpretation despite the desire to escape it and give a new law, a new signifier or Name-of-the-Father.

The chosen people, as Lacan noted, introduced the concept of the transbiological character of paternity, and in that tradition the Jewish secular prophecy of psychoanalysis seeks to become the new father of its own law. In Chapter 4, we noted Harry Wolfson's assertion that one of the important differences between the Philonic logos and its Patristic transformation was the Christian conception of the logos after a pagan model of generation: the father literally begets the son out of himself. In light of Lacan's insight about the Jewish introduction of transbiological paternity, this difference is decisive. And perhaps we can connect a transbiological paternity to a notion of meaning that is also *transbiological*, i.e., not pinned down to any fixed base, natural substratum, or founding father signified, which could ultimately lead to the reification of the word-become-flesh.

Transbiological paternity as Wolfson, Jonas, and others point out, is also the distinguishing characteristic of the Jewish Father—his transcendence from the universe which He creates. Herbert Schneidau writes that metaphor is a "fundamental mode of what was for the Hebrew idol-worship." The pagan gods were actually thought to be embodied in the forms that were metaphors of their powers, whereas the Jewish God is not in any of His appearances, which are only arbitrary creations. In Schneidau's formula, "Whereas myth is hypotactic metaphors, the Bible is paratactic metonymies."[19] Metaphor thus invites sacralization, whereas metonymy is connected with indeterminacy.

We have analyzed at length the kind of interpretive indeterminacy, multiplicity of signification, and play of signifiers that characterizes Rabbinic thought. Lacan, too, maintains the arbitrary connection between signifier and signified, and the polysemous property of language as the

foundation of logic. His method of deciphering the dream is entirely rhetorical:

> The important point begins with the translations of the text, the important
> part which Freud tells us is given in the [verbal] elaboration of the dream—in
> other words in its rhetoric. Ellipsis and pleonasm, hyperbaton or syllepsis,
> repression, repetition, opposition—these are the syntactical displacements;
> metaphor, catachresis, antonomasis, allegory, metonymy, and synec-
> doche—these are the syntactic condensations in which Freud teaches us to
> read the intentions. . . . out of which the subject modulates his oneiric
> discourse.[20]

Even more interesting is that Lacan, in the function of analyst whose
role it is to interpret this text of the unconscious, sees himself, like the
Rabbi, as careful guardian and preserver of the holy text: "We play a
recording role. . . . As a witness called to account for the sincerity of the
subject, depositary of the minutes of his discourse, references to his
exactitudes, guarantor of his straightforwardness, custodian of his testament, scrivener of his codicile, the analyst participates in the nature of a
scribe.[21]

But the faithful scribe is not merely the passive transmitter of the truth;
like Ezra, the scribe who returned the people to the Book, and gave its
sense, he presides over and amplifies it through his interpretive techniques.
"Above all," writes Lacan, the analyst "remains the master of the Truth of
which this discourse is the progress . . . . it is he who guarantees its
dialectic."[22] Psychoanalysis repeats while trying to displace its Rabbinic
predecessors. The analyst–Rabbi is a scribe, another link in the chain of
interpretation that the text itself produces. His interpretive displacements,
despite his attempts at mastery, only reinscribe him within the chain. In
Lacanian terms, the analyst wants to "bear witness to the unconscious
which speaks": he is its "messenger" and becomes the patient who suffers
in his question-and-answer dialogue with the patient as he tries to evoke
what is already there in the patient's unconscious.[23] Ostensibly, this is the
reason why Lacan's own prose so resembles the garbled but evocative and
hermetic language of the Unconscious itself. Lacan's reader, in turn, must
become analyst and interlocutor of Lacan's text, deciphering its enigmas.
Practically speaking, Lacan's text is another displacement: while at the
same time claiming to be merely a voice of the unconscious, it is a new Holy
Scripture for Lacan's disciples. Lacan claims only to return to Freud—but
in fact displaces him with a new prophetic message.

And like any new prophet, Lacan is zealous for his new Scripture.
While affirming his new law of the signifier, and its freedom from any
determination by the signified, Lacan nevertheless cautions—as do the
Rabbis—that ultimately "Interpretation is not open to any meaning":

> It is false to say, as has been said, that interpretation is open to all meanings
> under the pretext that it is a question only of connection of a signifier to a

signifier, and consequently of an uncontrollable connection. Interpretation is not open to any meaning. The fact that I have said that the effect of interpretation is to isolate in the subject a kernel, a *kern* to use Freud's own term, of non-sense, does not mean that interpretation is in itself nonsense. . . . Interpretation is a signification that is not just any sifnification. It comes here in place of the *s* [signified] and reverses the relation by which the signifier has the effect, in language, of the signified. It has the effect of bringing out an irreducible signifier. . . . What is essential is that he should see, beyond this signification, to what signifier—to what irreducible, traumatic, non-meaning—he is, as a subject, subjected.[24]

These signifying elements, kernels of nonsense, are loci which Freud calls "nodal pins." The nodal points correspond also to what Lacan calls the *point de capiton*, which he compares to the buttons on the mattress of a couch. The signifying letter of the unconscious, therefore, "insists."

Now one might conceive of midrash in an analogous sense, with the text as a kind of finite determinant and the interpretation as the indeterminate and free weave of play over it. The act of interpretation, in structural linguistic terminology, would be the moment of actual speech (*parole*) making concrete and evident the implicit abstract structure of the language (*synchrony*) in response to historical events and needs (*diachrony*). The implicit or latent constituents of the written law are the hidden structure, whose dialectical relation to the diachronic oral interpretation constitutes an inclusive system. In the same manner that the abstract structure of a language is implicit in its spoken and temporal manifestations, the Rabbis likened their interpretive activity to that of a man who has been given wheat from which to make fine flour and flax from which to make a garment; if the flax is the synchronic element, the garment is the diachronic weave. In the weaving process of interpretation the same elements are at work as in the weaving together of the dream as text, and the same indeterminate noncentered meanings. Rabbinic indeterminacy of belief is not the same as allegorical interpretation, where the hidden meaning is concealed as another essence in the figure; the flax, similarly, is not concealed by the garment.

Above all, both Freud and Lacan warn us not to consider the latent meaning as an essence, and both assert the necessity of continuous interpretation. "The fact remains," says Lacan, "that the Symbolic is something that cannot be possibly reified in any way at all,"[25] and the symbolic is the realm of psychoanalysis. The distance between meaning, desire, and object always remains.

Thus the Freudian and Rabbinic interpretations are far more historically oriented, as Lacan realized, the Bible alone among all claiming to be a historical book. For Freud, archaism was archaeology: he saw the nature of the psyche collectively and individually in historical terms. The history we choose to write, the analogies we selectively perceive, the interpretations we construct, are functions of desire, and that desire is ambivalent. Freud's interpretations of the dream and of his own Jewish heritage bear all the marks of these distortions of desire. Lacan's technique likewise maintains:

> In order to liberate the subject's Word, we introduce him into the language of his desire, that is into the primary language in which, beyond what he tells us of himself, he is already talking to us unbeknownst to him, and in the symbols of the system in the first place.
>
> . . . . What we teach the subject to recognize as his Unconscious is his *history*—that is to say, we help him to perfect the contemporary historization of the facts which have already determined a certain number of the historical turning points in his experience.[26]

And in that we may perceive an apt description of midrash as well, or of the attempts of Ezra to bring the Jews back to the promised land, to recover their history and make the laws contemporary, to adjust the structures of their present life to one that must never be forgotten, the story of which must be told from generation to generation: one long, elaborate talking cure.

7

Reb Derrida's Scripture

The Jew is an expert at unfulfilled time.

—Arthur Cohen

The work of Jacques Derrida is the latest in the line of Jewish heretic hermeneutics, but in contrast to Freud and Lacan, he openly preaches the doctrines of displacement, "dissemination," "deconstruction," and "difference." Derrida's deconstructive methodology is openly aimed at any of the "fathers" of philosophy or psychoanalysis who have preceded him. We can best begin to understand him by examining his polemics against Lacan, especially in their debate over the meanings of Poe's short story "The Purloined Letter."

Without becoming too deeply involved in the endless complexities of Lacan's and Derrida's readings and counter-readings of "The Purloined Letter," we might suggest nevertheless that the theme of the *purloined letter* can characterize our entire problem of Rabbinic versus Patristic hermeneutics. For as we have stressed, it was above all the question of the nature of the letter, the integrity of the text which was at stake. Stealing the "letter" is stealing the text, stealing Scripture, and transferring meaning elsewhere. It might be said that Paul stole the letter from the Jews and tried to abolish it by transcending it through the spirit. And Freud stole the letter from the Jews by displacing Moses, their greatest prophet, the father of their religion and giver of the letter of the law itself. Lacan reacts against the theft of the letter from Freud and tries to return it to its place. In his view, the moral of "The Purloined Letter" is that "a letter always arrives at its destination."[1] This Derrida attacks, accusing Lacan of the sins against which the Jewish prophets always inveighed: reification, pinning the signifier to the signified, and idol-worship—or ideal-worship—the idealization of this "transcendent signifier." But what will Derrida then do to counter Lacan's subtle theft of the letter? Erect a new religion of *Writing*, (although I think it would be better to translate Derrida's key term, *Écriture*, as *Scripture*, which it can also mean in French).

Derrida vs. Lacan

In the debate over Poe, Derrida accuses Lacan of a number of sins. Lacan's treatment of the letter, according to Derrida, implies a vision of truth dependent on two major (and according to Derrida, false) values. The first is that truth is defined in terms of "adequation in a circular return and proper course from beginning to end, from the place of detachment of the signifier to the place of its re-attachment."[2] This circuit guards the letter against any threat of loss. Since for Lacan, the "letter"—of both Poe's story and of the psyche in general—signifies the (missing) phallus, the "circle of adequation" guards this phallic doctrine of Lacan's as well. The phallus, as Lacan's signifier-of-signifiers, acquires, claims Derrida, an "ideality" which is, in effect, transcendental. When combined with Saussurian linguistics, which privilege spoken over written language, this evolves into what Derrida calls a "phallogocentric doctrine of the signifier."[3] We shall presently explain Derrida's theory of the Speech-versus-Scripture controversy, but here it will suffice to mention that in Derrida's view, Lacan is guilty of postulating a phallic doctrine of the signifier that is phonic, vocal, present, nonmutilatable.

The second value ascribed to Lacan by Derrida is what Derrida calls "veiling/unveiling as the structure of a lack."[4] In Lacan's doctrine of the phallus as signifier, castration—the missing phallus—implies that there is a "proper" place of the signifier, an origin and destination, which when unveiled shows nothing. The "proper place" of the truth operation is this place of lack-of-being from which the signifier is detached for its circuit.

These two values, in Derrida's view, are indissociable. Above all, the Lacanian letter must not be "lost," or in Derrida's word "disseminated." Returning it to its point of departure, as Lacan would do, is the old view of truth as "appropriation," "property," "univocal belonging," "self-identity"—values constantly criticized by Derrida in his attack on Western metaphysics (in Chapter 1, we have noted this same theme in his treatment of metaphor). Underneath Lacan's system lies a transcendental identity, guaranteeing the entire safe-circuit of truth, protecting it from disintegration, irrevocable loss, ambiguity, or infinite indivisibility. Derrida would instead mutilate the letter, diffract and free it from its rigid circuit, rebel against the law of the phallus. And that he does in the name of writing, free play, the hymen, dissemination. Derrida would break Lacan's covenant of unity between signifier and signified, abolish any illusory point of stability, which is some present signifier underlying all others, or some ideal *full word*.

> The letter can always not arrive at its destination. Its "materiality" and its polysemy result from its divisibility, its ever-possible partition. It can always be broken up irrevocably and this is what the system of the symbolic, castration, of the signifier, of truth, of the contract and so forth try to shield it from. . . . dissemination threatens the law of the signifier and of castration as a contract of truth. Dissemination mutilates the unity of the signifier i.e. of the phallus.[5]

Mutilation of the phallus (perhaps by circumcision), rebellion, irrevocable loss, breaking the covenant—again, all these are themes of the Jewish heretic hermeneutic we have been tracing from Freud. Nowhere do these themes coalesce so much as in Derrida's theory of writing, the cornerstone of his thinking. Derrida claims that Lacan's letter is above all a vocal letter, a present, spontaneous, nondivisible speech: "Lacan's word is (full) of itself, of its presence, of its essence," guaranteeing the circular return to itself. Its self-identity is an ideal meaning within the unity of the spoken word, or, to put it more bluntly, "The insistence of the Lacanian letter is the sublation of writing in the system of speech."[6] Derrida will "reclaim" the purloined letter by defining it "properly," through his notion of writing. In effect, what we have in Derrida's polemics is another version of the Scripture-versus-Logos controversy, quite openly stated. Derrida's destruction, fragmentation, dissemination of the "letter" is part of his attempt to replace it with the structure of writing. Barbara Johnson perceptively remarks that Derrida actually recommits the sin of which he accuses Lacan: "filling in of a blank," Lacan's blanks, and the blanks of signification in general—despite all of Derrida's protests to the contrary. To be honest, Johnson says, Derrida's infinite play of the signifier would require him to play beyond the *seme* (a minimal semantic feature in a system of sign-production) of writing itself. Isn't Derrida, in effect, transforming "writing" into "the written"? she asks.[7]

The Curtained Torah

The question is most suggestive. Derrida's choice of the seme "writing" to oppose to the logocentrism that he takes as the fundamental sin of Western thought is curious. Why such an investment in *Écriture—Scripture?* In *Glas,* in an obviously autobiographical passage, Derrida writes,

> In Algeria, in the middle of a mosque that the colonists had changed into a synagogue, the Torah once out from *derrière les rideaux,* is carried about in the arms of a man or child. . . . Children who have watched the pomp of this celebration, especially those who were able to give a hand, perhaps dream of it long after, of arranging there all the bits of their life.
>
> What am I doing here? Let us say that I work at the origin of literature by miming it. Between the two.[8]

Glas was written shortly after the death of Derrida's father, just as *The Interpretation of Dreams* was written after the death of Freud's father, facts which have much to do with the nature and structure of both works. Indeed, what *is* Derrida doing here: unveiling the veiled scroll, the veiled writing, and here arranging all the bits of his life? Gayatri Spivak interprets this passage as the Jewish child's inspiration at the absence of the Father, or truth behind the veil, an inspiration that allows him to place his autobiography in that place, producing the "origin" of literature.[9] We would also again find here the displacement of the Father, and reappropriation-repetition (miming the origin) of his Scripture. Like Freud, like Paul, like Jesus, Derrida, in spite of all, is another in the line of Jewish prodigal sons, who try to perpetuate the law in its own transgressions, indeed who make the very concept of "perpetuating the law through its transgressions" the center of their theory. Derridean deconstructionism, like psychoanalysis, is a repetition of the structure it seeks to analyze. In deconstructionism, we have again Holy Scripture, the return of the Rabbinic repressed. Like Freud, Paul, and so on, Derrida's displacements of fathers–founders–Text in the name of *free play* and opening the closed system of metaphysics becomes an ideology that forecloses anything outside itself. Derrida's project is not simply an overthrow of Western metaphysics, but a subtle subversion of the possibility of any thought outside his own. The doctrine may be free play and dissemination, but the application is a grinding of any and every text through the deconstructive machine in endlessly laborious, predictable, and repetitive reading. Derrida repeats/reappropriates Freud's repetitive/appropriative dream: to be the father–founder of the Text. And, as Derrida tells us: "There is nothing outside the text."[10]

Derrida's Freud is eminently a man of texts. Tracing the evolution of Freud's thought about the nature of the psyche in the well-known essay "Freud and the Scene of Writing," Derrida stresses Freud's abandonment of a mechanical model for one of a writing machine in Freud's essay "Notes upon the Mystic-Writing Pad" (1925). For Derrida's Freud, finally, "Psychical content will be represented by a text whose essence is irreducibly graphic. The structure of the psychical apparatus will be represented by a writing machine."[11] The neurological pathway is the effect of "traces," deferred, inscribed, and reconstituted from memory signs. Perception is inscription. The "trace," the sign of the absent other, becomes the constituent factor of memory. The mechanism of consciousness is "deferral"; in the beginning is postponement, not presence. For Derrida, the "effects of deferment" constitute the essence of Freud's discoveries about the psyche and culture in general.

The key to *The Interpretation of Dreams,* Derrida claims, is its dominant metaphor of writing to describe the psychic apparatus and the dream text—the dream as preverbal lithography, an alogical and metaphonetic script, a palimpsest. The dream's displacements are a new form of writing, a secret writing, which Freud's acts of reading attempt to decipher. But Freud knows that there is no fixed key, no univocal meaning for each symbol, and that meaning must be determined as much by context as by content. Such insights fit well into Derrida's theory of Writing, a theory which is not dominated by any authoritative logos and where the signifier and signified cannot be radically distinguished. Freud's method is not a decoding by which one can merely substitute the proper signified for the signifier, but one that allows for the play of signifiers. Moreover, the materiality of the signifier does not disappear before the signified in any kind of "translation" of the dream language.

The Freudian conscious appears to Derrida not as a transcription of an unconscious text, for one cannot say that there is a preexistent text, or a text "somewhere else." Ultimately, the unconscious is a text woven of traces, difference, presences constituted by deferment. The danger is to misunderstand Freud, freeze the energy of the writing machine, and attempt final translations or ends to interpretation. The dream is polycentered and follows a nonlinear spatiotemporal logic; it must not, therefore, be read as a language following the linear progressions of speech, but rather as a kind of hieroglyphic writing capable of endless reverberation and meaning.

Derrida's theory of Writing is most clearly articulated in the first part of his major work, *On Grammatology*. In Derrida's view, the whole history of metaphysics from the pre-Socratics to Heidegger has assigned truth to the logos and has debased and repressed writing. The spoken word has been considered closer to the immediacy of inner truth, and the written word dismissed merely as a secondhand, exterior, and insubstantial double, a "fallen secondarity" (this attitude is most evident in Aristotle's first chapter of *De Interpretatione*, examined in Chapter 1). It is Derrida's intent to break the link of truth with logos, destroy the science of signification, which privileges the phonic signifier, and redeem writing from its fallen condition. Above all, writing is the realm not of presence—to which the voice is so intimately linked—but of absence, deferment, difference, all of which become value terms for Derrida. Phonocentrism and logocentrism, on the other hand, depend on the determination of being as presence, whether it be the presence of the thing to sight; or presence as substance, essence, or existence; or the self-presence of the cogito, consciousness, or subjectivity, and so forth.

The immediacy of speech, the proximity of voice and being, lends itself to this privileging of the *phone* as the nonexterior, noncontingent, nonempirical signifier. A whole series of oppositions thereby arises: worldly–nonworldly, outside–inside, ideality–nonideality, universal–nonuniversal, transcendental–empirical. The dead-writing–full-speech opposition located by Derrida as the underlying demon has its direct counterpart in all those issues in the conflict of interpretation that we have so far traced, especially the letter–spirit debate at the heart of the Jewish–Christian encounter. Derrida at every point stresses what he calls the "onto-theological" basis (and bias) of Western thought.

The very act of differentiating between signifier and signified, and postulating their exteriority to one another, belongs to the "epoch of [the institution of metaphysics and especially to the epoch] of Christian creationism and infinitism when these appropriate the resources of Greek conceptuality." Derrida is at pains to uncover the "metaphysical –theological roots" of sign theory, in his view a theory entirely dependent on the distinction between *sensible* and *intelligible*. This distinction leads to a differentiation of signifier and signified, and postulates a signified that is purely intelligible: an absolute, ideal logos, or the infinite creative subject in medieval theology: "The sign and divinity have the same place and time of birth. The age of the sign is essentially theological."[12] In this epoch, the signifier is castigated as a mediated exteriority, which becomes the exteriority of writing in general. The signified is always related immediately to the logos and only mediately with the signifier, i.e., writing.

Derrida's claims are doubtless true for the Christian tradition. What we have stressed as unique about Rabbinic thought, however, is its escape from precisely this Greco-Christian ontotheological mode of thinking. Writing, the Holy Text, is the privileged term in Rabbinic thought; it not only precedes speech, but precedes the entire natural world. Rabbinic thought does not move from the sensible to the ideal transcendent signified, but from the sensible to the Text. And that is Derrida's path as well, a movement from ontology to grammatology, from Being to Text.

And yet Writing has been viciously condemned and despised, and the letter castigated as a carrier of death. We are of course familiar with this stigma in Christian polemics against the Jews, but Derrida traces it from Greek philosophy to Rousseau, Saussure, Husserl, and even Lévi-Strauss. Fallen, literal, dead writing is contrasted to a natural, living, metaphoric writing, which is venerated: such as the "voice of conscience" as divine law, or writing of the heart, etc. Such a natural writing, however, is not grammatological, but "pneumatological."[13] Of course, this position is eminently Christian, though Derrida does not explicitly say so. This natural metaphoric writing was prepared for by the concept of the Book of Nature in medieval theological thought. However, the grounds for this position were laid in the letter–spirit polemics of Paul. The contrast of the writing of the soul as opposed to that of the body, of interior to exterior, consciousness to passions, and so forth, dictates that one must return to the "voice of Nature" that merges with the divine inscription. The significance of this stance for the romantic goes without saying.

Derrida's analysis is especially intriguing because he shows the persistence of this ontotheology even in the likes of such as Saussure. Writing is seen not merely as exterior, but as a threatening exterior from which spoken language must be protected, a corrupt menace that can erupt and disrupt the self-enclosed interiority of the soul. "Saussure," Derrida tells us, "sees writing as perversion, debauchery, dress of corruption and disguise, a festival mask that must be exorcised, i.e., warded off by the good word," even as "original sin." Derrida is a vigorous polemicist, adept at contorting the arguments of others to fit his own needs, but his particular ironic use of passages and adjectives to characterize negative attitudes towards writing is curious: "the perverse cult of the letter-image," "the sin of idolatry," "perversion that engenders monsters," "deviation from nature," "principle of death," "deformation, sacrilege, crime," "the wandering outcast of linguistics," "expatriated, condemned to wandering and blindness, to mourning," "expelled other." The descriptions are overtly theological, and the logos described as the "historical violence of a speech dreaming its full self-presence, living itself as its own resumption. . . . auto-production of a speech declared alive . . . a logos which believes itself to be its own father, being lifted above written discourse,"[14] is obviously the Christian logos, the son dreaming himself to be his own father, born into the flesh and elevated above all texts and written discourses. And that exiled, wandering, mourning, condemned outcast, accused of unredeemed original sin, is the Jew, the carrier of the letter, the cultist of Writing.

It is odd that Derrida does not mention this most obvious point, especially since he is so much at pains to uncover the theological assumptions of this privileged logos. In essays written earlier than or contemporaneously with *Of Grammatology* and collected in *Writing and Difference,* Derrida quite clearly makes the connection between the Jewish–Christian polemic and the history of philosophy. Derrida discusses this question in his essay on Edmond Jabès, in pieces on the French Jewish philosopher Emmanuel Levinas, and in the final essay of the collection, specifically written for the book, "Ellipsis." In this piece, he argues for a "negative atheology," a writing that transcends the closure of "the book" for the openness of "the text," and signs the essay, "Reb Derissa," this signature becoming the last words of the book. The change from *Derrida* to *Derissa,* from *-ridda* to *-rissa* in French could be one of those word plays of which Derrida is so fond. If we take *risée* to mean *laughing* or *laughable,* Derrida might be trying to have the last laugh on us as *Reb,* or Rabbi, Derrida in an elliptical Rabbinic–commentary–text–play. (*Derrière les rideaux* in the aforementioned passage about the taking out of the Torah scroll in Algeria also contains the syllables of the name *Derrida*.)

But before we let Derrida have the last laugh, which so many contemporary critics seem all too willing to do, let us take him a little more at his word. Derrida, of course, would object, since his very theory of free play, part of his inheritance from Nietzsche, demands that we not take him at his word, for there is no proper, single, absolutely true meaning, and thereby Derrida can evade any theoretical attack and again assert his mastery over all critics. So let us take Reb Derissa, the laughing Rabbi, more in the spirit of midrash than Nietzsche, viewing his play as serious play, as a commentary, that is, as an extension of the text. As Gayatri Spivak writes, one of the distinguishing characteristics of Derrida's method, which he inherits from Freud, is an interpretive process in which attention is paid to the minute details of a text, to syntax, to the shapes of words—the dream's treatment of words as things.[15] This is in effect a species of midrashic play, which makes Derrida's deconstructions so different from Heidegger's or Nietzsche's destructions. Geoffrey Hartman writes of *Glas:*

> Derrida lets language be, not by nonchalance but by giving it its "to be," as he deconstructs a text or moves within, rather than simply against equivocation and the multiple register of words. . . . Let no one mistake this nonbook: *Glas* is of the House of Galilee.
>
> Who else but Reb Derissa could go from the dissemination/castration of flower/sword theme to the Warburg dictionary (59 ff.), and by an error . . . as bewildering as any semanticist has traced, show how sword and lily lie together (lis/lit) in 'glaieuil' (gladiolus:schwertlilie) with its *blütenstaub* of phonic or dialectic resonances: glageuil ("klage," "deuil"?); glaudius, claudio, gaudio ("joy"?); glaviol ("viol"?); glaive, glai, englasi, ("terrify," "freeze," "glaze"?); glai, glace, glisser?[16]

In a more serious moment, laughing Reb Derissa asks at the end of his essay on Levinas:

> Are we Jews? Are we Greeks? We live in the difference between the Jew and the Greek, which is perhaps the unity of what is called history. We live in and of difference, that is, in hypocrisy. . . .
>
> Are we Greeks? Are we Jews? But who are we? Are we (not a chronological, but a prelogical question) *first* Jews or *first* Greeks? And does the strange dialogue between the Jew and the Greek, peace itself, have the form of the absolute speculative logic of Hegel, the living logic which *reconciles* formal tautology and empirical heterology. . . . Or, on the contrary, does this peace have the form of infinite separation and of the unthinkable, unsayable transcendence of the other? To what horizon of peace does the language which asks this question belong? From whence does it draw the energy of its question? Can it account for the historical *coupling* of Judaism and Hellenism? And what is the legitimacy, what is the meaning of the *copula* in this proposition from perhaps the most Hegelian of modern novelists: "Jewgreek is greekjew. Extremes meet?"[17]

The history of philosophy, then, is ultimately an argument between Jews and Greeks. Levinas, in his many influential philosophical works, has taken up the side of the Jews. The influence of Levinas on Derrida is not often mentioned. Derrida openly acknowledges it in his long essay on Levinas, "Violence and Metaphysics: An Essay on the Thought of Emmanuel Levinas," which he opens with Matthew Arnold's famous quotation from *Culture and Anarchy* about Hebraism and Hellenism being the two major forces of culture. Philosophy, Derrida points out, is Greek in the most ethnocentric sense, and even Husserl and Heidegger, who seek to subordinate and transgress this metaphysical tradition, are not free from its Greek elements. "Here," writes Derrida, "the thought of Levinas can make us tremble. At the heart of the desert, in the growing wasteland, this thought, which fundamentally no longer seeks to be a thought of Being and phenomenality, makes us dream of an inconceivable process of dismantling and dispossession." In Levinas, Derrida finds an attempt to "dislocate the Greek logos" and thus to dislocate our identity and the principle of identity in general, which is a summons to depart from Greece, to liberate thought from the "oppression" of the same and the one, an "ontological, or transcendental oppression," which Derrida claims is the source of all oppression in the world.[18]

With Levinas, we have a "parricide of the Greek father Parmenides,"[19] as Derrida puts it; the theme of murdering the primal father and usurping origins again resurfaces here, in Derrida as in Freud. As pyschoanalysis was a species of parricide and giving of a new law, so Derridean deconstructionism will murder the father–founders of philosophy and disseminate a new writing, which, in the wake of the overthrow of the same and the one, celebrates pluralism, otherness, distance, and difference. Parmenides' disregard of the other is "totalitarian" and tautologous according to Levinas and Derrida, and the rebellion against the Greeks is a species of liberation.

To Love the Torah More than God

In place of presence, or *ousia,* Derrida will put his writing, which is "more 'metaphysical' than speech."[20] The writer can absent himself better, address himself more effectively to the other, can better defer, delay, multiply signs, and renounce the immediacy of violence. And Levinas teaches Derrida that Hebraism in its connection to the letter has much to show us. He quotes three passages from Levinas:

> To admit the action of literature on men—this is perhaps the wisdom of the West, in which the people of the Book will be recognized.

> The spirit is free in the letter, and subjugated in the root.

> To love the Torah more than God [is] protection against the madness of a direct contact with the sacred.[21]

The latter quotation Derrida takes from Levinas' *Difficile Liberté: Essai sur le Judaism,* which is worth examining somewhat more closely for the Judaic sources of some of Derrida's ideas. "To love the Torah more than God," is the title of the essay, a title which has its source in the famous statement found in Midrash and Talmud: "So should it be that you would forsake me, but would keep my Torah" (Yer. *Hag.* 1:7; *Eichah Rab.,* intro. ch. 2). The statement is striking and eminently Rabbinic—the Torah, the Law, Scripture, God says, are even more important than He. We might say that Freud, Derrida, and the other practitioners of Jewish heretic hermeneutics do precisely that: forsake God but perpetuate a Torah, Scripture, or Law in their own displaced and ambivalent way. Derrida, above all, keeps faith with the poor exiled scapegoat, writing.

Levinas, it should be noted, writes a specifically post-Holocaust French Jewish philosophy. He is himself a survivor of the camps, and the experience of the absence of God is the main concern of the aforementioned essay. The absent God of the Holocaust, the God who obscures His face, paradoxically becomes for Levinas the condition of Jewish belief. The loss of a consolatory childish heaven, the moment when God withdraws from the world is the moment which calls for what Levinas describes as an "adult" faith. In this faith, the adult can triumph only in his own conscience and suffering, a suffering that is no "mystic expiation of the sins of the world" but an ordeal of an adult, responsible man, "a suffering of the just for a justice without triumph, [which] is lived as Judaism."[22] The relation of man and God in Judaism is

> not a sentimental communion in the love of an incarnate God, but a relation between spirits, through the intermediary of a teaching, the Torah. It is precisely a *discourse, not* embodied in God that assures us of a living God among us. . . . [To love the Torah more than God is] protection against the madness of direct contact with the Sacred without the mediation of reason.
>
> . . . . The spiritual does not present itself as a tenable substance but, rather, through its absence; God is made real, not through incarnation, but, rather, through the Law.[23]

Judaism is then defined as this trust in an absent God.

In his commentary on this essay, Richard Sugarman makes the important point that in Levinas, absent justice does not mean that justice is nonexistent, and goes on to say:

> This decisive metaphysical distinction between the phenomenon of absence and that of non-existence, so long obscured in the history of philosophy, is central to Levinas' analysis and needs to be made more explicit. Absence is not that which is merely somewhere else, convertible into presence by a change of position, perspective, or interpretation. That which is absent is not necessarily an entity in another place, hidden from view, or unintelligible. Rather, the phenomenon of absence positively informs our understanding of everyday events with considerable concrete significance.[24]

This point is crucial to understanding the schism between Jews and Greeks, and between Derrida and the history of philosophy: *absence does not equal nonexistence*. Absence, otherness, the "trace," all of Derrida's primary terms, comprise a vocabulary that seeks to evade the either/or trap of being-or-nonbeing of Greek philosophy. Derrida's reality is not being, but absence; not the one, but the other; not unity but plurality, dissemination, writing, and difference. Reb Derissa, too, claims that "the spiritual does not present itself as a tenable substance, but, rather, through its absence," and he is the new high priest of the religion of absence.

Derrida agrees with Levinas that hearing is higher than seeing, for seeing the face is presence, *ousia*. And it is in discourse with God, the absent other, that Levinas founds his metaphysics. Writes Derrida in his commentary:

Via the passageway of this resemblance, man's speech can be lifted up toward God, an almost unheard of *analogy* which is the very moment of Levinas's discourse on discourse. Analogy as dialogue with God. "Discourse is discourse with God. . . . Metaphysics is the essence of this language with God." Discourse with God, and not in God as *participation*. Discourse with God, and not discourse on God and his attributes as *theology*. And the dyssymmetry of my relation to the other, "curvature of intersubjective space signifies the divine intention of all truth." It "is perhaps the very presence of God." Presence as separation, presence–absence—again the break with Parmenides, Spinoza, and Hegel, which only "the idea of *creatio ex nihilo*" can consummate. Presence as separation, presence–absence as resemblance, but as a resemblance which is not the "ontological mark" of the worker imprinted on his product, or on "beings created in his image and resemblance" (Malebranche), a resemblance which can be understood neither in terms of communion or knowledge, nor in terms of participation and incarnation. A resemblance which is neither a sign nor an effect of God . . . "trace of God."[25]

Derrida's analysis of Levinas is also an apt summary of the trends of Rabbinic thought discussed in the second chapter: a hermeneutic developed independently of ontology, a text whose writing is precisely this presence-as-separation, and which is structured not around a hierarchical great chain of being, but conceives of metaphysics as a discourse with God, an endless dialogue, disputation, interpretation, and reinterpretation. Christianity, on the other hand, is bound to a Greek ontology, in which beings are related to Being via participation, not discourse, incarnation, not interpretation, and in which absence is intolerable. In the reconciliation of the logos with itself, what is other must be returned to the same. If Judaism is the experience of the infinitely other, it is precisely this irruption of the totally other that threatens the Greek logos, and the Christian holy family as well. Like writing, the Jew is historically the castigated other, intruder, threat, scapegoat, exile, idolater, and it is surely no accident that those who take up arms against the paternal logocentrism of Western thought would be Jews; though secularized, though having forsaken the Jewish God, they "keep the Scripture."

But Derrida would go further than Levinas. What if the world is not the effect of the "trace of God," but the reverse: what if "God is the effect of the trace," he asks.[26] Elsewhere, Derrida acknowledges his debt to Levinas for relating the concept of the trace to the critique of ontology.[27] In replacing ontology and semiology with grammatology, Derrida claims that "difference" precedes all similarity; and the trace, which is pure difference, does not "exist" as a presence outside of plenitude, but is the condition of that plenitude and anterior to all signs: "The trace is in fact the absolute origin of sense in general. Which amounts to saying once again that there is no absolute origin of sense in general. The trace is the difference which opens appearance and signification."[28] The language of Derrida here is, to say the least, a kind of mystification, an attempt to transcend a system of thought he discredits by using its own tools, in a species of via negativa.

The origin is this "trace," which is the ultimate signified, a presence–absence that "carries in itself the problems of the letter and the spirit, of body and soul, and of all the problems whose primary affinity I have recalled." The entire history of metaphysics, with all its dualisms and monisms, has striven to reduce the trace and subordinate it to the full presence of the logos, and thereby humble writing. This onto-theology determined the meaning of being as presence, *parousia,* life without difference, from Plato to infinitist metaphysics: "We must not therefore speak of a 'theological prejudice,' functioning sporadically when it is a question of the plenitude of the logos; the logos as the sublimation of the trace is *theological.*"[29]

But is not the reinstitution of the trace also theological, one may ask Derrida. Is not the trace dialectically related somehow to all it negates? Well aware of these objections, Derrida tries to warn against any "return to the Book" in the final essay on Jabès at the end of *Writing and Difference.* The book must finally be closed and the text opened, for "If closure is not end, we protest or deconstruct in vain," says Derrida, echoing Paul's "If Jesus is not risen, our faith is in vain" (1 Cor. 15:14). The echo of Paul is most revealing; it is a variation on Jewish heretic hermeneutic. This time, however, it is not something so crass as an incarnate god which will supplant Scripture, but something more subtle and far more Jewish: a Text, a "writing beyond the Book." This writing "feigns, by repeating the book, inclusion in the book," but does not let itself be enveloped within the volume. It is "the writing of the origin, writing that retraces the origin, tracking down signs of its disappearance, the lost writing of the origin."[30] What takes place of the origin is not absence but a trace; this is origin by means of which *nothing* has begun. And thus another slaying of Moses, dispossession of the father and reappropriation of the father and origin, a new writing, but this time one that seeks to secure itself from all future displacement by concocting a mystifying nonterminology, which at every instant eludes definition.

Derrida's specific form of Jewish heresy is not metonymy become metaphor but metonymy run amuck, metonymy declaring itself to be independent of all foundations and yet claiming to be the origin and law of everything. *Difference* means *to differ* and *to defer or postpone.* Whereas Levinas claims that at some point there must be an unveiling and redemption—though postponed, it must come—Derrida chooses to stay in exile, to infinitely defer and differ—to play. Derrida will play in the interval between book and book, play with the "center," and decenter origin through writing. He will define the center as only a hole; writing the hole "we plunge into the horizontality of a pure surface, which itself represents itself from detour to detour."[31] Derrida will have the last laugh on all pretenders to his new throne of writing. No one can slay this new Moses. At any point, he can take another detour, or choose to differ. Derrida's feigning the book is also a feigning of philosophy, feigning seriousness, feigning play.

Derrida is the prodigal son, but unrepentant, enjoying his escapade. Geoffrey Hartman notes this theme in Derrida's theory of "dissemination," the play with "that which does not return to the father. . . . It is a word cast on the waters, a prodigal without hope of return. The 'imitation of nature' now takes nature literally and substitutes the image of a creative self-scattering for the 'collected' imitation of a divine pattern: the 'legein' of the logos."[32] This logos cannot return to the father, and no text can return to its author. Thus Derrida, too, is free from the sins which his own prodigal texts might commit. He is secure from all attack and reproach. This new setting aside of the father frees him from the original sin to which Freud was so grimly tied in his own theory of parricide. Derrida will joyfully carry out his "cruci-fiction of the Word," as Hartman puts it,[33] with no remorse. He will remain in exile, and exile the logos with him. He would not come home and he would not welcome the Messiah.

If psychoanalysis might be seen as one attempt to cure the neurosis of the Jew in exile, deconstructionism could be thought of as another. Kafka's comments about the exilic character of psychoanalysis could be adapted to Derrideanism: "It is no pleasure to busy oneself with psychoanalysis, and I keep as far away from it as possible, but it has at least as much reality as this generation. The Jews have always produced their joys and sorrows at almost the same time as the Rashi commentary relating to them, and here again they have done so."[34] Marthe Robert comments on this remark that Kafka finds the meaning of Freud in the context of the present-day joys and sorrows of Jewish life, which is unique in that "it is obliged since time immemorial to provide its own commentary, it has always been a written life, produced not before but almost *at the same time* as the writings that explain it."[35]

Let the commentary then, says Derrida, the writing developed in the endless delay of exile, be all, and be playful. Let exile subvert being and logos entirely. "Encounter is separation," Derrida writes, echoing Levinas in a proposition that "breaks the unity of Being. . . . by welcoming the other and difference into the source of meaning." This "original exile from the Kingdom of Being, signifies exile as the conceptualization of Being, and signifies that Being never is, never shows *itself*, is never *present*, is never *now*, outside difference. . . . Whether he is Being or the master of beings, God himself is, and appears as what he is, within difference, that is to say, as difference, and within dissemination."[36]

In his essay on "Jabès and the Question of the Book," Derrida traces the connection between the Jew and writing, defining Judaism precisely as "the birth and passion of writing. . . . the love and endurance of the letter itself." "The Jew who elects writing which elects the Jew, in an exchange responsible for truth's thorough suffusion with historicity and history's assignment of itself to its empiricity." For the Jew—and the poet—the book becomes folded and bound to itself, infinitely self-reflective, its own subject and its own representation. The home of the Jew and the poet is the text; they are wanderers, born only of the book. But the freedom of the poet depends, in Derrida's interpretation, on the breaking of the tablets of the law (slaying Moses again): "Between the fragments of the Broken Tablets the poem grows and the right to speech takes root. Once more begins the adventure of text as weed, as outlaw far from the 'fatherland of the Jews,' which is a 'sacred text surrounded by commentaries.' "[37]

Both the poet and the Jew must write and must comment, because both poetry and commentary are forms of exiled speech, but the poet need not be faithful nor bound to any original text. For Jabès, the law, after the breaking of the tablets, becomes a question, and to interrogate becomes a duty. For Jabès it also represents a negativity and difference in God, a dissimulation and hiding of His face, which is the origin of our freedom—and of our writing. Derrida is here attracted to the same theme as found in Levinas: the Judaic sense of the absence of God as His presence, and God's duplicity, His hiding and obliqueness. God's detours are borrowed by man; this infinite detour, or "Way of God," is "preceded by no truth, and thus lacking the prescription of truth's rigor, is the way through the Desert. Writing is the moment of the desert as the moment of Separation."[38]

Here Derrida, too, takes up residence and pitches his tent; between the fragments of the tablets he has destroyed, his texts grow up like "weeds," "outlaws," imitating the ruses and absences and infinite detours of a hiding God. Derrida flourishes in the absent spaces *between* the tablets, *between* Jew and Greek, Rabbi and poet. Absence, Derrida claims, is the "letter's ether and respiration"; signification arises through absence, rupture, fragmentation, the discontinuity of the letter:

> The caesura makes meaning emerge. It does not do so alone, of course; but without interruption—between letters, words, sentences, books—no signification could be awakened. *Assuming* that Nature refuses the *leap,* one can understand why Scripture will never be Nature. It proceeds by leaps alone. Which makes it perilous. Death strolls between the letters. To write, what is called writing, assumes an access to the mind through having the courage to lose one's life, to die away from nautre.[39]

For Derrida, absence is the ground and the content of the letter. This wandering life of the letter expresses itself above all in metaphor, metaphor as the origin of language, beyond being and nothing: "Metaphor, or the animality of the letter, is the primary and infinite equivocality of the signifier as Life. The *psychic* subversion of inert literality, that is to say, of nature, or of speech returned to nature."[40] This mode of metaphor does not return to its natural or proper univocal meaning, but subverts nature. Such a metaphorical letter or word could never become flesh, incarnate, and will not "return speech to nature," as does the Christian logos. Derrida will yet wander among the infinite play of letters of Scripture, between the lines. He is more at home in Scripture than nature, as are the Rabbis.

But Derrida, as we have seen, cannot reconcile himself to remaining somehow within the book; he would pose a final question to Jabès' *Book of Questions,* a question that would finally free him from the epoch of the book and make it no longer the model of meaning. Instead, he will ask if the meaning of being is not a "radical illegibility." This radical illegibility of an era other than the book is not, Derrida claims, "irrational," or something defined by relation to logic and the book. It is, rather, prior, an "original illegibility," which is the very possibility of the book. "The Being that is announced within the illegible is beyond these categories, beyond, as it writes itself, its own name."[41] Again the passion to displace origins, the Jewish heretic hermeneutic, surfaces in Derrida, who places a radical unintelligibility at the origin of his thought, a radical illegibility that constitutes, in fact, his own work. He, too, tries to write beyond the finitude of his own "proper name" with his fantasy of a disseminated name, which he places at the origin. Like Freud, he has his own species of family romance within the family of philosophy, where he can subvert his Jewish–Greek origins and evade any attempt to catch him by taking up residence in the absent spaces between his lines. Derrida will always choose to differ, but he leaves no empty spaces for any others who would differ with him.

He has both foreclosed the history of philosophy and even appropriated the blanks, the nonmeanings, the space of illegibility. Even here, however, he will dissimulate in order to disseminate himself. The ultimate questions he asks of the Book must, he says, sleep. "Writing would die of the pure vigilance of the question, as it would of the simple erasure of the question. Is not to write, once more, to confuse ontology and grammatology?"[42] Derrida has too much to lose if writing should die. He must defer his own questions, or else his radical attack on origins and the Book would lead to his own dissolution and silence. Like Freud, whose murder of Moses was an attempt to recapture his own origins and ward off death, to make himself his own father, Derrida must somehow perpetuate the law, at least be the father of writing lest the parricide become an inadvertent suicide.

Derrida's dissemination is as much a dissimulation as Freud's pretended exegesis of the Biblical text in *Moses and Monotheism.* But the Jewish prodigal sons cannot completely forego Scripture. To attack the European psyche and the Holy logos, to attempt to overturn Western man from within and without is an act of revenge by the exiles—and yet again a defense of the Jewish father. They will try, nevertheless, to recapture the "purloined letter," to redeem Scripture from the abuses it has suffered at the hands of Greeks and Christians. And they will accomplish their victory, above all, through acts of interpretation.

"The original opening of interpretation essentially signifies that there will always be rabbis and poets. And two interpretations of interpretation," writes Derrida.[43] There will always perhaps be war between Jews and Greeks, war over Scripture.

The Talmud (*Av. Zar.* 18a) relates that when the Romans came to take R. Hanina ben Teradion to be burned to death for teaching Torah despite their prohibition, they found him in the act of reading the Torah. As they took him, his daughter began to weep, and he questioned her why. She answered, "I weep for the Torah that is to be burned with you." He answered, "The Torah is fire, and no fire can burn fire itself." They seized him and wrapped him in the scroll of the Torah, heaped faggots around him and lit the pyre. In the moment of his agony, his disciples asked him, "Rabbi, what do you see?" He replied: "I see the parchment consumed by fire, but the letters of the Scriptures are flying upwards."

8

The Critic as Kabbalist: Harold Bloom and the Heretic Hermeneutic

> Hebraism and Hellenism—between these two points of influence move our world. At one time it feels more powerfully the attraction of one of them, at another time of the other; and it ought to be, though it never is, evenly and happily balanced between them.
>
> —Matthew Arnold

> He who is willing to work gives birth to his own father.
>
> —Kierkegaard

The wars between Jews and Greeks, so long fought on Mediterranean and European soil, have come, finally, to America. American literary theory, so long under the sway of the New Critics who came to prominence in the 1930s and 1940s, has been radically transformed in the postwar period. The character of the New Critics, led by such figures as John Crowe Ransom, Allen Tate, Robert Penn Warren, and Cleanth Brooks, was predominantly Southern, agrarian, conservative, and Christian. And T. S. Eliot's neo-Catholicism had left its mark on them all. The New Critical Gospel of formalism—that one must pay attention solely to the formal structures of the words on the page—might be summed up in the famous phrase that Wimsatt and Beardsley took from Archibald MacLeish: "A poem should not mean but be."[2]

The New Critics intended to do away with the sloppy excrescences of "meaning" produced by such unhealthy considerations as, in Ransom's terms: "personal registrations, which are the declaration of the effect of the art-work upon the critic as reader," "historical studies," "linguistic studies," "moral studies," "any other special studies which deal with some abstract or prose content taken out of the work."[3] Criticism must be "scientific," "precise," "objective," respectful of the autonomy of the work of art. Underlying this vision, of course, is a Hellenistic dream of logic, order, form, and lucidity.

For thinkers like the New Critics, the intellectual movements that have swept through Europe since World War II—existentialism, phenomenology, psychoanalysis, structuralism, deconstructionism—are anathema. Yet while the Yale University English Department harbored the New Critics Warren, Brooks, and Wimsatt, it has also more recently nurtured Harold Bloom, Geoffrey Hartman, Paul de Man, and J. Hillis Miller. And this new generation of Yale scholars has been one of the main conduits through which these recent trends in European literary theory—especially Freud–Lacan–Derrida—have entered the United States. The Yale school has met with much resistance from the American literary heartland, and has been resented as a kind of literary mafia, trying to infiltrate and dominate the plain, honest, objective tradesmen of literary criticism. To the plain folk of criticism, the baroque abstraction of these strange imported European fashions—the attempt to erase the distinction between literary commentary and literature itself, and to subvert the traditional hierarchies of author–text–critic–student—seem arbitrary, irrational, willful, and esoteric.

G. Douglas Atkins points out that the Yale school so threatens and unsettles because its underlying aim is, in his words, to "de-Hellenize" literary criticism.[4] Atkins rightly contends that our contemporary battle of the books is not between ancients and moderns, but between Hebrews and Hellenes. The plainstyle critics, as he calls them, have an implicit faith in logic, reason, and order, i.e., in the classic Hellenistic view of things; the Yale school questions the very possibility of order and unity and turns toward a speculative, visionary, and hermeneutic style. Atkins discerns that the Yale critics' "opposition to Hellenism and the classical logos derives from notions strikingly similar to Hebraic and biblical thought."[5] The Yale critics are by no means unaware of these Hebraic tendencies. Bloom is perhaps their most striking representative. With Bloom, the heretic hermeneutic attains full systematic theoretical self-realization. Bloom focuses his efforts on something we have barely touched upon in the authors studied so far: the will-to-power of interpretation. Commentary and exegesis are not innocent. Intensively studying Bloom can bring us to a final fuller definition of the heretic hermeneutic, and to uncover the dynamic that links Rabbinic thought to its prodigal sons.

From the Visionary to the Revisionary Company

Everyone who now reads and writes in the West . . . is still a son or daughter of Homer. As a teacher of literature who prefers the morality of the Hebrew

Bible to Homer, indeed who prefers the Bible aesthetically to Homer, I am no happier about this dark truth than you are.[6]

Chances are that the majority of readers whom Bloom so familiarly addresses here do not in fact consider their Homeric heritage a "dark truth." Bloom, however, has openly declared poetic and critical warfare against the Greeks: in the past decade, he has produced a series of books in which his explicit aim has been to "de-idealize" literature and literary criticism. One of Bloom's central axioms is that making and reading poetry is not a highly refined, humanistic endeavor, but a fierce Oedipal struggle, an open warfare conducted between poets and their precursors, as well as readers and their poets: a battlefield in which the combatants are all engaged in trying to create some kind of original space for themselves. The processes of reading and writing well are not, to Bloom, "polite": "Reading is always a defensive process . . . is defensive warfare."[7]

> Strong poets . . . should always be condemned by a humanist morality, for strong poets are necessarily perverse . . . perverse in relation *to the precursor.* . . .
> If the imagination's gift comes necessarily from the perversity of the spirit, then the living labyrinth of literature is built upon the ruin of every impulse most generous in us. So we are wrong to have founded a humanism directly upon literature itself, and the phrase "humane letters" is an oxymoron. . . . the strong imagination comes to its painful birth through savagery and misrepresentation.[8]

Reading is a defensive act of battle against a precursor text, a necessary misreading.

For such interpretive battles, Bloom arms himself—not with Aristotle and Plato, classical logic or New Critical formalism; he looks not to the idealizing tendencies of Northrop Frye, nor to the despiritualized theories of structural linguistics, nor the nihilistic aspects of deconstructionism—but to Jewish mysticism, to Kabbalah.

Bloom has written over a dozen books in the past two decades, beginning with studies of the major figures of the romantic era: *Shelley's Mythmaking; The Visionary Company: A Reading of English Romantic Poetry; Blake's Apocalypse; Yeats;* and *The Ringers in the Tower.* But in 1973, Bloom published the first of four theoretical books, which have proposed startling new theories of criticism: *The Anxiety of Influence* (1973); *A Map of Misreading* (1975); *Kabbalah and Criticism* (1975); *Poetry and Repression: Revisionism from Blake to Stevens* (1976); and even a novel—*The Flight to Lucifer: A Gnostic Fantasy* (1979). Though some might not think it too large a step from Shelley to Gnostic fantasies, Bloom's path from the visionary to the revisionary company has been long and involved.

Perhaps the best place to begin is *The Anxiety of Influence,* in which Bloom first fully articulated his new, radical "manifesto for an antithetical criticism," before he discovered Kabbalah. The key to this work, I think, is Bloom's quotation from Kierkegaard: "He who is willing to work gives birth to his own father."[9] Like Freud and Derrida, Bloom is obsessed with the question of origins.

At the root of Bloom's anxiety in *The Anxiety of Influence* is the despair over not having been self-begotten, at not being one's own father; for the question of birth is ultimately an attempt to overcome death. The primal wound for Bloom is to have been "thrown" into a world not one's own; the primal passion is to reverse one's fall by recreating that world in one's own image, by recreating and rebegetting oneself, thereby becoming one's own father, capturing the power of giving life. Hence the themes of *Anxiety* are belatedness, revisionism, discontinuity, subversion, interpretive reversal—themes that inform all of Bloom's work (and Freud's as well). And hence Bloom considers Milton's Satan "the greatest really Modern or Post-Enlightenment poet in the language. . . . Satan like any strong poet, declines merely to be a latecomer. His way of returning to origins, of making Oedipal trespass, is to become a rival creator to God-as-creator. He embraces Sin as his Muse, and begets upon her the highly original poem of Death, the only poem that God will permit him to write."[10]

In Bloom's vision, poetry is a conflict with God, an attempt at rival divination. The modern poet is heroic because like Satan he refuses the "incarnation of God's son," refuses the creation as ordered by God. Poetic election is a kind of curse, then, because it means belated and ultimately impossible rebellion against one's powerful precursor poet, who functions as God, as it were: a rebellion against culture, history, tradition, all of which exert tremendous influence over the new poet, blocking his own creativity. "The Sphinx, as Emerson saw, is nature and the riddle of our emergence from nature, which is to say that the Sphinx is what psychoanalysts have called the Primal Scene. But what is the Primal Scene for a poet as poet? It is his Poetic Father's coitus with the Muse. There he was begotten? No—there they failed to beget him. He must be self-begotten, he must engender himself upon the Muse his mother. . . . To beget here means to usurp."[11]

The process of this attempted usurpation—Bloom's analysis of the development of the new poet, or *ephebe* as Bloom calls him—becomes the pattern for all acts of reading (and especially the heretic hermeneutic), for essentially what the new poet does in order to clear space for himself is to misread his precursor. Intrapoetic relations are a struggle between fathers and sons, as in the classic Freudian family romance; and the necessary misreadings are at the same time (Freudian) defensive maneuvers of psychic survival. The reader's encounter with the text is no different, in effect, than the new poet's encounters with his predecessor texts, and this encounter is governed by the same Bloomian laws: "The influence relation governs reading as it governs writing, and reading is therefore a miswriting, just as writing is a misreading. As literary history lengthens, all poetry becomes verse-criticism, just as all criticism becomes prose-poetry."[12]

The boundaries, then, between commentary and text dissolve—the ephebe is as much a commentator on previous poems as is the critic. Both in effect are exegetes, grapplers with a Text, which each tries to appropriate for himself in a manner wherein the belated commentary somehow gains power over and appropriates the power of the initial Text, reversing the roles so that, in Wordsworth's famous phrase, "The child is father to the Man." Though Bloom's academic specialty was indeed romantic poetry, finally it is not Wordsworth who guides him along the path to rebirth, but more ancient intimations of immortality—the great revisionist interpretive systems of Gnosticism and Kabbalah: "An implied anguish throughout this book is that Romanticism, for all its glories, may have been a vast visionary tragedy, the self-baffled enterprise not of Prometheus but of blinded Oedipus, who did not know that the Sphinx was his Muse."[13]

The Revisionary Ratios

What, then, are the laws that govern the anxiety of influence, the birth and development of a poet, a reader, a commentary, a text—terms that all become interchangeable in the process? In his first attempt to "map" the process in *Anxiety of Influence,* Bloom proposed six "revisionary ratios."[14] I paraphrase them as follows:

1. *Clinamen (swerve).* Bloom takes this term from Lucretius, who defines it as the *swerve* of atoms that allows for change in the universe. In the universe of poetry, it is the swerve or movement *away* from the precursor by the new poet: a corrective movement asserting that the precursor has been accurate only up to a point, and that the ephebe will now move in the direction the precursor failed to follow.

2. *Tessera (completion and antithesis).* This term is taken from the ancient mystery cults, where it denoted a token of recognition. In Bloom's schema, this is a further development of clinamen. Here the new poet "completes" his precursor by retaining the precursor's terms but meaning them in another sense, taking them further.

3. *Kenosis (emptying out).* The word comes from Paul, for whom it referred to Jesus' emptying himself out of his own godhood, his humbling himself to become human. In this phase, the later poet, so to speak, empties himself of his own imaginary divinity, seeming to cease being a poet. However, this act simultaneously empties the precursor as well, and is subtly another maneuver for power, which Bloom calls a "breaking-device similar to the defense mechanisms our psyches employ against repetition—compulsions; *kenosis* then is a movement towards discontinuity with the precursor."[15]

4. *Daemonization.* This is a Neoplatonic term for the movement which is the new poet's attempt to set up a Sublime counter to that of the

precursor. He seeks a power in the parent–poem that in his view does not belong to the precursor, but lies just beyond him.

5. *Askesis*. This term, taken from the practice of pre-Socratic shamans such as Empedocles, denotes a movement of self-purgation towards solitude, in which the later poet yields up part of himself in order to separate himself from others, including the precursor. But in so doing, he simultaneously effects an *askesis,* a truncation of the precursor's poem.

6. *Apophrades* (the Athenian unlucky days when the dead returned to inhabit their former homes). In this final state, the later poet returns from his solipsism to open his poem to the precursor, but in a new way—out of strength rather than weakness—and the effect is such that the later poet appears to have written the earlier poet's work.

At first glance, these terms might appear confusing and difficult. Bloom has continually revised them in his subsequent three books, refining his concepts but nevertheless keeping their basic structure. In *A Map of Misreading* he elaborates the insight, barely touched upon in *The Anxiety of Influence,* that "the Revisionary Ratios have the same function in intrapoetic relations that defense mechanisms have in our psychic life."[16] He matches the Freudian schema of defense mechanisms to each of his revisionary ratios: reaction formation to clinamen; reversal and turning against the self to tessera; undoing to isolation, regression to kenosis; repression to daemonization; sublimation to askesis; and introjection and projection to apophrades.[17] Bloom then adds a third set of parallels, matching each revisionary ratio and psychic defense with the classical rhetorical tropes. Clinamen, for example, corresponds to the trope of irony, tessera to synecdoche, kenosis to metonymy, daemonization to hyperbole, and askesis to metaphor.

After writing *The Anxiety of Influence,* Bloom came across the work of Gershom Scholem, the famed scholar of Jewish mysticism. Bloom claims that he then realized he had been working on a Kabbalistic model all along, and proceeds in *A Map of Misreading* and *Kabbalah and Criticism* to further complicate his already baroque schema by matching up the revisionary ratios, psychic defenses, and tropes with a fourth parallel series: terminology from the kabbalistic theory of creation. But we are getting ahead of ourselves.

It is not yet necessary to examine Bloom's overt advocacy of Jewish mysticism as an interpretive paradigm to perceive his Rabbinic tendencies; they seem to me already evident in *The Anxiety of Influence.* Bloom is unusual only in being more acutely aware of and unembarrassed about his dependence on and exploitation of theological models than others. Part of the way I want to read Bloom is through *his* relationship to *his* precursors— that is, through his *own* revisionary ratios. He, along with Paul, with Freud, with Derrida, belongs to the tradition of heretic hermeneutics I began to define in the previous chapter. The kinds of displacements and discontinuities, the need to slay Moses and give the New Law, to rewrite origins and usurp the father, to make the son one with the father—above all through acts of revisionary interpretation—ties all these figures together. The heretic hermeneutic as a complex of identification and displacement is, I think, ultimately what Bloom maps in his misreadings.

That Bloom locates this subversive revisionary impulse in Kabbalah and Gnosticism, instead of within Rabbinic tradition, itself is a misreading we will later have to investigate; for, in essence, the Rabbinic tradition contains within it, even in the legalistic writings, the mechanism for its own interpretive reversals, a mechanism clearly at work, for example, in the famous Talmudic passage about R. Eliezer's dispute with the sages. In that passage, the majority of Rabbis force God to say, "My sons have defeated me, my sons have defeated me." In fact, one of the keys to understanding what some perceive as the bewildering excesses and fantastic nature of Rabbinic thought—especially in its midrashic form—is precisely the concept of revisionism. And it is Bloom who has given us our most profound insight into revisionist philosophy and psychology.

The Revisionary Warfare of Christian Exegesis

Indeed, Bloom's revisionary ratios may also be the most accurate guide to the interpretive warfare between Jews and Christians which we traced earlier. The movements of clinamen and tessera correspond to the Christian striving to correct and complete Hebrew Scripture. The New Testament declares emphatically that it is *new* and the Hebrew Scriptures now *old;* that is, though chronologically prior, they are no longer complete, authoritative, primary. The birth and figure of Jesus constitutes a decisive *swerve* that serves to complete the precursor text. As Bloom writes, tessera is the "later poet's attempt to persuade himself and us that the precursor's Word would be worn out if not redeemed as a newly fulfilled and enlarged Word of the ephebe."[18] Jesus comes, the Gospel of Matthew assures us, not to destroy but to *fulfill* the law (Matt. 5:17). The incarnation of the poet in Bloom's schema corresponds to the incarnation of the new Christian god. Clinamen and tessera depend on an act of "poetic misprision" (a necessary misreading and misinterpretation of the precursor text). And so, the apostle Paul tells us, the Greeks and Jews know not whereof they speak, no longer possess the true meaning, the correct interpretation. With Jesus only is the veil rent, and the true sense of the Bible now made manifest; without Jesus, all is yet darkness. To the Jews, of course, this is all extreme misreading of the text.

Kenosis and daemonization work to repress the memory of the dead.[19] The very term *kenosis* is taken from Paul to describe Jesus' *emptying out* his divinity to become human, an action which simultaneously empties the "Old" Testament of its divinity. Its words are now superseded by the centrality of the Incarnational Event. This act also isolates the ephebe and undoes the father–precursor. In Bloom's succinct formula, echoing Freud: "Where the precursor was, there shall ephebe be, but by the discontinuous mode of emptying the predecessor of *his* divinity, while appearing to empty himself of his own."[20]

Further following Bloom's schema, the New Testament sets up its own "counter-sublime" to the Hebrew vision as part of the attempt to repress its precursor; the New Testament constructs an entirely new image of the divine and relation of divinity to the world. But complete repression of the precursor is never possible, according to Bloom. Using Freud's insight that tradition is "equivalent to repressed material in the mental life of the individual," Bloom claims that daemonization allows the ephebe to "augment repression, by absorbing the precursor more thoroughly into tradition than his own courageous individuality should allow him to be absorbed."[21] In parallel fashion, the Old Testament is not discarded, but absorbed, and seen as a foreshadowing of the New Gospel.

The next movement, of askesis, or purgation, involves a kind of struggle for sublimation, and an ensuing solipsism. Askesis is the "contest proper, the match-to-the-death with the dead." (Though Bloom, in his own revisionary reading of his precursor Freud, asserts that poetic sublimation is not—as Freud would have it—the sublimation of the *sexual* instincts, but of the *aggressive* instincts.) With energy turned on himself, the new poet wrestles with his precursors to attain a new solitude and independence. Using Freud's insight from *The Ego and the Id* that sublimation is related to identification with the object, but a distorted identification which can even transform into the opposite, Bloom sees poetic sublimation as a kind of "self-curtailment which seeks transformation at the expense of narrowing the creative circumference of precursor and ephebe alike."[22] This movement involves a certain sacrifice and estrangement from the precursor and all other selves in its harsh egocentric expression of the new poetic will.

But finally comes apophrades, the return of the dead, the reincorporation of the precursor. For strong precursors can never be entirely repressed, nor do they completely die, but maintain a power over their successors, returning to haunt them. This final revisionary ratio accomplishes a last inversion by which the former becomes later, and the later earlier. The tyranny of time is reversed: "The triumph of having so stationed the precursor in one's own works, that particular passages in *his* work seem not to be presages of one's own advent, but rather to be indebted to one's own achievement, and even (necessarily) to be lessened by one's greater splendor. The mighty dead return, but they return in our colors, and speaking our voices." The ephebe fulfills "his precursor's prophecies by fundamentally re-creating those prophecies in his own unmistakeable idiom."[23] Similarly, in the Christian revision of the Hebrew Scriptures, the "Old" Testament remains, but now speaking the Christian message, its glory lessened.

The interpretive tradition of *figura,* which became so important for New Testament writers and the Church Fathers, is obviously relevant here. The central idea is that the figures of the Old Testament somehow fore-shadow, predict, and are fulfilled in the New Gospel. Bloom is well aware of this tradition of Scriptural interpretation and its influence on secular literature. He is, however, quite critical of it and argues against its use and advocacy by Auerbach, Tertullian, and the Christian interpreters.

> The basic principle of poetic misprision is: No later poet can be *the fulfillment of any earlier poet*. He can be the reversal of the precursor, or the deforma-tion of the precursor, but whatever he is, to revise is not to fulfill. Unlike *figura,* poetic misprision must be seen as the troping or erroring it is. But so, of course, contra Auerbach and Tertullian is *figura,* and it is surely time to see that *figura* was always a revisionary mode, and so a lie against time. The Old Testament is far too strong, as poetry, to be fulfilled by its revisionary descendent, the self-proclaimed New Testament. "New" means "Early" here and "Old" means "Late" and precisely what the New Testament lacks in relation to the Old is a transumptive stance, which is why the New Testament is a weak poem.
>
> We may wonder whether the idea of figura was ever more than a pious self-deception.[24]

The idea of figura is piously self-deceiving because in defining the connection between two terms, texts, poets, or Scriptures, it postulates a harmless and idealized relation, wherein the second term is the canonical, fulfilling truth; the first term merely signifies itself and foreshadows the second. Figura pretends that this relation is free of anxiety, power-play, misreading, will and counterwill, the agonies of history, and the anxieties of creation.

> The New Testament purports to "fulfill" the Old. Blake came, he sometimes thought, to "correct" Milton. Eduard Bernstein, founder of the modern science of "revisionism," anticipated many after him supposedly seeking to fulfill and correct Marx, a double quest since undertaken with respect to Freud by Jung and many heresiarchs after him. All revisionists, however irreligious, are anagogists, though frequently shallow in their anagogy. Spiri-tual uplift too frequently is exposed as the drive towards power over the precursors, a drive fixed in its origins and wholly arbitrary.[25]

Bloom's intense hostility towards the idea of fulfillment is perhaps a reflection of the Jewish mentality of exile, which we also noted in Freud and Derrida. There is truth, somehow, only in deferment, mediation, interpretation, yearning, agon—but there can be no fulfillment: the Mes-siah has not come. At the same time, Bloom as revisionist must, by his own terms, also be an anagogist; with whom is his struggle for power—what original father, precursor text?

Bloom comes to the critical arena to bring not peace, but a sword, and to expose the power struggle of poetic and critical relations and the illusion of fulfilling idealizations:

Poets no more fulfill one another than the New Testament fulfills the Old. It is this carry-over from the tradition of figural interpretation of Scripture to secular literature that has allowed a curious over-spiritualization of texts canonized by poetic traditions. Since poets also idealize themselves, and their relations to other poets, there is already an excessive self-regard in poetic and critical tradition. Modern theories of mutually benign relations between tradition and individual talent, including those of T. S. Eliot and Northrop Frye, have added their idealizations, so that it becomes an enormous labor to clear away all of this noble obfuscation. [26]

Bloom's intent is to again de-idealize the conventional view of literature and criticism. Eliot and Frye are Bloom's obvious targets here, and Bloom places them in an essentially Christian tradition of Scriptural interpretation.

The Conflict of Literary Traditions: Genteel Classical versus Judaic Antithetical

Eliot's famous essay "Tradition and the Individual Talent," to which Bloom alludes above, articulated Eliot's immensely influential "Impersonal Theory of Poetry." Eliot argued that the poet must, in effect, surrender his personality and individuality to the past tradition. Here there are no dialectical struggles, no Oedipal agonies, no will-to-power. Simply put, in Eliot's words: "The progress of an artist is a continual self-sacrifice, a continual extinction of personality" to what Eliot calls the "mind of Europe," defined as "the whole of the literature of Europe from Homer." This great tradition is composed of a timeless, simultaneous order, whose "existing monuments form an ideal order among themselves." Eliot intends to purge romantic self-expression; the poet, in his famous analogy, is similar to a piece of plantinum that acts as a catalyst, combining chemical elements. He is not a personality, but rather a neutral medium, combining emotions and experiences. Just as in the chemical reaction, the platinum remains "inert, neutral, and unchanged . . . the more perfect the artist, the more completely separate in him will be the man who suffers and the mind which creates." [27]

Bloom considers Eliot's idea of tradition—as a simultaneous order through which one attains freedom through sacramental communion and self-immolation—a "fiction," a "noble idealization, and a lie against time that will go the way of every noble idealization." Bloomian tradition, in contrast, is an agony of conflict, dialectical struggle, a family history of struggles with "inversion, incest, sado-masochistic parody. . . ." Tradition is the anxiety of influence, a passing down, surrender, and betrayal, and Bloom says he would rather model it after the mishnah, the Jewish Oral tradition, than the mind of Europe from Homer. [28]

Jewish tradition, as we have seen, is a study in exile, catastrophe, weeping, endless commentary on a Sacred Text, which alone gave its people a means to endure and a meaning to endure. In tracing the etymology of the word *meaning,* Bloom finds that it is related to *moaning,* and concludes: "A poem's meaning is a poem's complaint."[29] Poetry for Bloom is a Wailing Wall—the place of moaning and meaning. (The Western—or "Wailing"—Wall, of course, is the fragment left of the ancient Temple in Jerusalem where Jews have come for two thousand years to weep their sorrows.)

Where exactly Scripture fits into Eliot's *tradition* is uncertain, though his later return to Anglo-Catholicism, of course, leaves an important place for the New Testament. (Of Eliot's personal feeling about Jews, the less said the better.) But Eliot's tradition certainly had no place for Jewish weeping, wandering, midrashic excess, Kabbalistic speculation, meaning and moaning. Poetry, asserts Eliot, "is not a turning loose of emotion, but an escape from emotion; it is not the expression of personality, but an escape from personality. But, of course, only those who have personality and emotion know what it means to want to escape from these things."[30] Eliot's flight from emotion led him not to the couch of Sigmund Freud, but to the bosom of the Church.

Bloom certainly knows what it means to have personality and emotion, but his response—as has traditionally been that of the Jews in their various agonies, ecstasies, and catastrophes—is to passionately open the Sacred Text to the sorrows of time and history. That precisely is the response of revisionist interpretation. Bloom is so attracted to the Kabbalah of the sixteenth century specifically because, following Scholem, he sees it as a response to historical catastrophe (the expulsion from Spain), and as a solution to the problem of how to accomodate new religious insight in catastrophic times when confronted with a massive and already canonized and interpreted tradition:

> Their [the Kabbalists'] stance in relation to all this tradition, becomes, I think, the classic paradigm upon which Western revisionism in all areas was to model itself ever since, usually in rather indirect emulation. For the Kabbalists developed implicitly a *psychology of belatedness,* and with it an explicit rhetorical sense of techniques for opening Scripture and even received commentary to their own historical sufferings, and their own new, theosophical insights. [Emphasis in original.][31]

For Bloom, the important fact is that Kabbalah is a model for strong poetry and criticism because it forcefully manipulates, opens, misreads, revises the tradition in accordance with its own catastrophic vision—which is exactly what the strong poet and reader must do to their texts. The central principle of his argument, Bloom says, is that

> Poetic influence—when it involves two strong, authentic poets—always proceeds by a misreading of the prior poet, an act of creative correction that is actually and necessarily a misinterpretation. This history of fruitful poetic

influence, which is to say the main tradition of Western poetry since the Renaissance, is a history of anxiety and self-saving caricature, of distortion, of perverse, willful revisionism without which modern poetry as such could not exist.[32]

No trace here of Eliot's extinction of personality, of submission to an ideal, static, ahistorical order—or of merger with Frye's archetypal myths. Eliot and Frye follow an essentially Christian vision wherein the appearance of Jesus, in an act of fulfilling incarnation that is ultimately ahistorical, abrogates the long dialectical agonies of Jewish history. (Of course, Frye comes to literary criticism from divinity school and an overt Christian background. One may also see the Freud–Jung battle over the use of archetypes as a Jewish–Christian struggle.)

In sum, Bloom's anxieties of influence and Kabbalistic paradigms are part of his assault on the entire concept of tradition represented by Eliot and Frye, and this tradition is, above all, Christian and Classical.

Eliot, in fact, makes his relationship abundantly clear in his essay "The Function of Criticism." The difference between classicism and romanticism, asserts Eliot, is "the difference between the complete and the fragmentary, the adult and the immature, the orderly and chaotic." He then approvingly cites Middleton Murray's definition of classicism: "Catholicism stands for the principle or unquestioned spiritual authority outside the individual; that is also the principle of Classicism in literature."[33] Classicism, Catholicisim, tradition, piety, and criticism form one genteel (and Gentile) whole.

Against this compact majority, Bloom formulates his "Manifesto for an Antithetical Criticism." By "antithetical," Bloom means a dialectical principle which is achieved by continual conflict with its opposite, and which, like Nietzsche's "antithetical will," opposes itself to ascetic idealization. Criticism also needs to be antithetical in the rhetorical sense of the word: "the juxtaposition of contrasting ideas in balanced or parallel structures, phrases, words."[34] Furthermore, Bloom also intends Freud's use of the term in Freud's description of the dream-work's disregard for the principle of negation: the dream-work operates antithetically in its juxtapositions and expressions of contraries by identical means of representation.

For Bloom, of course, the poet is by no means an autonomous ego—that, in fact, is the poet's desperate, doomed dream; and the tradition is by no means an ideal, genteel order. The poet is inextricably enmeshed in a complex dialectic with his precursor; and the poet's imagination must necessarily misinterpret his precursor, antithetically swerve. And since criticism is for Bloom but another form of poetry, criticism must also become antithetical, must itself swerve, misinterpret, correct, revise, in acts of "creative misunderstanding." Bloom requires the critic to first read the precursor as the ephebe read him, and then read the ephebe as if he—the critic—were the ephebe's disciple, compelled to revise and correct him in order to claim a living space. "We never read a poet as poet, but only read one poet in another poet.''[35] What we read, in effect, is the poet's entire family romance.

To Wimsatt and Beardsley's formula, "A poem should not mean but be," Bloom counters: "The meaning of a poem can only be another poem." Against Eliot's ideal simultaneous order, Bloom asserts: "Every poem is a misinterpretation of a parent poem"; against Eliot's demand for the poet's self-sacrifice and escape from emotion is Bloom's formula: "A poem is not an overcoming of anxiety, but is that anxiety." "How do we understand anxiety? By ourselves becoming anxious." And despite Eliot's desire for scientific objectivity and impersonal poetry, Bloom maintains, "There are no interpretations but only misinterpretations." Poetry, in sum, "is the anxiety of influence, is misprision, is a disciplined perverseness. Poetry is misunderstanding, misinterpretation, misalliancé."[36]

Later, in *Kabbalah and Criticism,* Bloom will take his theories to the logical extreme. For if there are only misreadings and no poems-in-themselves or poets-in-themselves (only, in his terms, "intertexts" and inter-poets"), he concludes: "If there are no texts, then there are no authors. . . . But we must go further yet—there are no poems, and no poets, but there is also no reader, except in so far as he or she is an interpreter. 'Reading' is impossible because the received text is already a received interpretation, is already a value interpreted into a poem." Bloom will inform us that "the sad truth is that poems don't have presence, unity, form, or meaning."[37] What fragments would T. S. Eliot have shored against these ruins?

Satanic Criticism

Obviously, Bloom's Revisionism would be critical heresy to Eliot—and here we can return to the theme of Bloom as heretic hermeneutician. For antithetical criticism defines itself by its battle with what Bloom calls *canonical* reading. To Bloom, canonical reading is a mere copying of the text, making it identical with itself. And, of course, the notions of copy, mirror, and self-identity all involve the Greek dream of mimesis. But canonical reading, Bloom reveals, is actually a "misreading by religious example" to which poets and critics, as well as scribes and clerics, are all too prone.[38] Bloom's criticism would set interpretation against canon, text against text, meaning against meaning, poet against precursor, and critic against poet.

In this battle against canonization and father texts, it is no wonder that Bloom exalts the figure of Milton's Satan as the "archetype of the modern poet at his strength."[39] Bloom, like Satan in Milton's poem, is clearly in conflict with God over the power of creation; and, like Satan, his rebellion is a product of despair and jealousy at God's attribute of being Himself uncreated. Satan establishes himself as rival creator of his own doomed antithetical kingdom in *Paradise Lost,* and of this action Bloom, who is certainly one of the most well-read critics alive, writes: "I respond to Satan's speeches more strongly than to any other poetry I know."[40] Satan is precisely the state a strong poet or critic must appropriate.

Why, however, does Satan possess this overwhelming inner resonance for Bloom? Does Bloom's appropriation of this particular character—taken from one of the central theological poems of Protestantism—indicate something crucial about the theological warfare at the heart of his critical theory? The step from Bloom as "Satan" to the Protestant tradition (and Bloom sees British and American poetry since Milton as "displaced Protestantism"[41]) to Bloom as Kabbalistic Rabbi is not so far as it may seem. There is, of course, the deep sense in which the Jew has been the "Satan" of Christianity—imagined as the Judas, the apostate, the heretic, the great denier. The Jew is the stubborn rebel who refuses the redemption and fulfillment of the New Testament. Cast onto the margins of society and into exile, the Jew was, whether he like it or not, "antithetical man." We have seen the effects of this cultural and psychological position on Freud; Bloom's relation to the gentile culture of poets in which he is immersed is just as ambivalent, I think, as Freud's relation to scientific Vienna. Even the eclectic terminology of Bloom's revisionary ratios is a curious commingling of Gnostic, Kabbalistic, Hellenistic, and psychological terms. Why the impulse to make what seem like such strained equations between Greek tropes and Kabbalistic categories, which Bloom maintains are also simultaneously Freudian defense mechanisms? Bloom's "simultaneous order" juxtaposes Greeks and Jews in strange intercomminglings in contrast to Eliot's simultaneous order of staid literary monuments. As Derrida puts it, "Are we Jews? Are we Greeks? We live in the difference between the Jew and the Greek, which is perhaps the unity of what is called history. We live in and of difference, that is in hypocrisy."[42]

Bloom's concern is not so much with "difference" as with "discontinuity," though perhaps that is another way of saying the same thing. Why, then, the attempt to assert *continuities* between tropes, Kabbalah, defense mechanisms, poetic images? "Continuity" is that reassuring, non-traumatic, peaceful passage from father to son, the idealized illusory dream of tradition which Bloom is intent on unmasking. It is what he calls the "covering Cherub" that blocks creativity, inhibits and imprisons. Cries Bloom: "Discontinuity is freedom." The clinamen—the swerve from the father—constitutes "creative revisionism."[43] And to Bloom, all poetry since the Enlightenment is precisely a questing for discontinuity, a questing to appropriate a space, and to relieve itself of the vast burden of Eliot's "tradition."

Above all, the new poet must defend against tradition-as-repetition. Bloom's Freudianism is clearly evident here. We have noted that for Freud one of the key therapeutic tasks was changing repetition to remembrance. In *Beyond the Pleasure Principle,* Freud traces the repetition compulsion to the regressive death instinct; repetition is death. In the characteristically

Jewish mode, Freud replaces repetition by recollection, whereas the Christian vision involves a concentration on repetition of the Christian sacrifice. The centrality of the repetitive acts leads to a certain kind of textual repetition—to making meaning identical with itself, utterly present because it constantly and centrally reflects the Incarnational Event. Rabbinic Judaism's central movement is to change repetition to remembrance; that is, with the catastrophic loss of the Temple, the Rabbis instituted rules of remembering through study and interpretation of the Temple laws. From ritual repetition to excessive interpretation is Bloom's path for poetry and criticism as well.

Bloom defines the new poet's task as living the discontinuity of "undoing" repetition, but at the same time living the continuity of recollecting forwards.[44] This recollecting forwards enables the new poet to break forth, while yet tied to the precursor. Recollecting forwards as misreading and misplacement, as discontinuity, enable the new poet to swerve and simultaneously affirm and deny the precursor.

Like the ancient Rabbis, Bloom's task is to open interpretation of the tradition to the present sufferings, catastrophes, and dreams of the generation of sons. The god of poets is not Apollo, says Bloom, not the Greek rhythms of recurrence, but the "bald gnome Error, who lives in the back of a cave."[45] Illumination, Bloom seems to be saying, now comes to Plato's cave not from the front, but from the back, from the darkness itself. The illumination Bloom brings to literary theory also comes, in a sense, from the caves: the subterranean caves of Jewish history and Kabbalah. Interestingly, and coincidentally, Jewish tradition holds that the Zohar, one of the central works of Kabbalah, was composed by R. Shimon bar Yochai, who, in flight from the Romans, is said to have lived in a cave for twelve years: from the dark caves of those in flight from the Greeks and Romans comes freedom, through revivifying interpretation. Bloom, too, is a kind of Judas Maccabeus of criticism, coming forth from the caves to cleanse the defiled Temple (of literature) of its Hellenist conquerors.

In summary, then, Judas Maccabeus and Judas Iscariot—Satan, the refuser, the betrayer. For we have seen Bloom affirm that the modern poet–critic must adopt the stance of Milton's Satan: "The incarnation of Poetic Character in Satan begins when Milton's story truly begins, with the Incarnation of God's Son and Satan's rejection of *that* incarnation."[46] Bloom, too, will reject that incarnation, and replace it with interpretation— the pattern we have seen as one of the distinguishing marks of the Jewish–Christian schism: Christianity replaces the endless discourses of Rabbinic interpretation with the decisive act of presence: incarnation. Bloom, however, like Derrida, does not want this salvation. He, too, prefers to remain faithful to exile, to displacement, to discontinuity; to defer and differ, to assuage his sorrow through rereading—not transcending—the text.

But Bloom is far more gloomy, far less playful, and far more skeptical about the possibility of "deconstructing" the onto-theological tradition of the West, and undoing repression. Interpretation, for Bloom is, finally, a way of opening the text to one's own sorrow—but the precursor can never be done away with entirely. The dead return. Is there any sorrow like unto his sorrow? Bloom thus sees criticism "in danger of being over-spiritualized by the heirs of Auerbach and Northrop Frye, and being excessively despiritualized by the followers of the school of deconstruction." While taking lessons from the deconstructionists, Bloom ultimately positions himself against them; he seeks to "recenter," not "decenter," to "restore and redress meaning."[47]

Like Milton's Satan, Bloom will try to erect what he knows to be a doomed antithetical kingdom of the depths, valiantly carrying on his rebellion against father–precursor–poet–texts, despite the massive forces allied against him. Poetry begins, says Bloom, with the same pattern as *Paradise Lost*—the awareness of the poet that he is falling, that he lies in Hell: "There and then, in this bad, he finds his good; he chooses the heroic, to know damnation and to explore the limits of the possible within it. The alternative is to repent, to accept a God altogether other than the self, wholly external to the possible. This God is cultural history, the dead poets, the embarrassments of a tradition grown too wealthy to need anything more."[48]

Satan becomes the heroic model for the modern poet and critic by refusing to mourn, by organizing the chaos, rousing his minions, "finding what must suffice, while knowing nothing can suffice." In refusing his belatedness and rebelling, Satan, though doomed, attempts to be a rival Creator. If we follow Bloom's logic, what, then, is the ultimate difference between heresy and revisionism—if revisionism is an attempt to overcome the father–precursor–canon through purposeful misreading? To beget and free oneself by swerving? While acknowledging that the "ancestor of revisionism is heresy,"[49] Bloom maintains that heresy alters the *balance* of received doctrine, while revisionism alters the stance through creative correction. This distinction, however, seems to me somewhat tenuous. Bloom, though, claims that the "secular canon" is presumably more open to change than the sacred one; that the secular canon can absorb a new vision, say, of Wordsworth, which will alter the relation between it and the poem. Religious tradition, he thinks, is not so open, cannot subsume heresy, and is thrown off balance. The new vision necessarily becomes another religion, as in the case of Luther's break with Catholicism.

Bloom illustrates some of his observations about canonical readings and misreadings with the Biblical books of Koheleth (Ecclesiastes) and Ben Sirach, the former canonized after a struggle between two Rabbinic factions, the later consigned only to the Apocryphal literature. For Bloom, the irony here is that the canonized Koheleth is in fact a strong revisionist misreading of Orthodox Judaism, a skeptical humanism not at all orthodox. Ben Sirach, Koheleth's "ephebe," is, on the other hand, very doctrinaire: "Koheleth is a revisionist poem, a strong misprison of the Torah, which suffered the happy irony of being absorbed by the precursor against whom it had rebelled, however ambivalently." "The revisionist work, through canonization, is misread by being overfigurated by the canonically informed reader. The derivative orthodox work, left uncanonized because of its belatedness, is misread by being overliteralized by those who come after it, ourselves included."[50]

The case of Koheleth is not, however, merely a "happy irony," an accident, a mistake that slipped past the Rabbis, but represents what I take to be a crucial aspect of the dynamic of Rabbinic thought: the *ability to produce and absorb its own inversions*. The precursor–father–text, in this case Scripture, reasserts its priority by embracing its own revision. Perhaps we can call this the Seventh Revisionary Ratio, to which Bloom—because of his own revisionary stance towards Jewish tradition—is blind. This ability to absorb its rebelling sons is in fact one of the distinguishing characteristics of Rabbinic interpretation; that is, to absorb interpretive reversal and the sufferings of history back into itself, making it appear as if they had been hidden in he father–text all along, awaiting only the proper time for revelation. (This, of course, is the aspect of Rabbinic thought that Christianity appropriates and takes to an extreme.) In other words, if *Paradise Lost* had not been a Protestant poem, and if Milton's Satan had been Jewish, would he, instead, have merely set up another Rabbinical academy and written another commentary, instead of laboring in the domain of Hell?

How, for example, do the Rabbis deal with the case of the literal rebellious son of the Bible (Deut. 21:18–21), whom the text declares in no uncertain terms must be put to death? They claim that the law applies only if the son committed the transgression within three months of the age of thirteen, and only if the trial were completed in the same time . . . needless to say, a difficult set of conditions to fulfill. About this verse, they wrote: "There never has been a stubborn and rebellious son, and never will be. Why then was the law written? That you may study it and receive reward."[51] The literal rebellion, an occasion of denial of the text's authority, is transformed through an act of interpretation into—another occasion for interpretation.

Another example of redeeming rebellion through interpretation is the Rabbinic manner of dealing with other criminal cases that required strict punishments. According to Rabbinic law, the court had to find proof that the defendant committed the crime with malice aforethought; and in order to prove malicious intent, the court demanded that the person in question had to have been explicitly warned before committing the crime that it was forbidden and punishable by death. Moreover, the potential criminal had then to say, "I know and take it upon myself." Only these factors could prove malicious intent. There are so many other limitations and restrictions that a court which in fact was able to pass down a death sentence once in every seven years was called "the killing court."[52]

Through interpretive allowances the figurative faithless sons, wives, rebels, murderers are given as much leeway as possible. Opposing opinions, midrashic speculation, seemingly heretical books such as Koheleth, the Song of Songs, Job, are included in the canon. Up, of course, to a point. What is the point at which revisionism slides over into heresy? Where does symbolic or figurative interpretation of Scripture reach its limit? Where exactly is the point at which New Testament figurations of the Old Testament are not acceptable, and will not be absorbed—where the "old" becomes "new" and the Jews who follow Jesus irrevocably break from the Rabbinic circle, all the time claiming that they, too, are redeeming rebellion through interpretation? Is redeeming rebellion through interpretation the utmost act of piety, or the utmost act of heresy? For there is a point where what the Christians read as "only" figurative, the Rabbis insist on as unalterably literal. The Messiah, for example, must literally restore the Jews to their land and literally rebuild the Temple in Jerusalem, not just "the temple of the spirit." And often what the New Testament writers take as literal, the Rabbis see as figurative.

To be able to answer these questions in full would take us far beyond the scope of our present inquiry. Their function here is to illuminate the ambiguous critical positions of Bloom in relation to Rabbinic thought. For ultimately Bloom's interpretive revisions as prodigal son have the function not of cutting him off, but of returning him to the tradition of his forefathers in that doubly dialectical and ambivalent movement we have traced in Freud and Derrida as well. Bloom indeed recognizes that despite Derrida's posture as arch-deconstructionist and playful nihilist, Derrida too is performing Rabbinic revisions, creative corrections of Western philosophy, by substituting *davar* for *logos:* "Though he nowhere says so, it may be that Derrida is substituting davhar for logos, thus correcting Plato by a Hebraic equating of the writing-act and the mark-of-articulation with the word itself. Much of Derrida is in the spirit of the great Kabbalistic interpreters of Torah, interpreters who create baroque mythologies out of those elements in Scripture that appear least homogeneous in the sacred text."[53]

The reason Bloom takes up Kabbalah as the key to his interpretive system has to do with the way he perceives the intricate relation of revisionism and heresy in Kabbalah. Kabbalah, of course, is a large body of collected mystical teachings and writings accumulated and transmitted over thousands of years, and considered by its students to be a revelation of the inner, hidden mysteries of God, the universe, and the Torah. According to Orthodox Jewish tradition, Kabbalah was known only to those certain select figures in every generation who were on a high enough level of sanctity to receive it, such as the Patriarchs, prophets, and certain Rabbis of the Talmudic period. Kabbalah flourished particularly in Spain in the thirteenth and fourteenth centuries. After the expulsion of the Jews from Spain in 1492, it took root again in the sixteenth-century school of R. Isaac Luria in Safed, Palestine. There were numerous restrictions set about learning it: one had first to be an accomplished Talmudist, married, and of mature age. Kabbalah was difficult, required long years of study, and was potentially quite dangerous in the wrong hands.

One of the most interesting crises in Jewish history, the false Messianism of Shabbatai Sevi in the late seventeenth century, was based on distorted versions of certain Kabbalistic ideas. Shabbatai Sevi, however, captured the imagination of Jews all over Europe and the Middle East. The ensuing disappointment of their hopes when he converted to Islam under pressure of the reigning Sultan was catastrophic. Certain of his die-hard followers, however, Kabbalistically interpreted his apostasy as his necessary descent into the realm of evil to redeem the "fallen sparks" of holiness there embedded—again redeeming apostasy through interpretation. Gershom Scholem has written the magnum opus on the subject, *Shabbatai Sevi: The Mystical Messiah, 1626–1676.*

The debacle of Shabbatai Sevi caused the Rabbis to be even more cautious and restrictive about Kabbalah. When the Chassidic movement arose in the late seventeenth century and openly spread Kabbalistic ideas among the masses, it was fiercely opposed by many Rabbinic authorities, and a civil war of sorts arose in Judaism. With the Enlightenment and emancipation of the Jews from the ghettoes, the mythic, mystical, symbolic, and nonrational world of Kabbalah fell into disrepute, especially among reforming Jewish leaders and historians, who saw in it the worst extremes of the irrational, manic, messianic parochialism of the Jewish temper. Scholem, from 1920 to the present, has undertaken to resurrect Kabbalah and make it respectable to the secular and academic world. His life's work has been the study of the religious genius of Kabbalah and the elucidation of Jewish mysticism.

It is Gershom Scholem on whom Bloom completely depends for his understanding of Kabbalah. And if we are to follow Bloom's own principles for reading, then we must look not only for Bloom's misreadings of Kabbalah via Scholem, but Scholem's as well. If, according to Bloom, there are no texts, but only readings and misreadings, then Scholem's Kabbalah is also not a text in itself, but the misreading of another strong reader. Bloom in fact calls Scholem a "Miltonic" figure in relation to *his* precursors. Before we look more closely at Bloom's adoption and integration of technical Kabbalistic concepts into his poetic theory, we need first to understand Scholem, the precursor. And in doing so we will further clarify the relation of Kabbalah, heresy, and revisionism.

Scholem, Kabbalah, and Heresy

Scholem's reading of Kabbalah is most instructive in helping us understand Bloom's own misprision, not only because Bloom is so dependent on Scholem's work, but also because Scholem's own position as an assimilated German Jew maturing in the years of World War I parallels the equally ambivalent positions of Freud, Derrida, and Bloom towards their own Jewishness. Moreover, Scholem's stance towards the nineteenth-century mode of secular academic Jewish scholarship was emphatically one of rebellion and revision (as Freud's is to nineteenth-century science, Derrida's to the history of Western philosophy, and Bloom's to the literary tradition of the New Critics). David Biale, in his book *Gershom Scholem: Kabbalah and Counter-History,* has exhaustively studied the work of Scholem as historiography; he examines Scholem's work in Kabbalah as Scholem's revolt against and tranformation of the study of Judaism as it had been practiced by the nineteenth-century academic school of the *Science of Judaism (Wissenschaft des Judentums).*

Scholem's study of Kabbalah would be, in Bloom's term, "antithetical"—or as Biale calls it, "counter-history." It intentionally ran counter to the nineteenth-century scholarly view that Judaism was a dogmatic rational religion. In doing so, Scholem simultaneously revolted against the bourgeois assimilated German Jewish culture in which he was raised. Kabbalah and its various manifestations and distortions, including the heretical and disastrous Sabbatian movement, had been dismissed by the dominant scholars of the rationalist school as aberrations in Jewish history—irrational and dangerous excesses. Scholem, in presenting Kabbalah and Sabbatianism not only as valid subjects for scholarly study, but in fact as the very vivifying heart of Judaism, overturned the values and concepts of the *Wissenschaft* scholars entirely.

Scholem's stance towards *his* precursors was, in Biale's words, an act of "radical revision." Biale understands this act of rebellion, however, as also, paradoxically, Scholem's way of "returning to Judaism from a secular background but without adopting Orthodoxy."[54] Biale further shows how Scholem's stance towards his precursors is modelled after what Scholem conceived to be the stance of Kabbalah in relation to the Scriptural tradition of "normative, halakhic" Judaism. Biale's analysis is worth examining in detail because it will ultimately reveal a model for the stances toward Jewish tradition of the major Jewish figures discussed in this book: Freud, Derrida, and Bloom. And it will also help us clarify Bloom's own complicated relation to Jewish tradition, revisionism to heresy, and Rabbinic thought to its own rebellious sons.

Biale calls Scholem's work "counter-history" because Scholem investigates what had been consigned to what Scholem calls the "cellar" of Jewish history: a subterranean, suppressed, subversive, esoteric tradition that had run "counter" to the official version of Judaism created by the historians, and often counter to the official version of Judaism created by the Rabbis. In this cellar, Scholem finds "anarchic breezes," irrational, destructive, heretic, demonic impulses, and Gnostic myths. But a cellar is also the foundation of the house, and Scholem's startling assertion is that these impulses are the very foundation of Jewish existence and vitality;

that they exist at the heart of monotheism; that in this dark cellar lies the secret of Jewish survival. In Bloomian terms, Scholem's revisionist history follows the movements of clinamen and tessera, daemonization and the counter-sublime. For Scholem does not completely abolish the work of his historical precursors, but affirms that their work is incomplete, because they have neglected the true vital forces of the history they describe.[55]

The parallels to Freud, of course, are obvious. Freud also looked, so to speak, into the cellar of the psyche, and wrote the counter-history of the individual; he also found irrational, demonic, mythical secrets in the heart of reason. Scholem, like Freud, is also an eminently dialectical thinker, especially in his view of the relation between the rational and the irrational. Scholem, however, takes a somewhat more positive view than Freud of these irrational forces, though he recognizes, as did Freud, their inherent dangers: especially the danger of trying too harshly to suppress them. The key for Scholem, as for Freud, is to recover the suppressed tradition and harness its vital forces, to recognize the dialectical nature of creation and destruction. Hence Scholem's project, according to Biale, is to revitalize Jewish monotheism (as did the Kabbalists) by fusing rational and irrational, monotheism and myth; for precisely this constant dialectic of contradictory trends and ideas is for Scholem what constitutes Judaism. Freud was also compelled, as we have seen earlier, to this same combination of rational and irrational, science and subjectivity, medicine and myth; but he viewed with less optimism the dialectical tensions that besiege the psyche and society.

This study of Kabbalah, Gnosticism, and Sabbatianism became, in Biale's words, "a powerful weapon for Scholem in shattering dogmatic definitions of Judaism by showing how censored 'heresies' in Jewish history were just as legitimate as the normative tradition. The argument that the Sabbatian messianic heretics were part of Jewish history became the cornerstone of his counter-history."[56] Scholem's critics saw in this revision of Jewish history, however, a manifestation of Scholem's own antinomianism, an attempt to disguise his own subversion by reinterpreting the tradition itself as subversive, and a project to make his own secular interpretation of Judaism part of the normative Jewish tradition. If we disregard the judgmental aspect of these critics, though, and take their statements as descriptive rather than prescriptive, they are extremely suggestive. In interpreting "heretical" as truly a "normative" part of Jewish history, Scholem's "antinomianism" is here a *return to* tradition. And we can say that so also the "heretical" impulses of Freud, Derrida, and Bloom are likewise a dialectical return to Jewish tradition. Scholem's heretic hermeneutic results, not in a break from tradition, but in a vision of heresy as deeply traditional; and he demonstrates this through a special kind of interpretive commentary on Scripture. (What could be more traditional?) The paradox is, via heresy to return to tradition. And this movement is precisely what Scholem locates as the center of Kabbalah, which created, in his words, an "Orthodox Gnosticism"—an oxymoronic term that well expresses this paradox.

Gnosticism, in brief, was a late Hellenistic religious movement that posited a dualistic universe, a hidden beneficent God, and an evil demiurge, responsible for creating the material world and identified as the creator God of Scripture. Salvation would come through gnosis, special knowledge which would allow the redeemed to be free of the shackles of material existence and to attain unity with the good hidden God. The Church Fathers waged a fierce battle with the Gnostics, whom they considered a most pernicious sect.*

Gnosticism, Scholem believes, was appropriated, transformed, and infused into Jewish monotheism as the basis of Kabbalah. This was most certainly a potentially anarchic and explosive move which, in Scholem's view, eventually erupted into the heretical Sabbatian movement, and its later distortion into the theology of "redemption through sin."[52] Scholem maintains, moreover, that Sabbatian heresy and antinomianism were also the real inner destructive forces of Judaism, and the true, though hidden, causes of the breakdown of medieval Judaism and subsequent secular apostasy of Jews in the Enlightenment. At its point of greatest influence, however, Kabbalah was able to revitalize Judaism "by appropriating the normative tradition and transforming it." This method of appropriation and transformation is Scholem's as well, as Biale extensively shows; that is, Kabbalah as a counter-historical interpretation of normative Judaism becomes the model for the secular modern historian's attempt to also place himself within the continuity of Jewish tradition, and through his historical work, revitalize Judaism.[58]

How can heresy and tradition, which are so antithetical, be reconciled? This question is also central for our study of Freud, Derrida, and

---

*Gnosticism, nevertheless, had much influence on both Christianity and Judaism. Rosemary Reuther, following Hans Jonas, perceives Gnosticism as the expression of an alienated, Near Eastern intelligentsia, afflicted with a spiritual malaise because of the collapse of the symbols of the ancestral faith and culture and the suppression of national culture by Roman imperialism.

This group inverted Greek philosophy, the Jewish Bible, and ancient religions in an antithetical, negative, and demonic vision of what had been previously considered sacred. Jewish Gnosticism, Reuther asserts, is the result of a kind of psychic breakdown of those unable to manage the tensions of the conflict with Hellenistic culture; they diabolized one pole of the conflict.

Her analysis illumines the twentieth-century's renewed interest in Gnosticism—especially that of Bloom. The situation is strikingly parallel. "An alienated intellegentsia unable to cope with the conflicts of Hellenistic [secular Western] culture, suffering from a suppressed cultural identity" well describes the predicament of many a post-Enlightenment assimilated Jew (and many a modern non-Jewish alienated intellectual). The result: a diabolizing and inversion of tradition—in Bloom's case, literary tradition. See Reuther, *Faith and Fratricide*, pp. 48–52. See also the classic work of Hans Jonas on Gnosticism, *The Gnostic Religion* (Boston: Beacon Press, 1958), and, more recently, Elaine Pagels, *The Gnostic Gospel* (New York: Vintage, 1980).

Bloom. Scholem puts heresy at the heart of tradition, thus developing a heretic hermeneutic that claims to continue, even as it abrogates, that tradition: tradition becomes something continuous and discontinuous at the same time. This dialectic is exactly what we have been tracing in Freud, Derrida, and Bloom . . . and may serve as a model for understanding how their respective heretic hermeneutics can be part of tradition while simultaneously rebelling against it. Derrida, for example, appropriates scripture while trying to undo the notion of the central text; Bloom appropriates Kabbalah itself both to affirm and deny his links to Jewish thought, attracted to Kabbalah because in his view it is "antithetical" to both "normative" Judaism and "normative" literary criticism.

But herein is Bloom's own misreading. Scholem is more perceptive because he is far more intimate with Talmudic and Kabbalistic literature than Bloom; Scholem knows that the Kabbalists did not consider themselves heretics, but merely receivers of the *tradition*—which is what the Hebrew word *kabbalah* literally means. The great Kabbalists were the very same teachers who created the extensive system of Talmudic law. At issue is the very concept of *tradition*—the key term retranslated by Bloom as *influence*—around which all his theoretical work centers.

Revelation and Tradition

In a key essay entitled "Revelation and Tradition as Religious Categories in Judaism,"[59] Scholem analyzes the development of the concept of tradition—the oral Torah—in Jewish thought. In this essay are reviewed and broadened some of the concepts discussed earlier, in Chapters 2 and 3; it contains insights through which heretic hermeneutics can be further understood. In Scholem's view, the unique Rabbinic concept is that of "revelation including within itself as sacred tradition the later commentary concerning its own meaning"—which, taken to its ultimate extreme, means that "revelation comprises everything that will ever be legitimately offered to interpret its meaning." To Scholem, this classic Rabbinic stance is itself a product of *historical* development. The Rabbis, on the other hand, held that this inseparable relation of revelation and tradition (written and oral Torah) was the atemporal eternal essence of Torah. Scholem, however, postulates a time in Jewish history in which revelation and tradition were separate, in which the concept of revelation, as in all other religions, "referred to the concrete communication of positive, substantive, and expressible content."[60] In other words, the written scriptures alone originally contained this communication; revelation existed first *without* tradition.

Assuming that there once existed within Judaism a revelation or scripture without tradition, Scholem then argues that historical change, the need to transmit the revelation from generation to generation, and especially the need to apply it to the concrete details of life, resulted in the beginnings and growth of a tradition of interpretation. The process intensified in the formative period of Rabbinic Judaism, which Scholem dates from the fourth or third pre-Christian centuries to the second century C.E. That is, not until the time of the Second Temple does the intensely reciprocal relation between written and oral Torah emerge, and only then does tradition begin to itself acquire new religious value, becoming a category of religious thought in its own right, and a medium for creative forces.

In the next step, according to Scholem, tradition acquires religious authority and proclaims certain things to be Torah, thus beginning to invalidate the idea of revelation as a one-time, already established, complete communication. These two sources of authority, written and oral Torah, coexist. But in the third step, the scribes and exegetes include within revelation not just new legal ordinances, but their *own discussions* on all matters ethical, historical, and so forth. What is extraordinary here is their expansion of the concept of the written Torah (revelation) to embrace *their very attempts* to understand it. And they now attempt to deduce and derive the oral Torah (tradition) *from* the written Torah. The process of interpreting the written Torah is the process of unfolding:

> The unfolding of the truths, statements and circumstances that are given in or accompany revelation becomes the function of the Oral Torah, which creates in the process a new type of religious person. . . . The biblical scholar perceives revelation not as a unique and clearly delineated occurrence, but rather as a phenomenon of eternal fruitfulness to be unearthed and examined. . . . Out of the religious tradition, they bring forth something entirely new, something that commands religious dignity: commentary. Revelation needs commentary in order to be rightly understood and applied—and this is the far from self-evident religious doctrine out of which grew both the phenomenon of biblical exegesis and the Jewish tradition which it created.[61]

This commentary is distinctive, moreover, because it is now viewed as being implicit within the written Torah—in Derridean terms, "always already there." Commentary and exegesis of the Torah attain the same status as Torah; they are considered to be latent within revealed Scripture, needing only to be drawn forth by the ongoing generation of scholars. Exegesis and interpretation of Scripture now themselves become Scripture, and emanate, claim the Rabbis, from the same divine source as the written Torah.

Scholem labels this claim "patently absurd" and "fictitious"[62] but understands it as a result of the desire for historical continuity—which is, in fact, the essence of "tradition." Much of contemporary literary theory, however, would view this breakdown of the distinction between text and commentary as quite sophisticated. From the viewpoint of the modern literary theorist, Scholem's conception of the possibility of a pure text without an accompanying interpretation is itself a product of a naive historicism. Like Kant's thing-in-itself, the pure text-in-itself is unknowable; the text, in Derridean terms, is "always already" its interpretation. Geoffrey Hartman, for example, propounds the view that any absolute distinction between literary criticism and literature is naive, and that "There is no absolute knowledge but rather a textual infinite, an interminable web of texts or interpretations:"[63]

> The line of exegesis will therefore tend to be as precariously extensible as the line of the text. The subject matter of exegesis, is, in fact, this "line." Yet criticism as commentary *de linea* always crosses the line and changes to one *trans lineam*. The commentator's discourse, that is, cannot be neatly or methodically separated from that of the author: the relation is contaminating and chiastic; source text and secondary text, though separable, enter into a mutually supportive, mutually dominating relation.[64]

> The interpreter enters the text: there is no pure praxis.[65]

This symbiotic relation precisely characterizes the dynamic between oral and written Torah, or tradition and revelation as Scholem describes it. But in his view, "the achievement of every generation, its contribution to tradition, was projected back into the eternal present of the revelation at Sinai."[66] In Bloomian terms, this movement is the final revisionary ratio of the strong reader, the "metalepsis" or transumption where what comes later is projected backwards to become early, thus enabling the ephebe to transume his precursor. To Bloom, this is the final act, which every strong reader must accomplish. All this occurs, we should note, within the realm of "normative" Rabbinic Judaism; we are not yet in Kabbalistic spheres. Scholem, unlike Bloom, considers this radical stance of the Rabbis (that revelation includes everything offered to interpret it, even the commentary concerning its own meaning) to contain the logic only later taken by Kabbalah to its extreme conclusion. This point is most important, for this normative Rabbinic view of commentary ultimately opens the text to the Kabbalistic revisionary interpretation that Bloom finds so attractive.

We can also here note the striking similarities of these concepts of revelation and tradition, or text and commentary, to those of Freud—especially the notion that revelation unfolds in history through the medium of the interpretive tradition, in Scholem's words, "only because everything that can come to be known has already been deposited in a timeless substratum." In Freud, that timeless substratum is the unconscious, and the process of uncovering what is already there through the language of analysis is the central task. These ideas lead, moreover, to a specific Rabbinic conception of truth, which, as formulated by Scholem, links Freud, Lacan, Derrida, and Bloom (and describes much modern literary theory): (1) that "truth must be laid bare in a text in which it already pre-exists"; (2) that "not system but *commentary* is the legitimate form through which truth is apprehended."[67] All these figures are obviously

engaged in bringing forth truth from the text: be it the text of the unconscious, the text of being, or the text as father–precursor with whom one
must struggle by interpretive misreading. And the form each uses is precisely commentary. In his preface to an anthology of essays by critics in the
Yale school, Hartman comments on the way in which they all move
towards a theory of commentary:

> They expose the difficulty of locating meaning totally within one textual
> source. (Derrida's double analysis is an emblem of this, an expanding hendi-
> adys, exegesis within or upon exegesis.) Each text is shown to imbed other
> texts by a most cunning assimilation whose form is the subject of psychoana-
> lytic and purely rhetorical criticism. Everything we thought of as spirit, or
> meaning separable from the letter of the text, remains within an "intertex-
> tual" sphere; and it is commentary that reminds us of this curious and
> forgettable fact.[68]

In this light, the traditional Rabbinic emphasis on the letter of the text,
so scorned by Christian commentators, clearly becomes part of a larger
sensibility about language and meaning shared by Freud, Lacan, Derrida,
Bloom, and the Yale school. Moreover, when commentary crosses the line
and itself becomes text, we are simultaneously at the point of greatest
piety—and greatest impiety. As Hartman also makes clear, this crossing
over is also a transgression of boundaries, a "contamination," and implies
a fundamental indeterminacy of meaning.[69] This movement Scholem locates at the heart of Kabbalah; and, I would say, it also constitutes the
heretic hermeneutic.

Scholem points out how the interpreter's activity and spontaneity in
opening the text in the context of his own times leads inevitably to a variety
of interpretation—even contradictory interpretation. Rabbinic tradition
accomodates and records conflicting opinions in the oral Torah. But how
far does the opening of interpretation extend? How many contradictory
opinions can be encompassed before the plethora of differing authorities
nears anarchism? Where is the boundary line that finally *cannot* be
crossed? Scholem is not concerned with this line of demarcation; his
position, according to Biale, is one of "religious anarchy." As defined by
Biale anarchy is not a nihilistic destruction of all authority, but a belief in a
plurality of authorities.[70] Infinite interpretation means many authorities.

Scholem clearly understands that the Kabbalists themselves were by
no means heretical anarchists; they believed fully in the laws of orthodox
Judaism.[71] In his view, however, their relentless investigations into the
meaning of tradition and the nature of revelation subtly transformed the
classical Rabbinic viewpoint and opened it to potential heresy and anarchy
. . . . which finally manifested itself in the Sabbatian movement. The
Sabbatians, according to Scholem, essentially *carried to the extreme conclusion what was implicit in normative Rabbinic Judaism*. To Scholem, the
essence of Judaism is precisely a dynamic of constantly contradictory
elements: text and interpretation, reason and unreason, law and mysticism, which are all dialectically interrelated.

How, then, did the Kabbalists—albeit unintentionally—unleash this anarchic potential that finally finds expression in Harold Bloom's Gnostic fantasies? Scholem finds the key in their concentration on the nature of the divine language when they attempt to penetrate the inner meanings of the text. The complex Kabbalistic theory of language has been considered elsewhere.[72] Relevant to Scholem's analysis is the Kabbalistic concept that the divine language of the written Torah was *itself already mediated*—and that the essence of the divine language was the mystical "name of God," which was encoded in the text. Thus the actual text of Scripture is thought to be composed of the various combinations and permutations of this mystical name.

Scholem understands the Name of God to be somehow equivalent to God's essence; he considers it an emanation and creative power that transcends any human language, grammar, or understanding. Itself "above or beyond" meaning—"meaningless," as Scholem puts it—this mystical name is nevertheless the inexhaustible source of all meaning, and thus opens out into infinite interpretation: "This absolute word is originally communicated in its limitless fullness, but—and this is the key point—this communication is incomprehensible!"[73] It bcomes comprchensible only as it is mediated through the interpretations of tradition. (Scholem's concept of the mystical name sounds like Derrida's trace—that elusive originating–nonoriginating mark of meaning.)

Scholem is intent upon making a radical distinction between this mystical "meaningless" word, and the words of Scripture and tradition that interpret and unfold it; for who can know the meaning of the ultimately "meaningless" word? The radical consequence, which according to Scholem the Kabbalists veil, but which he claims to reveal, is finally that there is "no such thing as Written Torah in the sense of an immediate revelation of the divine word":

> The Written Torah is itself mediated; there is thus only and already interpreta-
> tion, only Oral Torah. This Oral Torah, however, still retains the character of
> the absolute, and bears the process of infinite interpretation. As opposed to
> the idea of revelation as a specific communication, revelation which has yet
> no specific meaning is that in the word which gives an infinite wealth of
> meaning. Itself without meaning, it is the very essence of interpretibility. For
> mystical theology, this is a decisive criterion of revelation.[74]

If we substitute for the word *Torah* here its contemporary secular equivalent, *text,* this description of a "meaningless" origin producing endless other text interpretations could have been written by Derrida or Barthes.

Therefore, the only revelation we can know, unless we are prophets or mystics ourselves, is the historical interpretation of continuously unfolding tradition: "The Kabbalistic idea of tradition is founded upon the dialectic tension of precisely this paradox: it is precisely the absoluteness that effects the unending reflection in the contingencies of fulfillment. . . . There is no immediate undialectic application of the divine word. If there were, it would be destructive."[75] Moreover, this unfolding of tradition through the scholar's inquiries is a highly creative process wherein the fullness of the word can encompass contradictions: wherein, indeed, contradictions play a creative role.

Scholem, then, through his interpretation of Kabbalah, has in effect made tradition a creature of history, and history the only divinity we can know. As historian, he then himself becomes part of the tradition. His interpretations are not merely secular analyses, but also part of the ongoing creative process of tradition; his voice becomes part of the voice still speaking from Sinai. He is both inside and outside at the same time. And this is the aim of his research as well; to make the outside inside, and the heretical the traditional. Thus Scholem's fascination with Shabbatai Sevi, and his attempt to place Sevi at the heart of Jewish tradition. And thus Scholem's analysis of Kabbalah as the absorption and transformation of Gnostic heresy into a myth of monotheism.

Freud, Derrida, and Bloom also play the role of outsiders to their respective traditions—scientific, philosophic, and literary. They, too, look to the cellars of self, of existence, and of poetry, seeking there suppressed hidden movements that are heresy to normative views of self, of being, and of literature. In uncovering these secret anarchic forces, they subvert what had been the normative orthodox view and make the outside inside. Heresy becomes tradition, and Freud, Derrida, and Bloom attain a priority and authority over those traditions to which they were heirs. Derrida undoes the very origins of Western philosophy; Freud uncovers the heretical desires at the origins of the self; and Bloom destroys the gentilized tradition of Eliot et al. by uncovering the fierce Oedipal warfare at the heart of poetry. All of these acts are seizures of the original texts of tradition, inversions of the texts through feats of interpretation, and, at the same time, affirmations of fidelity to the secret tradition—which then becomes the real tradition; and these masterly interpreters become the Moses figures who bring the revelation to the people from the flaming mountain.

These interpretive mediations—however secular—become the only revelation possible. We know the unconscious only as mediated through the analyst's interpretation; we know the world only through the free play of interpretation, which has no center; we know a poem only through our misreading of that poet's misreading of a precursor: "The interpretation of a poem is necessarily always interpretation of that poem's interpretation of other poems. . . . All interpretation depends upon the antithetical relation between meanings, and not on the supposed relation between a text and its meaning."[76] This statement by Bloom compares strikingly to Biale's description of Scholem's view: "There is no pure experience of revelation but only a tradition of interpretation of revelation to which one can refer."[77] The tradition of interpretations—as analytic constructions, free play, or Oedipal misreadings—comprise a secular oral Torah, which moves from the status of commentary to revelation, claiming not only equal authority with the text they come to interpret, but asserting that they are its secret and true heart.

In this shadowy area, interpretation *crosses the line,* edges over into revelation; revisionism edges into heresy, and heresy into tradition. This heretic hermeneutic in effect continues, even as it attempts to abrogate tradition. And this is precisely the pattern of revisionary ratios traced by Bloom. But can the rebellion ultimately overthrow tradition? Does the mechanism that opens the tradition allow for the return of the heresies into itself? Perhaps in this book I have been saying the same thing as Scholem, but from another angle: he uncovers the heresy at the heart of tradition in part to justify his own secular exegeses as part of tradition; I suggest that, especially in the cases of Freud, Derrida, and Bloom, there is tradition at the heart of heresy, a tradition that is compelling and reembracing. At the chiasmus, the crossing point, identities reverse. This would be a Seventh Revisionary Ratio (or perhaps Chiasmal Reversal), which Bloom does not mention—a return of the dead to reclaim the prodigal sons. Even Scholem affirms, finally, the value of tradition, which he says "legitimately represents the greatest creation of Judaism." "The tradition is one of the great achievements in which relationship of human life to its foundation is realized. It is the living contact in which man takes hold of ancient truth and is bound to it, across all generations, in the dialogue of giving and taking."[78]

In his view, only one who submits himself to the continuity of tradition of interpretive history gains the freedom and legitimacy to creatively interpret.[79] For Scholem, then, there is no singular authority in the tradition, but rather many centers, many contradictory voices. God, so to speak, has left His text to its interpreters.

Scholem's stance vis-à-vis tradition, finally, is ambivalent—and characteristic of many post-Enlightenment assimilated German Jewish intellectuals, struggling with their new secular identities and yet yearning for a lost Judaism. In this category are figures such as Freud, Martin Buber, Walter Benjamin (a close friend of Scholem's), Kafka, Ernst Bloch, Hermann Cohen, Franz Rozenweig. The Zionist movement, which Scholem fiercely supported (he emigrated to Palestine in 1923), shared this temperament: "The desire for a violent break with all of Jewish history mingled uneasily with the romantic urge to find a revolutionary tradition hidden in Jewish history itself."[80]

Scholem's redefinition of tradition was thus a combination of rebellion and continuity—and this is also characteristic of Freud, Derrida, and Bloom, each in his own way. What Biale says of Scholem's Zionism and work in Jewish historiography also applies to Bloom's Kabbalah, Derrida's text play, and Freud's midrashic interpretations: they "are part of his personal solution to the problem of Judaism in a secular age, a solution nourished by his profound desire for both rebellion and continuity." Counter-history becomes a path back to tradition; rebellion and submission to tradition are dialectically related—in a dialectic made possible, claims Scholem, by the inner dialectic of Jewish tradition itself. Are Freud, Derrida, and Bloom, though, inside this dialectic, or outside; or does outside become inside through the revisionist's attempt to overpower his precursor? Scholem clearly perceives his work as an extension of the tradition of Rabbinic commentary; modern historical science thus becomes part of Jewish tradition, and the Kabbalists, with their revisionary opening of tradition, his precursors.[81]

Revisionary Blindness

Here we can return to our discussion of Bloom's use of Kabbalah, for despite his dependence on Scholem, and his use of the Jewish mystical tradition, Bloom—in an unacknowledged reenactment of his own revisionary ratios—is filled with the anxiety of influence over Kabbalah and never confronts the problem of his own belatedness and adoption of the Kabbalistic model: "I did not set out upon this enterprise with a Kabbalistic model consciously in view. But it was there nevertheless, as I groped to explain to myself why I had become obsessed with revisionary ratios, and then with tropes and defenses of limitation and substitution."[82] For one who has proclaimed that there are no texts in themselves, and has traced the inevitable dialectical agonies of poets, it is strange to hear that Kabbalah was somehow "just there." There is obviously some blindness towards his own relation to texts that Bloom seeks not (at least openly) to overcome.

Bloom, however, challenges every other modern theorist to stand and unfold himself. Be they structuralist, spiritualist, or deconstructionist, they are all alike, claims Bloom, "in refusing to see the degree of revisionary compensation that psychically informs their work." The inescapable truth, he warns, is that "purpose or aim—that is to say, meaning—cleaves more closely to origins the more intensely it strives to distance itself from origins."[83]

But this aphorism applies as much to Bloom as to those he criticizes, and after our study of Scholem, we can more clearly understand Bloom's own antithetical revisionism in his use of Kabbalah. For if we are all belated, all anxious, all struggling ephebes—so is Harold Bloom. What, precisely, is *his* degree of revisionary compensation? How do we read Bloom through his own revisionary ratios? Who is his precursor and to whom is he ephebe? Whom is he defensively misreading, and what father is he rewriting? No one, claims Bloom, who is human can escape what he calls the *scene of instruction,* the scene of authority and priority; one always has an instructor and if one rejects all instructors, one condemns oneself to that earliest of all scenes of instruction: "The clearest analogue is necessarily Oedipal; reject your parents vehemently enough, and you will become a belated version of them, but compound with their reality, and you may partly free yourself."[84]

And so Harold Bloom becomes a belated version of Kabbalists, who in turn are belated interpreters of the belated chosen people in exile . . . .

cleaving to his origins even as he strives to distance himself. But all this remains unacknowledged. He does not discuss his own swerves, counter-sublimes, return of the dead. After commenting that R. Moshe Cordovero's Kabbalistic scheme of God's emanations reveals the structure of images, defenses, and tropes in the central revisionary texts of the last three centuries, Bloom somewhat disingenuously writes:

> This assertion on my part is so weird, as I am aware, that I become a little anxious myself *[sic]*, and must assert that I myself am no Kabbalist, and hold no theosophical beliefs of any kind. I am merely a skeptic, and want only to show the shape of Cordovero's configurations, and put off until later my own surmises as to how these structural resemblances between Kabbalism and Post-Enlightenment poetry could have been produced, aside of course from the doubtless pertinent consideration that whatever misprision of both Kabbalism and poetry is involved, in this analogizing, is of course my own belated and revisionist creation, my own misreading.[85]

And that disclaimer is all. This passage is itself an abbreviated revisionist tract, following the formula of the revisionary ratios. Bloom swerves, attempts to complete his precursors, empties himself out, erects a counter-sublime, and faces a return of the dead. "I am no Kabbalist"—Bloom asserts his swerve from Jewish tradition; he is only a literary critic specializing in romantic poetry. And in this, Bloom follows a familiar pattern, for secular literature has been the refuge of many belated Talmudists and post-Enlightenment Jews. It is part of the attempt to correct and complete (tessera) the now somewhat discredited sacred canon. "I am merely a skeptic"—he empties himself out (kenosis) in the face of these grand sacred and secular canons. But Kabbalah becomes his demonical counter-sublime, the antithetical tradition he opposes both to Jewish and New Critical orthodoxy. And when Bloom asserts that a medieval Jewish mystic has uncovered the structural patterns of modern poetry, he most certainly isolates himself (askesis) from the critical establishment. Finally comes the recognition, though, that his own belated misreading of Kabbalah and poetry, his own personal entanglement with tradition, has returned to haunt him (apophrades) and make him anxious.

We must then put Bloom's own question to him: "the invariable question that antithetical criticism learns always to ask of each fresh instance of the Sublime. What is being freshly repressed? What has been forgotten, on purpose, in the depths, so as to make possible this sudden elevation to the heights?"[86] To answer this question fully, we need now to turn to a more detailed scrutiny of Bloom's use of Kabbalah as the paradigm for modern criticism.

> We need to read more strenuously and more audaciously, the more we realize that we cannot escape the predicament of misreading. Kabbalists read and interpreted with excessive audacity and extravagance; they knew that the true poem is the critic's mind, or as Emerson says, the true ship is the shipbuilder.[87]

For Bloom, as we have seen, the extravagance of Kabbalistic interpretation is an indication of strength, an assertion of the interpreter's claim of authority and priority over the text. It is partly this stance towards the precursor text that makes Kabbalah, for Bloom, the "ultimate model for Western revisionism from the Renaissance to the present." For the precursor text is in this case The Text—Scripture—the ultimate divine writ, which possesses an authority and priority unmatched by any other in the West. Kabbalah, as Bloom reads it, is a massive misprision of Scripture, an enormous labor of interpretation aimed at freeing itself from the burdens of a massive canon, long closed, weighing heavily on all future generations. In Kabbalistic techniques of opening Scripture, in its revisionary misreadings and displacements, Bloom locates "the largest single source for material that will help us to study the revisionary impulse and to formulate techniques for the practice of an antithetical criticism."[88]

With our previous analysis of Scholem in mind, we can now see how Bloom misreads Kabbalah, which he wants to define solely as a rebellion against traditional Rabbinic methods of reading. In contrast to Scholem, Bloom defines "normative" Rabbinic literature as an already "closed commentary" confronting a "closed book," which leaves all successors painfully belated.[89]

> The first principle that revisionism or historical belatedness insists upon is best stated by a double rhetorical question of Novalis: "Who has declared the Bible completed? Should the Bible not be still in the process of growth?" . . . . Of course we all know, as he did, that the authority of institutional and historical Judaism and Christianity declared the Bible completed. Unlike the canon of secular literature, the Scriptures of the West are not still in the process of growth.[90]

Bloom is not aware of the subtleties in Scholem's analysis of the Rabbinic concepts of revelation and tradition, Bible and interpretation. Why does Bloom so obstinately insist upon separating Kabbalah from what he calls "normative Judaism," an absolute distinction not made by Scholem? Many of the most profound students of Kabbalah were also the greatest masters and compilers of Talmud and Jewish law. (R. Joseph Caro, for example, the compiler of the formidable *Shulchan Aruch,* the classic, compact, and authoritative code of Jewish law, was also a member of the Safed circle of Kabbalists, and enjoyed his full share of mystical experiences.) Bloom, it appears, has a special stake in making Kabbalah entirely "antithetical" in all senses of the word, and, in particular, antithetical to Rabbinic Judaism. For only then can Kabbalah become for Bloom a paradigm of his revisionist criticism. Bloom, that is, can accept and incorporate Judaic thought by alienating it from its root, trying to make it discontinuous with Rabbinic tradition and displacing it. Then Bloom's Kabbalah can become a kind of new Torah, which encompasses reality, a paradigm for interpretation to the extent of asserting that the "Zohar, most influential of Kabbalistic books, is the true forerunner of post-Enlightenment strong poetry."[91] We have seen Freud and Derrida performing the same maneuver: taking structural elements of Rabbinic thought, displacing them in an attempt to invert them against their Sacred origins, then reappropriating them as New Laws. Would Bloom be so interested in Kabbalah, one wonders, if he could not so neatly separate it from normative Judaism, could not misprise it as rebellion, as a Jewish Gnosticism trying to free itself from the anxiety of Sacred Scripture?

"Interpretation is revisionism," writes Bloom, "and the strongest readers so revise as to make every text belated and themselves as readers into children of the dawn, earlier and fresher than any completed text ever could hope to be."[92] And this seems to be Bloom's project in relation to Jewish tradition—to revise and invert so that he, Bloom, can become earlier and fresher than the Bible; to reappropriate for himself its authority and anteriority. Or, to use Cynthia Ozick's words, Bloom, like Blake, means to erect a subversive system and to become "the writer, via misprision, of a new Scripture based on discontinuity of tradition."[93]

Ozick, however, accuses Bloom of "idol-making" and "idol-worship" in her fierce denunciation of him:

> But the idol-maker envies the Creator, hopes to compete with the Creator, and schemes to invent a substitute for the Creator; and thereby becomes satanic and ingrown in the search and research that is meant to prise open the shells holding the divine powers. This is the work of "misprision," the chief Bloomian word. Misprision is to Bloom what Satan is to Milton. It is not an accident that the term—before Bloom exercises revisionary misprision upon it—denotes "felony," "wrongdoing," "violation."[94]

Geoffrey Hartman also notes that Bloom's theories form a kind of "counter-theology," and that *The Anxiety of Influence* is a kind of *Paradise Lost* transformed into satanic scholarship: "The eternal Hell revives."[95] It is clear that for Bloom, in his later work, Kabbalah is to Scripture as Satan is to *Paradise Lost*—and more. Kabbalistic revisionism is, in his words, "a reaction to the double priority and authority of both text and interpretation, Bible and the normative Judaism of Rabbinic tradition. Kabbalah can therefore be viewed as a rebellion against the Jewish version of a Scene of Instruction . . . which means that Kabbalah is a collective, psychic defense of the most imaginative medieval Jews against exile and persecution pressing on them *inwardly*."[96] What is appealing for Bloom is that Kabbalah as "Gnostic exegesis of Scripture is always a salutary act of textual violence, transgressive through-and-through."[97]

On the other hand, Bloom recognizes that Kabbalah, despite its mythopoetic symbolism and theosophical speculation, is distinguished from all other Eastern or Western brands of mysticism by a Rabbinic emphasis on *interpretation*. It is "more of a mode of intellectual speculation than a way of union with God. Like the Gnostics, the Kabbalists sought *knowledge,* but unlike the Gnostics they sought knowledge in the Book." Kabbalah can then become for him a "critical tradition" unusual for its inventiveness.[98] Elsewhere, Bloom expresses the ambivalence of the heretic hermeneutic by further saying that "Gnosis and Kabbalah, though heterodox, are at once traditional and yet also de-idealizing. . . ."[99] Thus Kabbalah is at once traditional and transgressive, Rabbinic and Gnostic, sacred and secular.

Geoffrey Hartman perceptively traces the confusion in Bloom's thought:

> Bloom's theory is vulnerable because *priority* (a concept from the natural order) and *authority* (from the spiritual order) are not clearly distinguished; in fact, they merge and become a single, overwhelming *proton pseudos*. By seeking to overcome priority, art fights nature on nature's own ground, and is bound to lose. Nothing *could* grow in the shadow of this first principle except by delusion or misrepresentation. The awareness of a prior greatness is unanswerably strong, and the argument that art—or its survival—is based on misprision looks suspiciously like one which holds that blasphemy is an acknowledgement of God. Disconnection proves to be impossible: each slap is an antithetical embrace.[100]

Indeed, Bloom's "blasphemy" is not simple. It involves what Hartman terms an "antithetical embrace." And when Bloom applies Jewish mystical concepts to poetry, he sticks to a fairly straightforward, nontransgressive version of Kabbalah.

The Theory of Literary Influence and Kabbalistic Terminology: Sefirot, Behinot, Tzimtzum

Bloom focuses on three major aspects of Kabbalah: (1) the doctrine of the ten *sefirot*, or "emanations of God"; (2) R. Moshe Cordovero's discussion of the six *behinot*, the individual and interrelated aspects of the sefirot; and (3) R. Isaac Luria's catastrophe theory of creation through *tzimtzum, shevirat ha-kelim,* and *tikkun—contraction, breaking of the vessels,* and *restoration.*

Luria, in whom Bloom is so interested, comes relatively late in Jewish history (1534–1572). The doctrine of the sefirot, however, is quite ancient. Scholem dates it to around the second century c.e., where it is found in an early Kabbalistic text, the *Sefer Yetzirah (Book of Creation)*. Roughly, the sefirot are conceived as emanations, attributes, lights, crowns, garments of God. The word *sefirah* comes from a Hebrew root *safar,* which is related to *sapar (number), sefer (book), siper (tell, relate), sapir (sapphire, brilliance),* and *separ (boundary).*[101] This intriguing and suggestive etymology indicates that the sefirot are both attributes and sayings—or things and language—at the same time. Bloom and Scholem are especially interested in this linguistic aspect of the sefirot. Using his literary background, Bloom further infers that the sefirot are "complex figurations for God," "tropes or turns of language that substitute for God," not to be confused with allegorical personifications. To Bloom, they are powers of signification, like poems implying commentaries, and rhetorically include the classical tropes from metaphor, metonymy, synechdoche, etc. Bloom perceptively summarizes the character of the sefirot by saying that they "are neither things nor acts, but rather relational events."[102]

Kabbalah speaks of ten sefirot, organized in three triads plus one. These sefirot are not only attributes, but as active emanations are posited as the instruments of creation bridging the infinite God with the finite world. That is, they are not only a topology of the intradivine life, but the underlying structural principles of the world.[103] As such, the sefirot also correspond to man the microcosm: to the organs of the body and man's psychological and intellectual attributes as well. In sum, the interactions of the sefirot simultaneously describe in a series of corresponding reflections: (1) the intradivine life and cosmogony; (2) the psychic and intellectual structure of man; and (3) the literal physical structure and organic existence of man and the universe. To further complicate matters, each sefirah is dialectically compounded of all the others. The complex and infinitely variable relations of the sefirot, their multifarious patterns of combination and recombination from which all things evolve, intrigues Bloom. His insight is that these patterns constitute a theory of influence which is a "direct portrayal of the mind-in-creation."[104] The pathways the sefirot follow are for Bloom the central highways on his map of misreading.

Bloom's Map of Misreading

Dialectic of Revisionism	Images in the Poem	Rhetorical Trope	Psychic Defense	Revisionary Ratio
Limitation	Presence and Absence	Irony	Reaction Formation	Clinamen
Substitution	↕	↕	↓	↕
Representation	Part for Whole or Whole for Part	Synecdoche	Turning against the Self Reversal	Tessera
Limitation	Fullness and Emptiness	Metonymy	Undoing, Isolation, Regression	Kenosis
Substitution	↕	↕	↕	↕
Representation	High and Low	Hyperbole, Litotes	Repression	Daemonization
Limitation	Inside and Outside	Metaphor	Sublimation	Askesis
Substitution	↕	↕	↕	↕
Representation	Early and Late	Metalepsis	Introjection, Projection	Apophrades

At first glance, of course, it is difficult to see how these esoteric theosophic categories relate to poetic influence. Bloom finds the direct connection in R. Moshe Cordovero's analysis of the figurations within and between each sefirah. According to Bloom, Cordovero's theories make him, in effect, a "philosopher of rhetoric" and "dialectician of influence."[105] Bloom finds that Cordovero's six *behinot* (inner *sefirotic* structures) correspond to the six revisionary ratios: just as the ratios map the inner life of the poet, and at the same time his dialectical relation to his precursor, Cordovero's behinot trace the dialectical interplay of aspects within each sefirah, and between sefirot. They chart influence-as-emanation in the process by which each sefirah emanates out from the preceding one. It is important to understand that the sefirot give rise to and emanate from each other in a chain-like formation. The image of links in a chain is taken from Kabbalah *(hishtalshelut)*; the idea is that the lower link of the upper becomes the upper link of the next lower link in an interlocking relation.

Bloom is intrigued by the dialectical interplay between sefirot as a model for the relation between poems, precursors, and ephebes. He also make analogical identifications of the behinot with rhetorical tropes, and with psychic defense mechanisms. Cordovero, Bloom declares, "uncovered the normative structure of images, of tropes, and psychic defenses, in many central revisionary texts, including many poems of the last three centuries."[106] To understand this startling assertion we need to enter with Bloom the strange world of Kabbalah. The following explication of Bloom's intricate analyses attempts to be as clear as possible. In effect, one never can merely "read" Bloom; his own texts are labyrinthine, aphoristic, enigmatic, and oracular. They, too, are poems, which demand commentary.

1. Concealment within the preceding sefira. In the first behina in Cordovero's scheme, as understood by Bloom, we start, not with the sefira itself in question, but with the one that *precedes* it in the linked chain of emanations. The first behina, then, is its hidden aspect in the sefira that precedes it. Bloom parallels this idea to the ephebe's initial relation to the precursor:

> That is to say, in literary terms, the initial trope or image in any new poem is closely related to the *hidden presence* of the new poem in its precursor poem. . . . We are speaking here of the greatest apparent puzzle in poetic influence. . . . A poem is a deep misprision of a previous poem when we recognize the later poem as being absent rather than present on the surface of the earlier poem, and yet still being *in* the earlier poem, implicit or hidden *in* it, nor yet manifest, and yet *there*.[107]

(Bloom's description of this relation well describes the Rabbinic conception of the relation of the oral to the written Torah, of interpretation to text, or of tradition to revelation—that is, interpretation is not something separate, but originally somehow latent in the text, hidden, not yet manifest.

That perhaps is one of the meanings of the famous Talmudic statement, "Every new idea a great scholar will conceive in the future was already given to Moses at Sinai.") For Bloom, the "latency" principle of this first behina helps to explain why so many strong post-Enlightenment poems open with dialectical images of absence and presence, rhetorical ironies, and defensive reaction-formations—this is due to the hiddenness of their origins in their precursors.[108]

2. Revelation within the preceding sefira. The second behina is the new sefira's (or poem's or poet's) emergence from concealment *in* the preceding one. It is still, however, *in* the earlier sefira (or poem). In literary terms, Bloom parallels this movement to synecdoche, where it is also accompanied poetically by images of part and whole. In practice, here a part of a poem seems prophetic of a poem to come.

3. Emergence of the sefira in its own right. In literary terms, Bloom claims, this corresponds to the poem's attempt to attain an illusory self-sufficiency; in psychic terms it corresponds to the defenses of undoing and isolation.

4. Reversal of power to project the sefira outwards. The fourth behina returns a power to the preceding sefira to enable it to emanate the next sefira outwards. As Bloom notes, a reversal of cause and effect is here involved, making the power of emanation dialectical. The corresponding trope is hyperbole, with its reversal of high and low; and the analogous defense mechanism is repression.[109] Here the sefira must repress its own emerging force to make the precursor stronger, or, conversely, must repress the precursor's force to make itself stronger. This reversal of cause and effect sets up reciprocal channels between sefirot, poems, poets, commentaries, texts.

5. Beginning of the emanation of the next succeeding sefira concealed within the newly emanated sefira as the process begins again. This aspect enables the new sefirah, now fully emerged after the preceding four steps, to emanate in its turn, the next sefirah concealed within *it*. The inside–outside movement corresponds to the trope of metaphor and the defense of sublimation.[110]

6. The emanation of the next succeeding sefirah to its place, at which point the process begins again. Lest this become too confusing, we are now talking about a *third* sefirah (poem or poet). The ephebe has now established himself and in his turn has given rise to others—in relation to whom he is precursor. The behinot, as Bloom traces them, reinforce and supplement the six revisionary ratios he formulated in *The Anxiety of Influence*, and like the ratios they are both psychic and linguistic, both mechanisms of defense and tropes.

For his over-arching dialectic of revisionism, however, Bloom turns to the creation theory of Luria, Cordovero's disciple. The behinot are aspects of the larger organizing principles, the sefirot; and the sefirot, while the instruments of creation, do not explain the *ultimate* origins of the world.

Luria provides the cosmogony. For Bloom, the behinot and the Lurianic vocabulary comprise a rhetoric of two distinct set of tropes: (1) the six tropes, corresponding to the six behinot—irony, metonymy, metaphor, synecdoche, hyperbole, and metalepsis; and (2) three Bloomian tropes corresponding to the three major movements in Lurianic cosmogony— *tzimtzum, shevirat ha-kelim,* and *tikkun,* or, as Bloom retranslates them: *limitation, substitution,* and *representation.*

Tzimtzum is perhaps the most innovative of Luria's ideas, because it defines the radical act that makes creation possible, not as an expansive breaking out, but as a withdrawal or contraction of God into Himself, whereby He creates the empty space from which the world can arise. For how else, ask the Kabbalists, could a finite world arise from the infinite presence of God? This emptiness is, in effect, a *concealment* of God, which allows the world to exist without being nullified in its source. Bloom connects tzimtzum to the trope of irony, for it means the opposite of what it appears to say: concealment is revelation; for by withdrawal, contraction, and concealment, God is able to manifest Himself in creation. "The image of His absence is one of the greatest images ever found for His presence." Translated into poetic terms, Bloom interprets tzimtzum as a loss-in-meaning for poetry, and a sense that "representation cannot be achieved fully, or that representation cannot fill the void out of which the desire for poetry arises."[111] Psychically, it means the arousal of defenses.

The second step in Lurianic theory is *shevirat ha-kelim (breaking of the vessels).* Needless to say, these concepts are extremely complex, and we are here giving but the barest outline. The catastrophic breaking of the vessels refers to the inability of a primordial pattern of sefirot to endure, their breakage and fall, which led to the scattering of sparks of light in the physical universe. Redemption—of the Jewish people, the world, and the cosmos—comes through the restoration of these sparks to their supernal source, through the performance of the religious commandments and directives of the Torah. This restorative activity is called *tikkun,* the third movement in the Lurianic dialectic; the term means *reparation, restitution,* literally *mending.*

Bloom connects the breaking of the vessels to the trope of *substitution,* because, he argues, here an original pattern yields to another one . . . that is, one verbal figure is substituted for another. Tikkun corresponds, in his view, to *representation;* the Latin etymology of *repraesentare,* he indicates, is "to bring something absent into presence." But *Kabbalistic tikkun* is not representation in the classical Greek mode. Bloom reads Kabbalah deconstructively: tikkun is not presence as fulfillment (as in the Christian mode of redemption), or presence as being (in the Greek sense), but a work of mending, which is the interminable labor of exile: "What is being mended cannot be meaning, or presence, or form, or unity. Poems don't have any of these, and cannot be transformed into what poems have never been . . . Poems cannot restitute, and yet they can lie against time."[112]

There is, Geoffrey Hartman observes, a strong theological aspect to the concept of representation. As Derrida and his followers show, representation is connected with mimesis, with the image as icon, with Greco-Christian concepts of beings and logos. Bloom and the Yale school share the belief that, as Hartman puts it, "The work of reading is a sullen art reacting against modern iconomania." Or more succinctly: "Art is a radical critique of representation, and as such is bound to compete with theological and other, ritual or clinical, modes of purification." In deconstructing the image, Hartman undoes the connection between aesthetic experience, knowledge, and perception: "Perceptibility—that all things can be made as perceptible as the eye suggests—may itself be the great *classic* phantasm, the mediterranean fantasy, continued even by Romantic and Modernist artists."[113]

In this light, it is easy to see why poststructuralist critical theory mates so easily with the Jewish esotericism of Kabbalah. Kabbalistic description of God's emanations—the sefirot, behinot, tzimtzum etc.—is decidedly nonrepresentational; as Bloom continually emphasizes, it is rhetorical, linguistic, anti-iconic. Kabbalah does not present itself as mystical vision but as commentary, another interpretation, not a new image. Bloom also reads tzimtzum as a deconstruction, so to speak, of an overdetermined tradition; it is a radical definition of God's absence and withdrawal as his presence. (Here again the parallels to Derrida's critique of the classical notion of presence are quite obvious.) In similar Derridean fashion, Bloom interprets the breaking of the vessels as a kind of "separating out and re-forming by and through difference," and thereby the factor which "accounts for the self-negating factor in every poem, the quest for origins that goes against the poem's own intentions,"[114] and explains its word consciousness.

Bloom does note, however, that despite his interpretation, tikkun ultimately represents a final unification and fulfillment (though yet delayed) for the Kabbalists. He chooses, however, to retain (misread) poetic tikkun as only a gesture towards an impossible fulfillment. Kabbalah is, finally, a grand cosmic myth of redemption; but that is not what interests Bloom. He focuses only on its dark side; he reads–misreads *tzimtzum* as *abyss, shevirat ha-kelim* as *catastrophe, tikkun* as a *never-ending labor of meaning* condemned to nonfulfillment. Kabbalistic literature, though, does not read like Satan's speeches in *Paradise Lost*. It is not an impassioned narrative, but a nondramatic discussion of the events it describes. Kabbalah is written in the form of Rabbinic commentary without *Sturm und Drang*.

Bloom, however, is interested in Kabbalah only as a theory of exile, not redemption; anxiety, not fulfillment; cosmic catastrophe, not potential cosmic unity. The ultimate significant fact about Kabbalah for Bloom is that it is a theory in which creation itself becomes exile.[115] Bloom makes his own conscious revision of Kabbalah with the novel proclamation that "tzimtzum was God's anxiety"[116]—His sublimation, purgation, askesis and self-truncation. This Bloomian God—now as anxiety-ridden and isolated as His chosen people—becomes the ultimate model for the poet, who must also pass through the tortuous dialectics of contraction, catastrophe, and mending in an equally regressive process. And this Lurianic theory, asserts Bloom, is "the best paradigm available for the way poets war against one another in the strife of Eternity that is poetic influence."[117] In short, poetic creation comes about through contraction of an internalized precursor: The precursor poem or poet (or even, in Bloom's case, read here "Jewish tradition") undergoes tzimtzum, a contraction or concentration, and is made to vacate part of itself or himself. Since, however, he has been internalized by the ephebe, this is simultaneously the new poet's own self-contraction, and the process of mending (tikkun)—the final complete aesthetic representation—is impossible.[118]

In his own revisionary completion of Freud, Bloom goes so far as to say that the Kabbalistic paradigm is more ultimate than the Freudian.[119] Among other reasons, Kabbalah is superior because of its innate rhetoricity and special belief in the power of language, its view of rhetorical substitution as a kind of magic. Bloom and Scholem do not appear to recognize, however, just how self-conscious this rhetoricity is; moreover, it is precisely this self-conscious rhetoricity that links Kabbalah to normative Judaism—as has, of course, been one of the central arguments of this book. It is at least partially because of the new comprehension of the rhetoricity of language that the sophisticated rhetoricity of the Rabbinic approach to language and texts reappears in contemporary critical theory. This new understanding emerges from the desire to conceive the world in non-Greek, nonclassical philosophic and religious ways.

Kabbalah especially, Bloom points out, "thinks in ways not permitted by Western metaphysics, since its God is at once *En Sof* and *Ayin* [Endless, Infinite, and Nothing], total presence and total absence, and all its interiors contain exteriors, while all of its effects determine its causes." He also perceives that Kabbalah is a radical theory of writing, one that Derrida fails to recognize (revisionary blindness again?) in Derrida's assertion that all Western methods of analysis and interpretation fail to pose the radical question of writing.[120] And in a stunning insight, Bloom reveals that Reb Derissa also has more in common with Isaac Luria than it appears:

> Language, in relation to poetry, can be conceived in two valid ways, as I have learned slowly and reluctantly. Either one can believe in a magical theory of all language as the Kabbalists, many poets, and Walter Benjamin did, or else one must yield to thoroughgoing linguistic nihilism, which in its most refined form is the mode now called Deconstruction. But these two ways turn into one another at their outward limits. . . . Is there a difference between an

absolute randomness of language and the Kabbalistic magical absolute, in which language is totally over-determined?[121]

Analogical Transformation

But to what extent are Bloom's complicated analogical readings of behinot as Greek-tropes-as-psychic-defenses inexact, strained, and suspicious? If Kabbalah is "the most dialectical and negative of theologies that can be found"[122] and for that reason the supreme model for modern poetry, then why the arduous attempt to retranslate its categories back into metaphor, syncecdoche, metalepsis, and so forth? This movement in Bloom's thought is, like everything else he propounds, dialectical. With such analogical correspondences, Bloom's ratios present themselves less as an alternate rhetoric and metaphysics (such as Derrida formulates in his new terminology of "trace," "difference," "écriture," etc.), and become reabsorbed into familiar, classical schemata.

This inversion is another twist of Bloom's endless revisionary reversals, and perhaps reflects his anxiety as the Jewish high critical priest of the romantic poets. After a lifetime of passionate study of romantic poetry, Bloom makes what must be a most painful confession in *Map of Misreading:* "At the center of the Romantic vision is the beautiful lie of the Imagination. . . . but what is the imagination unless it is the rhetorician's greatest triumph of self-deception?"[123] What is the answer except to make Wordsworth a Kabbalist?

> The language of Post-Enlightenment poetry in English, betrays the patterns that were systematized by Moses de Leon in his *Sefirot,* Moses Cordovero in his *Behinot,* and Isaac Luria in his *Parzufim.* As William Wordsworth surely never in his life had heard of Moses Cordovero, I am simply out of it by the canons of the carrion-eaters, Old Style, of my own belated (and benighted) profession. How can the *Intimations of Immortality* Ode show a patterning of images, tropes, defenses, and ratios of revision worked out nearly three centuries before Wordsworth, by thaumaturgical rabbis of whom he had never heard?[124]

Not only Wordsworth, but Browning, Keats, Shelley, Tennyson, Emerson, Whitman, and Stevens—and all major romantics, Bloom shows—follow the patterns set forth by the "thaumaturgical rabbis"; *A Map of Misreading, Poetry and Repression,* and *Wallace Stevens: The Poems of Our Climate* are devoted to showing precisely that.

Kabbalah possessed and dispossessed by Bloom is like Moses possessed and dispossessed by Freud. As Freud both identified with and rebelled against Judaism, taking revenge on the Gentile world with the Jewish science of psychanalysis and usurping the Jewish father at the same time—so Bloom identifies with Kabbalah and uses it to revenge himself on the parental New Critical gentry, the classical Hellenizing idealists of literature who take no account of anxiety, belatedness, the oppressiveness of exile. Yet he also revises–misreads Kabbalah with terms from Greek rhetoric, literary analysis, and Freud. He admits that his reading of Kabbalah is obviously a "displacement" and not direct translation.

These inversions and constant dialectical shifts in Bloom, these leaps of identification and associations, are hallmarks of his theories as well as stylistic characteristics of his prose. They also reflect what he calls the foundation of an antithetical criticism: the "analogical principle": "I seek to take from Freud . . . what he himself took from the poets . . . 'tropism of meaning' or 'wandering signification'. . . . a thinking-by-synecdoche."[125] Via the analogical principle of juxtaposing balanced rival ideas, Bloom can make his central assertion that tropes are mechanisms of defense and vice versa, and that these correspond to Lurianic categories and poetic images. Thus he can instantaneously leap from Kabbalistic tzimtzum as "limitation" to the trope of irony, to the defense mechanism of reaction-formation, to the poetic image of presence-and-absence, to the revisionary ratio of clinamen. Bloom's associationist logic is certainly removed from Aristotelian syllogism; it is more—like Freud's—a Rabbinical midrash over a text. In fact, Bloom would have us learn the following: "The great lesson that Kabbalah can teach contemporary interpretation is that meaning in belated texts is always wandering meaning, even as the belated Jews were a wandering people. Meaning wanders, like human tribulation, or like error, from text to text, and within a text from figure to figure."[126]

The exile of interpretation reappears, but there is something more to this wandering, and to the analogical method, whether in Bloom, Freud, Derrida, midrash, or Kabbalah. Wandering is also displacement, discontinuity, and these are terms of great importance to Freud, Derrida, and Bloom. For each of these thinkers discontinuity and displacement mean inversion, usurpation, in the ambivalent obsession with origins. Analogical thinking helps make possible these revisionary inversions, for in analogy one can neglect the strict laws of continuity and logic, the laws that effect must follow cause, son must follow father, commentary must follow text, critic must follow poem, late must follow early. Analogical wanderings can reverse relations, disrupt normal unities, juxtapose and maintain contradictory thoughts and ideas. This wandering, says Bloom, is governed by "defense"[127] and is a weapon of sorts:

> Meaning, whether in modern poetry or in Kabbalah, wanders whenever anteriority threatens to take over the whole map of misreading, or verbal universe. . . . Meaning swerves, enlarges oppositely, vacates, drives down so as to rise up again, goes outside in the wan hope of getting itself more on the inside, and at last attempts to reverse anteriority by forsaking the evasions of mental space for those of mental time.[128]

The analogical method, then, is Bloom's defense as well: his restless wandering among texts, meanings, Scriptures, religions. The texture of

Bloom's prose is in this sense both midrashic and Miltonic, restlessly moving from allusion to allusion, trope to trope, a feat whose aim appears to be a transumption, a reversal in which Bloom and his theory come to precede all others; and all his precursors, including Freud, Nietzsche, Valentinus, the second-century Gnostic, R. Isaac Luria, and so on are shown to be incomplete. "Transumption," writes Bloom, "murders time, for by troping on a trope, you enforce a state of rhetoricity or word-consciousness and you negate fallen history."[129]

The wandering analogical method allows for sudden shifts, undoings, and recombinations of identities. It also allows Bloom to play out Freud's family romance, which Bloom also takes as the poet's myth of origins. In the family romance, the child fantasizes a changed relation to his parents; he imagines, for example, that he is a foundling, really born of royalty. The fantasy results from the pressure of the Oedipal situation. Writes Bloom, "A changeling-fiction is one of the stances of freedom. The changeling is free because his very existence is a disjunction, and because the mystery of his origins allows for Gnostic reversal of the natural hierarchy of parents and children."[130] The poet similarly makes himself free by altering his relation to his parent poems, changing his stance, revising, becoming a changeling, trying to fictively alter the condition of his birth. And this is Bloom's project as well—and Freud's—and Derrida's—sons of a Rabbinic heritage, which is burdensome and yet unavoidable. Jacob Freud becomes Oedipus the Greek king, not petty bourgeois but royalty, yet at the end Freud returns to meditate on Moses, who the Bible tells us, was himself a changeling.

What shift or change in identity does Bloom seek to accomplish by his anxiety of influence, Kabbalistic dialectics, and revisionary heretic hermeneutics? What simultaneous affirmation and disavowal of origins? If, as Bloom says, the wandering of meaning is governed by defense, then is this the defense of negation, defined by Bloom as a "demonic repressed which is revealed and disavowed simultaneously"?—an act in which "the ego expresses a repressed thought or desire, but continues the defense of repression by disavowing the thought or desire even as it is made overt."[131] And if Bloom cites Freud's notion of "tradition" as the equivalent of repressed material in the mind, then Bloom's analogical method, his restless wandering meaning must be his defense against Jewish tradition, which he simultaneously expresses through Kabbalistic imagery and disavows through rhetorical troping and transumption. And is not this defense as painful and unfulfilling as the long Jewish exile? Ultimately, Bloom recognizes: "No newly strong poet can reduce the significance of the precursor's mastery, because it is not possible for the new or belated poet to transcend the oppositional relationship that is ultimately a negative or dialectical identification with the precursor. . . . There are no dialectics of liberation that will work on the world of the antithetical."[132] The only salvation is not to become a poet.

Like Freud and Derrida, Bloom's identification with Jewish tradition is negative and dialectical. His misreadings of Kabbalah come, I think, from his own attempt to resolve the problem of his own belatedness, his own exile from Scripture, from Judaism; his exile as critic from text, as commentator from creativity. In part, this exile is resolved by the making of "exile" the precise metaphor for the act of creation and interpretation. This is a resolution in the Jewish mode, not as fulfillment of signs in the incarnate word, but as the raising of the Jewish historical condition into a paradigm of existence: to be is to be in exile; to create is to endure catastrophe; to make texts is to already interpret; absence is presence.

And Bloom knows well how full of painful self-contradiction is this position. But self-contradiction, he claims, is the very language of poetry, and the theory of poetry, he asserts, must itself *be* poetry. In even stronger and more desperate language, Bloom proclaims that "the poetic ego is a kind of paranoid construct founded upon the ambivalence of opposition and identity between the ephebe and the precursor."[133] In such a state, misreading is a vital maneuver; how else can one endure the pain of this self-contradiction: "Schizophrenia is disaster in life and success in poetry."[134] Ultimately, then, the poem is a lie—about itself, its precursor, and time . . . but a lie necessary to live.

And so, finally, we must read Bloom the way he instructs us. Literary history becomes a species of biography in which what we trace are one poet's defensive misreadings of another. We have traced Bloom's defensive misreadings of Jewish Scripture as the key to his poetics. We can only leave him with his own grim formula: Reject your parents vehemently enough, and you will become a belated version of them, but compound with their reality and you may partly free yourself. Bloom sees few prospects for freedom in misreading and shares none of Derrida's playfulness; for Bloom, misreading is not free play, but an unrelenting agon of the exiled, who yet yearns to return home.

There is no end to exile for Bloom—or for Derrida—or for Freud. Or perhaps in reaction to a Scripture that endlessly promises but never fulfills, and a God whose absence must suffice for presence, they will make of their exile an antithetical promised land, a "Criticism in the Wilderness," to use Geoffrey Hartman's term, a phrase inspired by Matthew Arnold. Arnold, who so clearly saw the agon of Hebrew and Hellene, wrote of the unfulfilled position of criticism in his era: "There is the promised land, toward which criticism can only beckon. That promised land will not be ours to enter and we shall die in the wilderness."[135]

* * * *

How are we to understand, finally, this complicated interweaving of tradition, revision, and heresy? Only the language of parable, at last, can capture it. Kafka, who so painfully shared Bloom's anxieties of influence and Scholem's secular–religious dilemmas, tells the story in a chilling parable: "Leopards break into the temple and drink the sacrificial chalices dry; this occurs repeatedly, again and again: finally it can be reckoned on beforehand and becomes part of the ceremony."[136]

Kafka's parable is an uncanny description of Freud, Derrida, Bloom, and the Jewish heretic hermeneutic. The Jewish Temple was in fact broken into several times, destroyed twice, and its devotees sent into exile . . . displaced, yet forever yearning to return. In the long interim of exile, study and interpretation of the laws and rituals of the Temple replace the literal sacrifices. In exile, a broken people try to heal themselves through ever more complicated figuration, opening, troping of their Sacred Text . . . trying somehow to make the facts of their historical catastrophe agree with the exalted promises of their Sacred Book. And this can be accomplished only through feats of subtle interpretive reversal: somehow the leopards have entered the Temple and must be accomodated without being allowed to triumph. Excessive troping, transgressive interpretation, Kabbalistic inversion and displacement all appear under the guise of extension and application of the Sacred Book, part of its unfolding interpretation. Bloom is so attracted to Kabbalah as a paradigm for all revisionist thought and as a model for intrapoetic wars precisely for this reason; he recognizes the excesses of Rabbinic interpretation as survival strategies, "necessary misreading" not only against historical catastrophe, but against an overwhelming, authoritative paternal sacred text that can never be overcome.

The leopards—the rebellious, profaning, heretical forces—have become part of the holy ritual itself, through interpretation. *Displacement* not only describes such extreme misreading, is not only a technique of interpretation; it is the only way to survive the endless displacements of Jewish history. Displacement is a necessary re-vision and re-creation of a text which is the only anchor of a people displaced in space. Displacement, in other words, is both the *condition* of and the *answer* to exile. The leopards become part of the ritual. In the school of heretic hermeneutics, holy and profane intermingle; there is something sacred about writing, commentary, and texts, yet these notions are displaced into the profane fields of literature, philosophy, and psychoanalysis. At the same time, under the guise of revisionary interpretation, the Temple and Scripture are profaned. The lines become crossed: who knows now which is the holy, and which the profane: which the leopards and which the priests?

Appendix

Rabbi Ishmael's Rules Four Through Eleven: General and Particular

In the first instance—which is Rule Four of R. Ishmael *(clal u-frat)*—the provision is made that when a general rule is followed by an explicit particular, the rule is *limited* to the specified particular. This means that particulars in question are not to be taken as merely illustrative examples of the general, but that the contents of the latter are to be *restricted* solely to those particulars. An example may be taken from Deut. 22:11, "Thou shalt not wear a *mingled stuff [shatnez]*, wool and linen together." The general term *mingled stuff* is followed by two particulars, *wool* and *linen*, and the Rabbis thus infer that the prohibition of *shatnez* refers only to a mixture of wool and linen *(Mishnah Kilayim* 10:1).

In the second case—R. Ishmael's Rule Five *(prat u-clal)*—when the specification is followed by a *general* rule, *all* that is included in the general applies; the preceding particulars in this case are taken as merely illustrative examples of the general, in contrast to the previous case in Rule Four. The text of Exod. 22:9 states, "If a man delivereth to his neighbor an ass, or an ox, or a sheep, or any beast to keep, and it dies. . . ." Here the particulars, *ass, ox,* and *sheep* precede the general term *beast.* The inference is thus made that the law refers to *any kind* of animal which is delivered to be guarded.

Rule Six *(clal u-frat u-clal)* concerns the case where the order is general–particular–general. When a general rule is followed by a specification and then again by a general rule, the law is applicable to *only* such cases which are similar to the *specification.* The particular between the two general terms is to be extended only to that which is similar to the contents of the particular. In Exod. 22:8, the rule concerning theft or embezzlement of property prescribes, "For every matter of trespass [general], whether it be for ox, for ass, for sheep, for raiment [particulars], or for any manner of lost thing [general] . . . he shall pay double to his neighbor." Applying the rule of general–particular–general, the law is then construed to mean that the restitution of the twofold value is to be made *only* for such property which resembles the enumerated particulars (ox, sheep, raiment, ass), insofar as it is *moveable* property and of *intrinsic* value (like ox, ass, etc.). The fine would not apply in the case of real estate (which is not moveable), nor for bills or notes (which have only a representative and not intrinsic value) *(B. Kamma* 62b).

Rules Seven through Eleven all modify the three preceding rules—typical of the Rabbinic tendency to relativize, scrutinize, and modify any general rules. The

225

first modification (Rule Seven) concerns Rules Four and Five: when a general rule requires an explicit specification *for the sake of clarity*, the general rule is *not* then limited to the specified particular, as was the case in Rule Four. Similarly, when a specification requires a generalization *for the sake of clarity*, the general rule is *not* then limited to the specified particular, as was the case in Rule Four. Similarly, when a specification requires a generalization for the sake of clarity, the generalization does *not* have the all-embracing effect as it does in Rule Five. (In technical terms, Rule Seven is stated thus: *clal she hu tzarich l'frat u'ferat u-ferat she hu tzarich l'clal*.) That is, where the general or specific terms are ambiguous, they cannot be treated in terms of *clal u-ferat*. When they need to be clarified by supplementation—when the general needs to be clarified through a particular, and the particular requires the supplementation of the general in order to express a clear and full meaning—the preceding rules concerning clal and prat do not apply.

In Lev. 17:3, the text states that he who "taketh in hunting any beast or fowl that may be eaten, he shall pour out the blood thereof, and cover it with dust."

At first glance, it might be thought that the verb *cover* is a general term and *with dust* a particular, and that according to Rule Four, the interpretation would be that the blood must be covered with dust and nothing else. Since, however, the Hebrew expression for *cover* (*kesseh*) is here ambiguous, and could have different meanings such as *hide, conceal,* or withdraw as well as *cover, overlay,* or *envelop*, the expression requires a defining particular. It could otherwise mean merely *to be put out of sight* or *concealed in a vessel. With dust* here serves to define the general. Hence the rule of *clal u-ferat* cannot be applied and *with dust* should not be taken in its strictest sense, but may be extended to include anything resembling dust (*Chul.* 88b).

The second modification—Rule Eight of R. Ishmael—states that when a particular case that is included in a general law is singled out to instruct us concerning something new, it is singled out not only to teach concerning its own case, but is to be applied to the *whole* of the general law *(kol davar she hayah b'clal ve-yatzah min ha clal lelamed lo lelamed al atzmoah yatzah, elleh lelamed al ha-clal coolo yatzah)*. Deut. 22:1–3 sets down the laws for returning found property to its owner. First the text speaks of animals, and then adds "And so shalt thou do with his garment, and so shalt thou do with every lost thing of thy brother's which he hath lost, and thou hast found." Ask the Rabbis, why does the text expressly single out *garment*, even though *garment* is already included in the general term *every lost thing?* They answer: to indicate precisely what manner of lost thing requires one to advertise in order to restore it to the owner. Every garment had an owner and marks by which he could identify it. Hence these characteristics apply to the *whole* of the general law: the obligation to advertise found things refers *only* to such property, which obviously had an owner who will reclaim it and which has certain marks by which he would be able to identify it (*Mishnah B. Metzia* 2:5). (This rule modifies Rule Five, the case of particulars followed by a general, wherein the particulars are *only illustrations* and not *instructions* concerning the general rule.)

Rule Nine is a third modification of *clal u-ferat:* when a particular case that is included in a general law is singled out to add another provision similar to the general law, it is singled out in order to lessen, but not to increase, the severity of that provision. Exod. 35:3 states, "You shall kindle no fire throughout your habitations on the Sabbath day." The particular case of kindling fire is included in the general law that prohibits all labor on the Sabbath day. Why, then, is it here singled out, even though similar to the general law? According to this rule, it is for the purpose of lessening the severity of the prohibition, of alleviating the special case of kindling fire, so that he who does kindle fire on the Sabbath transgresses only a prohibitory law, but is not subject to the severe punishment which the verse prescribes for other kinds of labor (*Shab.* 70a; *Sanh.* 35b).

The fourth modification comprises Rule Ten: when a particular case that is included in a general law is singled out to add another provision which is unlike the general provision, it is singled out in order, in some aspects, to lessen, and in others to add to, the severity of the provision. The former rule considered the singling out of a provision similar to the general law; this rule deals with a provision dissimilar to the general law.

The fifth and final modification—Rule Eleven of R. Ishmael—states that when a particular case that is included in a general law is singled out with a new stipulation, the provisions of the general law no longer apply to it, unless the Torah expressly states that such is to be the case. Here the special case is provided with an entirely new provision, exempting it entirely from the general law.

The last two rules of R. Ishmael are concerned with the determination of meaning through context, not with the relations between particular and general. Rule Twelve states that the meaning of a passage may be deduced from its context or from a subsequent passage. Exod. 16:29 contains the law, "Abide you every man in his place, let no man go out of his place on the seventh day." Taken out of context, this verse would mean that one should not leave his place of abode at all. In the context of the preceding verse, however, it is interpreted to refer only to the manna gatherers, prohibiting them from going out on the Sabbath with the intention to seek manna. (The Talmud, in another interpretation of this passage, not according to context, deduced from the words of the text the general prohibition for an Israelite not to go farther than two thousand cubits from the place of his abode [*Eruv.* 51a].)

The last rule of R. Ishmael states that when two Biblical passages contradict each other, the meaning can be determined by a third Biblical text which reconciles them. For example, there seems to be a distinct contradiction between Exod. 13:6 and Deut. 16:8: the former states, "Seven days thou shalt eat unleavened bread"; the latter, "Six days shalt thou eat unleavened bread." One way the contradiction is removed is by the use of a third passage, Lev. 23:14, which contains a law concerning the prohibition of making any use of the new corn until the offer of an Omer of the first of the barley harvest on the morning after the first day of Passover. Thus unleavened bread made of the new corn could be eaten only during the six remaining days of the Passover festival, and it is this circumstance of which the passage in Deut. 16 speaks (six days), whereas the passage in Exod. 13 (seven days) refers to the unleavened bread prepared of the former year's harvest, which might be eaten for the full seven days (*Mekilta* "Bo" VIII; *Men.* 66a). Other Rabbis apply Rule Eight to Deut. 16:8 and conclude that just as eating unleavened bread on the seventh day was optional, so was it also on the first six days. The obligation to eat matzo referred then only to the first day, with the other days optional—though, of course, no leavened bread could then be eaten (*Pes.* 120a).

Glossary

aggadah. Rabbinic lore, legend, narrative; in general, the non-legal material of the Talmud in contrast to the legal material, or halacha.

al tikrei. "Do not read it thus, but thus." Alternate readings of Hebrew words through different possible vowel combinations.

binyan av. Method of deducing a general rule from a Biblical text; constructing a principle applicable to many instances based on one instance; inductive mode of reasoning.

Gemara. Rabbinic discussion, analysis, and debate on the Mishnah, the Jewish Oral Law. Gemara and Mishnah and their commentaries comprise the Talmud.

gematria. Rabbinic method of interpretation based on computing numerical values of words.

gezerah shavah. Second of the Thirteen Rules of R. Ishmael. Analogy between laws based on identical verbal expressions in the text; linguistic or philological principle of interpretation.

halacha. Lit. "going, walking, path." The Jewish legal system; also any practical Jewish law.

Kabbalah. Lit. "Received Tradition." Jewish mystical literature.

kal ve-chomer. One of the Thirteen Rules of R. Ishmael. Argument from "the light to the heavy"; argument a fortiori.

Midrash. Exegetical inquiry into Scripture, formally dating back to Ezra (fifth century B.C.E.) and collected in various works through approximately the tenth century. A major collection is the Midrash Rabbah, a commentary on the Pentateuch.

Midrash aggadah. Homiletic exegesis of the non-legal protions of Scripture.

Midrash halacha. Exegetical inquiry into the legal portions of Scripture.

Mishnah. Code of Jewish Oral Law, handed down independently of Scripture, codified by R. Yehudah ha-Nasi around 220 C.E.

notarikon. Rabbinic interpretive principle based on reading words as acronyms.

ribbuyin u-mi'yutin. "Inclusion and Exclusion." Method of inferring from grammatical particles and conjunctions in the text an amplification or limitation of certain provisions in the text. Counterpart to R. Ishmael's Rules of General and Particular.

smuchin. Method of inference from juxtaposition of passages.

Talmud. Lit. "Teaching, Learning." Compilation of the Oral Torah that includes the Mishnah and Gemara. The Jerusalem Talmud was compiled around the end of the 3rd century C.E., while the larger and more popular Babylonian Talmud was compiled and edited at the end of the 5th century C.E.

Thirteen Rules of R. Ishmael. Logical Principles of Rabbinic interpretation. Core of Rabbinic interpretive system detailing the relations of general and particular.

Torah. Lit. "Teaching." In the narrow sense, the Five Books of Moses. In the Comprehensive sense, the entire body of Jewish knowledge and literature (Bible, Talmud, Kabbalah, etc.). Jewish tradition holds that there are two Torahs, or two aspects to the Torah: Written (Bible) and Oral (the accompanying Rabbinic interpretation and amplification).

Notes

Methodological Preface

1. Jacques Lacan, "The Insistence of the Letter in the Unconscious," in *Structuralism*, ed. Jacques Ehrmann (Garden City, N.Y.: Doubleday & Co., 1970), p. 135. Also available in Lacan's *Écrits: A Selection*, trans. Alan Sheridan (New York: Norton, 1977).

2. Jacques Derrida, "Force and Signification," in *Writing and Difference*, trans. Alan Bass (Chicago: Univ. of Chicago Press, 1978), p. 10.

3. Jacques Lacan, "Radiophonie," *Scilicet* 2/3 (Paris, 1970) in Jeffrey Mehlman, "The 'floating signifier': Lévi-Strauss to Lacan," *Yale French Studies* 48 (1972): pp. 9–37.

4. Geoffrey Hartman, *Criticism in the Wilderness* (New Haven: Yale Univ. Press, 1980), p. 8.

5. Harold Bloom, *Kabbalah and Criticism* (New York: Seabury Press, 1975), p. 91.

6. Hartman, *Criticism in the Wilderness*, p. 145.

7. Ibid., p. 82.

8. Ibid., p. 84.

1. Greek Philosophy and the Overcoming of the Word

1. Hans-Georg Gadamer, *Truth and Method* (New York: Seabury, 1975), p. 366.

2. Ibid., p. 374.

3. Charles H. Kahn, "Language and Ontology in the *Cratylus*," in F. N. Lee, ed., *Exegesis and Argument: Studies in Greek Philosophy Presented to Gregory Vlastos* (Assen, Netherlands: Van Gorcum, 1973), p. 168.

4. William and Martha Kneale, *The Development of Logic* (Oxford: Clarendon, 1962), p. 20. This book (especially the first 100 pages) and Gadamer's have been very helpful in clarifying the issues discussed in this chapter.

5. Ibid., pp. 3–6.

6. This is not to say, of course, that Rabbinic thought is not also highly logical in a rational manner or is ignorant of such basics as the syllogism. The contrary is true. What I mean to stress here, however, is the development of an additional unique model of inference and logic.

7. Kneale and Kneale, *Development of Logic*, p. 31.

8. Gadamer, *Truth and Method*, pp. 423–24.

9. Tzvetan Todorov, "On Linguistic Symbolism," *New Literary History* 6 (1974): 120.

10. Norman Kretzmann, "Aristotle on Spoken Sound Significant by Convention," in John Corcoran, ed., *Ancient Logic and its Modern Interpreters* (Dordrecht, Netherlands and Boston: D. Reidel, 1974), p. 3.

11. Richard McKeon, "Aristotle's Conception of Language and the Arts of Language," in R. S. Crane, ed., *Critics and Criticism* (Chicago: Univ. of Chicago Press, 1952), pp. 187–88.

12. Sir David Ross, *Aristotle* (1923; reprint ed., New York: Barnes & Noble Books, 1966), p. 26.

13. In Ernest Kapp, *Greek Foundations of Traditional Logic* (New York: Columbia Univ. Press, 1942), p. 26.

14. Gadamer, *Truth and Method*, p. 392.

15. "History of Semantics," *The Encyclopedia of Philosophy*, Vol. 7 (New York: Macmillan-Free Press, 1967), p. 363.

16. Kneale and Kneale, *Development of Logic*, pp. 67–69.

17. Paul Ricoeur, *The Rule of Metaphor* (Toronto: Univ. of Toronto Press, 1978), pp. 12–13.

18. Ibid., pp. 9–10.

19. Ibid., p. 280.

20. Ibid., pp. 20–22.

21. Jacques Derrida, "White Mythology," *New Literary History* 6 (1974): 69.

22. Ibid., pp. 6–7.

23. Ibid., pp. 9–11.

24. Derrida, "White Mythology," p. 29.

25. Ibid., p. 48.

26. Ricoeur, *Rule of Metaphor*, p. 21.

27. Ibid., p. 22.

28. Gadamer, *Truth and Method*, pp. 390–92.

29. Ricoeur, *Rule of Metaphor*, p. 7.

30. Monroe Beardsley, *Aesthetics* quoted in *Rule of Metaphor*, p. 95, 194.

31. Emile Benveniste, *Problems in General Linguistics*, trans. Mary E. Meade (Coral Gables: Univ. of Miami Press, 1971), p. 165, cited in Jacques Derrida, "The Supplement of Copula: Philosophy *before* Linguistics," in Josue Harari, ed., *Textual Strategies* (Ithaca: Cornell Univ. Press, 1979), p. 115. See this essay of Derrida's, which is a deconstructionist reading of Benveniste's reading of Aristotle on the relation of thought and language.

32. Ricoeur, *Rule of Metaphor*, pp. 302–3.

2. Rabbinic Thought: The Divinity of the Text

1. Hans Jonas, *Philosophical Essays: From Ancient Creed to Technological Man* (Englewood, N.J.: Prentice-Hall, 1973), p. 29.

2. Ibid., pp. 29–30.

3. In Erich Auerbach, *Mimesis: The Representation of Reality in Western Literature* (Princeton, N.J.: Princeton Univ. Press, 1953).

4. Ibid., p. 6.

5. Ibid., p. 13.

6. Ibid., p. 15.

7. Ibid., p. 16.

8. Saul Lieberman, *Hellenism in Jewish Palestine* (New York: Jewish Theological Seminary, 1950), p. 27. Or as C. K. Barrett puts it:

> To the Greek philosopher, the existence of earlier literature was no more than incidental; at most it provided a useful confirmation of truths of which he was already persuaded on other grounds. . . . [For the Jewish writers, by contrast] the ancient scriptures were a constitutive and generative element in their religious life. Their system of thought was . . . not confirmed but created by their work on documents possessed of absolute authority. . . . The Jewish interpreters are distinguished from Greek by the fact that they take their stand under the authority of, and profess to be controlled by, their scriptural text. . . .

"The Interpretation of the Old Testament in the New," *Cambridge History of the Bible,* ed. P. R. Ackroyd and C. F. Evans. Vol. I, (Cambridge: Cambridge Univ. Press, 1970), p. 380.

9. Wilhelm Dilthey, The Rise of Hermeneutics," *New Literary History* 3 (1972): 234.

10. Isaac Rabinowitz, " 'Word' and Literature in Ancient Israel," *New Literary History* 4 (1972): 121.

11. Thorlief Boman, *Hebrew Thought Compared with Greek* (Philadelphia: Westminster Press, 1960), p. 68.

12. Ibid., p. 113.

13. Ibid., p. 117.

14. Ibid., p. 117.

15. Jean-François Lyotard, "Jewish Oedipus," *Genre* 10 (1977): 400–402.

16. Ibid., p. 406.

17. Ibid., p. 410.

18. Claude Lévi-Strauss, *The Raw and the Cooked,* trans. J. Weightman (New York: Harper & Row, 1969).

19. Boman, *Hebrew Thought,* p. 133.

20. Ibid., pp. 135–36.

21. Ibid., pp. 138–39.

22. Ibid., pp. 149.

23. Ibid., p. 146.

24. Louis Finklestein, "Introduction," to Solomon Schechter, *Aspects of Rabbinic Theology* (1909; reprint ed., New York: Schocken, 1961), pp. xix–xx.

25. Simon Rawidowicz, "On Interpretation," in Nathum Glatzer, ed., *Studies in Jewish Thought* (Philadelphia: Jewish Publication Society, 1974), p. 52. See also his longer essay in the same volume, "Israel's Two Beginnings: The First 'House' and the Second 'House.' " "On Interpretation" is also available in *Proceedings of the American Academy for Jewish Research* 26 (1957): 83–126.

26. Ibid., p. 52.

27. Ibid., p. 56.

28. Mark Zborowski and Elizabeth Herzog, *Life Is with People: The Culture of the Shtetl* (New York: Schocken, 1952), p. 109.

29. Roland Barthes, "From Work to Text," in Josue Harari, ed., *Textual Strategies* (Ithaca, N.Y.: Cornell Univ. Press, 1979), p. 81.

3. Some Philosophic Aspects of the Rabbinic Interpretive System

1. We must also distinguish between rules of interpretation applied to Scripture and those applied to Talmud. Though there is much overlapping, there are different methods for the interpretation of the Talmud itself which cannot all be covered in this survey. A distinction must also be made between rules for the interpretation and derivation of *halacha* (law) and *aggadah* (nonlegal material). Applied to legal portions of Scripture, the midrashic process is called *midrash halacha;* applied to the nonlegal portions, *midrash aggadah.* During the time of the redaction of the Mishnah and the Talmud, compilations of midrashim were also produced. Though these compilations first emerged around the second century, they contain oral traditions and teachings dating back to most ancient times. The Talmud makes frequent use of midrashim in its expositions. Approximately one-third of the Babylonian Talmud consists of entirely nonlegal matter. The aggadah includes religious philosophy, folklore, history, mathematics, astronomy, medicine, natural science, and so forth. Boaz Cohen writes in his "Introduction" to *Everyman's Talmud,* ed. A. Cohen (New York: Dutton, 1949), p. 4: "In fine, halakah is to the Jews what religion, ceremonies and civil law (to use Cicero's phrase, *De Oratore* I.10,39) were to the Romans. Haggada represents the imaginative, artistic and scientific literature of the Jews. The Haggadah, which embraces one third of the Talmud, is for the Jews what Latin literature was to the Romans." And more. The legal and nonlegal material is woven together in a way that precludes any rigid distinctions. The same teachers who labored over the intricacies of the civil law taught the aggadah.

There are, however, some important differences in exegetical method and in the binding force of halacha as opposed to aggadah. One was bound to follow the laws in practice, but not so bound to the aggadah. No legal inferences could be made from the aggadah. In halacha, a text could not bear any more than one halachic interpretation for the same author; in aggadah there was no such limit. Nevertheless, aggadah was approached as seriously as halacha. Says the midrash, "If you wish to know the One who spoke and brought the world into being, study the aggadah" (*Sifre* Deut. 11:29).

In summarizing the Thirteen Rules of R. Ishmael, I depend on the definitions of Hermann L. Strack, *Introduction to the Talmud and Midrash* (1931; reprint ed., New York: Atheneum, 1969), pp. 93–98, and Moses Mielziner, *Introduction to the Talmud* (1894; reprint ed., New York: Bloch, 1968), pp. 123–86. See also I. Heineman, *Darke Ha-Aggadah* (Jerusalem: 1949), and the German works of Willhelm Bacher. The general problem with most studies of Rabbinic methodology is that they do not deal with the *philosophic* issues of meaning. Most are classificatory and descriptive. Louis Jacobs, cited later, is one of the few philosophic analysts. Strack and Mielziner are skeletal and not up to date, but there it little else available to the English reader.

2. Louis Jacobs, *Studies in Talmudic Logic and Methodology* (London: Vallentine, Mitchell, 1961), p. 4.

3. Ibid., p. 7.

4. Arnold Kunst, "An Overlooked Type of Inference," *Bulletin of the School of Oriental African Studies* 10 (1942): 986.

5. Tzvetan Todorov, "On Linguistic Symbolism," *New Literary History* 6 (1974): 111–34.

6. Ibid., p. 119.

7. Ibid.

8. Paul Ricoeur, *The Rule of Metaphor*, p. 198.

9. Louis Jacobs, "Hermeneutics," *Encyclopedia Judaica* (New York: Macmillan, 1971), p. 367.

10. Adin Steinsaltz, *The Essential Talmud* (New York: Bantam Books, 1977), p. 230.

11. Ibid., p. 230.

12. Ibid., pp. 231–32.

13. Adin Steinsaltz, "The Imagery Concept in Jewish Thought," *Shefa Quarterly* 1 (1978): 56.

14. Ibid.

15. Ibid., p. 57.

16. Ibid., pp. 57–58.

17. Ricoeur, *Rule of Metaphor*, pp. 198–99 ff.

18. Jacobs, *Studies in Talmudic Logic*, p. 13.

19. Ibid., p. vii.

20. Steinsaltz, *Essential Talmud*, p. 97.

21. Max Kadushin, *The Rabbinic Mind* (New York: Bloch, 1952), p. 45.

22. *Encyclopedia Talmudica*, Vol. II, ed. Shlomo Yosef Zevin (Talmudic Encyclopedia Institute: Jerusalem, 1969), p. 36.

23. Mark Zborowski and Elizabeth Herzog, *Life Is With People*, pp. 122–23.

24. Steinsaltz, *Essential Talmud*, p. 232.

25. The Ba'al Shem Tov, the founder of Chassidism in the eighteenth century, explained the verse in Ps. 119:89, "Forever, O God, Your word stands firm in the heavens," to mean that the very words and letters which God spoke in the Ten Utterances through which the world was created ("Let there be . . .") themselves stand firmly forever within heaven to give life to the worlds. As explained further by his follower, R. Schneur Zalman, if the letters were to depart for an instant and return to their source, the heavens would revert to nought and nothingness, as before their creation through the Utterance, "Let there be a firmament." And the same is true of all created things, physical and spiritual. Shneur Zalman of Liadi, *Sha'ar ha-Yichud ve-ha-Emunah* (1799; reprint ed., London: Soncino, 1973), Ch. 1.

26. Henry Slonimski, "The Philosophy Implicit in the Midrash," *Hebrew Union College Annual*, Vol. 27 (1956; reprint ed., New York: Ktav, 1968), p. 236.

27. Jacob Neusner, *History and Torah: Essays in Jewish History* (New York: Schocken, 1965), p. 23.

28. Ibid.

29. Kadushin, *Rabbinic Mind*, p. 108.

30. Roman Jakobson, "Two Aspects of Language: Metaphor and Metonymy," in *European Literary Theory and Practice*, ed. Vernon Gras (New York: Delta, 1973), p. 121.

31. Ibid.

32. Ibid., p. 122.

33. Edward W. Said, *Beginnings: Intention and Method* (Baltimore: Johns Hopkins Univ. Press, 1975), p. 161.

34. Ibid., p. 162.

35. Ibid., p. 229.

36. Ibid., p. 176.

37. Roland Barthes, *The Pleasure of the Text* (New York: Farrar, Straus & Giroux, 1975), p. 27.

38. Roland Barthes, *S/Z* (New York: Farrar, Straus, 1974), p. 10.

39. Ibid., p. 4.

40. Ibid.

41. Roland Barthes, *Image–Music–Text* (New York: Farrar, Straus, 1977), p. 58.

42. Jacques Derrida, "Edmond Jabès and the Question of the Book," in *Writing and Difference,* trans. Alan Bass (1967; Chicago: Univ. of Chicago Press, 1978), pp. 64–65.

43. Ibid., p. 65.

44. Ibid.

45. Barthes, *Pleasure of the Text,* p. 36.

46. Barthes, *Image–Music–Text,* p. 160.

47. Mielziner, *Introduction to the Talmud,* p. 103.

48. Harry Wolfson, *From Philo to Spinoza* (New York: Behrman House, 1977), p. 17.

4. Escape from Textuality: The Fulfiller of Signs

1. Geoffrey Hartman, *The Fate of Reading and Other Essays* (Chicago: Univ. of Chicago Press, 1975), p. 5.

2. Edward Said, *Beginnings: Intention and Method* (Baltimore: Johns Hopkins Univ. Press, 1975), pp. 201, 218.

3. Quoted in Robert L. Wilken, *Judaism and the Early Christian Mind* (New Haven: Yale Univ. Press, 1971), p. 1.

4. D. C. Allen, *Mysteriously Meant: The Rediscovery of Pagan Symbolism and Allegorical Interpretation in the Renaissance* (Baltimore: Johns Hopkins Univ. Press, 1970), p. viii.

5. Harry Wolfson, *Philo,* Vol. I (Cambridge: Harvard Univ. Press, 1947), pp. 132–33.

6. James Shiel, *Greek Thought and the Rise of Christianity* (London: Longman's, 1968), pp. 48–49.

7. Boaz Cohen, "Letter and Spirit in Roman and Jewish Law," in Henry A. Fischel, ed., *Essays in Greco-Roman and Related Talmudic Literature* (New York: Ktav, 1977), p. 145. It also played quite an important role in Greek rhetoric. Aristotle used the contrast of letter and spirit with reference to the law and the consideration of equity which should, according to his view, enter into the law's interpretation when the law was defective. In the *Rhetorica* (1.13), Aristotle says that equity is justice that goes beyond the written law, and that the law could also be interpreted according to its intention rather than its letter. Above all, the law cannot be contrary to nature. Aristotle's philosophical understanding of the law had a deep influence on all subsequent thinking on the subject.

8. Harry Wolfson, "Greek Philosophy in Philo and the Church Fathers," in I. Twersky, ed., *Studies in the History of Philosophy and Religion,* Vol. 1 (Cambridge: Harvard Univ. Press, 1973), p. 74.

9. Harry Wolfson, *The Philosophy of the Church Fathers,* Vol. 1 (Cambridge: Harvard Univ. Press, 1956), p. 43.

10. Cohen, "Letter and Spirit," p. 9.

11. Wolfson, "Greek Philosophy," p. 74. For further discussion of early Christian exegetical methods discussed in this chapter, see the works of J. Bonsirven, Jean Daniélou, David Daube, R. M. Grant, R. P. C. Hanson, Henri deLubac, C. H. Dodds, E. R. Goodenough. A comprehensive bibliography on Christian tradition may be found in Jaroslav Pelikan's *magnum opus, The Christian Tradition: A History of the Development of Doctrine.* See especially the end of Volume I, *The Emergence of the Catholic Tradition (100–600)* (Chicago: Univ. of Chicago Press, 1971).

12. Margaret Ferguson, "Saint Augustine's Region of Unlikeness: The Crossing of Exile and Language," *Georgia Review* 29 (1975): 843–44.

13. Jean-François Lyotard, "Jewish Oedipus," *Genre* 10 (1977): 401–3.

14. Emmanuel Lévinas, *Quatre lectures talmudiques* (Paris: Editions de Minuit, 1968), pp. 73, 19.

15. Said, *Beginnings,* p. 210.

16. Ibid., p. 211.

17. Claude Lévi-Strauss, *The Savage Mind* (Chicago: Univ. of Chicago Press, 1962), p. 225. See also René Girard's extensive study of the ritual of sacrifice in *Violence and the Sacred* (Baltimore: Johns Hopkins Univ. Press, 1977).

18. *Glas* 99a, quoted in Gayatri Spivak, "Glas-Piece: A *Compte Rendu,*" *Diacritics* 7 (1977): 33.

19. *Glas* 67a, in Spivak, "Glas-Piece," p. 33.

20. Lévi-Strauss, *Tristes Tropiques* (1955; reprint ed., New York: Atheneum, 1974), pp. 230–31.

21. Ibid.

22. Lévi-Strauss, *Savage Mind,* p. 228.

23. Wolfson, "Greek Philosophy," p. v.

24. Ibid., p. vi.

25. Wolfson, *Philo,* Vol. 1, p. 3.

26. Ibid., pp. 139–45.

27. Wolfson, *Philosophy of the Church Fathers,* Vol. 1, p. 71.

28. Wolfson, *Philo,* Vol. 1, p. 133.

29. Frederic W. Farrar, *History of Interpretation* (1885; reprint ed., Grand Rapids, Mich.: Baker Book House, 1961), pp. 22–26.

30. Beryl Smalley, *The Study of the Bible in the Middle Ages* (1940; reprint ed., New York: Philosophical Library, 1952), p. 14. For comprehensive studies of Origen, see the classic scholarly studies of him by Jean Daniélou, *Origen* (New York: Sheed & Ward, 1955); R. P. C. Hanson, *Allegory and Event* (London: SCM Press, 1959); Henri de Lubac, *Histoire et Esprit* (Paris: Aubier, 1950).

31. Wolfson, *Philosophy of the Church Fathers,* Vol. 1, pp. 11–12.

32. Wolfson, "Greek Philosophy," p. 75.

33. N. R. M. deLange, *Origen and the Jews* (Cambridge: Cambridge Univ. Press, 1976), p. 7.

34. *Origen: On First Principles,* ed. G. W. Butterworth (New York: Harper & Row Pubs., 1966), p. 269.

35. Ibid., p. 297.

36. For the extensive treatment of this topic on which the analysis in this section depends, see Wolfson, *Philo,* Vol. 1, pp. 208–94.

37. Wolfson, "Greek Philosophy in Philo," p. 78.

38. Wolfson, *Philosophy of the Church Fathers*, Vol. 1, p. 159.
39. Ibid., pp. 288–89.
40. Ibid., p. 307–19.
41. Ibid., p. 361.
42. Ibid., p. 363.
43. Hans Jonas, *Philosophical Essays: From Ancient Creed to Technological Man* (Englewood, N.J.: Prentice-Hall, 1973), p. 29.
44. Kenneth Stein, "Exegesis, Maimonides, and Literary Criticism," *Modern Language Notes* 88 (1973): 1134–54.
45. Moses Maimonides, *Guide to the Perplexed*, trans. Shlomo Pines, quoted in Stein, "Exegesis," p. 1139.
46. Maimonides, quoted in Stein, "Exegesis," p. 1139.
47. Ibid., pp. 1139–43.
48. Wolfson, *Philosophy of the Church Fathers*, Vol. 1, p. 314.
49. Ibid., pp. 374–85.
50. Michael McCanles, "The Literal and the Metaphorical: Dialectic or Interchange," *PMLA* 91 (1976): 279.
51. Ibid., p. 281.
52. Ibid., pp. 283, 284.
53. Smalley, *Study of the Bible*, p. xi.
54. Farrar, *History of Interpretation*, p. 277.
55. D. W. Robertson, *A Preface to Chaucer* (Princeton: Princeton Univ. Press, 1962), p. 303.
56. *Literary Criticism of Dante Alighieri*, trans. Robert S. Haller (Lincoln: Univ. of Nebraska Press, 1973), pp. 99, 112-13.
57. Smalley, *Study of the Bible*, p. 2.
58. Erich Auerbach, *Mimesis: The Representation of Reality in Western Literature* (Princeton: Princeton Univ. Press, 1953), pp. 48–49.
59. Henri deLubac, *The Sources of Revelation*, trans. L. O'Neill (New York: Herder & Herder, 1968), pp. 14–15.
60. Robertson, *Preface to Chaucer*, pp. 292–93.
61. Augustine, *On Christian Doctrine*, trans. D. W. Robertson (New York: Liberal Arts Press, 1958), p. x.
62. *On Christian Doctrine*, pp. 37–38.
63. Robertson, *Preface to Chaucer*, pp. 54–55.
64. B. Darrell Jackson, "The Theory of Signs in St. Augustine's *De Doctrina Christiana*," in R. A. Markus, ed., *Augustine: A Collection of Critical Essays* (Garden City, N.Y.: Doubleday & Co., 1972), p. 136.
65. R. A. Markus, "St. Augustine on Signs," in R. A. Markus, ed., *Augustine: A Collection of Critical Essays*, p. 64.
66. Jackson, "Theory of Signs," pp. 127, 134.
67. *On Christian Doctrine*, pp. 8–9.
68. Ibid., pp. 32–33.
69. Jackson, "Theory of Signs," p. 131.
70. Joseph Mazzeo, "St. Augustine's Rhetoric of Silence," *Journal of the History of Ideas* 23 (1962): 187, 189, 181.
71. John Freccero, "The Fig Tree and the Laurel; Petrarch's Poetics," *Diacritics* 5 (1975): 37.
72. Ibid., p. 38.

73. Jacques Derrida, *Of Grammatology,* trans. G. Spivak (Baltimore: Johns Hopkins Univ. Press, 1976), pp. 72–73.

74. The incarnation as expressive of a certain relationship between word and thing, an attempt to render presence, an extralinguistic immanence, has been of central importance for poetics as well as theology. Freccero traces the influence of Augustine on Dante and Petrarch, in whom may be found the origins of modern literature. In an article on the ground of postmodern poetics, Charles Altieri indicates further the influence of the metaphor of incarnation on modern poetics:

> The metaphor of incarnation has specifically poetic implications as well as axiological ones. Incarnation interpreted by Christian writers as diverse as Dante and Augustine, is a historical concrete event which mediates and guarantees the transformation of fact into allegory. Now while the New Critics were opposed to allegory, they did devote a lot of energy to explaining ways in which logical structure and local texture, the realm of discourse and the realm of particular experience are miraculously joined in the poem as concrete universal.
>
> While incarnation for the moderns exemplified the union of form and significant value on an otherwise empty and chaotic natural world, God for the contemporaries manifests himself as energy, as the intense expression of immanent power. . . . Consequently, sacramentalism takes on radically different implications. . . . To Scott and the contemporary poets sacrament equals radical presence while the more traditional humanist interpretation views it as essentially symbolic, structuring as well as intensifying experience.
>
> Symbolism, however, is always distrusted in Protestant cults of presence, and postmodern poetics are radically Protestant.

"From Symbolist Thought to Immanence: The Ground of Postmodern American Poetics," *Boundary* 1 (1973): 609–11.

75. Ferguson, "St. Augustine's Region," p. 861.

76. Augustine, *Confessions,* trans. R. S. Pine-Coffin (Baltimore: Penguin, 1961), p. 258.

77. Ferguson, "St. Augustine's Region," p. 856.

78. The corollary of this concept is Augustine's idea of the "inward hearing" in man which is responsive to the silent Word of God, circumventing textual and linguistic mediation, and preventing endless interpretation. According to Augustine, this "inward ear" is illuminated by God, the "Interior Teacher," and judges all words according to whether or not they promote charity. For how do we know when to take literal expressions literally, and when figuratively? Augustine answers in III:11: "Whatever appears in the divine Word that does not literally pertain to virtuous behaviour or to the truth of the faith you may take to be figurative. Virtuous behaviour pertains to the love of God and one's neighbor." The "Interior Teacher" is a necessary part of Augustine's theory because, as "Christ in the mind," it teaches by simultaneously displaying to the mind the reality to be known and the language which signifies it. Without this concept, there would again be no bridge between words and signs.

79. Ferguson, "St. Augustine's Region," pp. 843–44.

Prologue: The Book of Books and the Book of Nature

1. Hans-Georg Gadamer, *Truth and Method* (1960; trans. New York: Seabury Press, 1975), p. 154.

2. Ibid., p. 296.

3. Quoted in F. W. Farrar, *History of Interpretation* (1885; rpt. Grand Rapids, Michigan: Baker Book House, 1961), p. 328.

4. Quoted in Robert W. Grant, *A Short History of Interpretation of the Bible* (New York: Macmillan, 1948), p. 128.

5. Quoted in Farrar, *History of Interpretation,* p. 340.

6. Luther eventually came to question the canonicity of certain Books of the Bible according to the rule: "That which does not teach Christ is not apostolic" (Farrar, *History of Interpretation,* p. 336). Consequently, Paul was more Gospel for Luther than Matthew, Mark, and Luke. As might be expected, Luther and Calvin supplanted close grammatical readings for figural or typological interpretation in the Pauline manner, and both shared Paul's extreme antinomianism, his distaste for the law, and his gospel of faith through grace apart from the law. The law was seen as the negative of the Gospel.

7. Hans Frei, *The Eclipse of Biblical Narrative: A Study in Eighteenth and Nineteenth Century Hermeneutics* (New Haven: Yale Univ. Press, 1974), pp. 21, 23.

8. Sigurd Burckhardt, *Shakespearean Meanings* (Princeton: Princeton Univ. Press, 1968), pp. 285–86. Joseph Mazzeo also puts it in the following way: "Scripture was seen as an endless allegory and the world that Scripture described, those silent things, were a further wordless allegory of the eternal. Thus the whole created world was now conceived as a set of divine symbols. Nature is a poem whose silent voice is the Creator. Words point to things and those things are signs pointing to God. Nature is God's Book." Joseph Mazzaeo, "St. Augustine's Rhetoric of Silence," *Journal of the History of Ideas* 23 (1962): 183.

9. Burckhardt, *Shakespearean Meanings,* p. 288.

10. See Barbara Lewalski's admirable study of the relation of English lyric poetry of the seventeenth century to the new stimulus of Protestant emphasis upon the Bible as a book, *Protestant Poetics and the Seventeenth-Century Religious Lyric* (Princeton, N.J.: Princeton Univ. Press, 1979).

5. *Solomon-Sigmund, the Son of Jakob*

1. Hans-Georg Gadamer's *Truth and Method* is a brilliant exposition of this history. It is beyond our scope to further examine the development of modern philosophy from Protestant hermeneutics.

2. Gadamer, *Truth and Method,* p. x.

3. Sigmund Freud, *The Interpretation of Dreams* (1900; reprint ed., New York: Avon, 1965), p. 35.

4. W. W. Meissner, "Freud's Methodology," *Journal of the American Psychoanalytic Association* 19 (1971): 281.

5. *A Psycho-Analytic Dialogue: The Letters of Sigmund Freud and Karl Abraham, 1907–1926,* ed. H. Abraham and E. Freud (London: Hogarth Press–Institute of Psychoanalysis, 1965), p. 34.

6. Ibid., p. 36.

7. Sigmund Freud, *Moses and Monotheism* (1939; reprint ed., New York: Vintage, 1967), p. 52.

8. I stress the fundamentally Talmudic nature of Freud's hermeneutics to emphasize my difference from the thesis put forth by David Bakan in his book

Sigmund Freud and the Jewish Mystical Tradition (New York: Schocken, 1958). Bakan also recognizes the deep and significant structural affinities between the hermeneutics of the psychoanalytic method and the Rabbinic method of textual exegesis, but locates Freud within the Jewish mystical tradition instead. Bakan claims that psychoanalysis was secularization of Kabbalah, and Freud obscured his Kabbalistic ideas to make his work scientifically and culturally acceptable to his contemporaries, the Gentile anti-Semitic majority.

On the one hand, it is well-nigh impossible to prove that Freud ever knew anything about Kabbalah, or if he did that he consciously or unconsciously used it in formulating the methods and concepts of psychoanalysis. Moreover, all the methods of exegesis which Bakan cites as Kabbalistic are, in fact, Talmudic and belong to the vast array of traditional nonmystical methods that were openly available and commonly used by all the sages of the Jewish tradition. Kabbalah itself is most difficult to study. Bakan is limited to the few available works in English and is not intimate with the literature. We will trace the Kabbalistic connection in the final chapter, on Harold Bloom.

9. Quoted in Ernest Jones, *The Life and Works of Sigmund Freud* (New York: Basic Books, 1953–57), Vol. 2, p. 458.

10. Freud, "The Moses of Michelangelo," (1914) reprinted in *Character and Culture,* ed. Philip Rieff (New York: Crowell-Collier, 1963), pp. 82–83.

11. *Interpretation of Dreams,* pp. 299–300.

12. Freud, *The Psychopathology of Everyday Life* (1901; reprint ed., New York: Mentor Book, 1960), p. 119.

13. Ibid., p. 120.

14. *Interpretation of Dreams,* p. xxvi.

15. Marthe Robert, *From Oedipus to Moses: Freud's Jewish Identity,* trans. Ralph Mannheim (1974: Garden City, N.Y.: Doubleday & Co., 1976), p. 12.

16. Kafka, *Briefe 1902–1924* (New York: Schocken, 1958), p. 337, quoted in Robert, *From Oedipus,* p. 9.

17. Robert, *From Oedipus,* p. 141.

18. Ibid., pp. 151, 165–67.

19. Ibid., p. 6.

20. Harold Bloom, *The Anxiety of Influence* (New York: Oxford Univ. Press, 1975), p. 30.

21. Cynthia Ozick, "Judaism & Harold Bloom," *Commentary* (Jan. 1979), pp. 46–47.

22. Jean-Francois Lyotard, "Jewish Oedipus," *Genre* 19 (1977): 398, 401.

23. Ibid., p. 405.

24. Murrary Schwartz, "Critic Define Thyself," in Geoffrey Hartman, ed., *Psychoanalysis and the Question of the Text* (Baltimore: Johns Hopkins Univ. Press, 1968), p. 6.

25. Barbara Johnson, "The Frame of Reference: Poe, Lacan, Derrida," *Yale French Studies* 55/56 (1977): 498.

26. Ibid., p. 499.

27. Jacques Derrida, "Coming Into One's Own," trans. James Hulbert in Hartman, *Psychoanalysis and the Question of the Text,* pp. 116–18.

28. Ibid., pp. 131, 133–34.

29. Edward Said, *Beginnings: Intention and Method* (Baltimore: Johns Hopkins Univ. Press, 1975), p. 162.

30. Ibid., p. 163.

31. Ibid., p. 66.

32. Ibid.

33. *From Oedipus to Moses*, p. 20, at which page the quoted letter from Freud is also cited.

34. Freud, *The Origins of Psycho-Analysis: Letters to Wilhelm Fliess, Drafts and Notes: 1887–1902*, ed. Marie Bonaparte et al. (New York: Basic Books, 1954), p. 170.

35. *Moses and Monotheism*, pp. 51–52.

36. Ibid., p. 52.

37. Freud, "One of the Difficulties in Psychoanalysis" (1917), reprinted in Philip Reiff, *Character and Culture*, p. 189.

38. William McGuire, ed., *The Freud–Jung Letters*, trans. Ralph Mannheim and R. F. C. Hull, Bollingen Series XCIV (Princeton, N.J.: Princeton Univ. Press, 1974), pp. 196–97.

39. Paul Ricoeur, *Freud and Philosophy: An Essay on Interpretation* (New York: Yale Univ. Press, 1970), pp. 347, 257.

40. Gerard Radnitzky, *Contemporary Schools of Metascience*, Vol. 2 (Sweden: Scandinavian Univ. Books, 1968), p. 55.

41. *Interpretation of Dreams*, pp. 346–47.

42. Ibid., p. 311.

43. Ibid., p. 544–45.

44. Ibid, pp. 376–77.

45. Ricoeur, *Freud and Philosophy*, p. 35.

46. *Interpretation of Dreams*, p. 552.

47. Ibid., p. 311.

48. Ibid., p. 331.

49. Ibid., p. 266.

50. Ibid., p. 314.

51. Ibid., p. 143, n. 2. Freud writes this statement, in fact, at the point where he stops his analysis of the three female figures in the Irma dream, a curious and abrupt halt, and an unusual comment from one who boasted that the "secret of dreams" was revealed to him, that he had "solved the mystery." Erik Erikson, in his analysis of Freud's dream of Irma, intriguingly suggests that the centrality of the figure of the female might itself represent the "Mystery of the Dream which itself was the anxious prize of his persistence. . . . The dream may be a mother image; she is the one, as the Bible would say, to be 'known.' "

The dream as mysterious source of nurturance, creativity, knowledge, as "Promised Land," as Erikson puts it in another of his own Biblical metaphors, stands indeed in relation to Freud the interpreter as Holy Writ—mysterious, "royal," ultimately unfathomable, yet something to which he rigorously applies analytic technique and of which he makes rational scientific sense. The interpretive technique, though, involved such a personal revelation of self, of Freud's making himself his own patient, that Erikson perceives it in the context of Freud's milieu as a "feminine yielding" as opposed to "masculine precision," again placing Freud in a curious position vis-à-vis the scientists of his day. Again this relation of both yielding passively to the text and aggressively analyzing it is the Rabbinic relation to Holy Writ—at once the source of mysterious divine authority and subject to human interpretation. Erik Erikson, "The Dream Specimen of Psychoanalysis," in

Psychoanalytic Psychiatry and Psychology, Clinical and Theoretical Papers, Austen Riggs Center, vol. 1, ed. Robert P. Knight and Cyrus R. Friedman (New York: Hallmark-Hubner, 1954).

52. Oral statement reported by Ernest Jones, *The Life and Work of Sigmund Freud,* Vol. 3, p. 221, cited in Robert, *From Oedipus,* p. 37, n. 46.

53. Letter of January 17, 1938 to Ernst Freud, *Letters,* p. 440, cited in Robert, *From Oedipus,* p. 160, n. 46.

54. David Bakan, *Sigmund Freud and the Jewish Mystical Tradition,* (1958; reprint ed., Boston: Beacon, 1975), pp. 305-318.

55. Freud, *Moses and Monotheism,* p. 52. See also Robert, *From Oedipus,* pp. 145–67.

6. The Analyst as Scribe: Jacques Lacan and the Return of the Father's Name

1. Jacques Lacan, "The Insistence of the Letter in the Unconscious," in *Structuralism,* ed. Jacques Ehrmann (Garden City, N.Y.: Doubleday & Co., 1970), p. 117.

2. Jacques Lacan, "Radiophonie," in *Scilicet 2/3* (Paris, 1970), quoted in Jeffrey Mehlman, "The 'floating signifier': Lévi-Strauss to Lacan," *Yale French Studies* 48 (1972): 33.

3. Ibid., p. 32.

4. Ibid., p. 26.

5. Lacan, "Insistence of the Letter," p. 120.

6. Ibid., p. 118.

7. Ibid., p. 115.

8. Ibid., p. 116.

9. Ibid.

10. Ibid., p. 126.

11. Ibid., p. 123.

12. Ibid., p. 124.

13. Ibid., p. 86, 11.

14. Jacques Lacan, *The Language of the Self,* trans. Anthony Wilden (Baltimore: John Hopkins Univ. Press, 1968), p. 165.

15. Jacques Lacan, Seminar of March–April, 1957, quoted by Wilden in *Language of the Self,* p. 271.

16. Jacques Lacan, *The Four Fundamental Concepts of Psycho-Analysis,* ed. J-A Miller, trans. A. Sheridan (London: Hogarth Press–Institute of Psychoanalysis, 1977), p. 248.

17. Geoffrey Hartman, *Psychoanalysis and the Question of the Text,* p. 91.

18. Ibid., pp. 92–93.

19. Herbert Schneidau, *Sacred Discontent: The Bible and Western Tradition* (Berkeley: Univ. of California Press, 1976), pp. 290, 292.

20. Lacan, *Language of the Self,* p. 31.

21. Ibid., pp. 77–78.

22. Ibid., p. 78.

23. For a clear and detailed account of this idea, see Eugen S. Bar, "Understanding Lacan," in *Psychoanalysis and Contemporary Science* 3, ed. Leo Gold-

berger and Victor Rosen (New York: International Universities Press, 1974), p. 481.

24. *Four Fundamental Concepts,* pp. 250–51.
25. Lacan, *Actes,* p. 245, quoted by Wilden in *Language of the Self,* p. 125, n. 87.
26. *Language of the Self,* pp. 57, 23.

7. *Reb Derrida's Scripture*

1. Lacan, "Seminar on the 'Purloined Letter,' " *Yale French Studies* 48 (1972): 72.
2. Jacques Derrida, "The Purveyor of Truth," *Yale French Studies* 52 (1975): 82.
3. Ibid., p. 95
4. Ibid., p. 82.
5. Ibid., p. 65.
6. Ibid., pp. 93, 85.
7. Barbara Johnson, "The Frame of Reference: Poe, Lacan, Derrida," *Yale French Studies*, 55/56 (1977): 484.
8. Jacques Derrida, *Glas* (Paris: Éditions Galilée, 1974), 268b–269b, quoted in Gayatri Chakravorty Spivak, "*Glas*-Piece: A *Compte Rendu,*" *Diacritics* 7 (1977): p. 23.
9. Spivak, *Glas*-Piece," p. 23.
10. Derrida, *Of Grammatology* trans. Gayatri Spivak (1967; Baltimore: Johns Hopkins Univ. Press, 1976), p. 158.
11. Derrida, "Freud and the Scene of Writing," *Yale French Studies* 48 (1972): 75.
12. Derrida, *Of Grammatology*, pp. 13, 14.
13. Ibid., p. 17.
14. Ibid., pp. 35, 38–39, 44, 39.
15. Spivak, Introduction, Derrida, *Of Grammatology*, p. xlv.
16. Geoffrey Hartman, "Monsieur Texte: On Jacques Derrida, His *Glas,*" *Georgia Review* 29 (1975): 777–78. Expanded in Hartman's longer book on Derrida, *Saving the Text: Literature/Derrida/Philosophy* (Baltimore:Johns Hopkins Univ. Press, 1981).
17. "Violence and Metaphysics: An Essay on the Thought of Emmanual Levinas," Derrida, *Writing and Difference,* trans. Alan Bass (1967; Chicago: University of Chicago Press, 1978), p. 153. The quote ("Jewgreek is greekjew.") is from James Joyce.
18. Ibid., pp. 82–83.
19. Ibid., p. 89.
20. Ibid., p. 102.
21. Ibid.
22. Emmanuel Levinas, "To Love the Torah More than God," *Difficile liberté: Essai sur le Judaisme* in *Présences du Judaisme* (Paris: Albin Michel, 1963), trans. Helen A. Stephenson and Richard Sugarman, commentary by Richard Sugarman, *Judaism* 28 (1979): 218.
23. Ibid., p. 219.

24. Sugarman, "To Love the Torah More than God," p. 221.

25. Derrida, "Violence and Metaphysics," p. 108.

26. Ibid.

27. *Of Grammatology*, p. 70.

28. Ibid., p. 65.

29. Ibid., p. 71.

30. Derrida, "Ellipsis," *Writing and Difference*, pp. 294–295.

31. Ibid., p. 298.

32. Geoffrey Hartman, "Monsieur Texte II: Epiphony in Echoland," *Georgia Review* 30 (1976): 178. Expanded in *Saving the Text*.

33. Ibid., p. 192.

34. Letter to Franz Werfel, probably not mailed. Cf. the letters to Max Brod and Franz Werfel of December 1922, in *Breife 1902–24*, ed. Max Brod (New York: Schocken, 1958), p. 423 ff., cited in Robert, *From Oedipus to Moses*, p. 173, n. 12.

35. Marthe Robert, *From Oedipus to Moses*, p. 8.

36. Derrida, "Edmond Jabès and the Question of the Book," *Writing and Difference*, p. 74.

37. Ibid., p. 64–65, 67.

38. Ibid., p. 68.

39. Ibid., p. 71.

40. Ibid., p. 73.

41. Ibid., p. 77.

42. Ibid., p. 78.

43. Ibid., p. 67.

8. *The Critic as Kabbalist: Harold Bloom and the Heretic Hermeneutic*

1. Matthew Arnold, *Culture and Anarchy*, ed. J. Dover Wilson, (1869; reprint ed., Cambridge: Cambridge Univ. Press, 1960), p. 130.

2. "Ars Poetica" by Archibald MacLeish, quoted in W. K. Wimsatt and Monroe C. Beardsley, "The Intentional Fallacy," 1954; reprinted in *20th Century Literary Criticism*, ed. David Lodge (London: Longman's, 1972), p. 335.

3. John Crowe Ransom, "Criticism, Inc.," *The World's Body* (1938; reprint ed., Baton Rouge: Louisiana State Univ. Press, 1968), reprinted in Lodge, *20th Century Literary Criticism*, pp. 235–36.

4. G. Douglas Atkins, "Dehellenizing Literary Criticism," *College English* 41 (1980): 769.

5. Ibid., 769–70, 776.

6. Harold Bloom, *A Map of Misreading* (New York: Oxford Univ. Press, 1975), p. 33.

7. Harold Bloom, *Kabbalah and Criticism* (New York: Seabury Press, 1975), p. 104.

8. Harold Bloom, *The Anxiety of Influence* (New York: Oxford Univ. Press, 1973), pp. 85–86.

9. Bloom, *Anxiety*, p. 56.

10. Bloom, *Map*, p. 37.

11. Bloom, *Anxiety*, p. 37.

12. Bloom, *Map*, p. 3.

13. Bloom, *Anxiety,* p. 10.
14. Ibid., pp. 14–15.
15. Ibid., p. 14.
16. Ibid., p. 88.
17. *Map,* p. 84.
18. *Anxiety,* p. 67.
19. Ibid., p. 122.
20. Ibid., p. 91.
21. Ibid., p. 109.
22. Ibid., pp. 122, 119.
23. Ibid., pp. 141, 152.
24. Bloom, *Poetry and Repression* (New Haven: Yale Univ. Press, 1976), pp. 88–89.
25. *Map,* p. 83.
26. *Poetry,* p. 95.
27. T. S. Eliot, "Tradition and the Individual Talent" (1919; reprinted in Lodge, *20th Century Literary Criticism),* pp. 72–74.
28. *Map,* pp. 30, 32.
29. Bloom, "The Breaking of Form," in Harold Bloom et al., *Deconstruction and Criticism* (New York: Seabury, 1979), p. 1.
30. Eliot, "Tradition," p. 76.
31. Bloom, *Kabbalah,* p. 4.
32. *Anxiety,* p. 30.
33. T. S. Eliot, "The Function of Criticism" (1923; reprinted in Lodge, *20th Century Criticism),* p. 79.
34. Ibid., p. 65.
35. Ibid., pp. 93–94.
36. Ibid., pp. 94–96.
37. Bloom, *Kabbalah,* pp. 114–15, 122.
38. *Poetry,* p. 29.
39. *Anxiety,* p. 19.
40. *Map,* p. 37.
41. *Anxiety,* p. 152.
42. Jacques Derrida, "Violence and Metaphysics: An Essay on the Thought of Emmanuel Levinas," *Writing and Difference,* trans. Alan Bass (1967; Chicago: Univ. of Chicago Press, 1978), p. 118.
43. *Anxiety,* pp. 35, 39, 42.
44. Ibid., p. 83.
45. Ibid., p. 78.
46. Ibid., p. 20.
47. *Map,* pp. 79, 175.
48. *Anxiety,* p. 21.
49. Ibid., pp. 22, 28.
50. *Poetry,* pp. 33–34.
51. *Sanh.* 71a; see also "Interpretation," *Encyclopedia Judaica,* p. 1,423.
52. *Mishnah Makkot* I; see also Adin Steinsaltz, *The Essential Talmud* (New York: Bantam, 1977), pp. 168–69.
53. *Map,* p. 43.
54. David Biale, *Gershom Scholem: Kabbalah and Counter-History* (Cambridge: Harvard Univ. Press, 1979), pp. 1–2.

55. Biale, *Gershom Scholem,* p. 11.

56. Ibid., p. 155.

57. Ibid., p. 191.

58. Ibid.

59. Gershom Scholem, "Revelation and Tradition as Religious Categories in Judaism," in *The Messianic Idea in Judaism* (New York: Schocken, 1971), pp. 282–303.

60. Scholem, "Revelation and Tradition," pp. 288–89, 284.

61. Ibid., p. 287.

62. Ibid., pp. 288–89.

63. Geoffrey Hartman, *Criticism in the Wilderness* (New Haven: Yale Univ. Press, 1980), p. 202.

64. Ibid., p. 206.

65. Ibid., p. 156.

66. Scholem, p. 289.

67. Ibid., p. 289–90.

68. Geoffrey Hartman, Preface, in *Deconstruction and Criticism,* by Harold Bloom et al., p. viii.

69. Hartman, *Criticism,* p. 207.

70. Biale, *Gershom Scholem,* p. 80.

71. Scholem, "Revelation and Tradition," p. 292.

72. For extended discussions, see Gershom Scholem's works, including *Major Trends in Jewish Mysticism* (1941; reprint ed., New York: Schocken, 1961); "The Meaning of the Torah in Jewish Mysticism," in *On The Kabbalah and Its Symbolism* (1960; reprint ed., New York: Schocken, 1969), pp. 32–86; "The Name of God in the Linguistic Theory of the Kabbalah," *Diogenes* 79 (1972): 59–80; and 80 (1972): 164–94; "Revelation and Tradition." See also Biale's discussion in *Gershom Scholem,* pp. 79–122.

73. Scholem, "Revelation and Tradition," p. 294.

74. Ibid., p. 295.

75. Ibid., p. 296.

76. Bloom, *Map,* p. 75–76.

77. Biale, *Scholem* p. 94.

78. Scholem, "Revelation and Tradition," pp. 297–98, 303.

79. Biale, *Scholem,* p. 94.

80. Ibid.

81. Ibid., p. 206.

82. Bloom, *Kabbalah,* p. 87.

83. Bloom, *Map,* p. 62.

84. Ibid., p. 38.

85. *Kabbalah,* p. 66.

86. *Poetry and Repression,* p. 236.

87. *Kabbalah,* p. 35.

88. *Map,* p. 4.

89. *Kabbalah,* p. 72.

90. Ibid., p. 98.

91. *Map,* p. 4.

92. *Kabbalah,* p. 126.

93. Cynthia Ozick, "Judaism and Harold Bloom," *Commentary,* January 1979, p. 46.

94. Ibid., p. 50.

95. Geoffrey Hartman, "War in Heaven: A Review of Harold Bloom's *The Anxiety of Influence: A Theory of Poetry*," in *The Fate of Reading* (Chicago: Univ. of Chicago Press, 1975), pp. 44–45.

96. Bloom, *Kabbalah,* p. 153.

97. Bloom, "Breaking of Form," p. 6.

98. Bloom, *Kabbalah,* pp. 33, 47.

99. Bloom, "Breaking of Form," p. 6.

100. Hartman, "War in Heaven," p. 49.

101. For full explanation of Kabbalistic terms used in this section, see Scholem's works as cited in n. 72. In *On the Kabbalah and Its Symbolism,* see also pp. 87–157. See also Scholem's summary of his life's work in the expanded version of the articles he wrote for the *Encyclopedia Judaica* on Kabbalah and published later as a separate book, *Kabbalah* (New York: New American Library, 1974). For another description and point of view, see Rabbi Jacob Immanuel Schochet, "Mystical Concepts in Chassidism: An Introduction to Kabbalistic Concepts and Doctrines in *Igeret HaKodesh,*" in R. Schneur Zalman, *Likutei–Amarim–Tanya* (1797; reprint ed., London: Soncino, 1973), pp. 794–887. Bloom also provides his own summary in *Kabbalah and Criticism.*

102. Bloom, *Kabbalah,* pp. 25, 28.

103. Kabbalah speaks in general of three "intellectual" and seven "emotional" attributes. *Keter (Crown)* is the first sefirah—*primal will,* standing apart from the others as their originating force. *Hochmah (Wisdom), Binah (Understanding),* and *Da'at (Knowledge)* are three intellectual functions. The seven emotional attributes include: (1) the triad of *Chesed (Kindness), Gevurah (Might, Severity),* and *Tiferet (Beauty, Mercy*—a synthesis of *Chesed* and *Gevurah);* (2) the second triad of *Netzach (Endurance, Permanence, Victory), Hod (Splendor),* and *Yesod (Foundation).* The last sefirah is *Malchut (Sovereignty, Kingship).* In certain schemes, *Keter* is the first sefirah and *Da'at* is omitted.

104. Bloom, *Kabbalah,* p. 52.

105. Ibid., p. 65.

106. Ibid., p. 68.

107. Ibid., pp. 66–67.

108. Ibid., pp. 67–68.

109. Ibid., p. 70.

110. Ibid., p. 70.

111. Ibid., p. 74.

112. Ibid., pp. 86–87.

113. Hartman, *Criticism in the Wilderness,* pp. 151, 115, 25.

114. *Kabbalah,* pp. 83, 85.

115. Ibid., p. 83.

116. Ibid.

117. *Map,* p. 5.

118. *Kabbalah,* p. 80.

119. For Bloom's rereading of Freud via Kabbalah and rhetoric, see his "Freud and the Poetic Sublime: A Catastrophe Theory of Creativity," *Antaeus,* No. 30/31 (Spring, 1978): 355–77; and "Freud's Concepts of Defense and the Poetic Will," in *The Literary Freud: Mechanism of Defense and the Poetic Will, Psychiatry and the Humanities,* Vol. 4, ed. Joseph H. Smith (New Haven: Yale Univ. Press, 1980), pp. 1–28.

120. *Kabbalah,* p. 53.

121. Bloom, "Breaking of Form," p. 4.

122. Bloom, *Poetry and Repression,* p. 14.

123. *Map,* p. 66.

124. *Kabbalah,* pp. 87–89.

125. *Map,* pp. 168, 89.

126. *Kabbalah,* p. 89.

127. Ibid.

128. Ibid.

129. *Map,* p. 138.

130. Bloom, "Breaking of Form," *Deconstruction,* p. 3.

131. *Poetry and Repression,* pp. 227, 224.

132. Ibid., p. 146.

133. Ibid., p. 145.

134. Bloom, *Kabbalah,* p. 11.

135. Matthew Arnold, "The Function of Criticism at the Present Time," epigraph in Hartman, *Criticism,* p. ix.

136. Franz Kafka, as cited in Hartman, *Criticism,* p. 55.

Selected Bibliography

Ackroyd, P. R., and Evans, C. F., eds. *From the Beginnings to Jerome*. The Cambridge History of the Bible, vol. 1. Cambridge: Cambridge Univ. Press, 1963.

Allen, Don Cameron. *The Legend of Noah: Renaissance Rationalism in Art Science, Letters*. 1949, Reprint. Urbana, Ill.: Univ. of Illinois Press, 1963.

———. *Mysteriously Meant: The Rediscovery of Pagan Symbolism and Allegorical Symbolism in the Renaissance*. Baltimore: John Hopkins Univ. Press, 1970.

Alter, Robert. *The Art of Biblical Narrative*. New York: Basic Books, 1981.

Altieri, Charles. "From Symbolist Thought to Immanence: The Ground of Postmodern Poetics." *Boundary* 1 (1973): 605–37.

———. "Wittgenstein on Consciousness and Language: A Challenge to Derridean Literary Theory." *Modern Language Notes* 19 (1976): 1397–423.

Aquinas, Thomas. *Summa Theologica*, vol. 1. Translated by Thomas Gilby. London: Blackfriars; New York: McGraw Hill, 1964.

Aristotle. *Categories & De Interpretatione*. Translated by J. L. Ackrill. London: Oxford Univ. Press, 1963.

———. *Poetics*. Translated by Gerald F. Else. Ann Arbor: Univ. of Michigan Press, 1967.

———. *Rhetoric*. Translated by W. Rhys Roberts. Oxford: Clarendon Press, 1946.

Armstrong. A. H., and Markus, R. A. *Christian Faith and Greek Philosophy*. New York: Sheed & Ward, 1960.

Atkins, G. Douglas. "Dehellenizing Literary Criticism." *College English* 41 (1980): 769–79.

Auerbach, Erich. *Mimesis: The Representation of Reality in Western Literature*. Princeton, N.J.: Princeton Univ. Press, 1953.

———. "Figura." In *Scenes from the Drama of European Literature*. 1944. Reprint. New York: Meridian, 1959.

Augustine. *Confessions*. Translated by R. S. Pine-Coffin. Baltimore: Penguin, 1961.

———. *On Christian Doctrine*. Translated by D. W. Robertson. New York: Liberal Arts Press, 1958.

Baeck, Leo. *Judaism and Christianity*. Translated by Walter Kaufman. 1958, Reprint. New York: Meridian, 1961.

Bakan, David. *Sigmund Freud and the Jewish Mystical Tradition*. 1958. Reprint. Boston: Beacon, 1975.

Bar, Eugene S. "Understanding Lacan." In *Psychoanalysis and Contemporary Science 3*, edited by Leo Goldberger and Victor H. Rosen. New York: International Universities Press, 1974.

Barthes, Roland. *Image–Music–Text*. Translated by Stephen Heath. New York: Hill & Wang, 1973.

———. *The Pleasure of the Text*. Translated by Richard Miller. New York: Hill & Wang, 1973.

———. *S/Z*. Translated by Richard Miller. 1970, New York: Hill & Wang, 1974.

Bashford, Bruce. "The Rhetorical Method in Literary Criticism." *Philosophy and Rhetoric* 9 (1976): 133–46.

Bercovitch, Sacvan, ed. *Typology and Early American Literature*. Amherst: Univ. of Massachusetts Press, 1972.

Biale, David. *Gershom Scholem: Kabbalah and Counter-History*. Cambridge, Mass.: Harvard Univ. Press, 1979.

Bloom, Harold. *The Anxiety of Influence: A Theory of Poetry*. New York: Oxford, 1973.

———. et. al. *Deconstruction and Criticism*. New York: Seabury, 1980.

———. *Kabbalah and Criticism*. New York: Seabury, 1975.

———. *The Flight to Lucifer: A Gnostic Fantasy*. New York: McGraw Hill, 1979.

———. "Freud and the Poetic Sublime: A Catastrophe Theory of Creativity." *Antaeus*, No. 30/31 (1978): pp. 355–77.

———. "Freud's Concepts of Defense and the Poetic Will." In *The Literary Freud: Mechanisms of Defense and the Poetic Will. Psychiatry and the Humanities*, edited by Joseph Smith, vol. 4. New Haven, Conn.: Yale Univ. Press, 1980.

———. *A Map of Misreading*. New York: Oxford Univ. Press, 1975.

———. "Poetic Crossing: Rhetoric and Psychology." *Georgia Review* 30 (1976): 495–526.

———. *Poetry and Repression: Revisionism from Blake to Stevens*. New Haven, Conn.: Yale Univ. Press, 1976.

———. *Wallace Stevens: "The Poems of Our Climate."* Ithaca, N.Y.: Cornell Univ. Press, 1977.

Bowker, John. *Targums and Rabbinic Literature*. Cambridge: Cambridge Univ. Press, 1969.

Bloomfield, Morton W. "Allegory as Interpretation." *New Literary History* 3 (1972): 301–18.

———. "Symbolism in Medieval Literature." *Modern Philology* 56 (1958): 73–81.

Bochenski, I. M. *Ancient Formal Logic*. 1951, Amsterdam: North Holland Pub. Co., 1963.

Boman, Thorlieff. *Hebrew Thought Compared with Greek*. Philadelphia: Westminster Press, 1954.

Burckhardt, Sigurd. *Shakespearean Meanings*. Princeton, N.J.: Princeton Univ.Press, 1954.

Burghardt, Walter J. "On Early Christian Exegesis." *Theological Studies* 11 (1950): 78–116.

Caplan, Henry. "The Four Senses of Scriptural Interpretation and the Medieval Theory of Preaching." *Speculum* 4 (1929): 282–90.

Chaitin, Gilbert. "The Representation of Logical Relations in Dreams and the Nature of Primary Process." *Psychoanalysis and Contemporary Science* 1 (1978): 477–502.

Chajes, Z. H. *The Student's Guide through the Talmud*. 1860, Reprint. New York: Feldheim, 1960.

Chayes, Irene. "Revisionist Literary Criticism." *Commentary* 61 (1976): 65–69.

Cohen, A. *Everyman's Talmud*. New York: E. P. Dutton, 1949.

Corcoran, John, ed. *Ancient Logic and Its Modern Interpreters*. Dordrecht, Netherlands & Boston: D. Reidel Pub. Co., 1974.

Cuddihy, John Murray. *The Ordeal of Civility: Freud, Marx, Lévi-Strauss and the Jewish Struggle with Modernity*. New York: Basic Books, 1974.

Curtius, Ernst Robert. *European Literature and the Latin Middle Ages*. Translated by Willard Trask. 1948, Princeton, N.J.: Princeton Univ. Press, 1953.

Daube, David. *The New Testament and Rabbinic Judaism*. London: Univ. of London Press, 1956.

———. "Rabbinic Methods of Interpretation and Hellenistic Rhetoric." *Hebrew Union College Annual* 22 (1949): 239–64.

Davies, W. D. *Paul and Rabbinic Judaism: Some Rabbinic Elements in Pauline Theology*. 1948, Reprint. New York: Harper Row Pub., 1967.

DeLange, N. R. M. *Origen and the Jews: Studies in Jewish–Christian Relations in Third-Century Palestine*. Cambridge: Cambridge Univ. Press, 1976.

DeLubac, Henri. *The Sources of Revelation*. Translated by L. O'Neil. New York: Herder & Herder, 1968.

DeMan, Paul. *Blindness and Insight: Essays in the Rhetoric of Contemporary Criticism*. New York: Oxford Univ. Press, 1971.

———. "The Rhetoric of Temporality." In *Interpretation: Theory and Practice*, edited by Charles S. Singleton. Baltimore: John Hopkins Univ. Press, 1969.

Derrida, Jacques. "Coming into One's Own." In *Psychoanalysis and the Question of the Text*, edited by Geoffrey Hartman. Baltimore: John Hopkins Univ. Press, 1978.

———. *L'écriture et la différance*. Paris: Éditions du Seuil, 1967.

———. "Freud and the Scene of Writing." *Yale French Studies* 48 (1972): 74–117.

———. *Glas*. Paris: Éditions Galilée, 1974.

———. *Of Grammatology*. Translated by Gayatri Chakravorty Spivak. 1967, Baltimore: John Hopkins Univ. Press, 1976.

———. *"The Purveyor of Truth."* Yale French Studies 52 (1975): 31–113.

———. "Structure, Sign, and Play in the Discourse of the Human Sciences." In *The Structuralist Controversy*, edited by Richard Macksey and Eugenio Donato. Baltimore: John Hopkins Univ. Press, 1970.

———. "The Supplement of Copula: Philosophy *before* Linguistics." In *Textual Strategies: Perspectives in Post-Structuralist Criticism*. Edited by Josue V. Harari. Ithaca, N.Y.: Cornell Univ. Press, 1979.

———. "White Mythology." *New Literary History* 6 (1974): 5–74.

———. *Writing and Difference*. Translated by Alan Bass. 1967, Chicago: Univ. of Chicago Press, 1978.

Diesing, Paul. *Patterns of Discovery in the Social Sciences*. Chicago: Aldine-Atherton, 1971.

Dilthey, Wilhelm. "The Rise of Hermeneutics." Translated by Frederick Jameson. *New Literary History* 3 (1972): 229–44.

Dobshutz, Ernst von. "Interpretation." 1961 ed. *Encyclopedia of Religion and Ethics*, vol. 7. New York: Scribner.

Dungey, Kevin, R. "Christian Hermeneutic Styles." Ph.D. Dissertation, Stanford Univ., 1980.

Epstein, I. ed. *The Babylonian Talmud*. London: Soncino, 1938.

Erikson, Erik. "The Dream Specimen of Psychoanalysis." In *Psychoanalytic Psychiatry and Psychology: Clinical and Theoretical Papers*, vol. 1, edited by Robert P. Knight and Cyrus R. Friedman. New York: Hallmark, Hubner, 1954.

Farrar, Frederic W. *History of Interpretation*. 1885, Reprint. Grand Rapids, Mich.: Baker Book House, 1961.

Ferguson, Margaret W. "Saint Augustine's Region of Unlikeness: The Crossing of Exile and Language." *Georgia Review* 29 (1975): 842–64.

Fishbane, Michael. "The Teacher and the Hermeneutical Task: A Reinterpretation of Medieval Exegesis." *Journal of the American Academy of Religion* 43 (1975): 709–21.

Fischel, Henry A., ed. *Essays in Greco-Roman and Related Talmudic Literature*. New York: Ktav, 1977.

Foucault, Michel. *The Order of Things: An Archaeology of the Human Sciences*. New York: Random House, 1970.

Frankel, Israel. *Peshat in Talmudic and Midrashic Literature*. Toronto: LaSalle Press, 1956.

Freccero, John. "The Fig Tree and The Laurel: Petrarch's Poetics." *Diacritics* 5 (1975): 34–40.

Frei, Hans. *The Eclipse of Biblical Narrative: A Study in Eighteenth and Nineteenth Century Hermeneutics*. New Haven, Conn.: Yale Univ. Press, 1974.

Freud, E. and Abraham, H. *A Psycho-Analytic Dialogue: The Letters of Sigmund Freud and Karl Abraham, 1907–1926*. London: Hogarth Press and Institute for Psychoanalysis, 1965.

Freud, Sigmund. "Analysis Terminable and Interminable." In *Therapy and Technique*, edited by Philip Rieff. 1937. New York: Crowell-Collier, 1963.

———. "Beyond the Pleasure Principle." In A *General Selection from the Works of Sigmund Freud*, edited by John Rickman. 1920. New York: Doubleday & Co., 1957.

———. "Constructions in Analysis." In *Therapy and Technique*, edited by Philip Rieff. 1937. New York: Crowell-Collier, 1963.

———. "Freud's Psychoanalytic Method." In *Therapy and Technique*, edited by Philip Rieff. 1904. New York: Crowell-Collier, 1963.

———. *The Interpretation of Dreams*. Translated and edited by James Strachey. 1900. New York: Avon, 1965.

———. *Moses and Monotheism*. 1939, Reprint. New York: Vintage, 1967.

———. "The Moses of Michelangelo." In *Character and Culture*, edited by Philip Reiff. 1914. New York: Crowell-Collier, 1963.

———. "On Psychotherapy." In *Therapy and Technique*, edited by Philip Rieff. 1904. New York: Crowell-Collier, 1963.

———. "One of the Difficulties of Psychoanalysis." In *Character and Culture*, edited by Philip Rieff. 1917. New York: Crowell-Collier, 1963.

———. *The Origins of Psychoanalysis: Letters to Wilhelm Fleiss, Drafts and Notes: 1887–1902*. Edited by Marie Bonaparte et al. New York: Basic Books, 1954.

———. *An Outline of Psychoanalysis*. 1917, Reprint. New York: Norton, 1949.

———. "Psychoanalysis." In *Character and Culture*, edited by Philip Rieff. 1922. New York: Crowell-Collier, 1963.

————. *Psychopathology of Everyday Life.* 1901, Reprint. New York: Mentor Books, 1960.

————. "Recommendations for Physicians on the Psychoanalytic Method of Treatment." In *Therapy and Technique*, edited by Philip Rieff. 1912. New York: Crowell-Collier, 1963.

————. *Totem and Taboo.* Translated by A. Brill. 1913, New York: Vintage, 1946.

Frye, Northrop. *Anatomy of Criticism.* Princeton, N.J.: Princeton Univ. Press, 1957.

Gadamer, Hans-Georg. *Truth and Method.* 1960, New York: Seabury, 1975.

Garver, Newton. "Derrida on Rousseau on Writing." *Journal of Philosophy* 74 (1977): 663–73.

————. Preface to *Speech and Phenomena: And Other Essays on Husserl's Theory of Signs*, by Jacques Derrida. Translated by David B. Allison. Evanston, Ill.: Northwestern Univ. Press, 1973.

Ginzberg, Louis. *On Jewish Law and Lore.* Philadelphia: Jewish Publication Society, 1955; reprint ed., New York: Atheneum, 1970.

Gordis, Robert. "Midrash—Its Method and Meaning." *Midstream*, September 1959, pp. 91–96.

————. "The Two Faces of Freud." *Judaism* 24 (1975): 194–200.

Grant, Robert M. *A Short History of Interpretation of the Bible.* New York: Macmillan Pub. Co., 1948.

Gras, Vernon W., ed. *European Literary Theory and Practice: From Existential Phenomenology to Structuralism.* New York: Dell Pub. Co., 1973.

Grassi, Ernesto. "Rhetoric and Philosophy." *Philosophy and Rhetoric* 9 (1976): 200–16.

Green, W. S., ed. *Approaches to Ancient Judaism: Theory and Practice.* Brown Judaic Studies, vol. 1. Missoula, Mon.: Scholars Press, 1978.

Hanson, R. P. C. *Allegory and Event.* London: SCM Press, 1959.

Harari, Josue V., ed. *Textual Strategies: Perspectives in Post-Structuralist Criticism.* Ithaca, N.Y.: Cornell Univ. Press, 1979.

Hartman, Geoffrey. *Beyond Formalism: Literary Essays 1958–70.* New Haven, Conn.: Yale Univ. Press, 1970.

————. *Criticism in the Wilderness: The Study of Literature Today.* New Haven, Conn.: Yale Univ. Press, 1980.

————. *The Fate of Reading and Other Essays.* Chicago: Univ. of Chicago Press, 1975.

————. "Monsieur Texte: On Jacques Derrida, His *Glas.*" *Georgia Review* 29 (1975): 759–97.

————. "Monsieur Texte II: Epiphony in Echoland." *Georgia Review* 30 (1976): 169–97.

————. *Psychoanalysis and the Question of the Text: Selected Papers from the English Institute, 1976–77.* Baltimore: John Hopkins Univ. Press, 1978.

————. *Saving the Text: Literature/Derrida/Philosophy.* Baltimore: John Hopkins Univ. Press, 1981.

Hatch, Edwin. *The Influence of Greek Ideas on Christianity.* New York: Harper & Bros., 1957.

Heinemann, J. "Profile of a Midrash." *Journal of the American Academy of Religion* 39 (1971): 141–50.

Hengel, Martin. *Judaism and Hellenism: Studies in Their Encounter in Palestine during the Early Hellenistic Period.* Philadelphia: Fortress Press, 1974.

"Hermeneutics." *Encyclopedia Judaica.* New York: Macmillan Pub. Co., 1971.

"History of Semiotics." *Encyclopedia of Philosophy.* New York: Macmillan Pub. Co., 1967.

"Interpretation." *Encyclopedia Judaica,* New York: Macmillan Pub. Co., 1971.

Jackson, B. Darrell. "The Theory of Signs in St. Augustine's *De Doctrina Christiana.*" In *Augustine: A Collection of Critical Essays,* edited by R. A. Markus. New York: Doubleday & Co. 1977.

Jacobs, Louis. *Studies in Talmudic Logic and Methodology.* London: Vallentine, Mitchell & Co., 1961.

Jaeger, Werner. *Early Christianity and the Greek Paideia.* Cambridge, Mass.: Harvard Univ. Press, 1961.

Jakobson, Roman. "Two Aspects of Language: Metaphor and Metonymy." In *European Literary Theory and Practice.*, edited by Vernon Gras. New York: Dell Pub. Co., 1973.

Jameson, Frederic. *The Prison-House of Language: A Critical Account of Structuralism and Russian New Formalism.* Princeton, N.J.: Princeton Univ. Press, 1972.

Johnson, Barbara. "The Frame of Reference: Poe, Lacan, Derrida." *Yale French Studies* 55/56 (1977): 457–505.

Johnson, W. R. "Isocrates Flowering: The Rhetoric of Augustine." *Philosophy and Rhetoric* 9 (1976): 217–31.

Jonas, Hans. *Philosophical Essays: From Ancient Creed to Technological Man.* Englewood Cliffs, N.J.: Prentice-Hall, 1974.

Jones, Ernest. *The Life and Works of Sigmund Freud,* edited by Lionel Trilling and Steven Marcus. 1953. New York: Basic Books, 1961.

Kadushin, Max. *The Rabbinic Mind.* 1952, Reprint. New York: Bloch, 1972.

Kahn, Charles H. "Language and Ontology in the Cratylus." In *Exegesis and Argument: Studies in Greek Philosophy Presented to Gregory Vlastos,* edited by F. N. Lee et al. Assen, Netherlands: Van Gorcum & Co., 1973.

Kapp, Ernst, *Greek Foundations of Traditional Logic.* New York: Columbia Univ. Press, 1942.

Kermode, Frank. *The Genesis of Secrecy: On The Interpretation of Narrative.* Cambridge, Mass.: Harvard Univ. Press. 1979.

Kneale, William and Martha. *The Development of Logic.* Oxford: Clarendon Press, 1962.

Krieger, Murray, and Dembo, L. S. *Directions for Criticism: Structuralism and Its Alternatives.* Madison: Univ. of Wisconsin Press, 1977.

Kunst, Arnold. "An Overlooked Type of Inference." *Bulletin of the School of Oriental African Studies* 10 (1942): 976–91.

Lacan, Jacques. *Écrits: A Selection.* Translated by Alan Sheridan. New York: Norton, 1977.

———. "The Insistence of the Letter in the Unconscious." Translated by Jan Miel. In *Structuralism,* edited by Jacques Ehrmann. New York: Doubleday & Co., 1970.

———. *The Four Fundamental Concepts of Psycho-Analysis,* edited by J.-A. Miller. Translated by A. Sheridan. London: Hogarth Press and Institute for Psychoanalysis, 1977.

————. *The Language of the Self: The Function of Language in Psychoanalysis.* Translated by Anthony Wilden. Baltimore: John Hopkins Univ. Press, 1968.

————. "Seminar on the Purloined Letter." *Yale French Studies* 48 (1972): 38–72.

Lampe, G. W. H., ed. *The West from the Fathers to the Reformation.* Cambridge History of the Bible, vol. 2. Cambridge: Cambridge Univ. Press, 1969.

Lauterbach, Jacob Z. *Rabbinic Essays.* 1951, Reprint. New York: Ktav, 1951.

Lentricchia, Frank. *After the New Criticism.* Chicago: Univ. of Chicago Press, 1980.

Lewalski, Barbara. *Protestant Poetics and the Seventeenth-Century Religious Lyric.* Princeton, N.J.: Princeton Univ. Press, 1979.

Levinas, Emmanuel. *Quartres Lectures Talmudiques.* Paris: Éditions de Minuit, 1968.

————. "To Love the Torah More than God." Translated by Helen A. Stephenson and Richard I. Sugarman. *Judaism* 28 (1979): 216–23.

Lévi-Strauss, Claude. *The Savage Mind.* 1962, Reprint. Chicago: Univ. of Chicago, 1966.

————. *Structural Anthropology.* New York: Basic Books, 1963.

————. *Tristes Tropiques.* 1955, Reprint. New York: Atheneum, 1974.

Lieberman, Saul. *Hellenism in Jewish Palestine.* New York: Jewish Theological Seminary, 1950.

Lodge, David, ed. *20th Century Literary Criticism: A Reader.* London: Longman's, 1972.

Loewe, R. "The Jewish Midrashim and Patristic and Scholastic Exegesis of the Bible." In *Studia Patristica,* edited by Kurt Alard and F. L. Cross. Vol. 1. Berlin: Akademic-Verlag, 1957.

Lorenz, Kuno, and Mittlcstrauus, Jurgen. "On Rational Philosophy of Language: The Programme in Plato's *Cratylus.*" *Mind* 76 (1967): 1–20.

Lynch, William F. *Christ and Apollo: The Dimensions of the Literary Imagination.* New York: New American Library, 1960.

Lyotard, Jean-François. "Jewish Oedipus." *Genre* 10 (1977): 395–411.

Macksey, Richard, and Donato, Eugenio. *The Structuralist Controversy.* Baltimore: John Hopkins Univ. Press, 1970.

————. *Velocities of Change: Critical Essays from MLN.* Baltimore: Johns Hopkins Univ. Press, 1974.

Maimonides. *Introduction to the Talmud: A Translation of the Rambam's Introduction to His Commentary on the Mishna.* Translated by Zvi L. Lample. New York: Judaica Press, 1975.

Markus, R. A., ed. *Augustine: A Collection of Critical Essays.* New York: Doubleday & Co., 1977.

————. "St. Augustine on Signs." *Phronesis* 3 (1957): 60–83.

Mazzeo, Joseph A. "St. Augustine's Rhetoric of Silence." *Journal of the History of Ideas* 23 (1962): 175–96.

McCanles, Michael "The Literal and the Metaphorical: Dialectic or Interchange." *PMLA Proceedings of the Modern Language Association* 91 (1976): 271–90.

McGuire, William, ed., and Mannheim, Ralph, trans. *The Freud–Jung Letters.* Bollingen Series 94. Princeton, N.J.: Princeton Univ. Press, 1974.

McKenna, Andrew. "Biblioclasm: Joycing Jesus and Borges." *Diacritics* 8 (1978): 15–29.

McKeon, Richard. "Aristotle's Conception of Language and the Arts of Language." In *Critics and Criticism: Ancient and Modern*, edited by R. S. Crane. Chicago: Univ. of Chicago Press, 1952.

————. "Canonic Books and Prohibited Books: Orthodoxy and Heresy in Religion and Culture." *Critical Inquiry* 2 (1976): 781–806.

————. "Rhetoric in the Middle Ages." In *Critics and Criticism*, edited by R. S. Crane. Chicago: Univ. of Chicago Press, 1952.

Mehlman, Jeffrey. "The 'floating signifier': from Lévi-Strauss to Lacan." *Yale French Studies* 48 (1972): 10–37.

Meissner, W. W. "Freud's Methodology." *Journal of the American Psychoanalytic Association* 19 (1971): 265–309.

Midrash Rabbah, Genesis, edited by H. Freeman and M. Simon. Vol. 1. London: Soncino, 1939.

Mielziner, Moses. *Introduction to the Talmud.* 1894, Reprint. New York: Bloch, 1968.

Moussaie, J., and Masson, E. "Buried Memories on the Acropolis: Freud's Response to Mysticism and Anti-Semitism." *International Journal of Psychoanalysis* 59 (1978): 199–208.

Muller, John P., and Richardson, William J. "Toward Reading Lacan." *Psychoanalysis and Contemporary Thought* 1 (1978): 325–53.

Nemetz, Anthony. "Literalness and the Sensus Litteralis." *Speculum* 34 (1959): 76–89.

Neusner, Jacob. "Form and Meaning in Mishnah." *Journal of the American Academy of Religion* 45 (1977): 27–54.

————. *History and Torah: Essays on Jewish Learning.* New York: Schocken, 1965.

————. *Invitation to the Talmud.* New York: Harper & Row Pubs., 1973.

Origen. *On First Principles.* Translated by G. W. Butterworth. New York: Harper & Row Pubs., 1966.

Ozick, Cynthia. "Judaism and Harold Bloom." *Commentary* 67 (1979): 43–51.

Palmer, Richard E. *Hermeneutics: Interpretation Theory in Schleiermacher, Dilthey, Heidegger, and Gadamer.* Evanston, Ill.: Northwestern Univ. Press, 1969.

Patai, Raphael. *The Jewish Mind.* New York: Scribner, 1977.

Patte, Daniel. *Early Jewish Hermeneutic in Palestine.* Missoula, Mont.: Society of Biblical Literature and Scholars Press, Univ. of Montana, 1975.

Pelikan, Jaroslav. *The Christian Tradition: A History of the Development of Doctrine.* 2 vols. Chicago: Univ. of Chicago Press, 1971, 1978.

The Pentateuch and Rashi's Commentary: A Linear Translation into English. Translated by Benjamin Sharfman and Abraham Ben-Isaiah. Brooklyn, N.Y.: S. S. & R. Pub. Co., 1949.

Plato. *The Dialogues of Plato.* Translated by B. Jowett. Vol. 30. 1871, Reprint. Oxford: Clarendon Press, 1953.

Rabinowitz, A. H. *The Jewish Mind: A Study in Halachic Expression.* Jerusalem: Hillel Press, 1978.

Rabinowitz, Isaac. " 'Word' and Literature in Ancient Israel." *New Literary History* 4 (1972): 119–30.

Radnitzky, Gerard. *Contemporary Schools of Metascience,* vol. 3. Sweden: Scandinavian Univ. Books, 1968.

Randall, John Herman. *Aristotle.* New York: Columbia Univ. Press, 1960.

Rawidowicz, Simon. "On Interpretation." In *Studies in Jewish Thought*, edited by N. Glatzer. Philadelphia: Jewish Publication Society, 1974.

Reuther, Rosemary., *Faith and Fratricide: The Theological Roots of Anti-Semitism*. New York: Seabury, 1974.

Ricoeur, Paul. *The Conflict of Interpretations: Essays in Hermeneutics*. Edited by Don Ihde. Evanston, Ill.: Northwestern Univ. Press, 1974.

———. *Freud and Philosophy: An Essay on Interpretation*. New Haven, Conn.: Yale Univ. Press, 1970.

———. *The Rule of Metaphor: Multi-Disciplinary Studies of the Creation of Meaning in Language*. Toronto and Buffalo: Univ. of Toronto Press, 1977.

Robert, Marthe. *From Oedipus to Moses: Freud's Jewish Identity*. Translated by Ralph Mannheim. 1974, Reprint. New York: Doubleday & Co. 1976.

Robertson, D. W. *A Preface to Chaucer: Studies in Medieval Perspective*. Princeton, N.J.: Princeton Univ. Press, 1962.

Robinson, James M., ed. *The New Hermeneutic*. New York: Harper & Row Pubs., 1964.

Rorty, Richard. "Derrida on Language, Being, and Abnormal Philosophy." *Journal of Philosophy* 74 (1977): 673–82.

———. "Philosophy as a Kind of Writing: An Essay on Derrida." *New Literary History* 10 (1978): 141–60.

Rosenblatt, S. *The Interpretation of the Bible in the Mishnah*. Baltimore: Johns Hopkins Univ. Press, 1935.

Ross, Sir David. *Aristotle*. 1923, Reprint. New York: Barnes & Noble, 1966.

Said, Edward. *Beginnings: Intention and Method*. Baltimore: John Hopkins Univ. Press, 1975.

Schechter, Solomon. *Aspects of Rabbinic Theology*. 1909, Reprint. New York: Schocken, 1961.

Schneerson, Rabbi Menachem M. *On the Essence of Chassidus*. Translated by S. Handelman and H. Greenberg. Brooklyn: Kehot Pub. Society, 1978.

Schneidau, Herbert N. *Sacred Discontent: The Bible and Western Tradition*. Berkeley: Univ. of California Press, 1976.

Schneur Zalman of Liadi. *Likutei Amarim-Tanya*. New York and London: Kehot Pub. Society, 1973.

Scholem, Gershom. *Kabbalah*. New York: New American Library. 1974.

———. *Major Trends in Jewish Mysticism*. New York: Schocken, 1941.

———. *The Messianic Idea in Judaism and Other Essays on Jewish Spirituality*. New York: Schocken, 1971.

———. "The Name of God and the Linguistic Theory of the Kabbalah." *Diogenes* 79 (1972): 59–80, 164–194.

———. *On Jews and Judaism in Crisis*. Edited by Werner J. Dannhauser. New York: Schocken, 1976.

———. *On the Kabbalah and Its Symbolism*. Translated by Ralph Mannheim. 1960, Reprint. New York: Schocken, 1969.

———. *Shabbatai Sevi: The Mystical Messiah, 1626–1676*. Translated by R. J. Z. Werblowsky. Princeton, N.J.: Princeton Univ. Press, 1973.

Schwartz, Leo. *Great Ages and Ideas of the Jewish People*. New York: Modern Library, 1956.

Schwartz, Murray. "Critic, Define Thyself." In *Psychoanalysis and the Question of the Text*. Edited by Geoffrey Hartman. Baltimore: Johns Hopkins Univ. Press, 1978.

Schiel, James. *Greek Thought and the Rise of Christianity*. London: Longman's, 1968.

Shestov, Lev. *Athens and Jerusalem*. Translated by Bernard Martin. Athens: Ohio Univ. Press, 1966.

Siddur Tehillat Ha-Shem Nusach Ha-Ari-Zal. Translated by Nissen Mangel. Brooklyn, N.Y.: Merkos L'Inyonei Chinuch, 1978.

Simonson, Solomon. "The Idea of Interpretation in Hebrew Thought." *Journal of the History of Ideas* 8 (1947): 467–74.

Slonimsky, Henry. "The Philosophy Implicit in the Midrash." *Hebrew Union College Annual* 27. 1956, Reprint. New York: Ktav, 1968.

Smalley, Beryl. *The Study of the Bible in the Middle Ages*. 1940, Reprint. New York: Philosophical Library, 1952.

Spivak, Gayatri Chakravorty. *"Glas-Piece: A Complete Rendu."* Diacritics 7 (1977), 22–43.

Stein, Kenneth. "Exegesis, Maimonides, and Literary Criticism." *Modern Language Notes* 88 (1973): 1134–54.

Steiner, George. *On Difficulty and other Essays*. 1972, Reprint. New York: Oxford Univ. Press, 1980.

Steinsaltz, Adin. "The Imagery Concept in Jewish Thought." *Shefa Quarterly* 1 (1979): 56–62.

———. *The Essential Talmud*. Translated by Chaya Gadai. New York: Basic Books, 1976; reprint ed., New York: Bantam Books, 1977.

Strack, Hermann L. *Introduction to the Talmud and Midrash*. 1931, Reprint. New York: Atheneum, 1974.

Strauss, Leo. *Persecution and the Art of Writing*. Glencoe, Ill: Free Press, 1952.

Todorov, Tzvetan. "On Linguistic Symbolism." *New Literary History* 6 (1974): 11–34.

Trosman, Harry. "Freud's Cultural Background." In *Freud: The Fusion of Science and Humanism: The Intellectual History of Psychoanalysis*, edited by John E. Gedo and George H. Pollack. New York: International Universities Press, 1976.

Turkle, Sherry. *Psychoanalytic Politics: Freud's French Revolution*. New York: Basic Books, 1978.

Vogel, Leon. "Freud and Judaism: An Analysis in Light of His Correspondence." *Judaism* 24 (1977): 181–93.

Wilken, Robert L. *Judaism and the Early Christian Mind: A Study of Cyril of Alexandria's Exegesis and Theology*. New Haven, Conn.: Yale Univ. Press, 1971.

Wolfson, Harry. *From Philo to Spinoza: Two Studies in Religious Philosophy*. New York: Behrman House, 1977.

———. "Greek Philosophy in Philo and the Church Fathers." In his *Studies in the History of Philosophy and Religion*, edited by I. Twersky. Vol. 1. Cambridge, Mass.: Harvard Univ. Press, 1973.

———. *Philo: Foundations of Religious Philosophy in Judaism, Christianity, and Islam*, vol. 1. 1947, Reprint. Cambridge, Mass.: Harvard Univ. Press, 1962.

———. *The Philosophy of the Church Fathers: Faith, Trinity, Incarnation*, vol. 1. Cambridge, Mass.: Harvard Univ. Press, 1956.

Wolheim, Richard. "The Cabinet of Dr. Lacan." *New York Review of Books*, 25 January 1979, pp. 36–45.

Wood, James E. *The Interpretation of the Bible*. London: G. Duckworth, 1958.
Zborowski, Mark, and Herzog, Elizabeth. *Life Is with People: The Culture of the Shtetl*. 1952, Reprint. New York: Schocken, 1962.
Zevin, Shlomo Yosef. *Encyclopedia Talmudica: A Digest of Halachic Literature and Jewish Literature from the Tannaitic Period to the Present Time*. Jerusalem: Talmudic Encyclopedia Institute, 1969.

Index

Abraham, Karl, 132
Akiba, Rabbi, 38, 42, 45, 51, 70
Alexandria, school of exegesis of, 93-100.
 See Origen; Patristic Thought; Philo
Allegory, 14-16; and Alexandrian school of
 exegesis, 93-99; in Classical rhetoric,
 84-85; in Clement, 97; in Middle Ages,
 109-10; and Midrash, 75; in Origen,
 96-99; in Paul, 85-91; in Philo, 93-96;
 typological, 87-88. *See* Augustine; Bible,
 exegesis of; Logos; Letter versus Spirit;
 Origen; Patristic Thought; Paul; Philo
Alter, Robert, 30
Altieri, Charles, 239n. 74.
Al tikrei, 71, 73, 74
Antioch, school of exegesis of, 99
Aquinas, Saint Thomas, 109
Aristotle: and Bible, 28-29; concept of
 Unity, 104-105; Derrida's critique of,
 16-21, 167; influence on history of interpretation, 6-15; logic of, 6-13, 28; logos
 of, 8-9; on metaphor, 16, 54-55; nous, 8;
 ontology of, 7-8; philosophy of language,
 6-15, 71; and Plato, 7-8; rhetoric and
 poetics of, 9-16; subject-predicate prepo-
 sitions of, 6-13; syllogism of, 6-7, 15,
 53-56; theory of signs, 114; Todorov's
 critique of, 54-55. Works: *Analytica
 Priora,* 6, 14; *De Anima,* 8; *De Interpretatione,* 9, 10, 12; *De Generatione et
 Corruptione,* 9; *Metaphysica,* 13, 17, 21,
 104; *Poetica,* 16, 19, 54, 71; *Rhetorica,*
 11, 15, 31, 55
Arnold, Matthew, 3, 170, 179, 222
Atkins, G. Douglas, 180
Auerbach, Erich, 29-33, 111, 187

Augustine, Saint, 5, 85; and allegory, 107-
 114; and Aristotle, 115-16; background
 of, 111-12; fourfold sense of Scripture,
 108-109; "Interior Teacher," 239n. 78;
 and Jewish interpretation, 117; on language, 119-200; literal and figurative
 meaning, 116-18; and medieval aesthetics, 112-13; obscurity of Scripture,
 112; rhetoric of silence, 116; and Scripture, 112-13; semiotics of idolatry, 117-
 20; theory of signs of, 113-20. Works:
 Confessions, 108, 112, 119; *On Christian
 Doctrine,* 108, 11-12, 114, 116

Bakan, David, 151, 240-41n.8.
Barrett, C. K., 233 n.8
Barthes, Roland, 49-50, 79-81
Benveniste, Emile, 24
Beardsley, Monroe, 24
Benjamin, Walter, xviii
Biale, David, 198-99, 204, 206
Bible: and Aristotle, 28; Book of Books and
 Book of Nature, 124-26; and Freud,
 144-45; and Greek thought, 27-37, 86,
 139, 233 n.8; and Homer, 21-24, 29-34;
 indeterminacy in, 29-30; metaphor and
 metonymy in, 158-9; philosophical impli-
 cations of creationism in, 28-9, 39; and
 Rabbinic interpretation, 31, 36-37; in
 Reformation, 123-26; and scientific inter-
 pretation, 125-26; space-time in, 36-37;
 word in, 32. *See* Allegory; Freud; Letter
 versus Spirit; Patristic Thought; Rabbinic
 Interpretation.
Bloom, Harold: analogical mthod of, 219-
 22; antithetical criticism of, 190, 206, 210;